ENGAGING WITH SOCIAL RIGHTS

With a new and the most comprehensive account of the South African Constitutional Court's social rights decisions to date, Brian Ray argues that the Court's procedural enforcement approach has had significant but underappreciated effects on law and policy and challenges the view that a stronger substantive standard of review is necessary to fulfill their potential. Drawing connections between the Court's widely acclaimed early decisions and the more recent second-wave cases, Ray explains that the Court has responded to the democratic-legitimacy and institutional-competence concerns that consistently constrain it by developing doctrines and remedial techniques that enable activists, civil society, and local communities to press directly for rights-protective policies through structured, court-managed engagement processes. *Engaging with Social Rights* shows how those tools could be developed to make state institutions responsive to the needs of poor communities by giving those communities and their advocates consistent access to policy-making and planning processes.

BRIAN RAY is the Joseph C. Hostetler-BakerHostetler Professor of Law at Cleveland-Marshall College of Law, Cleveland State University. He has published widely on social rights and judicial review, and his work has appeared in leading journals, including the *Stanford Journal of International Law*, the *South African Journal of Human Rights*, and the *Constitutional Court Review*.

COMPARATIVE CONSTITUTIONAL LAW AND POLICY

Series Editors

Tom Ginsburg
University of Chicago

Zachary Elkins
University of Texas at Austin

Ran Hirschl
University of Toronto

Comparative constitutional law is an intellectually vibrant field that encompasses an increasingly broad array of approaches and methodologies. This series collects analytically innovative and empirically grounded work from scholars of comparative constitutionalism across academic disciplines. Books in the series include theoretically informed studies of single constitutional jurisdictions, comparative studies of constitutional law and institutions, and edited collections of original essays that respond to challenging theoretical and empirical questions in the field.

Books in the Series

Engaging with Social Rights Brian Ray
Making We the People Chaihark Hahm and Sung Ho Kim
Radical Deprivation on Trial Cesar Rodríguez-Garavito and Diana Rodríguez-Franco
Unstable Constitutionalism edited by Mark Tushnet and Madhav Khosla
Magna Carta and Its Modern Legacy edited by Robert Hazell and James Melton
International Courts and the Performance of International Agreements: A General Theory with Evidence from the European Union Clifford Carrubba and Matthew Gabel
Reputation and Judicial Tactics: A Theory of National and International Courts Shai Dothan
Constitutions and Religious Freedom Frank Cross
Constitutionalism in Asia in the Early Twenty-First Century edited by Albert Chen
Social Difference and Constitutionalism in Pan-Asia edited by Susan H. Williams
Constitutions in Authoritarian Regimes edited by Tom Ginsburg and Alberto Simpser
Presidential Legislation in India: The Law and Practice of Ordinances Shubhankar Dam
Social and Political Foundations of Constitutions edited by Denis J. Galligan and Mila Versteeg
Consequential Courts: Judicial Roles in Global Perspective edited by Diana Kapiszewski, Gordon Silverstein, and Robert A. Kagan
Comparative Constitutional Design edited by Tom Ginsburg

ENGAGING WITH SOCIAL RIGHTS

Procedure, Participation, and Democracy in South Africa's Second Wave

BRIAN RAY

CAMBRIDGE
UNIVERSITY PRESS

CAMBRIDGE
UNIVERSITY PRESS

University Printing House, Cambridge CB2 8BS, United Kingdom

Cambridge University Press is part of the University of Cambridge.

It furthers the University's mission by disseminating knowledge in the pursuit of education, learning, and research at the highest international levels of excellence.

www.cambridge.org
Information on this title: www.cambridge.org/9781107029453

First published 2016

A catalogue record for this publication is available from the British Library

ISBN 978-1-107-02945-3 Hardback

CONTENTS

ACKNOWLEDGMENTS

I have taken far longer than I anticipated to complete this book, and I am grateful to many people and institutions for support, advice, and good counsel along the way. Funding for the research was generously provided by the Fulbright Commission, the Cleveland State Faculty Scholarship Initiative, and the Cleveland-Marshall Fund.

My interest in South African constitutional law was sparked by Richard Goldstone's serendipitous invitation to apply for a foreign clerkship with him at the Constitutional Court in 2003. Jim Brudney is responsible for arranging that invitation (and for turning me into an academic). I will be forever grateful for that opportunity and for Richard's and Jim's support and mentorship throughout my career.

I first learned of the remarkable meaningful engagement remedy in conversations with Stuart Wilson and Jackie Dugard at the 2006 Law and Society Conference, when both were at the Centre for Applied Legal Studies, and Stuart, before he was a lawyer, was in the midst of negotiating the favorable settlement that resulted from the very first engagement process in the *Olivia Road* case. Both Stuart and Jackie have generously shared their expertise and insights over the years as I've grappled with the Court's social rights jurisprudence, and I could not have written this book without that assistance.

Penelope Andrews is the reason I was able to attend that conference as a new academic. I am grateful for her generosity (in that and many other instances) and to the rest of the African Collaborative Research Network, especially Mark Kende and Jonathan Klaaren, for welcoming me wholeheartedly into the fold. I am indebted to Jonathan Klaaren more specifically for repeatedly challenging me to think more critically about engagement's limits and for organizing a seminar at the University of Witwatersrand in 2008 that forced me to stop thinking about these issues in purely theoretical terms. During that same trip, David Bilchitz graciously arranged for me to present my early ideas on engagement at the South African Institute for Advanced Constitutional, Public, Human

Rights and International Law (SAIFAC). That was the first of several times I have profited from David's critical engagement with my work over the years.

I completed much of the book in 2013 while I was a Fulbright Scholar at the Socio-Economic Rights and Administrative Justice Research Project (SERAJ) at the University of Stellenbosch and the Socio-Economic Rights Project at the University of the Western Cape's Community Law Centre (CLC). Both institutions provided excellent facilities and stimulating intellectual environments. At Stellenbosch, Sandy Liebenberg graciously opened her home to me and my family and helped us navigate the complexities of the move to South Africa. Sandy and the talented faculty and graduate students at SERAJ, especially Geo Quinot, André van der Walt, and Shanelle van der Berg, were invaluable in helping me work through these ideas. The book is infinitely better for the many opportunities, both formal and informal, their gracious engagement with me and my ideas provided during that visit.

At the CLC, Ebenezer Durojaye, Gladys Mirugi-Mukundi, and Keathélia Sapto graciously incorporated me into their important work with several community organizations and gave me the opportunity to see how democratic engagement might work in practice. CLC hosted a community seminar on meaningful engagement co-organized by SERAJ that year, and I am indebted to them and the participants in the seminar who deepened my understanding of the challenges implementing engagement processes in practice.

During my Fulbright stay in South Africa, the inimitable Stuart Woolman invited me to participate in the 2013 Constitutional Court Review (CCR) conference. The crucible of that event helped me to sharpen my ideas on the eviction decisions and to identify them as part of the distinctive model this book describes. I owe a large debt to Stuart and the participants in that conference, in particular to David Bilchitz, David Landau, and Katie Young for providing thoughtful and critical commentary on my work, and to Stuart Wilson and Jackie Dugard for their deeply informed analyses of those same decisions.

A stimulating and extended e-mail exchange with Frank Michelman regarding the *Maphango* decision was the basis for the CCR piece. Frank's thoughtful engagement with the Court's decisions is a model I aspire to emulate, and the influence of his work permeates the book. I also rely extensively on Chuck Epp's work, and he graciously provided very helpful suggestions for refinements to Chapters 8 and 9.

My colleagues at Cleveland-Marshall provided helpful feedback on several draft chapters I presented at faculty colloquia. Eric Tucker, our distinguished visitor from Osgoode Hall Law School, gave me much needed encouragement and guidance throughout the process and provided insightful comments on several chapters. Eric also arranged for me to present these ideas to the Osgoode Hall faculty at a relatively early stage, which gave me confidence to pursue the book project. Our talented and dedicated librarians, in particular Amy Burchfield, Sue Altmeyer, and, more recently, Neeri Rao, went out of their way to respond to every request. Neeri also coordinated the excellent citation check and edit by the library's research assistant, Kyle Connell.

It was a real pleasure working with Cambridge University Press. John Berger was extremely helpful in guiding me through this process as well as patient with my delays. Steven Acerra put together a wonderful cover, and Anamika Singh and Holly Monteith were careful and thorough editors.

This manuscript developed out of two earlier articles: "Evictions, Aspiration and Avoidance," 5 *Constitutional Court Review* 173 (2014), and "Proceduralism's Triumph and Engagement's Promise in Socio-Economic Rights Litigation," 27 *South African Journal of Human Rights* 107 (2011). I am grateful to Juta for permission to adapt portions of each article, which appear in parts of Chapters 6 and 9. The CLC graciously permitted me to use the summary of the *Hlophe* decision in Chapter 8, which was published in "Courts, Capacity and Engagement: Lessons from Hlophe v City of Johannesburg," 14 *Economic and Social Rights Review* 3 (2013).

Finally, I am deeply indebted to my parents, Roy and Frances Ray, for their long support and to my wife, Kim, for too many things to list. I dedicate this book to her for all of those things, but especially for taking a chance on South Africa, and to my four children, Audrey, Iain, Evelyn, and Adrian, who make it all worthwhile.

1

Introduction

> It is clear, as we have stated above, that the socio-economic rights entrenched in [the new Constitution] are not universally accepted fundamental rights. For that reason, therefore, it cannot be said that their "justiciability" is required by CP II. Nevertheless, we are of the view that these rights are, at least to some extent, justiciable.[1]

South Africa's 1996 Constitution – the "final" constitution that was a key component of the negotiated settlement ending apartheid – includes an extensive range of socioeconomic or social rights. These rights to basic necessities, such as housing, health care, food, water, social security, and education, represent an important – perhaps the most important – aspect of the broad political, social, and economic transformation promised under the new constitutional order.

The South African Constitutional Court's first opportunity to address the social rights provisions came in the form of a challenge to the provisions' constitutionality. The two-stage process for drafting and adopting the final constitution included a unique procedure. It empowered the newly established Constitutional Court to decide whether each provision complied with a set of thirty-four constitutional principles the negotiations established.[2]

With the cautious assessment quoted in the epigraph, the Court rejected arguments that the novel social rights provisions violated the separation of powers and the justiciability requirements in the constitutional principles. It was not exactly a ringing endorsement of the social rights' transformative potential. The Court's tentative language reflected a set of

[1] *Ex Parte Chairperson of the Constitutional Assembly: In re Certification of the Constitution of the Republic of South Africa 1996*, 1996 (10) BCLR 1253 (CC) ("First Certification judgement"), [78].

[2] Ibid., [12–19]. The 34 principles are included in Annexure 2 of the judgment.

concerns raised during the constitutional drafting process over the wisdom and practical consequences of giving courts the power to reject and even dictate social-welfare policies in the new democracy.[3] Those concerns in turn reflected the terms of a long-running theoretical debate in the human rights and comparative constitutional law fields over whether social rights could properly be called rights at all and, even if they could, whether courts could ever legitimately enforce them.[4]

That debate over the justiciability of social rights centers on two related concerns: first, how to legitimate thrusting courts into the middle of complex and often contentious fiscal and policy debates that are the primary province of the legislature and the executive, and second, whether courts as institutions have the competence to craft remedies addressing those complex concerns and to issue orders that legislatures and executives either can or will follow.[5] These concerns arguably apply with greater force in transitional democracies like South Africa, where giving courts broad powers with potentially far-reaching fiscal consequences risks undermining the fragile commitment to constitutional democracy that those same courts are intended to protect and nourish.[6]

It is easy to trace the push and pull of these objections throughout the Constitutional Court's social rights decisions beginning with the infamous *Soobramoney* case, in which the Court rejected a claim for access to dialysis treatments because the allocation policy was rational and adopted in good faith. As Justice Sachs described the dilemma the Court faced in denying a dying man necessary care, "important though our review functions are, there are areas where institutional incapacity and appropriate constitutional modesty require us to be especially cautious."[7] Social rights advocates were deeply disappointed by that decision, in particular,

3 Theunis Roux, *The Politics of Principle: The First South African Constitutional Court, 1995–2005* (2013), 265–73.

4 *See* Sandra Fredman, *Human Rights Transformed: Positive Rights and Positive Duties* (2008), 1–3; Dennis M. Davis, "Socio-economic Rights: Has the Promise of Eradicating the Divide between First and Second Generation Rights Been Fulfilled?," in Tom Ginsburg and Rosalind Dixon (eds.), *Comparative Constitutional Law* (2011), 519–21.

5 E.g., Sandra Liebenberg, *Socio-Economic Rights: Adjudication under a Transformative Constitution* (2010), 10–11; Jeff King, *Judging Social Rights* (2012), 3–4, Chapter 5.II.C.

6 E.g., Cass R. Sunstein, "Against Positive Rights," in Andras Sajo (ed.), *Western Rights? Post-Communist Application* (1996) Ch. 12; Wojciech Sadurski, "Postcommunist Charters of Rights in Europe and the U.S. Bill of Rights," 65 *L. and Contemp. Prob.* 223, 227–32 (2002); David Beatty, *The Ultimate Rule of Law* (2004) 125–26.

7 *Soobramoney v Minister of Health (Kwazulu-Natal)* 1997 (12) BCLR 1696 (1997) ("*Soobramoney*") [58].

by the Court's adoption of an apparently deferential standard of review for social policies.[8] The Court's reputation took a further hit in the general public when Mr. Soobramoney died, literally on camera, in a media interview about his reaction to the decision.[9]

Three years later, in one of its most celebrated decisions, *Grootboom*, the Court did an apparent about-face when it held that the government's housing policies violated the access to housing right because those policies completely failed to address emergency needs of people like those in the displaced community where Irene Grootboom, who faced homelessness following eviction, lived.[10] Although the Court interpreted the housing right to impose a specific positive obligation on the state, it softened the effect of that pathbreaking interpretation in its remedy by refusing to specify even in general terms what policy changes the constitution required to meet this obligation.[11]

This was followed less than one year later by the equally famous *Treatment Action Campaign* (*TAC*) decision, in which the Court went even further and ordered the national government to expand a pilot program that provided antiretroviral drugs to prevent mother-to-child transmission of HIV. In terms miles distant from the First Certification judgment's modest acknowledgment that these rights are "at least, to some extent, justiciable," the Court unequivocally stated, "The question in the present case, therefore, is not whether socio-economic rights are justiciable. Clearly they are."[12] The Court dispelled any doubts about the scope of its authority, holding that "courts may – and if need be must – use their wide powers to make orders that affect policy as well as legislation."[13]

These three decisions form the core of the Court's well-deserved international reputation as a leading example of a national court that has developed new and potentially effective approaches to enforcing social rights without either diminishing the status of the constitution in general or unduly usurping the roles of the legislative and executive (or, perhaps

[8] *See* Craig Scott and Patrick Macklem, "Constitutional Ropes of Sand or Justiciable Guarantees? Social Rights in a New South African Constitution," 141 *U. Penn. L. Rev.* 91 (1992).

[9] Richard J. Goldstone, "A South African Perspective on Social and Economic Rights," 13 *Hum. Rts. Br.* 4, 5 (2006).

[10] *Government of the Republic of South Africa v Grootboom* 2000 (11) BCLR 1169 (CC) ("*Grootboom*").

[11] Ibid., [88–90].

[12] *Minister of Health and Others v Treatment Action Campaign and Others* 2002 (10) BCLR 1033 (2002) ("*TAC*") [25].

[13] Ibid., [113].

most significantly, bankrupting the state).[14] These decisions have been amply documented and analyzed by commentators both inside and outside of South Africa.

But a string of more recent decisions, beginning in 2008 with the housing-rights case *Olivia Road*, have garnered comparatively less attention, especially outside of South Africa.[15] Stuart Wilson and Jackie Dugard – activists and scholars who were key players in each litigation – recently identified these as the "second wave" of the Court's social rights jurisprudence.[16] The Court's formal doctrinal approach is nominally the same in both the first and second waves; however, the second-wave decisions display a distinctly different – and, in the view of most commentators, far less effective – approach to both interpretation and enforcement of the social rights provisions.[17]

The Court's water-rights decision, *Mazibuko*, is the most prominent – and most criticized – example of the strong procedural emphasis and self-consciously secondary role that the Court has adopted in the second-wave decisions.[18] *Mazibuko* recast the social rights as providing a primarily procedural set of protections that enforce a strongly participatory form of democracy rather than as a set of substantive guarantees.[19]

Analyses of *Mazibuko* and the second-wave decisions generally almost without exception conclude that the Court has retreated from even the modestly substantive version of the reasonableness standard of review it started to develop in its earlier, first-wave decisions.[20] There is a general

[14] *See* Theunis Roux, *The Politics of Principle: The First South African Constitutional Court, 1995–2005* (2013) 38–45.

[15] *Occupiers of 51 Olivia Road, Berea Township and 197 Main Street Johannesburg v City of Johannesburg and Others* 2008 (5) BCLR 475 (CC) (2008) ("*Olivia Road*").

[16] Stuart Wilson and Jackie Dugard, "Constitutional Jurisprudence: The First and Second Waves," in Malcolm Langford, Ben Cousins, Jackie Dugard, and Tshepo Madlingozi (eds.), *Socio-Economic Rights in South Africa: Symbols or Substance?* (2014) 35.

[17] Ibid., 37.

[18] *Mazibuko and Others v City of Johannesburg and Others* 2010 BCLR 239 (CC) (2009).

[19] Ibid., [71], [160].

[20] *See* Wilson and Dugard, *supra* note 16, 54–59; Liebenberg, *supra* note 5, 468–80; Kirsty McLean, "Meaningful Engagement: One Step Forward or Two Back? Some Thoughts on *Joe Slovo*," 3 Const. Ct. Rev. 223, 24–42; Danie Brand, "Judicial Deference and Democracy," in Sandra Liebenberg and Geo Quinot (eds.), *Law and Poverty: Perspectives from South Africa and Beyond* (2012); Marius Pieterse, "Procedural Relief, Constitutional Citizenship and Socio-Economic Rights as Legitimate Expectations," 28 *S. Afr. J. Hum. Rts.* 359, 362 (2012). One notable exception is Susan Rose-Ackerman, Stefanie Egidy, and James Fowkes, *Due Process of Lawmaking: The United States, South Africa, Germany and the European Union* (2015) 148–50.

consensus among the Court's critics that it should revise its interpretive framework by, at a minimum, infusing reasonableness review with "substantive analysis of the normative purposes and values" social rights represent.[21]

A. Arguments and methods

That background sets up the central questions this book attempts to address. At the broadest level, this book contributes to the debate over judicial enforcement of social rights. I follow the lead of most recent work in this area and start with the assumption that social rights are appropriately included in modern constitutions and justiciable by courts.[22] I closely examine the major arguments in the justiciability debate, but I do not seek to develop a full-fledged defense of constitutionalizing social rights. Instead, I am interested in understanding how the justiciability concerns construct and constrain the roles courts adopt when they address social rights claims and whether and how those roles directly and indirectly contribute to fulfilling social rights.

1. *Arguments*

I take the South African Constitutional Court as my subject because it is widely recognized as a leading example of a domestic court that has developed creative enforcement techniques that successfully navigate the justiciability objections. Focused as I am on a single court within a specific country, my objective is not to provide a comprehensive theory of the judicial role applicable to social rights enforcement generally. Instead, I offer a fairly thick and nearly comprehensive description of the Court's social rights decisions. I use that thick description to identify two promising models derived from the interpretive and remedial techniques the Court has developed that could be adapted to apply in other contexts. I describe and analyze how those models respond to the justiciability objections and also the jurisprudential and functional characteristics that fit the conditions sociolegal studies identify as necessary for court decisions to influence social and political change.

The consensus within South Africa over the disappointing limits of the Court's social rights jurisprudence is at odds with the Court's

[21] Liebenberg, *supra* note 5, 467; *see, also,* Pieterse, ibid., 362; Wilson and Dugard, *supra* note 16, 60.

[22] *See* King, *supra* note 5, 1.

international reputation for developing an innovative set of enforcement techniques that do not unduly strain either judicial legitimacy or competence. The disconnect between those views is due, in large part, to the relative lack of attention the Court's more recent social rights decisions have received outside of South Africa. This book's first contribution is to remedy that gap in the literature by providing one of the most comprehensive accounts of the Constitutional Court's decisions, including the second-wave decisions identified by Wilson and Dugard and a more recent string of consistently pro-poor eviction-related cases.

But that disconnect also reflects the persistent influence of the justiciability concerns in the theoretical debate over the appropriate role of courts in enforcing social rights. The international acclaim the Court received for its early decisions focused in part on the simple fact that the Court was willing to enforce social rights but also on the relative modesty the Court displayed by carefully structuring both its legal analysis and remedies to leave ample room for the legislature and executive to respond. This careful balance was often associated with weak-form or dialogic forms of review.

Domestic critics targeted that same modesty but argued, far from initiating a potentially productive dialogue over the substance of social rights, the Court was diminishing their transformative promise and its own authority to enforce that promise. The Court is widely perceived as having adopted an even more deferential approach in its second-wave decisions by continuing to avoid strong substantive interpretations of social rights and limiting itself to a set of procedural rights and remedies.

I use the detailed account of the Court's decisions and the debate over its interpretive framework and remedial choices to make three related arguments. First, the Court's critics are correct that it has developed a largely procedural enforcement approach and moved even further from the more substantive interpretations it adopted in the later first-wave cases. Second, despite that deepening proceduralization, the Court's international reputation as a leader in developing innovative and effective interpretive and remedial techniques is well deserved, but for different reasons than those most commentators identified following the Court's first-wave decisions.

Rather than a weak-form review model, in which the Court engages in a substantive dialogue with the political branches that democratize judicial enforcement, the second-wave decisions reveal that the Court has developed a largely procedural set of rights and remedies and has consistently sought to avoid developing the substance of social rights directly, preferring instead to rely on legislation and policy. Despite the significant substantive limitations to its approach, the Court has deployed these procedural techniques often in surprisingly authoritative ways that have contributed to the development of rights-protective policies.

Third, I use the examples of the Court's authoritative application of these procedural rights and remedies to describe two related enforcement models. The first of these, the "eviction model," comes from the Court's remarkably consistent record in finding procedural routes to delay or prevent evictions. In these decisions, the Court intervenes to stop temporarily an eviction or related action by the state and manages the situation to prompt the parties to reach a rights-protective outcome themselves, sometimes in ways that prompt broader policy and budget changes.

The second, "democratic engagement," expands the meaningful engagement requirement the Court has created to establish mechanisms that could give local communities and social rights activists more consistent access to policy-planning and budgeting processes. I argue that these models each could be expanded in ways that capitalize on the Court's more authoritative role and that have the potential to create even greater leverage for social rights activists, civil society, and local communities to press for policies that fulfill social rights.

2. *Methods*

This book draws on and connects with three closely related bodies of literature. First and foremost, it is part of the growing comparative constitutional law literature on judicial review of social rights, including discussions of alternative forms of judicial review and judicial–political dialogue over constitutional rights. Constitutional structures, interpretive approaches, and remedies that "weaken" judicial review or create opportunities for judicial-political dialogue feature prominently in the social rights literature because they offer theoretical solutions to the democratic-legitimacy and institutional-competence objections that are at the heart of the justiciability debate. The divergent assessments of the South African Constitutional Court's first-wave decisions center around whether the Court's interpretive framework and remedial choices represent creative applications of weak-form or dialogic review or an overly deferential abdication of the judicial role in a constitutional democracy.

Close analysis of both the first- and second-wave decisions shows that justiciability concerns play a consistently prominent role in the Court's decisions and result in a jurisprudence structured to avoid the development of strong abstract principles that could potentially commit the Court to taking the lead role in articulating, even at a fairly abstract level, the social policies required to fulfill the social rights. Indeed, in the second-wave decisions, the Court frequently relies on procedural techniques to avoid even the weaker judicial–political dialogue over the substance of the social rights that many argued it was initiating in its early decisions. At the same time, however, the Court in the second-wave decisions has relied on a strongly participatory conception of democracy to enforce the social rights in authoritative ways that both avoid outright deference to the political branches and have resulted in identifiable changes to social policy.

Second, this book takes up Ran Hirschl's challenge to comparativists to abandon the safe confines of doctrinal analysis and consider the political and social forces that constrain and shape judicial enforcement of constitutional rights, including social rights.[23] At the broadest level, I try to connect the legal–theoretical debate over social rights with the sociolegal literature on rights, litigation, and social change. The social rights field has long engaged in the realpolitik analysis Hirschl advocates, and several studies approach many of the South African Constitutional Court's decisions from social science and political science perspectives.

I don't attempt to replicate those analyses here. Instead, I draw on them first to complicate and enhance the detailed account of the Court's jurisprudence by considering how the political and social factors these studies identify help explain both the Court's own analysis and the outcomes in social rights cases. Second, I connect studies of social rights and the Constitutional Court's decisions with more general analyses of the conditions under which rights-based approaches and litigation have helped instigate social change to support the central claims I advance based on that description. The mix of social, political, and historical factors that have shaped the Court's decisions makes it unlikely that it will adopt a stronger interpretive framework in the short term. Nonetheless, the Court's substantively limited procedural approach already has influenced social policies in South Africa and contributed to rights-based mobilization in identifiable and significant ways. Relatively modest changes to that approach focused on institutional reforms, particularly at the local government level, could provide even more effective tools for enforcing social rights.

[23] Ran Hirschl, "From Comparative Constitutional Law to Comparative Constitutional Studies," 11 *Int'l J. Const. L.* 1 (2013).

To both analyze the Court's own approach and support the claim that it illustrates how procedural enforcement models could be effective in fulfilling social rights, I also draw on what Charles Sabel and William Simon call "democratic experimentalism" or "experimentalism" and related studies of participatory democracy.[24] The Court has explicitly connected the social rights to the South African Constitution's strongly participatory version of democracy and identified social rights litigation as a mechanism for individuals and communities to challenge political decisions directly outside of elections. The Court also has identified a set of procedural rights and remedies, including meaningful engagement, that give individuals and communities the right to participate in policy and budget decisions that affect them.

Democratic experimentalism and participatory democracy offer a set of empirically grounded models for operationalizing participatory democracy through institutional reforms designed to make public institutions more responsive to the people they serve and more effective in delivering those services. These models overlap with social science studies of the conditions under which rights- and litigation-based strategies are likely to instigate meaningful change. They share an emphasis on institutional reform and the critical role of policies and procedures that give outsiders structured and consistent access to generate those reforms. I analyze the Court's procedural innovations in light of these models and argue that they offer a set of principles and judicial techniques that could create leverage for local communities and social rights activists to use social rights to press for similar institutional reforms.

B. Outline

Part I identifies the theoretical and practical arguments in the justiciability debate and how those arguments shaped the Court's jurisprudence in the first-wave cases. Chapter 2 summarizes the theoretical debate over entrenching social rights, including the strong influence that theories of dialogic and weak-form review have had on that debate. It then outlines how that debate played out in the constitutional drafting process in South Africa in ways that continue to influence the Court's approach to interpreting and enforcing social rights.

[24] Charles F. Sabel and William H. Simon, "Destabilization Rights: How Public Law Litigation Succeeds," 117 *Harv. L. Rev.* 1016 (2004). Sabel and Simon use the terms "democratic experimentalist review" and "experimentalist review" as shorthand for experimentalist judicial approaches and "democratic experimentalism" or "experimentalism to refer broadly to both judicial and nonjudicial processes." Ibid., 1082–94.

Chapter 3 closely analyzes the first-wave decisions and identifies the strong influence of the justiciability concerns in those decisions. Those concerns contributed to the distinctive features of reasonableness review, in particular the Court's emphasis on context-specific interpretations that incorporate the progressive-realization and resources limitations into the substance of the rights.

Chapter 4 describes the strikingly divergent assessments of the first-wave decisions that centered on the distinctive features of reasonableness review.[25] Domestically, the Court faced serious criticism for its largely contentless application of the reasonableness review standard. Outside of South Africa, by contrast, several of the first-wave decisions – especially *Grootboom* and *TAC* – were hailed as innovative examples of judicial enforcement of social rights that avoided either preempting democratic control over policy and budgets or exceeding the institutional competence of courts.

Part II turns to the second-wave decisions, which have received far less attention outside of South Africa. Despite the substantive limitations evident in the second-wave cases, the Court has demonstrated increasing confidence and greater institutional authority when addressing social rights claims. That confidence has resulted in some remarkably assertive interventions and creative applications of the social rights.

I argue that these decisions are more significant than the first-wave decisions for several reasons. First, they demonstrate the strength of the Court's commitment to a proceduralized enforcement approach. Second, the Court in several of these decisions has carved out substantial judicial authority to enforce social rights and has used that authority in creative ways to uphold challenges to government social policy. Third, the distinctive features of the Court's approach in these decisions have the potential to develop into two related enforcement models that could effectively instigate rights-protective policy changes while allowing courts to maintain a largely procedural role.

Chapter 5 analyzes the five decisions that form the core of the second wave. The two eviction cases illustrate the Court's decisive shift away from *Grootboom*'s highly abstract application of section 26 toward a concrete, hands-on approach that uses section 26 and related legislation to manage individual evictions directly. A set of three service-delivery decisions, including *Mazibuko*, highlights the Court's explicit embrace of a

[25] Roux, *supra* note 14, 262.

proceduralized role and also its willingness to intervene in more authoritative ways when operating within those limits.

Chapter 6 examines the more recent remarkable string of rights-protective eviction-related decisions beginning with *Blue Moonlight*.[26] These decisions reinforce the limitations of the Court's approach in the second-wave decisions but also illustrate the Court's willingness to work within those self-imposed constraints to manage individual cases to reach rights-protective outcomes and identify a broad array of procedural powers for doing so. The Court's increasing confidence in managing individual cases and the array of procedural powers it developed in these decisions form the basis for the eviction model that Chapter 8 describes.

Chapter 7 identifies distinctive patterns in the second-wave decisions that consistently shape the Court's interpretive framework and remedial choices. It connects the internal dynamics of the Court's decisions to the political factors that Theunis Roux has argued consistently constrain the Court, but it also identifies factors that enable the Court to adopt a stronger, if still procedural, enforcement role.

My analysis of these factors challenges the view that a more effective model for enforcing social rights necessarily entails formal revision of the Court's standard of review and an explicitly substantive account of these rights. Instead, I argue that the proceduralized enforcement model the Court has developed in the second-wave decisions offers a potentially effective framework for enforcing social rights, but largely through political and administrative reforms rather than directly through judicial elaboration of substantive constitutional requirements. That framework not only responds to the theoretical objections to entrenching social rights but also could create leverage for local communities and social rights activists to influence policy and budget processes.

Part III identifies and develops two enforcement models that build on those more authoritative interventions but still work within the jurisprudential and political limits of the second-wave cases. Chapter 8 summarizes the two basic components of the first of these, the eviction model: (1) enforcing *Grootboom* through constitution-enforcing legislation by temporarily enjoining eviction until alternative accommodation is available and (2) expanding the procedural powers of courts in eviction cases to obtain information about housing planning and resources and manage

[26] *City of Johannesburg Metropolitan Municipality v Blue Moonlight Properties 39 (Pty) Ltd and Another* 2012 (2) BCLR 150 (CC) ("*Blue Moonlight*").

the cases in rights-protective ways that ensure access to temporary accommodation and could lead to broader policy change.

The enhanced procedural powers these cases establish strengthen the indirect positive-rights effects of enforcing section 26(3) by allowing a court to scrutinize the underlying policies at issue. Even greater substantive potential, however, lies in combining the strengthened procedural requirements these cases established with carefully structured meaningful engagement orders to directly address the broader housing-policy questions that the Court consistently has refused to revisit following *Grootboom*.

Chapter 9 describes the second enforcement model, democratic engagement. It first connects *Mazibuko*'s redefinition of social rights as tools for policing democratic accountability to the Court's broader participatory democracy jurisprudence to argue that both lines of cases reinforce a more authoritative role for judicial enforcement of procedural norms. It then analyzes the array of community-participation legislation and policies and argues that they provide a thick legal framework courts can rely on in combination with the meaningful engagement requirement to address the systemic problems that underlie both the lack of meaningful participation in local government and the bureaucratic failures that have undermined effective service delivery.

Chapter 10 concludes the book by considering both the eviction model and democratic engagement in light of the justiciability debate and the sociolegal literature on law and social change. It identifies the specific characteristics of these substantively limited, largely procedural enforcement approaches that could effect the kinds of diffuse and incremental changes case studies of effective legal mobilization identify. I argue that judicial approaches like these, focused on participatory processes and grounded in a commitment to deep democracy, could be effective in changing state institutions and processes.

PART I

Justiciability and the first wave

2

The justiciability debate and the 1996 Constitution

Writing in 2001, shortly after the South African Constitutional Court decided the celebrated housing-rights case *Grootboom*,[1] Cass Sunstein hailed the Court's "extraordinary decision" as establishing "a novel and promising approach to judicial protection for each person whose socio-economic needs are at risk."[2] Sunstein was referring to the Court's limited declaration that the state modify its housing policies to address the emergency needs of people like the applicants who faced homelessness following eviction without specifying the changes necessary to comply with constitution or retaining jurisdiction to review the results.[3]

For Sunstein – who only eight years earlier argued strongly *against* inclusion of social rights in developing East European democracies[4] – the "distinctive virtue" of the *Grootboom* approach was that it "suggests that such rights can serve, not to preempt democratic deliberation, but to ensure democratic attention to important interests that might otherwise be neglected in ordinary debate."[5] In a short response, Theunis Roux wrote that *Grootboom*'s limited remedy "was not extraordinary enough" because the Court's failure to, at a minimum, oversee compliance with even the very general terms of its order (much less provide any direct relief to the plaintiffs) fell far short of the expectations of advocates for the poor in South Africa and South African constitutional law experts more generally.[6]

1 *Government of the Republic of South Africa v Grootboom* 2000 (11) BCLR 1169 (CC) ("*Grootboom*").

2 Cass R. Sunstein, "Social and Economic Rights? Lessons from South Africa," 11 *Const. For.* 123, 131 (2001).

3 *Grootboom, supra* note 1, [99].

4 Cass R. Sunstein, "Against Positive Rights: Why social and economic rights don't belong in the new constitutions of Post-Communist Europe," 2 *East Eur. Const. Rev.* 35, 35–38 (1993).

5 Sunstein *supra* note 2, 131.

6 Theunis Roux, "Understanding Grootboom – A Response to Cass Sunstein," 12 *Const. For.* 41, 42 (2002).

That exchange captures the central divide in the debate over the Constitutional Court's approach to enforcing the social rights provisions in the 1996 Constitution. On one hand, many commentators like Sunstein (predominantly, but not exclusively, from outside of South Africa) have found in the Court's measured approach the potential to avoid judicial usurpation of legislative and executive power over budgets and core policy priorities while still enforcing these rights.[7] Critics, on the other hand, have charged the Court with failing to give social rights the teeth necessary to live up to their transformative mandate and in the process ignoring the harsh realities faced by the vast majority of South African citizens.[8]

This South African debate reflects the terms of a broader discussion over the legitimacy and effectiveness of entrenching social rights provisions in constitutions and, more specifically, over giving courts the power directly to enforce such provisions by ordering changes to social policy and budget allocations.[9] That broader discussion has developed several distinct strands that center on two core objections and a related practical concern: (1) court enforcement is deeply antidemocratic because it preempts legislative and executive authority over policy and budgets; (2) courts are institutionally ill-suited to deal with the complex and interrelated nature of social-welfare policies; and (3) relying on litigation and a rights-based approach to progressive social and economic change is an expensive and feckless distraction from the real work of social and political mobilization for pro-poor policies.

Unsurprisingly the terms of this debate have shifted as the Constitutional Court and other courts have decided an increasing number of social rights cases. The arguments have evolved away from whether constitutions should include these rights and courts should enforce them to

[7] E.g., Mark Tushnet, *Weak Courts, Strong Rights: Judicial Review and Social Welfare Rights in Comparative Constitutional Law* (2008); Mark Kende, *Constitutional Rights in Two Worlds, South Africa and the United States* (2009); Frank I. Michelman, "The Constitution, Social Rights, and Liberal Political Justification," 1 *Int'l J. Const. L.* 13 (2003).

[8] E.g., David Bilchitz, *Poverty and Fundamental Rights: The Justification and Enforcement of Socio-Economic Rights* (2007); Marius Pieterse, "Eating Socioeconomic Rights: The Usefulness of Rights Talk in Alleviating Social Hardship Revisited," 29 *Hum. Rts. Q.* 796 (2007); Danie Brand, "The Proceduralisation of South African Socioeconomic Rights Jurisprudence, or 'What Are Socioeconomic Rights For?'" in Henk Botha *et al.* (eds.), *Rights and Democracy in a Transformative Constitution* (2003); Sandra Liebenberg, "South Africa's Evolving Jurisprudence on Socio-Economic Rights: An Effective Tool in Challenging Poverty?," 6 *Law Dem. and Develop.* 159 (2002).

[9] Marius Pieterse, "Possibilities and Pitfalls in the Domestic Enforcement of Social Rights: Contemplating the South African Experience," 26 *Hum. Rts Q.* 882, 885 (2004).

how judicial enforcement can be both legitimate and effective. Starting with the assumption that courts will enforce social rights doesn't resolve the democratic-legitimacy and institutional-competence objections, but it changes the questions. Now we ask about the relative effects of different interpretive and remedial approaches. How preemptive of democratic prerogatives are they and to what extent do they strain or maximize the institutional advantages of courts? What effects does judicial enforcement have and how do we measure them?

Mark Tushnet's typology of weak-form review is one of the more influential theoretical models in the debate over social rights and the effects of different enforcement approaches. Weak-form review describes a range of interpretive stances and remedial techniques that "weaken" the judicial role to some extent by allowing for legislative or executive response to court decisions. A significant literature has developed analyzing how weaker approaches can both democratize judicial enforcement and also diminish institutional-competence problems by returning some control over policy choices to the political branches.[10]

The shift to the relative merits of different enforcement models also forefronts the practical concerns and challenges the relevance of the normative questions that long have dominated the debate.[11] Does it really matter whether judicial enforcement is more or less democratic? Isn't the more relevant question whether court enforcement of social rights can make any material improvement in the lives of poor people? It's not enough to theorize about the hypothetical competencies of courts versus legislatures or the executive. What really happens when a court intervenes?

[10] E.g., Katherine G. Young, *Constituting Economic and Social Rights* (2012); Kende, *supra* note 7; Rosalind Dixon, "Creating Dialogue about Socio-economic Rights: Strong-Form versus Weak-Form Judicial Review Revisited," 5 *Int'l J. Const. L.* 391 (2007); Cesar Rodriguez-Garavito, "Beyond the Courtroom: The Impact of Judicial Activism on Socio-economic Rights in Latin America," 89 *Tex. L. Rev.* 1669 (2009); Murray Wesson, "The Emergence and Enforcement of Socio-Economic Rights," in Liora Lazarus, Christopher McCrudden, Nigel Bowles (eds.), *Reasoning Rights: Comparative Judicial Engagement* (2014), Ch. 4; Xenophon Contiades and Alkmene Fotiadou, "Social Rights in the Age of Proportionality: Global Economic Crisis and Constitutional Litigation," 10 *Int'l J. Const. L.* 660 (2012). Sandra Liebenberg integrates some aspects of weak-form approaches in her prescriptions for revising reasonableness review. *Socio-Economic Rights: Adjudication under a Transformative Constitution* (2010) Ch. 4. For a critical perspective on weak-form review, *see* David Landau, "The Reality of Social Rights Enforcement," 53 *Harv. Int'l L. J.* 189 (2012).

[11] E.g., Octavio Luiz Motta Ferraz, "Harming the Poor through Social Rights Litigation: Lessons from Brazil," 89 *Tex. L. Rev.* 1643 (2011).

Do different interpretive frameworks or remedies change these outcomes? What conditions constrain or enable courts to intervene in these ways?

The social rights literature is only beginning to examine these difficult, largely empirical questions.[12] Weak-form review's theoretical response to the institutional-competence problem hypothesizes answers to some of these questions and several empirically grounded analyses have started to test those hypotheses against the "reality" of social rights enforcement with conflicting conclusions.[13]

This chapter first summarizes the debate over constitutional entrenchment and judicial enforcement of social rights – shorthanded as the "justiciability" debate. It then examines the literature on weak-form judicial review with a focus on a variant that Charles Sabel and several collaborators call "experimentalism" or "democratic experimentalist review."[14] These alternative forms of review arguably democratize judicial review and ease the strain on judicial competence by creating opportunities for legislative, executive, and, in the case of experimentalist review, popular responses to judicial decisions enforcing constitutional rights.

Weak-form review does not directly respond to the practical concerns and empirical questions raised by the third objection that rights-based approaches are at best ineffective in materially improving the lives of poor people. This argument is an aspect of the larger "myth-of-rights" debate – the divide between "realists" and "constructivists" over whether and how rights can effect meaningful social change. This chapter examines the connections between more recent analyses of weak-form review that engage with the myth-of-rights debate. Finally, I turn to the justiciability debate in South Africa focusing on the distinctive character these arguments assumed during the constitutional negotiation process.

12 Malcolm Langford, Ben Cousins, Jackie Dugard, and Tshepo Madlingozi (eds.), *Socio-Economic Rights in South Africa: Symbols or Substance?* (2013); Ran Hirschl and Evan Rosevear, "Constitutional Law Meets Comparative Politics: Socio-Economic Rights and Political Realities," in Tom Campbell, K. D. Ewing, and Adam Tomkins (eds.), *The Legal Protection of Human Rights: Skeptical Essays* (2011); Daniel M. Brinks and Varun Gauri, *The Law's Majestic Equality? The Distributive Impact of Litigating Social and Economic Rights*, World Bank Development Research Group Working Paper 5999 (March 2012); Varun Gauri and Daniel M. Brinks (eds.), *Courting Social Justice: Judicial Enforcement of Social and Economic Rights in the Developing World* (2010).

13 Landau, *supra* note 10; Rodriguez-Garavito, *supra* note 12; Brinks and Gauri, *supra* note 10.

14 E.g., Charles F. Sabel and William H. Simon, "Destabilization Rights: How Public Law Litigation Succeeds," 117 *Harv. L. Rev.* 1016 (2004); Michael C. Dorf and Charles M. Sabel, "A Constitution of Democratic Experimentalism," 98 *Col. L. Rev.* 267 (1998).

A. Objections to social rights

Most defenses of social rights begin with an argument that any just society must include a foundational commitment to assisting its members who cannot on their own obtain the basic necessities for survival. Including fundamental rights to these needs in a constitution first demonstrates that commitment in concrete terms and also, at least in theory, helps ensure that the political process consistently works to fulfill it.

It's this second function – shaping normal politics to ensure that those processes create policies and spend money in ways consistent with this fundamental commitment to provide basic needs for everyone that makes justiciable social rights controversial. Doing so seems to provide broad license for courts to second-guess almost every aspect of democratic decision-making from broad policy objectives to detailed budget plans. This, critics argue, is both deeply antidemocratic and foolishly unrealistic about the capacity of judges and the limits of litigation.[15]

1. *Democratic legitimacy*

Frank Michelman identifies the core of this objection as "the lack of any sufficiently decisive or formally realizable rule for saying when the correlative duties these rights impose has been met."[16] This defect typically is explained in comparative terms. A court can establish relatively concrete rules to identify when actions by government officials violate, for example, a constitutional prohibition against unreasonable searches and seizures. To be sure, there will be grey areas on the margins. Complicated scenarios or new technologies can create serious disagreements over where to draw the constitutional line. But the scope of that boundary is perceived as narrow, making it easy to identify the legitimate range of reasonable interpretations. And, once a court draws it, there is relatively little uncertainty for the government actor seeking to comply with the line or for the next court enforcing it.

Social rights, critics charge, are quite different. Court enforcement invites judicial inquiry into multiple, open-ended policy questions and

[15] E.g., Landau, *supra* note 10 at 206 (summarizing the critiques); Frank B. Cross, "The Error of Positive Rights," 48 *UCLA L. Rev.* 857 (2000); Aryeh Neier, "Social and Economic Rights: A Critique," in Henry J. Steiner *et al.* (eds.), *International Human Rights in Context: Law, Politics, Morals* (2008) 283.

[16] Frank Michelman, "The Constitution, Social Rights and Reason," 14 *S. Afr. J. of Hum. Rts.* 499, 506 (1998).

intervention in all aspects of economic and social policy.[17] This potentially places large areas of democratic decision-making under judicial control. An example illustrates this problem: I sue my local municipality, arguing that it has an obligation to provide me with temporary housing following an eviction. The city responds that it cannot because the amount earmarked for emergency housing is fully committed. Can a court inquire into the entire housing budget? What about the budgets for other social service programs? Is the city's tax policy relevant? Money is fungible and budgets are a zero-sum game and so there is no obvious limit to where a court's inquiry should end.

The problem extends beyond resources into policy decisions. What if the city – in an effort to address what it determines are the priority needs of inner-city residents occupying buildings with significant health and safety risks – decides to dedicate all of its emergency housing funding to relocating those people? Assume further that this decision is a key part of a broader plan to revitalize the inner city and attract businesses and higher-income residents to expand the tax base and increase revenues – revenues that could be used to increase social services generally. If a group of people threatened with eviction from private property sues to challenge that policy, what factors should a court use to assess those priorities?

2. *Institutional competence*

The indeterminacy of social rights raises another serious objection to courts getting involved in social-welfare policy: courts (and the litigation process more generally) are not well equipped to deal with the practical problems of deciding among competing potential routes of fulfilling these rights. The institutional-competence objection frequently draws on Lon Fuller's concept of "polycentric" disputes – multi-faceted disputes that are not amenable to the kind of issue-specific resolutions law and litigation are best suited to address.[18]

There is a related, practical argument against judicial enforcement of socioeconomic rights that suggests focusing on a rights-based approach to improving the lives of poor people is counterproductive. Even if courts are given the power to enforce social rights, they will be no more – and likely much less – able to ensure meaningful changes to social-welfare policy than if these rights did not exist.[19]

[17] E.g., Neier, *supra* note 15; Cross, *supra* note 15.
[18] Lon L. Fuller, "The Forms and Limits of Adjudication," 92 *Harv. L. Rev.* 353 (1978).
[19] *See* Cross, *supra* note 15; Ferraz, *supra* note 11.

The potential ineffectuality of judicial enforcement puts courts to "a hapless choice between usurpation and abdication, from which there is no escape without embarrassment or discreditation."[20] The first part of this "hapless choice" points to the fact that, even if courts were both able and willing to order the state to make substantial changes in social and economic policy in the face of substantial political resistance, the political branches are unlikely to comply with the orders in any meaningful way. Serious enforcement orders, thus, are likely to go unheeded and to embarrass the institution (as well as call into question the status of other constitutional rights).

Conversely, avoiding such confrontations with the other branches is likely to lead to serious underenforcement through reading down the substantive content of the right.[21] Some critics emphasize that the haplessness of the situation means that courts are no more likely than legislatures to robustly enforce these rights, even disregarding the institutional risks they take in doing so.[22]

This concern has broader dimensions. Even assuming litigation in some specific contexts could achieve substantial change in social policy, reliance on a legal process can be counterproductive in the long term. Reducing the complex social, political, and moral issues social rights raise to specific legal claims and arguments risks oversimplifying the fundamental causes of poverty. It also potentially marginalizes rights-holders by making them reliant on specialist lawyers and judges. Finally, it drives resources into an expensive, time-consuming effort that, as just noted, is likely to achieve limited substantive results at best.[23]

3. *The "myth" of rights*

The related concerns over institutional-competence and ineffectuality are not unique to the social rights literature. They are connected to a broader law-and-society debate over litigation and social change. Catherine Albiston describes the two sides of this broader debate as the "myth-of-rights"

[20] Frank I. Michelman, "Socioeconomic Rights in Constitutional Law: Explaining America Away," 6 *Int'l J. Const. L.* 663 (2008).

[21] Tushnet, *supra* note 7, at Ch. 3. [22] Cross, *supra* note 15.

[23] E.g., William Forbath, "Cultural Transformation, Deep Institutional Reform and ESR Practice: South Africa's Treatment Action Campaign," in Lucie E. White and Jeremy Pereleman (eds.), *Stones of Hope: How African Activists Reclaim Human Rights to Challenge Global Poverty* (2011) 51–2, 55 (summarizing and responding to these concerns). A related variant of this concern is the risk that judicial interventions in social policy are more likely to benefit the middle class because they have the resources to bring and win cases and also because judges are more likely to intervene in favor. *See* Landau, *supra* note 10.

camp and the "symbolic-strategic" camp.[24] Others characterize the sides as "realist" or "constructivist."[25] The most prominent example of the myth-of-rights/realist camp is Gerald Rosenberg's seminal book *The Hollow Hope: Can Courts Bring about Social Change?*[26] Rosenberg argues that courts can play a role in spurring social change but only under certain conditions and only in relatively incremental ways.[27] The conditions necessary for court-induced social change occur relatively infrequently, and the results courts are able to achieve are relatively small. Moreover, a critical mass of external political support is required to achieve legal change – support that could be mobilized more effectively to seek change directly through political channels rather than indirectly through courts.[28]

Ran Hirschl's hegemonic-preservation thesis offers an even more pessimistic assessment of the prospects for judicial enforcement to effect meaningful social change. Hirschl examines the effects of constitutionalization in Canada, New Zealand, Israel, and South Africa. According to Hirschl this dramatic trend toward constitutionalization and enhanced judicial power "is best understood as the product of a strategic interplay" between three groups of elites seeking to preserve their existing power in society – political elites threatened with a loss of power, economic elites seeking protection from democratic processes that might result in redistribution, and judicial elites seeking to enhance and preserve their national and international reputations.[29] Hirschl argues that the widespread view that constitutionalized rights promote progressive social change naively ignores these political realities. He marshals evidence in these four countries to show that constitutionalization has "utterly failed to promote progressive or egalitarian notions of distributive justice in any meaningful way."[30]

Hirschl is slightly more optimistic in his specific analysis of the South African Constitutional Court's early social rights decisions – citing the *Grootboom* and *Treatment Action Campaign* decisions as demonstrating

[24] Catherine Albiston, "The Dark Side of Litigation as a Social Movement Strategy," 96 *Iowa L. Rev. Bullet.* 61 (2011).

[25] Malcolm Langford, Jackie Dugard, Tshepo Madlingozi, and Ben Cousins, "Concluding Perspectives," in Langford *et al.* (eds.), *supra* note 12.

[26] Gerald N. Rosenberg, *The Hollow Hope: Can Courts Bring about Social Change?* (2nd edn, 2008).

[27] Ibid., 35–36. [28] Ibid.

[29] Ran Hirschl, *Towards Juristocracy: The Origins and Consequences of the New Constitutionalism* (2007) 12.

[30] Ibid., 14.

the Court "has been openly contemplating its position with regard to subsistence rights."[31] But these few counterexamples do not fundamentally undermine his view that judicial interpretations are limited by the dominant social and economic neoliberalism in these four countries and therefore that "constitutional rights appear to have only a limited capacity to advance non-market notions of social justice" in the areas social rights typically address such as basic housing, health care, education, employment, and welfare.[32]

More recently Hirschl, writing with Evan Rosevear, has argued that "there is no readily apparent correlation" between formal constitutional protection of social rights and their actual status. They point out that measures of income inequality and development indicators are similar across developing countries irrespective of whether a constitution contains social rights. Conversely, well-resourced countries with relatively generous social-welfare programs, like Canada, Sweden, Finland, and Denmark lack social rights.[33] In South Africa, they cite income inequality and government redistribution measures that show both net and gross inequality have increased in the postapartheid era.[34]

B. Alternative forms of judicial review

Social rights advocates argue that concrete experience with judicial enforcement of social rights has moved the debate beyond normative questions over whether constitutions should include social rights and into the details of the appropriate scope of the judicial role. Malcolm Langford's assertion that "the argument that [social] rights are somehow substantively different has withered" is characteristic of this view.[35] Mark Tushnet similarly argues "a consensus has emerged" that social rights are both "properly included in modern constitutions" and "enforceable to the same extent" as civil and political rights.[36]

[31] Ibid., 132–34. [32] Ibid., 218. [33] Hirschl and Rosevear, *supra* note 12, 211–13.

[34] Ibid., 219–21. The authors concede that the proportion of inequality offset by government redistribution has started to improve since 2000 but counter that the overall proportion of inequality offset through distribution remains well below the level in 1993–96. Ibid.

[35] Malcolm Langford, "The Justiciability of Social Rights: From Practice to Theory," in Malcolm Langford (ed.), *Social Rights Jurisprudence: Emerging Trends in International and Comparative Law* (2009) 30.

[36] Mark V. Tushnet, "Reflections on Judicial Enforcement of Social and Economic Rights in the Twenty-First Century," 4 *N.U.J.S. L. Rev.* 177, 177 (2011).

Others, like David Landau, contend that the normative concerns maintain some force but agree that "truth is somewhere in between" with social rights, raising concerns that are at least in degree if not in character sufficiently distinct to require separate consideration.[37] This view accepts that social rights more often – and possibly more intensely – raise justiciability concerns.

Notably, these responses don't argue that the democratic and institutional-competence questions are irrelevant; only that they either aren't insurmountable or don't in practice play out in any way distinguishable from enforcement of civil and political rights. In other words, they argue the debate has shifted from *whether* courts should enforce social rights to *how* they can enforce them in ways that are both legitimate and effective.[38]

1. *Weak rights and remedies*

Tushnet's typology of "weak-form" judicial review has played a prominent role in this discussion over legitimate judicial enforcement approaches. Weak-form review offers the possibility of democratizing rights enforcement by creating "mechanisms for the people to respond to [judicial] decisions that they reasonably believe mistaken that can be deployed more rapidly than the constitutional amendment or judicial appointment process."[39] Courts applying weak-form review "assess legislation against constitutional norms, but do not have the final word on whether statutes comply with those norms."[40] Instead the legislature has the opportunity to respond and that response is treated as equally authoritative.[41] This creates the possibility for "real-time" conversations between legislatures and courts over constitutional interpretation.

Weak-form review is part of dialogue theories of judicial review.[42] These theories each describe mechanisms that develop constitutional principles through extended exchanges between the courts and the political branches. This constitutional dialogue breaks up the judicial monopoly over constitutional interpretation that is assumed to exist under strong-form review. Engaging in dialogue requires courts to take into account – and in some manifestations defer to – the views of the democratically

[37] Landau, *supra* note 10, 195. [38] Tushnet, *supra* note 36, 187.

[39] Tushnet, *supra* note 7, 23. [40] Ibid., ix. [41] Ibid., 33–36.

[42] Mark Tushnet, "The Rise of Weak-Form Judicial Review," in Tom Ginsburg and Rosalind Dixon (eds.), *Comparative Constitutional Law* (2011) 326–27.

elected branches of government in cases where there is reasonable disagreement over the meaning of the constitution's text.[43]

Tushnet describes a range of both existing and hypothetical weak-form systems. He uses the legislative override provision in section 33 of the Canadian Charter of Rights and Freedoms, the interpretive mandate in the New Zealand Bill of Rights Act, and the "augmented" interpretive mandate in the UK Human Rights Act as principle examples.[44] He also considers the possibility of judges using weak-form review for certain constitutional provisions within otherwise strong-form systems.[45] In all of its potential forms, however, the appeal of weak-form review is that it "hold[s] out the promise of reducing the tension between judicial review and democratic self-governance, while acknowledging that constitutionalism requires that there be some limits on self-governance."[46]

Tushnet distinguishes between weak *substantive* rights and weak *remedies.* Rights can be substantively weak either because they explicitly provide or are interpreted by courts to provide broad discretion to the government and do not guarantee individual relief to particular plaintiffs.[47] When interpreting weak rights, courts give relatively strong deference to legislative action while still preserving the power to draw some constitutional limits. Weak rights require limited substantive definition and thus leave ample room for legislative response. They also emphasize case-by-case basis analysis of challenged programs or actions and avoid broad constitutional principles that substantially constrain future action.

Weak remedies create broad legislative or executive discretion in determining how to correct a constitutional violation. Examples include declaratory judgments that identify a constitutional violation without specifying how to correct it, requiring government to develop a plan for remedying the violation over a relatively short time, and judicial management of negotiations over resolving a constitutional-rights claim.[48] Courts can weaken a remedy in several ways, including issuing general orders and by relinquishing control over implementation.[49] But to satisfy

[43] Ibid., 322. [44] Tushnet, *supra* note 7, 23–33. [45] Ibid., 36–42, 75–76.

[46] Ibid., 23. [47] Ibid., 244. [48] Ibid., 248.

[49] Tushnet has suggested elsewhere that, at least in practice, the difference between even a structural injunction – the paradigmatic strong-form remedy – and weak-form remedies "may reflect temporal rather than analytical differences" because injunctions typically begin as relatively general orders reflecting weak-form characteristics. *See* Mark Tushnet, "A Response to David Landau by Mark Tushnet," at www.opiniojuris.org/2012/01/23/hilj_tushnet-responds-to-landau/.

as truly weak, a remedy must leave room for a legislative or executive response that does not merely implement a court order.

Tushnet acknowledges that the distinction between weak substance and weak remedies is slippery and that his description "regularly slides between identifying a standard of review, which goes to the strength of the right, and mentioning what courts do when they find violations of the weak or strong rights, which goes to the remedies available for violations."[50] But he maintains that the distinction is useful because it points toward the possibility of enforcing even strong rights through political mechanisms in ways that democratize judicial review. In a strong right–weak remedy combination it is the judicial role that weakens rather than the right itself. Rights enforced through politics rather than coercive court orders can be substantively "strong." That strength, however, depends on whether and to what extent the rights generate claims the legislature and executive feel compelled to address.[51]

Court judgments that deploy weak remedies can strengthen those political claims without directly coercing action in two ways. First, litigation provides a forum for drawing attention to constitutional failures by the government. Second, even the weakest remedy – a straight declaration – can create some purchase for making claims in either legislative or administrative processes. Somewhat stronger remedies, where a court stops short of specifying precisely how the government should address a violation but nonetheless structures a process for ensuring that it does so in a relatively short time frame, offer even greater possibilities for strengthening those claims.

As with a weak right, the central benefit of a weak remedy is the opportunity for constitutional norms to develop incrementally over time and through interactions – the supposed "dialogue" – between the courts and the legislature or executive. A weak remedy will sometimes dictate a timeline or mandate a process that could include consultation with parties to the case or other actors. Even stronger remedies might specify some substantive requirements but either at a very general level or for only certain aspects of a policy. In each case, however, the remedy leaves room for government response but requires the government to explain and justify that response in explicitly constitutional terms.

Tushnet suggests (with substantial caveats) that the strong right–weak remedy combination might offer the best opportunity for democratizing

[50] Tushnet, *supra* note 7, 248.

[51] Ibid., 250–51 ("A nation's constitutional culture, perhaps reinforced by court decisions can give particular rights a 'feeling' of strength").

judicial review while still maintaining some meaningful constitutional constraint on democratic politics.[52] The problem with weak substantive rights is that they push toward a deferential standard of review – at its weakest something close to rational-basis review as developed by the US Supreme Court. Weak rights thus potentially strike a balance between constitutionalism and democracy that overemphasizes democratic control at the expense of rights-based limitations because courts may find constitutional breaches for only clearly unconstitutional action. Weak rights also limit the possibility for the judicial–political dialogue that is the signature feature of weak-form review because they minimize substantive interpretation by courts. The relatively high threshold for finding legislative or executive action unconstitutional that weak rights require also leaves a smaller range of reasonable interpretations for cooperative development by the courts and the legislature.

2. *Democratic experimentalist review*

Charles Sabel, William Simon, and several collaborators have described a related judicial enforcement model they call "democratic experimentalist review."[53] The distinctive feature of experimentalist review is a reliance on a participatory and iterative remedial process in which parties and other stakeholders identify the specific solutions to the violation identified by a court. Experimentalist review "combines more flexible and provisional norms with procedures for ongoing stakeholder participation and measured accountability."[54] As with weak-form remedies generally, the court does not specify the precise remedy but manages a process of "ramifying, participatory self-revision" of the remedy by the parties themselves.[55]

At first glance, experimentalism appears to provide the strong right–weak remedy combination that Tushnet suggests could strike the most appropriate balance between judicial review and democratic control. An experimentalist court makes a liability determination that recognizes a strong but fairly abstract right with a weak remedy that imposes a process for experimenting with substantive standards to fulfill that abstract legal obligation rather than concretely identifying those standards. An

[52] Ibid., 252 (suggesting that a strong right–weak remedy combination might be the most attractive for enforcing social rights but then discussion potential problems with that approach).

[53] Dorf and Sabel, *supra* note 14; Sabel and Simon, *supra* note 14. Tushnet identifies experimentalist review as a weak-form variant. Tushnet, *supra* note 7, 249.

[54] Sabel and Simon, *supra* note 14, 1019.

[55] Ibid., 1020.

experimentalist court cedes control over the specific measures required to fulfill the abstract right to the participants; in the process it establishes and explicitly recognizes the need for those measures to change over time in response to the results of the experiment.[56]

Describing experimentalism in the abstract, however, masks the difficulty of cleanly distinguishing between rights and remedies that Tushnet acknowledges. In critical respects an experimentalist remedy fundamentally weakens the right a court recognizes because all the details that matter in terms of actual compliance are left to the experimental process. Further confounding this distinction, the experimentalist examples Sabel and Simon cite typically involved a structural injunction, the paradigmatic strong-form remedy.[57]

Regardless of whether we view experimentalism as weakening the right or the remedy (or both), however, one central benefit is that a participatory remedial process, like weak-form review generally, makes judicial enforcement more democratic. In contrast to Tushnet's main examples – including Canada's legislative override provision and the United Kingdom's Human Rights Act – experimentalism is an ad hoc, judicially created procedure. Rather than establishing a formal mechanism for political-branch response to judicial decisions, experimentalism democratizes judicial enforcement through the opportunities it provides for private parties and other interested stakeholders to participate in developing public-law norms by specifying concrete remedies for constitutional violations.[58]

Experimentalism also differs from Tushnet's other examples in that it targets executive institutions rather than the legislature. It thus creates a mechanism for democratizing executive decision-making processes as well as judicial rights enforcement. Indeed, Sabel and Simon identify the experimental remedial process in public-law litigation specifically as a mechanism for opening up entrenched bureaucracies that have become immune from democratic control. They characterize this effect as creating "destabilization rights" that force public institutions to engage with citizens and other stakeholders directly.[59]

[56] Ibid.

[57] Sabel and Simon emphasize that the stakeholders the court convenes rather than the court itself determine the "norms that define compliance" in an experimentalist process. Ibid. They also specifically focus on the ways responds to classic objections to structural injunctions in public-law cases. Ibid., 1090.

[58] Ibid., 1055–56. [59] Ibid., 1056.

C. Social rights and alternative forms of judicial review

1. *Theory*

The distinctive features of these alternative forms of review – lightly specified substantive content and/or weak remedies that do not involve directly coercive orders – respond directly to the justiciability concerns. If court enforcement of social rights leaves open the possibility for a political process to redefine their content or if the remedies courts employ do not outline specific policy changes but instead order some change (and possibly direct a process intended to create those changes), then judges are not required directly to take on the complexities of policy development. By the same token the perceived democratic costs of court incursion into legislative and executive territory is greatly reduced because the government retains some authority to develop rights-sensitive policies and can offer alternatives to court remedies.

The democratic payoff is fairly straightforward. Courts provisionally interpret social rights. Political actors are not completely free to ignore those interpretations, but they have the power to develop alternative interpretations in response. Weak remedies leave open alternative compliance options and so don't require that courts dictate detailed policies. The degree of democratic constraint will vary depending both on the extent to which the court specifies the substantive content and the degree to which it retains control over the remedy. Because of this the line between weak and strong enforcement may have a tendency to blur in some cases. But weak-form review offers the possibility of a relatively lighter constraint on the choices of political actors while still requiring those choices to reflect the obligations social rights impose.

Equally important, weak remedies create incentives for the legislature and executive to incorporate social rights obligations into legislation and policy. If the state passes legislation and develops policies that reflect reasonable approaches to fulfilling social rights obligations – and especially if the justifications expressly reflect those obligations – weak-form review requires courts to defer to those judgments even in the face of equally reasonable alternatives. This aspect of weak-form review can prod legislators and administrators to reframe legislative and policy discussions in constitutional terms and generate democratic deliberation over social rights.

Where a court upholds a social rights challenge, weak remedies can have the same effect. Instead of foreclosing debate over the specific policy best suited to satisfy the constitution, weak remedies like declaratory orders and structured negotiations create opportunities for focused discussion of what the constitution requires and how different alternatives might meet those requirements while still meeting other legislative priorities.

Rosalind Dixon describes the potential democracy-reinforcing effect of weak-form review as permitting courts to address legislative "blockages" or "blind spots."[60] Blind spots take three different forms. Legislators are tasked with a broad range of responsibilities in conducting the business of the people. Only some of those responsibilities directly or indirectly implicate the Constitution, and so even the most conscientious legislator may fail to take into account the Constitution's effect on a particular piece of legislation. This risk is potentially greater for social rights because legislators as a group are more likely to come from more affluent backgrounds and thus may fail to appreciate how a particular policy might affect poor people differently. Finally, even where legislators consider the Constitution, their inexperience – at least relative to courts – in balancing constitutional norms with policy objectives may make them unable to see alternative pathways that could accommodate the Constitution.[61]

Blockages are inherent in the legislative process. Legislators may be unable or unwilling to respond to constitutional requirements because the perceived political costs of doing so are too great or the perceived benefits of a different legislative approach sufficiently outweigh a more constitutionally responsive policy. Blockages also can arise within bureaucracies implementing legislation.[62] Experimentalism goes further and argues bureaucracies are even less unresponsive to democratic, or even legislative, control.[63] By addressing these blockages, weak-form review not only mitigates the antidemocratic nature of judicial review, it affirmatively improves the democratic process by making it more responsive either to representative institutions or, in experimentalism, directly to citizens.[64]

2. *Practice*

This theoretical account of these alternative forms of review suggests they offer direct and compelling responses to the core normative objections

[60] Dixon, *supra* note 10, 402. [61] Ibid., 403.

[62] Ibid., 404–5. [63] Sabel and Simon, *supra* note 14.

[64] Dixon, *supra* note 10, 403–6. Dixon distinguishes between the negative and positive dimensions of social rights. She argues that courts should operate at the strong end of the weak-form spectrum when enforcing the negative aspects by developing relatively strong interpretations and using stronger remedies but deferring to legislative sequels. Ibid., 408.

to judicial enforcement of social rights. Applying weak interpretations or remedies not only avoids undue interference with democratic choice; there are reasons to believe that weak-form courts actually can improve democratic results by refocusing democratic processes on fulfilling social rights while leaving open a broad range of policy options for addressing the complex and interrelated problems they raise.

Ideally those same techniques push courts to decide issues and craft remedies that generally play to their institutional strengths – in some cases instigating, structuring, or even managing processes that bring together adversaries (and at times other stakeholders) to resolve legal differences and in others simply declaring in general terms what the law requires while leaving the complex implementation details to the political process. At worst, they prevent courts from becoming hopelessly entangled in making uninformed decisions about complex policy and budget issues with potentially disastrous polycentric effects.

Concrete experience with alternative models has demonstrated that this neat theoretical picture is more complicated. On one hand, critics of weak-form models argue that the point of including justiciable social rights in constitutions is to give courts the power to test the results of the democratic process against a substantive set of norms adopted to constrain democratic excesses.[65] From this perspective weak-form review at best produces a watered-down set of constitutional protections that significantly – perhaps fatally – undermines their status as constitutional rights.

Others critique the theoretical defense of weak-form review. Rather than democratizing judicial enforcement, Sandra Liebenberg and Katherine Young argue that in practice, weak remedies further marginalize poor people.[66] Social rights recognize poor people lack the resources to participate in the very democratic processes that weak-form review expects them to successfully influence to gain those resources.[67] Litigation is expensive, and weak remedies make even judicial victories costly by requiring substantial and persistent follow-up through the political process. If the potential payoff for that expense is a weak right – enhanced procedural obligations as opposed to concrete benefits – then it's likely not worth

[65] E.g., Bilchitz, *supra* note 8; David Bilchitz, "Socio-economic Rights, Economic Crisis, and Legal Doctrine," 12 *Int'l J. Const. L.* 710 (2014); Landau, *supra* note 10.

[66] Sandra Liebenberg and Katherine G. Young, "Adjudicating Social and Economic Rights: Can Democratic Experimentalism Help?," in Helena Alviar García, Karl Klare, and Lucy A. Williams (eds.), *Social and Economic Rights in Theory and Practice: Critical Inquiries* (2015) Ch. 13.

[67] Ibid.

the expense and effort even for someone lucky enough to have access to outside support.

Landau raises a related objection to weak-form review. He argues that the political circumstances in developing countries, where the most social rights cases have been litigated, make weak-form review's idealized judicial–political dialogue unrealistic because "the intended recipient of the dialogue is unlikely to respond effectively."[68] Landau's point is the flip side of Liebenberg's and Young's. Dialogue requires capacity, resources, and willingness on both sides of the discussion. The robust and sustained exchange among courts, the political branches, and civil society over what social rights mean and how they should be enforced assumes those conditions exist. But experience in social rights cases demonstrates they are frequently lacking.

These objections to weak-form review shift the focus from the normative concerns in the justiciability debate to how well weak-form models work in practice. This forefronts the instrumentalist focus of the myth-of-rights debate. The weak-form review literature focuses primarily on the theoretical justifications for restructuring judicial review to make it more democratic, but these instrumentalist concerns are implicit in the discussion. Arguments over conditions and techniques that make court enforcement more democratic and those that make enforcement more likely to generate progressive legislation or policies are related and sometimes coincide.[69] Part of the intuitive appeal of weak-form review is that the political branches are more likely to comply with court orders that provide substantial discretion and that a judicial–political partnership will be both more legitimate and produce better results. Hirschl and Rosevear draw out this practical implication when they approvingly cite Tushnet's analysis of weak-form review as a rare example of an empirically engaged theoretical discussion of the effects of constitutionally entrenched social rights.[70]

Experimentalist review confronts these instrumentalist concerns directly. The participatory, iterative remedial process it prescribes is explicitly aimed at not only democratizing judicial review but also at better solving complex institutional problems than traditional "command-and-control" strong-form remedies.[71] Sabel and Simon acknowledge that experience with experimentalist models is insufficient to draw strong empirical

[68] Landau, *supra* note 10, 192. [69] E.g., Rodriguez-Garavito, *supra* note 10, 1679.
[70] Hirschl and Rosevear, *supra* note 12, 209.
[71] *See* Sabel and Simon, *supra* note 14, 1067–69.

conclusions regarding their superiority over alternatives but argue experimentalist approaches have "functional and jurisprudential properties that make them a distinctively promising to the dimension of uncertainty" that characterize complex public policy problems.[72]

Conversely, assessing judicial review's "actual capacity to induce, real, on-the-ground change, independently or in association with other factors," potentially pits effectiveness against democratic legitimacy.[73] The assertion that weak-form review creates a watered-down version of constitutional rights is premised at least in part on the assumption that a stronger interpretive approach and remedial techniques are more likely to be effective in fulfilling social rights.[74] From this perspective, weak-form review is at best a compromise where any increase in democratic legitimacy comes at the expense of diminishing the status and force of social rights. This also puts the institutional-capacity objection in a different light. Weak-form review solves the problem of judicial capacity to manage complex issues by creating new, unrecognized problems related to the capacity of poor communities to initiate and sustain a dialogue with a state that may itself lack the capacity, or at least the will, to respond.[75]

D. Justiciability and the 1996 Constitution

The 1996 South African Constitution's entrenchment of a broad range of social rights would seem to have resolved the justiciability objections in favor of legitimizing judicial enforcement. As we'll see in the following chapter, the Constitutional Court explicitly affirmed the justiciability of these guarantees in the First Certification judgment.[76] It did so, however, with important qualifications that reflect the influence of the justiciability debate.

The next several chapters trace the consistent influence those concerns have exerted on the Court's approach to interpreting and enforcing social

[72] Charles F. Sabel and William H. Simon, "Minimalism and Experimentalism in the Administrative State," 100 *Geo. L. Rev* 53, 78 (2011).

[73] Ran Hirschl, "From Comparative Constitutional Law to Comparative Constitutional Studies," 11 *Int'l J. Const. L.* 1, 7–8 (2013).

[74] *See* Landau, *supra* note 10, 190 ("the solution to the socio-economic rights problem is to make remedies stronger, not weaker"); *see generally*, Bilchitz, *supra* note 65; Stuart Wilson and Jackie Dugard, "Constitutional Jurisprudence: The First and Second Waves," in Langford *et al.* (eds.), *supra* note 12.

[75] Landau, *supra* note 10; Liebenberg and Young, *supra* note 66.

[76] *Certification of the Constitution of the Republic of South Africa* 1996 (10) BCLR 1253 (CC) (1996).

rights.[77] In each of its social rights decisions – although arguably to a greater degree in the more recent "second-wave" cases – the Court has consistently sought to carefully limit its role to avoid impinging on the power of the political branches and embroiling itself in issues beyond its institutional capacity. As noted earlier, the Court's preoccupation with the justiciability concerns and the limited enforcement role it has developed in its social rights cases frequently draws comparisons to weak-form models of review.[78]

This section first examines the debates over including social rights in the 1996 Constitution, the prominent role the justiciability concerns played in them, and the distinctive South African cast the politics of the transition gave them. It then analyzes the structure of social rights included in the 1996 Constitution and argues that they reinforce the emphasis on political enforcement reflected in the drafting debates. This emphasis on political enforcement likewise reflects the emphasis in both weak-form and experimentalist review on interpretive and remedial techniques that incorporate nonjudicial actors into the rights-enforcement process.

1. *Entrenching social rights*

The debates over including social rights in the 1996 Constitution provide important context for understanding how and why the Court has adopted a substantively limited enforcement role and how that role, although motivated by the same concerns over democratic legitimacy and institutional capacity, differs in key respects from weak-form and experimentalist review.

Justiciability concerns played a central role in the drafting debates, but those concerns were articulated in distinctive ways that reflected the new constitution's anticipated role in transforming South African society, the African National Congress's (ANC's) evolving views on judicial review, and South Africa's long history of parliamentary sovereignty.[79] This mix

[77] E.g., Danie Brand, "Judicial Deference and Democracy in Socio-Economic Rights Cases in South Africa," 3 *Stell L. Rev.* 614, 616 (2011) ("I assume that I do not have to defend the claim that a set of institutional concerns – concerns about the institutional capacity, legitimacy, integrity and security of courts and about classical separation of powers requirements . . . have centrally influenced the development of our courts' approach to deciding socio-economic rights").

[78] E.g., Tushnet, *supra* note 7; Landau, *supra* note 10; Dixon, *supra* note 10; Rodriguez-Garavito, *supra* note 10; Young, *supra* note 10; Sandra Fredman, *Human Rights Transformed* (2008) 113–23.

[79] Brand, *supra* note 77, 267 (noting the prominence of the democratic objection).

of influences helps explain the patterns that emerged in the Court's social rights cases, in particular its emphasis on political enforcement and social rights' role in ensuring democratic accountability.

One of the clearest illustrations of the prominent influence of justiciability concerns in the South African debate is a proposal drafted in 1992 by an influential group of lawyers and legal academics in the Western Cape.[80] The group was organized by Justice Kate O'Regan, at that time a professor at the University of Cape Town, and included Hugh Corder, a prominent participant in the constitutional drafting process.[81] The group proposed a comprehensive set of constitutional rights but recommended including social rights only as directives of state policy. The introduction to their proposal explained this recommendation in terms that directly track the justiciability debate: judicial enforcement of social rights would inappropriately intrude into legislative discretion to set budgets and policy, and "adjudication is ill-suited" to the polycentric issues social rights raise.[82]

In that same year the *South African Journal on Human Rights* devoted the bulk of an entire issue to the specific question whether the new constitution should include social rights.[83] The articles in that issue engage extensively with the justiciability concerns.[84] Etienne Mureinik's defense of social rights in that issue is among the most well known and arguably has had the strongest influence on the Court.[85] He acknowledged that courts enforcing social rights would have to defer to political judgments on how best to fulfill them.[86] This would mean limiting courts to "reviewing policy choices, not making them."[87] Limiting judicial review to existing programs and policies sidestepped the indeterminacy problem because the legislature and executive would fill in those details. Courts would extend a "substantial margin of indulgence" to those choices and thus mitigate the democratic-legitimacy and institutional-competence concerns that social rights raise.[88]

[80] Hugh Corder *et al.*, *A Charter for Social Justice: A Contribution to the South African Bill of Rights Debate* (1992).

[81] Ibid., 1. [82] Ibid., 21. [83] Volume 8, *S. Afr. J. Hum. Rts.* (1992).

[84] *See* Pieterse, *supra* note 9, 885–86 (summarizing the views exchanged in the issue); Theunis Roux, *The Politics of Principle: The First South African Constitutional Court, 1995–2005* (2013) 268–70 (same).

[85] Etienne Mureinik, "Beyond a Charter of Luxuries: Economic Rights in the Constitution," 8 *S. Afr. J. Hum. Rts.* 464 (1992). Theunis Roux argues that the Court essentially adopted Mureinik's framework as the only alternative to the minimum-core framework in international law. Roux, *supra* note 84, Ch. 7.

[86] Mureinik, ibid. [87] Ibid., 470. [88] Ibid., 474.

Even with these limits, however, courts could play a meaningful enforcement role by requiring the state to justify the policies it adopted in terms of the social objectives and priorities those rights established.[89] This would create important, but principally procedural, benefits: "even if the constitutional review of the kind suggested here proved to have no substantive bite at all – even, that is, if it resulted in the annulment of not a single programme – the procedural benefits would be immense."[90]

Another prominent defense by Nicholas Haysom focused specifically on the democratic-legitimacy question. Haysom argued that social rights were necessary for a legitimate democratic process in South Africa. But they also could improve democratic decision-making to make it more responsive to marginalized groups. Entrenched social rights would "enrich political contest and democratic participation – not by limiting political choice but by facilitating real participation in social and political life."[91] Judicial enforcement, on this view, would create "a forum in which members of other marginalized groups could stake their claims and exercise leverage through vigorous debate."[92]

Opponents of including social rights in the new constitution likewise framed their arguments in terms of the justiciability concerns. The most developed critique by Dennis Davis argued that social rights should be limited to the status of directive principles to avoid constraining the new democratic institutions and to prevent courts from overstepping their appropriate institutional boundaries.[93] Davis summarized the justiciability concerns described previously but acknowledged that Mureinik's justification approach provided several convincing responses. By requiring courts to respect rational and sincere government decisions, Mureinik's approach allowed for judicial review of social rights "without involving courts in a process that would be akin to a form of central planning."[94] It also encouraged courts "to do that which they perform best" by establishing a procedure for reviewing policies and programs for claims that they fail to take social rights seriously into account.[95]

For Davis, however, the indeterminacy of social rights raised specific risks in the South African context. He worried that courts might adopt

[89] Ibid. [90] Ibid., 470.

[91] Nicholas Haysom, "Constitutionalism Majoritarian Democracy and Socio-economic Rights," 8 *S. Afr. J. Hum. Rts.* 451, 459 (1992).

[92] Ibid., 463.

[93] Dennis M. Davis, "The Case against Inclusion of Socio-Economic Demands in a Bill of Rights Except as Directive Principles," 8 *S. Afr. J. Hum. Rts.* 475 (1992).

[94] Ibid., 482. [95] Ibid.

a more conservative interpretation than the newly elected government: "a transformed jurisprudence will not occur overnight. Our legal community is schooled in laissez faire positivism." As a result. "legislative assistance is needed to assist in the development of a transformed concept of equality."[96] Directive principles committed both the courts and the democratic process to socioeconomic transformation while putting the emphasis appropriately on realizing that transformation through politics, not law.[97]

2. *Politics and justiciability*

These articles were representative of the broader debate that had been developing in South Africa for some time. As Davis's article illustrates, the justiciability objections took on a specifically South African cast in that debate reflecting two important background assumptions: (1) an ANC-controlled government would be the most progressive force in the new constitutional democracy and lead the way in implementing the legal and political reforms necessary to transform South African society and (2) the legacy of South Africa's conservative legal culture and tradition of strong parliamentary sovereignty required transformation of the legal profession generally and the judiciary specifically for the new constitution to facilitate that transformation.

These assumptions were reflected in the evolution of the ANC's own position on social rights. The ANC encompassed a broad coalition with diverse views on the merits of including a bill of rights in the new constitution.[98] Even after the ANC publicly committed to the adoption of a judicially enforceable set of rights, an internal debate continued over how to structure the relationship between the political branches and the judiciary.[99] As Heinz Klug explains, "the architects of the ANC constitutional guidelines did not see the entrenchment of a bill of rights as altering the fundamental power of a democratically-elected legislature."[100] With respect to social rights, specifically, the ANC viewed their inclusion as necessary to empower the democratic government to implement

[96] Ibid., 487.

[97] Ibid., 489. Davis also argued that "empirical evidence suggests there is limited democratic success" in court-induced social change. Ibid.

[98] Roux, *supra* note 84, 152–61.

[99] Heinz Klug, *Constituting Democracy: Law, Globalism and South Africa's Political Reconstruction* (2000) 80–82.

[100] Ibid., 82.

reforms and also to counterbalance the neoliberal character of the civil and political rights.[101] But the more socialist wing of the party had long viewed social rights as a primarily political mandate "best realized through forms of participatory democracy in which the judiciary had no meaningful role to play."[102]

The expectation that an ANC government would play the leading role in implementing economic and social reforms shaped the way the justiciability concerns were framed. With respect to democratic legitimacy, the concern wasn't primarily that enforcing social rights would give courts license to impose progressive policies and reorder budgets, but instead that a conservative judiciary might enforce them in ways that put a brake on the ANC's capacity to implement progressive economic reforms.[103]

This sense that an unfettered ANC government might be better positioned to implement a robust reform agenda than one limited by a set of rights subject to judicial control is evident in Albie Sachs's early analyses of arguments for including social rights in the new constitution. Sachs was a member of the ANC's Constitutional Committee and played a leading role in developing the ANC's position.[104] Writing in 1989, shortly after the ANC published its "Constitutional Guidelines for a Democratic South Africa," in which it committed to a judicially enforceable bill of rights, Sachs analyzed the possible effect of entrenching social rights in precisely these terms. After asserting that Parliament is the appropriate institution for dealing with social rights, he observed that leaving social rights out of the new constitution might be more radically redistributive than including them: "in effect it would leave Parliament free to adopt any measures it saw fit in the socio-economic arena. The majority in Parliament would almost certainly have a mandate for moving as rapidly as possible towards elimination of the massive inequalities created by apartheid."[105]

[101] Ibid., 91; Roux, *supra* note 84, 155–56 and 265–73.

[102] Roux, *supra* note 84, 155–56. As Roux notes, this reading of the ANC's ambivalence toward judicially enforceable social rights is in tension with Tom Ginsburg and Rosalind Dixon's analysis that the ANC included the social rights in the final constitution as an "insurance swap" to offset the property-rights clause. *See* Tom Ginsburg and Rosalind Dixon, "The South African Constitutional Court and Socio-Economic Rights as 'Insurance Swaps,'" 4 *Const. Ct. Rev.* 1 (2011).

[103] Klug, *supra* note 99, 82.

[104] Roux, *supra* note 84, 267–68; Klug, *supra* note 99, 81–82.

[105] Albie Sachs, "A Bill of Rights for South Africa Areas of Agreement and Disagreement," 21 *Col. Hum. Rts. L. Rev.* 13, 25 (1989). Sachs's views evolved toward stronger support for judicially enforceable rights. *See* Roux, *supra* note 81, 267–68; Albie Sachs, *The Strange Alchemy of Life and Law* (2009) 165–73.

The concern that a robust set of constitutional rights might diminish the ANC's political authority to implement broad social transformation politically was heightened by perceptions that the existing judicial system and overall legal culture required its own transformation. At a minimum, the adoption of a judicially enforceable constitution established a new relationship between courts and Parliament that required judges to adopt a stronger, partially political role. The Constitution's commitment to a new normative framework and an extensive range of specific rights combined with the specific power it granted to courts to review legislation and develop the common law required, at a minimum "a rejection of the crude positivist view of law that had prevailed before 1994."[106]

These changes were not merely a matter of technical, legal reforms. They required a dramatic shift in understandings of the judicial role as well as adoption of new modes of legal argument and reasoning. That kind of transformation would take time to develop and posed a clear risk that even the most progressive judges would be implicitly influenced by this history and cultural legacy when interpreting the new constitution.[107]

3. *Text and structure*

The social rights included in the new constitution generally are structured in ways that reflect the assumption that the democratic process was committed to redressing the inequalities apartheid created and that the legislature and executive would take the lead in effecting that transformation. The final 1996 Constitution contains a broad range of social rights including qualified rights to access to housing, health care, social security, food and water in sections 26 and 27, as well as an unqualified right to basic education in section 29.[108] Section 28 also gives children the unqualified right to "basic nutrition, shelter, basic health care services and social services."[109]

Sections 26 and 27 – the two core social rights provisions – are identically structured with three main clauses.[110] The language and structure

[106] Roux, *supra* note 84, 209; Wilson and Dugard, *supra* note 74, 38.

[107] Ibid., 192. *See* also Pieterse, *supra* note 9, 905.

[108] S. Afr. Const. 1996 §§26–27, 29. [109] Compare S. Afr. Const. 1996 §§26 and 27.

[110] The rights in section 28 (children's rights) and section 29 (basic education) are structured differently and do not contain the limitations clause. The right to access to land in section 25(5) incorporates the resources-limitation language. *See Grootboom*, *supra* note 1, at [19] and nn. 15–18 (summarizing and quoting "the cluster of socio-economic rights" enshrined in the Constitution).

of these rights, although different in several respects, was deliberately modeled in the International Covenant on Economic and Social Rights (ICESCR).[111] The first clause provides an affirmative right to "access" these resources. The second clause, sometimes called the "internal" or "resources" limitations clause, imposes a qualified obligation on the state to "take reasonable legislative and other measures, within its available resources, to achieve the progressive realisation of this right."[112] The third clause, which the resources limitations clause does not qualify, prohibits specific actions related to each right.[113]

The second clause in each right both enables and constrains the democratic process. On one hand, it explicitly commits the state to a fairly robust set of social-welfare programs and limits the scope of legitimate political debate over redistribution in ways that Mureinik described. At the same time it recognizes that the legislature plays a central role in fulfilling each right and that the scope and pace of transformation in the short term will be constrained by budgets and competing priorities.

Both aspects take some of the edge off of the democratic objection to judicial enforcement because courts don't have to choose sides in a polarized political debate over first-order commitments.[114] Including these rights in the Constitution means that the only legitimate arguments are over the nature and scope of social assistance programs, not the more fundamental question whether the state should establish such programs. That still arguably leaves all of the hard practical decisions on the table, but it shifts the emphasis to the institutional-competence questions.

The sheer scope of poverty and depth of inequality that are apartheid's legacy put the institutional-competence issues in a different light as well. In some respects the competence issues are magnified. This especially is true when it comes to resources. The Court frequently cites the hard

[111] Liebenberg, *supra* note 10, 19; Roux, *supra* note 84, 270.

[112] S. Afr. Const. 1996 §§ 26(2) (housing); 27(2) (health care, food, water, and social security). This provision is referred to as an "internal" limitation to distinguish it from the general limitations provision in section 36, which creates a form of proportionality analysis that permits laws to limit constitutional rights in limited circumstances. *See* Kevin Iles, "Limiting Socio-Economic Rights: Beyond the Internal Limitations Clause," 20 *S. Afr. J. Hum. Rts.* 448 (2004); Young, *supra* note 10, 104.

[113] S. Afr. Const. 1996 § 26(3): "No one may be evicted from their home, or have their home demolished, without an order of court made after considering all the relevant circumstances. No legislation may permit arbitrary evictions."

[114] Roux makes this same point with respect to the qualified property rights in section 25, arguing that those qualifications clearly eliminated a classic liberal interpretation that strongly insulated private property from state control. Roux, *supra* note 84, 307–8.

reality of limited resources as a framing device in its social rights decisions.[115] This makes it particularly difficult for courts to address claims that government programs fail to deliver an adequate level of service. As we'll see later, the Court has been most comfortable enforcing the social rights to address categorical exclusions in social programs but consistently reluctant to identify – even as future targets for progressive realization – specific benefit requirements.

But the relatively high level of poverty also makes some aspects of the problem more obvious. The cases the Court has considered typically don't raise questions about the relative effectiveness of complex competing policies that would force it to reassess technical arguments already vetted in the political process. Instead they address clear gaps in policies, negative infringements or obvious failures to consider the social rights. Even in cases that directly challenge specific programs, the Court generally has framed the issues or structured its orders in ways that avoid having to make judgments over the relative adequacy of alternative policies.[116]

The politics of the transition and the Constitution's explicit mandate for transformation would seem to justify a strong judicial role and undermine the case for weak-form review in South Africa. There's no debate whether the state should be committed to a robust set of social service programs, only over the most effective way to structure those programs and the appropriate balance to strike among competing priorities. The political commitment to economic redistribution thus reduces weak-form review's signature benefit of democratizing constitutional interpretation. Rather than usurping democratic authority to decide difficult, contested questions over first-order commitments, judicial enforcement of social rights merely implements the central commitment "to the attainment of social justice and the improvement of the quality of life for everyone."[117]

Conversely, the assumption that the political process is committed to fulfilling the social rights arguably makes weak-form review more appropriate. From this perspective social rights operate as the kind of blueprint for political action that the socialist wing of the ANC favored. A weak-form judicial–political partnership that cooperates in translating

[115] E.g., *Grootboom, supra* note 1, [6]; *Mazibuko and Others v City of Johannesburg and Others* 2010 (3) BCLR 239 (CC) (2009) [3].

[116] The declaratory order in *Grootboom* is one example of this. *Grootboom, supra* note 1, [99].

[117] Ibid., [1].

constitutional norms into practical policies looks like an ideal institutional arrangement for implementing that blueprint.

Roux argues that the political circumstances in South Africa during the Constitutional Court's first two years of existence lent itself to precisely this kind of partnership. The ANC had a vested interest in making the new constitution work and needed a relatively independent Court to give legitimacy to the transition. Although the 1993 Interim Constitution did not contain the broad range of social rights eventually included in the final constitution, its text and structure committed South Africa to social and economic transformation that aligned closely with the ANC's own initial political agenda.[118] The ANC's 1994 Reconstruction and Development Programme established a broadly progressive agenda that included affordable housing, redistribution of agricultural land, and equal access for all to health care services and education.[119]

Circumstances changed, however, shortly after the final Constitution was adopted in 1996. Several political developments began to "cast serious doubts on the ANC's trustworthiness as a partner in the constitutional project."[120] Among these was a new set of fiscally conservative policies under the Growth, Employment, and Redistribution (GEAR) strategy. These strategies shifted the relationship between the ANC and social rights. Rather than a natural alliance in which social rights provided a blueprint and affirmative mandate for progressive legislation and policy, GEAR put the ANC in potential conflict with the Constitution's commitment to robust social and economic transformation.[121]

Later chapters will argue that, rather than engaging in the substantive dialogue that is characteristic of weak-form review, the Court typically resolves social rights cases in ways that cut off any possibility of repeated engagement with the political branches over constitutional substance. Very rarely this involves strong-form interventions. More often, it involves focusing on procedural issues and resolving substantive questions in narrow, context-specific ways. Although these context-specific resolutions might seem to invite dialogue in later cases that could lead to incremental development of broader principles, the Court instead has consistently maneuvered to avoid repeated engagements with similar issues that would establish a consistent interpretive framework.

[118] Roux, *supra* note 84, 173.

[119] Ibid.; African National Congress, *The Reconstruction and Development Programme: A Policy Framework* (1994).

[120] Roux, *supra* note 84, 177–78.

[121] Ibid., 178.

These patterns do not fit the standard account of weak-form review. On one hand, the Court's strong procedural focus looks like weak-form review because it cedes substantive interpretive authority over the social rights to the political process, but the Court's active avoidance of opportunities to engage in explicitly constitutional terms with the political response eliminates weak-form's characteristic judicial–political dialogue. At the same time, the Court's increasingly strong procedural interventions trade interpretive authority for an expanded judicial role managing individual cases that opens up possibilities for influencing the underlying policy decisions and processes.

This substantively thin but procedurally strong role also shares strong affinities with democratic experimentalist review but shorn of the strong remedial control experimentalist examples typically feature. The Court has frequently relied on procedural interventions and enhanced citizen participation to open up public institutions and policy processes to popular influence in ways that look much like the experimentalist interventions described by Sabel and Simon.[122] But, even when it relies on procedural, experimentalist remedies, the Court has articulated a role that deliberately minimizes substantive interpretation of social rights and issued participatory remedies that operate largely outside of judicial control. It also has consistently refused to issue structural injunctions in social rights cases and has generally been reluctant to maintain jurisdiction in other ways to oversee the procedures it mandates.

E. Conclusion

This chapter began by surveying a set of theoretical and practical objections to entrenching social rights and the response that weak-form review and its variant experimentalism provide to those objections. It then described the ways the justiciability concerns emerged in the debates over including social rights in the 1996 South African Constitution and the final form those rights took.

This history illustrates that the democratic-legitimacy and institutional-competence objections played a prominent role in South Africa, but that they were shaped differently by the prevailing political situation and South Africa's legal culture. In particular, the assumption that the ANC would lead the way in implementing a progressive reform agenda and the concern that more conservative courts might seek to limit or

[122] Sabel and Simon, *supra* note 14.

oppose that agenda put an emphasis on political enforcement of the social rights. The social rights were part of a new constitutional framework designed to radically transform South African society both politically and economically.[123] That transformation, however, was expected to come primarily through the democratic process under the ANC's leadership.

The next several chapters describe and analyze the Court's first-wave social rights jurisprudence in light of this general theoretical debate and the ways it manifested in South Africa. This mix of influences has resulted in the Court generally characterizing its enforcement role in terms that range from outright deference to the kind of partnership weak-form review anticipates. Even in that more active, partnership mode, however, the Court has deliberately avoided engaging in a substantive, even weak-form, dialogue. That partnership role has taken forms that more closely resemble experimentalist review by identifying defects in government processes and recognizing procedural rights and remedies but without the more direct judicial control that characterizes the examples of experimental judging Sabel and Simon describe.

[123] *See* Liebenberg, *supra* note 10, 16–19. This history also undermines Hirschl's argument that the 1996 Constitution fits the hegemonic preservation model. *See* Roux, *supra* note 84, 178, n. 116.

3

The first-wave cases

Chapter 1 described the prominent role the justiciability concerns over democratic legitimacy and institutional competence played in the South African debate over entrenching social rights and how the expectation that the ANC would lead the way in fulfilling them framed those concerns in distinctive ways. The persistent influence of that debate is evident through the first wave of the Constitutional Court's social rights decisions.[1] The Court's First Certification judgment rejected a wholesale challenge to the social rights provisions in language, suggesting that the judicial role might be limited. The Court's first substantive decision – addressing the health care rights in section 27 – appeared to confirm that limited role by adopting an apparently deferential standard of review.

In a string of three later cases, however, the Court began to take a progressively stronger role. Beginning with *Grootboom*, where the Court rejected the state's housing policy, through *Khosa*, where it directly altered social-assistance legislation in part on the basis of section 27, the Court appeared to gain increasing confidence in its ability to manage the justiciability concerns.

Even as the Court began to intervene in stronger ways, however, it carefully structured those interventions to limit their effects. The Court consistently avoided developing strong substantive interpretations of the social rights provisions or engaging with arguments over the relative adequacy of existing programs.[2] The Court also deployed interpretive

[1] Several members of the new Court actively participated in the drafting debates over social rights. Theunis Roux argues that in these new cases "the judges were not so much interpreting these rights for the first time as continuing a process of thinking and deliberation that had begun some years before." Theunis Roux, *The Politics of Principle: The First South African Constitutional Court, 1995–2005* (2013) 266.

[2] Sandra Liebenberg, *Socio-Economic Rights: Adjudication under a Transformative Constitution* (2010) 163–64 (summarizing critiques); Marius Pieterse, "Possibilities and Pitfalls in the Domestic Enforcement of Social Rights: Contemplating the South African Experience," 26 *Hum. Rts. Q.* 882 (2004); David Bilchitz, "Towards a Reasonable Approach to the

and remedial techniques that contain weak-form and experimentalist elements either because they created room for real-time legislative or executive response or because they relied on political processes to flesh out the substantive requirements for enforcing social rights.

In each of these cases, the Court nominally applied the same standard of review – the famous "reasonableness" standard – and articulated the scope of that standard in generally deferential terms that reflect an internalization of the justiciability concerns. Both this formal continuity in doctrinal approach and the tendency to avoid strong substantive interpretations set up the stronger turn to proceduralization evident in the second-wave cases. This culminated in the deeply disappointing water-rights decision, *Mazibuko*, where the Court drew on the formal framework it established in these early cases but applied that framework in a more deferential way that put procedural concerns at the center of reasonableness review.[3]

This chapter analyzes the Court's early cases and identifies the groundwork they laid for this turn to proceduralization and how that groundwork is tied to the concerns central to the justiciability debate. We can trace these concerns back to the constitutional drafting history and the prominent role the justiciability objections played in that process. Those concerns also reflect what the Court's critics describe as a conservative, usually formalist, understanding of law and the judicial role that is rooted in the apartheid-era legal culture.[4] Later chapters will show that, rather than revealing a change in approach, the second-wave cases reflect these same persistent concerns but feature a more explicit embrace of procedural rights and remedies as the solution.

A. The First Certification judgment

The 1993 Interim Constitution was the result of a multiparty negotiating process that allowed for a peaceful transition to a fully representative democracy.[5] The settlement included a set of thirty-four constitutional

Minimum Core: Laying the Foundation for Future Socio-economic Rights Jurisprudence," 19 *S. Afr. J. Hum. Rts* 1 (2003).

3 *Mazibuko and Others v City of Johannesburg and Others* 2010 (3) BCLR 239 (CC) (2009).

4 E.g., Pieterse, *supra* note 2, 903–4.

5 *See* Liebenberg, *supra* note 2, 14–15; *see generally*, Richard Spitz and Matthew Chaskalson, *The Politics of Transition: A Hidden History of South Africa's Negotiated Settlement* (2000); Heinz Klug, *Constituting Democracy: Law, Globalism and South Africa's Political Reconstruction* (2000).

principles that the final Constitution was required to incorporate.[6] A newly created Constitutional Court would have the power both to enforce the interim constitution and to review the final constitution for consistency with the constitutional principles.[7]

The challenges to the 1996 Constitution in the First Certification judgment included three objections to the social rights provisions: (1) they were not "universally accepted fundamental rights," which Constitutional Principle II required; (2) they violated the separation of powers required by Constitutional Principle VI; and (3) they were not justiciable because of the budget issues they raise violating another aspect of Principle II.[8] The Court rejected these challenges in two brief paragraphs. Its analysis, however, showed clear indications that the Court accepted, at least to some degree, the concerns these challenges raised.

First, the Court agreed that social rights were not universally accepted rights but found that Principle II permitted the drafters to include rights outside of that class. In reaching this conclusion, the Court rejected the analysis prepared by the Bill of Rights technical committee advising the drafters.[9] To dismiss the separation-of-powers objection, the Court noted that civil and political rights sometimes raise these same concerns. Social rights did not put courts in a role "*so different* from that ordinarily conferred upon them by a bill of rights *that it results in a breach of the separation of powers.*"[10]

The Court interpreted Principle II to require justiciability only for universally accepted rights.[11] Because the Court had already found that social rights were not universally accepted, Principle II did not bar social rights *even if they were not justiciable.* The Court emphasized that this analysis did not necessarily mean courts lacked any power to enforce them: "nevertheless, we are of the view that these rights are, at least to some extent, justiciable." But at this point the Court was willing to recognize

[6] *Certification of the Constitution of the Republic of South Africa* 1996 (10) BCLR 1253 (CC) (1996) ("First Certification judgment"). Sandra Liebenberg provides an insider's analysis of the drafting process and the key issues in the First Certification judgment related to the social rights provisions. *See* Liebenberg, *supra* note 2, 16–21.

[7] S. Afr. Const. (Interim) 1993, Ch. 5, 7.

[8] First Certification judgment, *supra* note 6, [76–77].

[9] Ibid., [76]. The technical committee advising the Bill of Rights drafting committee issued a report during the drafting process that concluded precisely the opposite – that social rights were universally accepted fundamental rights within the meaning of Principle II. *See* Liebenberg, *supra* note 2, n. 103.

[10] First Certification judgment, *supra* note 6, [77] (emphases added).

[11] Ibid.

only the possibility that social rights could be "negatively protected from improper invasion."[12]

Put differently, the Court determined that the constitutional principles did not preclude social rights only because social rights are different from universally accepted rights and therefore do not require court enforcement.[13] Those differences did not exclude social rights from the new constitution, and they were not so extreme that courts could not enforce social rights at all. They nonetheless raised serious questions about the scope of the courts' enforcement power, especially with respect to their potential "positive" dimensions.

B. *Soobramoney*

The Court's first substantive engagement with the social rights seemed to fulfill fears that the Court would adopt a deferential review standard.[14] *Soobramoney* involved a man dying from kidney disease who was denied access to dialysis services at a public hospital. The provincial medical service's policy rationed dialysis service on the basis of several criteria, including whether an individual was likely to benefit either directly from dialysis or because dialysis would make her eligible for a kidney transplant. Mr. Soobramoney's condition was chronic, and dialysis would at best prolong his life.[15] In unanimous judgment with two separate concurrences, the Court rejected Mr. Soobramoney's claim that this policy violated his health care rights.

As Chapter 1 explained, the health care rights are part of section 27, which also provides rights to food, water, and social security. Recall that sections 26 and 27 are identically structured with three clauses.[16] The first clause in section 27 guarantees access to health care, food, water, and social security. The second requires the state to progressively realize those rights within its available resources. Mr. Soobramoney relied on the third clause, which is unqualified by the second and states that "[n]o one may be refused emergency medical treatment."[17]

[12] Ibid., [78].

[13] Others have characterized the Court's analysis differently. E.g., Pieterse, *supra* note 2, 886 (arguing this same language "powerfully dismissed" the justiciability argument and showed that the Court "did not in principle distinguish between the enforcement of civil and social rights"); Liebenberg, *supra* note 2, 20–21.

[14] *Soobramoney v Minister of Health (Kwazulu-Natal)* 1997 (12) BCLR 1696 (1997) ("*Soobramoney*").

[15] Ibid., [2–4]. [16] S. Afr. Const. 1996 §§ 26, 27. [17] Ibid., § 27(3).

The Court held that section 27(3) does not apply to people suffering from chronic diseases like Mr. Soobramoney.[18] It went on to consider and reject the possibility that the dialysis-allocation scheme violated the qualified right to access to health care in section 27(1). Three aspects of this analysis are particularly important because they established the core features of the Court's general approach that many have criticized: (1) insisting that the substantive rights in the first clause are always read together with the internal limitations clause; (2) a flexible but generally deferential "reasonableness" standard of review that reflects the democratic and institutional-competence objections; and (3) a focus on programmatic rather than individual enforcement.

First the Court made what likely is its most criticized interpretive decision with respect to these rights. After emphasizing that resource constraints require extreme caution when interpreting sections 26 and 27, it stated that "the corresponding rights themselves are limited by reason of the lack of resources."[19] In other words, the Court would read the substantive rights together with the internal limitation clause. Rather than identifying what each right requires in the abstract and then going on to consider possible arguments that the state lacks sufficient resources to completely fulfill those obligations, the Court would collapse the two steps.

Sandra Liebenberg explains that this is markedly different "from the traditional two-stage approach to Bill of Rights litigation" the Court uses when applying the general limitations provision in section 36 to other rights. Under section 36, which establishes a proportionality analysis applicable to all the rights in the Constitution, the Court first defines the right in the abstract and then considers the state's arguments for limiting the full scope of the right.[20] There is some debate over how section 36 interacts with the internal limitations imposed by sections 26(2) and 27(2), but the clauses are clearly related and allow the state to justify legislation and actions that infringe on constitutional rights.[21]

Collapsing the first and second clauses when interpreting sections 26 and 27 establishes an analytical framework that merges those two steps. Rather than a defense the state raises to justify its failure to meet a standard the court establishes, this analysis requires the court itself to take into account resource constraints and progressive-realization considerations

[18] *Soobramoney*, *supra* note 14, [19–20]. [19] Ibid., [11].

[20] Liebenberg, *supra* note 2, 141.

[21] Kevin Iles, "Limiting Socio-Economic Rights: Beyond the Internal Limitations Clause," 20 *S. Afr. J. Hum. Rts.* 448 (2004).

when determining what the right requires. That, in turn, requires contingent, fact-specific interpretations that limit the scope of each right. It also shifts the focus to questions of what resources are available and how they should be deployed – questions the Court has consistently said require caution when second-guessing legislative and executive decisions.

Section 27(3)'s "negative" protection against denial of emergency services is not subject to the resources limitation in 27(2). Nonetheless, the Court in *Soobramoney* went on to say that it would interpret section 27(3) taking into account the state's capacity to immediately fulfill those obligations.[22] This extended a de facto resources limit to even this unqualified right and reduced the inquiry, as the Court summarized it, to whether "bureaucratic requirements or other formalities" inappropriately prevented access to available emergency services.[23]

The Court also substantially narrowed the class of people entitled to access even available services by defining emergencies to exclude chronic conditions. It justified this limited reading in institutional-competence and separation-of-powers terms emphasizing that resource-allocation "involve[s] difficult decisions to be taken at the political level in fixing the health budget, and at the functional level in deciding upon the priorities to be met."[24] This requires considerable deference to the political branches when courts address social rights claims: "a court will be slow to interfere with rational decisions taken in good faith by the political organs and medical authorities whose responsibility it is to deal with such matters."[25]

In its next three cases, the Court would apply this same standard of review in very different ways. But it would repeat these same concerns and describe the standard as premised on the need to respect both separation of powers generally and the substantial institutional limitations of courts to deal with the complexity of social policies and budgets.

Despite the constrained role the Court articulated, the majority judgment as well as the two concurrences show a Court deeply concerned about the human suffering and social inequalities that Mr. Soobramoney's situation represented and a strong desire to find ways to make social rights address those problems within these limitations.

22 *Soobramoney, supra* note 14, [11].

23 Ibid., [20]. *See* Craig Scott and Philip Alston, "Adjudicating Constitutional Priorities in a Transnational Context: A Comment on Soobramoney's Legacy and Grootboom's Promise," 16 *S. Afr. J. Hum. Rts.* 206, 238 (2000).

24 *Soobramoney, supra* note 14, [29]. 25 Ibid.

Justice Albie Sachs's concurrence went the furthest in this direction and set the stage for the stronger proceduralist interventions the Court would develop later. Sachs acknowledged the same justiciability concerns as the majority in characterizing the Court's role: "there are areas where institutional incapacity and appropriate constitutional modesty require us to be especially cautious."[26] But he framed this "constitutional modesty" as part of a larger reconfiguration of the "traditional legal context" that requires courts to develop approaches to "take account of the special problems created by the need to provide a broad framework of constitutional principles governing the right of access to scarce resources and to adjudicate between competing rights bearers."[27]

Sachs's emphasis on developing substantive principles and adjudicating competing rights claims suggests a stronger role for the Court than the simple deference to political-branch decisions that the majority's language implies. Courts can't legitimately assume the power to set policies, but they can establish principles and a constitutional framework for the political decision-making process.

C. *Grootboom*

Coming three years after the deeply disappointing *Soobramoney* decision, social rights proponents viewed the *Grootboom* case with great anticipation.[28] Would the Court persist in the limited role it assumed in *Soobramoney* or was *Soobramoney* an artifact of its difficult facts – a claim for expensive health care services that, as the Court emphasized, would at best extend but not preserve life?[29]

Grootboom involved a community of close to 900 people, including Ms. Irene Grootboom, who had resettled on a public sports field outside Cape Town following their eviction from private land slated for housing development. They sued the municipal, provincial, and national governments seeking an order requiring the government to provide temporary housing and other basic services.[30] They relied on both the right to access

[26] Ibid., [58]. [27] Ibid., [54].

[28] *Government of the Republic of South Africa v Grootboom* 2000 (11) BCLR 1169 (CC) ("*Grootboom*").

[29] Pierre DeVos argues that the difference in the resource each plaintiff claimed explains the apparent difference in the Court's approach in *Soobramoney* and *Grootboom*. "Grootboom, the Right of Access to Housing and Substantive Equality as Contextual Fairness," 17 *S. Afr. J. Hum. Rts.* 258, 259–60 (2001).

[30] *Grootboom*, *supra* note 28, [4].

adequate housing in section 26 and, because more than half of the community were children, the right of every child "to basic nutrition, shelter, basic health care services and social service" in section 28(1)(c).[31] The section 28 claim was strategically important because that provision does not contain the same resources and progressive-realization qualifiers that the Court in *Soobramoney* said limited the scope of section 26.

Judge Dennis Davis – who had famously argued against including justiciable social rights in the new Constitution – drafted the High Court opinion and held that the community's situation violated section 28(1)(C) but not section 26.[32] Judge Davis's order declared that the children and their parents in the community were entitled to shelter, required immediate provision of tents, portable toilets, and water and required the government respondents to submit a report explaining how it would implement the order.[33]

The government parties appealed the High Court's order directly to the Constitutional Court. As the case progressed two developments reconfigured the issues in important ways that shaped the Constitutional Court's resolution of the case and the famous declaration that the state's housing policy was unconstitutional. First, the South African Human Rights Commission and the University of the Western Cape's Community Law Centre intervened as *amici curiae*, arguing the Court should interpret section 26(1) to include a minimum core that was violated in this case. This both reopened and broadened the section 26 argument beyond the immediate facts of the case.[34] Second, following an offer by the government, the Court ordered provision of basic services to the community, including water, toilets, and building materials to improve their shelters.[35] This effectively addressed the community's immediate needs and shifted the focus to the general housing policies.

Justice Zak Yacoob authored the Court's decision. He first highlighted the "considerable jurisprudential and political debate" over social rights' justiciability, citing the major South African academic commentary. He then quoted the First Certification judgment saying it put to rest the threshold question whether social rights were at all justiciable, but left open the "very difficult issue" of "how to enforce them in a given case."[36]

[31] Ibid., [13]. [32] *Grootboom v Oostenberg Municipality* 2000 (3) BCLR 277 (C) [23].

[33] Ibid., [26–27]. [34] Roux, *supra* note 1, 285–86.

[35] *Grootboom, supra* note 28, [5]; Constitutional Court order CCT 38–00 (September 26, 2000).

[36] *Grootboom, supra* note 28, [20].

This resolved the easy question of whether courts have any role to play in enforcing social rights but the nature and extent of that role was an issue "which must be carefully explored on a case-by-case basis."[37]

Minimum Core. The most prominent enforcement model available to the Court was the minimum core approach used to enforce similarly worded obligations under the ICESCR. As just noted, several *amicus curiae* argued that the Court should adopt the minimum core in *Grootboom.*[38] Justice Yacoob rejected their arguments, emphasizing that the Court played a very different role and had access to much less information: "the committee developed the concept of minimum core over many years of examining reports by reporting states. This Court does not have comparable information."[39]

After noting some minor textual differences between the treaty and section 26. Yacoob found that "[t]here are difficult questions relating to the definition of minimum core in the context of a right to have access to adequate housing, in particular whether the minimum core obligation should be defined generally or with regard to specific groups of people."[40] He then identified "the real question in terms of our Constitution" as "whether *the measures taken by the state* to realise the right afforded by section 26 are reasonable."[41] In other words, the Constitution focuses on the legislative and executive fulfillment, and court review begins with assessing those measures rather than an abstract standard.

Turning to section 26, Yacoob explicitly adopted the interpretive approach *Soobramoney* identified in which the housing right in section 1 and the resources and the limitations in section 2 "are related and must be read together."[42] But, in marked contrast to *Soobramoney*'s analysis that repeatedly emphasized the limited scope of both sections 27(3) and 27(1), Yacoob proceeded to analyze section 26(1) in expansive terms without referencing resource constraints. Liebenberg cites this elaboration as a paradigmatic – but unusual – example of the Court embracing its obligation to substantively interpret the social rights provisions.[43]

In a remarkable series of paragraphs, Yacoob relied on section 26(1)'s inclusion of the single word "*access*" to adequate housing – contrasting it with the ICESCR's, in his view, more limited right specifically to "adequate

[37] Ibid.

[38] The South African Human Rights Commission and the Community Law Centre of the University of the Western Cape argued in favor of the minimum core standard. Ibid., [17].

[39] Ibid., [32]. [40] Ibid., [33]. [41] Ibid. (emphasis added).

[42] Ibid., [34]. [43] Liebenberg, *supra* note 2, 177.

housing" – to establish a broad-based obligation on the state to develop a comprehensive legislative and regulatory framework that would enable both public and private housing development. This framework requires the state not only to provide housing directly but extends to providing land and essential services such as water, sanitation, electricity, roads, and financing.[44] It also includes the obligation to create conditions necessary for private development of both market-rate and low-income housing. Critically, these expansive obligations require the state to recognize the different economic levels in society and to provide for the special needs of poor people within this comprehensive framework.[45]

Reasonableness Review. After laying out what was essentially an extensive analysis of the unqualified scope of section 26(1), Yacoob reintroduced the limitations in section 26(2), explaining that the provision contains "three key elements that are considered separately: (a) the obligation to 'take reasonable legislative and other measures'; (b) 'to achieve the progressive realisation' of the right; and (c) 'within available resources.'"[46]

The first of these, "reasonable legislative and other measures," is the core of the famous "reasonableness review" standard the Court has applied in all of its social rights decisions following *Grootboom*. Reasonableness first requires that a housing plan "must be a comprehensive one determined by all three spheres of government in consultation with each other as contemplated by Chapter 3 of the Constitution."[47]

Courts have the power to ensure such a plan is in place at all levels of government but, reverting to the deferential language that characterized *Soobramoney*, Yacoob emphasized that "the precise contours and content of the measures to be adopted are primarily a matter for the legislature and the executive."[48] Courts applying this standard "will not enquire whether other more desirable or favourable measures could have been adopted, or whether public money could have been better spent." Instead, they must "recognise that a wide range of possible measures could be adopted by the state to meet its obligations."[49]

The second component of section 26(2) turns out, somewhat surprisingly, to expand the state's obligations. Echoing his discussion of section 26(1), Yacoob noted that the language requires "legislative *and* other measures."[50] Legislation is only the starting point and must be "supported by appropriate, well-directed policies and programmes implemented by the executive." Courts can assess programs for reasonableness "both in

44 *Grootboom, supra* note 28, [35]. 45 Ibid., [34–37]. 46 Ibid., [38].
47 Ibid., [40]. 48 Ibid., [41]. 49 Ibid. 50 Ibid., [42] (emphasis original).

their conception and their implementation." Significantly, although a court is substantially limited in assessing a program's conception because it's specifically barred from examining alternatives, it can ask whether the state is living up to the standards the program establishes: "an otherwise reasonable programme that is not implemented reasonably will not constitute compliance with the state's obligations."[51]

The main criteria for assessing whether a program is reasonably conceived is whether it addresses "[t]hose whose needs are the most urgent and whose ability to enjoy all rights is most in peril."[52] Reasonable implementation incorporates several features. First, a program reasonable at one point can be rendered unreasonable by subsequent changes later in time.[53] Second, reasonableness enforces the right to human dignity that "requires that everyone be treated with care and concern" and therefore courts can go beyond statistical evidence of progress to assess the individual effects of programs: "if the measures, though statistically successful, fail to respond to the needs of those most desperate, they may not pass the test."[54]

Turning to the progressive-realization requirement, Yacoob adopted wholesale the interpretation in paragraph 9 of general comment 3 to the ICESCR. Under this interpretation, progressive realization gives the state flexibility to fulfill each right over time but also "imposes an obligation to move as expeditiously and effectively as possible." "[D]eliberately retrogressive measures" that scale back existing programs require heightened justification by the state.[55] Like Yacoob's expansive interpretation of access to housing, this was another distinct departure from *Soobramoney* that expanded the Court's authority to review legislative and executive action. Puzzlingly, it also incorporated the ICESCR's approach after rejecting the minimum-core model earlier.

Why would the Court accept the ICESCR's interpretation of progressive realization while rejecting the minimum-core approach? It appears that the minimum core crossed a key line the Court has consistently drawn for itself. Adopting the minimum core would have required the Court to take the lead in developing substantive standards for section 26(1). Applying heightened scrutiny for retrogressive measures, by contrast, carves out power that relies on comparative assessment of standards the legislature or executive has already adopted.

Thus, in a clear departure from the strongly deferential and analytically thin approach the Court used to analyze section 27 in *Soobramoney*,

[51] Ibid. [52] Ibid., [44]. [53] Ibid., [43]. [54] Ibid., [44]. [55] Ibid., [45].

Grootboom established a framework that set important boundaries for challenging government action under section 26. *Grootboom* applied that framework to hold that the state "was not meeting the obligation imposed on it by section 26(2)" because it lacked provision for addressing the emergency needs of people like those in the case who faced the prospect of imminent homelessness from eviction.[56] As we will see in later chapters, the Court has continued to rely on this framework in housing-rights cases, and *Grootboom* is now recognized as perhaps its most substantive social rights decision because the Court appealed "to a second-order principle, which gave some definition and purpose to the positive aspect of" section 26(1).[57]

Several aspects of the decision, however, reflect the continued influence of the justiciability concerns. These features are at the center of the continuing debate over *Grootboom* as well as its reputation as a leading example of weak-form review. First, despite its broad interpretation of housing under section 26(1), the Court confirmed the analytical marching order it established in *Soobramoney* where the internal limitations clause determines the substantive scope of the right in each case. Notably, the Court's conclusion that the housing program here was unreasonable flowed directly from its analysis of the section 26(2) limitation factors – principally the government's complete exclusion of a "significant segment of society" from its housing policies. Relying on section 26(2) to frame the analysis first allowed the Court to expressly limit the scope of the reasonableness inquiry to existing legislative and executive measures. Noting that "the precise contours and content of the measures to be adopted are primarily a matter for the legislature and the executive," the Court said that "[a] court considering reasonableness will not enquire whether other more desirable or favourable measures could have been adopted or whether public money could have been better spent."[58]

Following the pattern it established in *Soobramoney*, the Court also imported implicit limits into the textually unqualified children's rights claims in the case. Yacoob rejected the High Court's interpretation that section 28 provided children and their parents a direct and enforceable right to housing as "anomalous" and at odds with "the carefully

[56] Ibid., [69].

[57] Stuart Wilson and Jackie Dugard, "Taking Poverty Seriously: The South African Constitutional Court and Socio-Economic Rights," in Sandra Liebenberg and Geo Quinot (eds.), *Law and Poverty: Perspectives from South Africa and Beyond* (2012) 227.

[58] *Grootboom, supra* note 28, [41].

constructed constitutional scheme for progressive realisation" of social rights.[59] Instead, Yacoob found that section 28 served as a kind of backstop protection that obligated the state to provide shelter to children only where their parents are unable.[60]

Finally, the Court structured its limited remedy directly in response to the justiciability concerns. Instead of identifying the specifics of a constitutionally compliant housing policy, the Court stopped with this declaration and left it to the government to develop its own solution in light of the principles the Court had articulated. The order was further limited to a declaration that the overall housing *program* – not the government's conduct in seeking to evict the individual plaintiffs – was unconstitutional. Although the Court earlier took the municipal government to task for the manner in which it conducted the evictions, it specifically held that "[n]either section 26 nor section 28 entitles the respondents to claim shelter or housing immediately upon demand."[61] Thus section 26 (and section 28) do not provide direct relief for individual plaintiffs and impose only programmatic obligations on the government.

In combination these aspects of the decision – limiting section 26 to programmatic rather than individual relief, assessing reasonableness within the context of existing legislation and policy, imposing only secondary obligations on the government to fulfill the unqualified children's rights, and relying on a purely declaratory order – worked together to significantly ameliorate the concerns raised in the justiciability debate even in a decision that upheld a positive-rights challenge to government policy. Following *Grootboom*, similar challenges would now address only the government's own policies for implementing the housing right, and, at least in this case, the government was responsible for devising its own solution to the unconstitutional gap the Court identified. The Court limited its role to identifying that gap based on a highly general set of constitutional principles.

D. *Treatment Action Campaign*

Grootboom established the Court as an international leader in social rights enforcement.[62] But the Court's limited order and refusal to retain

59 Ibid., [71]. 60 Ibid., [77].

61 Ibid., [88–90] (criticizing the eviction process), [95] (quotation).

62 E.g., Heinz Klug, "*Grootboom* at Home and Abroad: Adventures in the Construction of the Global Constitutional Canon," 1–2 (2012) (describing *Grootboom* as a "canonical"

jurisdiction to monitor compliance drew strong criticism at the time of the decision. Those same critiques continue to circle around discussions of *Grootboom*'s legacy frequently punctuated by the observation that Irene Grootboom died homeless in 2008, eight years after the Court ordered the state to design and implement a new policy.[63]

The Court's next social rights decision, *Treatment Action Campaign*, cemented its international reputation in the social rights field and also appeared to answer some of the domestic criticisms leveled at *Grootboom.*[64] The Court's analysis clearly featured a higher level of scrutiny and, for the first time, it enforced a social right to order direct changes to an existing program.

The plaintiffs in *TAC* challenged restrictions the government had placed on a program for preventing mother-to-child transmission of the HIV virus at birth through a single-dose of the antiretroviral drug nevirapine as unreasonable under section 27. Despite a five-year commitment by the drug's manufacturer to provide nevirapine for free, the government had limited provision of the drug to a small number of research and training sites and banned the use of it outside of these sites.[65]

Although the Court formally applied the same reasonableness standard, its analysis was much more searching and less deferential than in either *Soobramoney* or even *Grootboom.* It also issued a direct remedy that, for the first time, ordered specific changes to a government program. Notably, those changes were to a health care program supported by the same kind of scientific evidence and arguments that the Court in *Soobramoney* had said require substantial deference to government prerogatives and expertise.[66] As we will see, the Court has applied this stronger version

decision in comparative studies of positive rights and citing treatments of it), http://digitalcommons.law.umaryland.edu/schmooze_papers/150/.

63 Pearlie Joubert, "Grootboom Dies Homeless and Penniless," *Mail and Guardian* (August 8, 2008), www.mg.co.za/article/2008–08–08–grootboom-dies-homeless-and-penniless; Edwin Cameron, "What You Can Do with Rights," *The Fourth Leslie Scarman Lecture* (2012) [29] ("It has become a commonplace taunt directed at the Court's socio-economic rights rulings that [Ms. Grootboom] died without a home"), www.lawcom.gov.uk/wp-content/uploads/2015/05/Scarman_2012_Justice_Cameron_What_you_can_do_with_rights.pdf.

64 The Court issued two decisions in this litigation. The first dealt with an interlocutory order. *See Minister of Health and Others v Treatment Action Campaign and Others*, 2002 (10) BCLR 1075 (2002). The second is the main judgment. *Minister of Health and Others v Treatment Action Campaign and Others* 2002 (10) BCLR 1033 (2002) ("*TAC*"). Roux argues that *TAC* and *Grootboom* gained the Court a strong international reputation for its social-rights jurisprudence. Roux, *supra* note 1, 215–16, 262–63.

65 *TAC*, *supra* note 64, [19].

66 *Soobramoney*, *supra* note 14, [30].

of reasonableness review arguably in only one other case, *Khosa*, where substantial equality arguments make it difficult to tease out the manner in which the Court applied reasonableness review.

Both observers and participants in *TAC* have cited a range of factors to explain the stronger role the Court adopted. Prominent among these are the political context – in particular the increasing marginalization created by President Thabo Mbeki's position on the link between HIV and AIDs – and TAC's successful multi-prong strategy that combined strategic litigation with grassroots and political organizing.[67] But at least part of the explanation lies in the confluence of factors that allowed the Court to issue this direct order but still avoid reordering the state's budget, second-guessing its technical judgments or forcing the state to adopt a court-selected policy over its own. In other words, the Court was able to sidestep the justiciability concerns that a strong intervention like this typically would raise. In addition, although *TAC* has had a tremendous practical effect on HIV-AIDs policy within South Africa, in terms of interpreting the health care rights in section 27, these same factors also significantly limited the substantive scope of the decision.

The Court began its discussion by deliberately characterizing the issues in the case as both uncontroversial and limited. After summarizing the parties' arguments the Court obliquely referred to the political backdrop by noting that "[i]n our country the issue of HIV/AIDS has for some time been fraught with an unusual degree of political, ideological and emotional contention."[68] This "contention and emotion" the Court observed could have "rendered the resolution of the case more difficult." But, instead "we have found it possible to cut through the overlay of contention and arrive at a straightforward and unanimous conclusion" because "[t]he essential facts, as we see them are not in dispute."[69]

Separation-of-powers issues opened the substantive discussion with the Court acknowledging that "these considerations are relevant to the manner in which a court should exercise the powers vested in it under the Constitution" but rejecting the possibility that "they are relevant to the question of justiciability."[70] Citing *Soobramoney* and *Grootboom* the Court reiterated that social rights are not unique in raising these concerns

[67] E.g., Roux, *supra* note 1, Ch. 7.4; William Forbath, "Cultural Transformation, Deep Institutional Reform and ESR Practice: South Africa's Treatment Action Campaign," in Lucie E. White and Jeremy Pereleman (eds.), *Stones of Hope: How African Activists Reclaim Human Rights to Challenge Global Poverty* (2011); Mark Heywood, "Preventing Mother-to-Child HIV Transmission in South Africa," 19 *S. Afr. J. Hum. Rts.* 278 (2003).

[68] *TAC, supra* note 64, [20]. [69] Ibid., [20–21]. [70] Ibid., [22].

and so section 27 was clearly justiciable. But, as in *Grootboom*, it said the appropriate starting point is "the measures adopted by the government" and whether they fell "short of its obligations under the Constitution."[71]

Minimum core. In an extensive discussion the Court reinforced its rejection of the minimum-core approach and confirmed the interpretive collapse of sections 27(1) and 27(2) as well as the programmatic character of social rights. This analysis repeated the justiciability concerns and concluded with a description of a carefully circumscribed judicial role specifically designed to minimize those concerns.

The analysis first emphasized that "courts are not institutionally equipped to make the wide-ranging factual and political enquiries" the minimum core entails "nor for deciding how public revenues should most effectively be spent."[72] More broadly, courts "are ill-suited to adjudicate upon issues where court orders could have multiple social and economic consequences for the community." For these reasons the Court concluded the "Constitution contemplates rather a restrained and focused role for the courts." Decisions applying reasonableness review, thus, "may in fact have budgetary implications, but are not in themselves directed at rearranging budgets."[73]

Notably the Court started this discussion of its limits by describing its role in procedural terms citing the founding democratic values in the Constitution: "courts will guarantee that the democratic processes are protected to ensure accountability, responsiveness and openness, as the Constitution requires in section 1."[74] Although considering alternatives to government policy is beyond the scope of reasonableness review, investigating the democratic sufficiency of the processes that lead to those decisions is not.

This concern with ensuring that government procedures are open, inclusive, and accountable – what the Court refers to as "participatory" democracy – extends beyond the social rights cases. The idea that the social rights are tools for promoting democratic accountability played a supporting role in the first-wave cases. But the Court would forefront it as their primary purpose as part of the stronger proceduralization in the second wave.

The result. The Court framed its justifications for intervening directly to change the government's policy in terms that featured the same justiciability concerns it cited to justify its limited interpretive approach. But the close scrutiny it employed in analyzing the government's

[71] Ibid., [25]. [72] Ibid., [37]. [73] Ibid., [38]. [74] Ibid., [36].

reasons for limiting the program featured very little of the deference those concerns imply. Cost was "not an issue" because the nevirapine protocol was "admittedly within the resources of the state."[75] The government had already established the safety and efficacy of the protocol amply demonstrated by the fact that "the drug is being provided by the government itself to mothers and babies at pilot sites in every province."[76] And the protocol was "potentially life-saving" for a particularly vulnerable group of people – children born to HIV-positive mothers dependent on the public health-care system.[77]

Unlike in *Soobramoney*, the Court here accorded little or no deference to the government's scientific evidence and arguments.[78] The government argued that the two-year pilot programs were necessary to determine first, whether a single-dose therapy was effective on its own and whether there was a risk of retransmission without a more comprehensive program that included provision of formula to prevent infected mothers from later breastfeeding their children, a process known as "sero-conversion." Second, it claimed that there was a risk that the therapy would contribute to the development of drug-resistant strains of HIV. Finally, the government raised questions about the long-term safety from administration of nevirapine. To support these arguments, the government submitted affidavits from several scientific, medical, and public health experts.[79]

Concerning the efficacy of nevirapine in preventing mother-to-child transmission of HIV and the risk of sero-conversion, the Court rejected the conclusion of the government's scientific expert as unsupported by the data.[80] Instead, the Court independently assessed "the wealth of scientific material produced on both sides," finding it clearly demonstrated that nevirapine "remains to some extent efficacious in combating mother-to-child transmission even if the mother breastfeeds her baby."[81]

When it came to the risk of developing drug-resistant strains of HIV, the Court determined – without citing any evidence from either

[75] Ibid., [71], [73] ("Where counseling and testing facilities exist, the administration of nevirapine is well within the available resources of the state").

[76] Ibid., [72].

[77] Ibid., [72–73], [78]. In contrast to *Grootboom*, here the Court found that the program's restriction implicated children's rights under section 28 because only the government not parents could provide nevirapine. Ibid., [74–79].

[78] Klug notes in his analysis of the lower court decision in *TAC* that the government specifically cited *Soobramoney* to argue that decisions related to health-care policy were essentially unreviewable. Heinz Klug, "Access to Health Care: Judging Implementation in the Context of AIDS," 18 *S. Afr. J. Hum. Rts.* 114, 117 (2002).

[79] *TAC, supra* note 64, [7]. [80] Ibid., [58]. [81] Ibid.

side – that "this mutation is likely to be transient" and therefore that the risk of a drug-resistant strain developing "is small in comparison with the potential benefit of providing a single tablet of nevirapine to the mother and a few drops to her baby at the time of birth."[82]

The Court then rejected the government's safety concerns as "no more than a hypothetical issue" finding that "[t]here is . . . no evidence to suggest that a dose of nevirapine to both mother and child at the time of birth will result in harm to either of them." In harsh terms, the Court noted that the government's decision to roll out the pilot program on such a large scale was inconsistent with any genuine concern with safety: "these sites cater for approximately 10% of all births in the public sector and it is unthinkable that the government would gamble with the lives or health of thousands of mothers and infants."

The remedy. The Court's searching scrutiny of the government's scientific arguments for limiting the nevirapine program was clearly in tension with the justiciability concerns the Court cited earlier in describing the limits of its enforcement role. But those concerns resurfaced in the Court's discussion of the appropriate remedy and appeared to drive its careful crafting of its final order.

The Court first rejected the government's position that the separation-of-powers concerns limit the remedies available for social rights. Instead, in an extensive discussion that canvassed its own precedents and a range of foreign jurisdictions, the Court found that it had the power in social rights cases to craft even highly intrusive remedies like mandatory injunctions with continuing court oversight.[83]

After establishing that its remedial powers were no different for social rights, the Court nonetheless declined to exercise the full scope of those powers here. Noting that "the executive is always free to change policies where it considers it appropriate to do so" and that "court orders concerning policy choices made by the executive should therefore not be formulated in ways that preclude the executive from making such legitimate choices," it refused to either issue a mandatory injunction or retain oversight to enforce the terms of its order.[84]

The Court also reiterated *Grootboom*'s principle that these rights provide only programmatic relief and don't create individual entitlements. Here that limited the effect of the order: it did "not mean that everyone can immediately claim access" to the nevirapine treatment, only that the

[82] Ibid., [59]. [83] Ibid., [98–114]. [84] Ibid., [114], [127].

government had to "make every effort" to make the treatment universally available as soon as reasonably possible.[85]

The specific terms of the order reflected this concern with preserving executive prerogative to set and change policy. The order required the government to expand the nevirapine policy but gave the government express permission to change the policy if necessary: "the orders made in paragraph 3 do not preclude the government from adapting its policy in a manner consistent with the constitution if equally appropriate or better methods become available for the prevention of mother-to-child transmission of HIV."[86]

If not everything that social rights advocates had hoped for due to the scaled-down remedy, *TAC* nonetheless was a significant advance in the Court's enforcement approach. The Court for the first time ordered direct changes to a specific social-welfare program. In doing so, the Court also put to rest questions whether it would limit the remedies available for social rights – questions that the First Certification judgment's cautious endorsement had left open. This seemed to promise more expansive judicial interventions in later cases.

But these advances were not unqualified, and it was those qualifications that would turn out later to dominate the Court's approach. On a doctrinal level, the Court's application of the same interpretive approach under reasonableness review limited the substantive scope of the decision. Although the Court's searching scrutiny of the government's arguments in *TAC* exhibited far less deference than its abstract description of reasonableness review seemed to allow, its substantive analysis of section 27 was limited by the continued integration of the internal limitations clause and insistence on starting with the challenged policy or legislation. In *TAC* that approach allowed the Court to focus only on the details of the nevirapine policy and the reasonableness of the government's arguments for limiting that particular program.[87] As a result, *TAC* provides very little guidance for applying section 27 in other contexts. Indeed, as a substantive precedent it arguably establishes nothing more than the same

85 Ibid., [125]. 86 Ibid., [135].

87 Wilson and Dugard classify *TAC* with *Soobramoney* and *Khosa* as cases that relied on an administrative-law-related rationality principle to evaluate the exclusion of certain classes of people from a particular program. Relying on that generic principle allowed the Court to evaluate each program "without importing any particular conception of the purposes served by the rights" at issue. Stuart Wilson and Jackie Dugard, "Constitutional Jurisprudence: The First and Second Waves," in Malcolm Langford *et al.* (eds.), *Socio-Economic Rights in South Africa: Symbols or Substance?* (2014) 43.

generic requirement as *Grootboom*: government policy cannot unreasonably exclude a vulnerable class of people.

It was *TAC*'s extensive discussion of the justiciability concerns and the legitimate role those concerns play in shaping its enforcement approach rather than its bold assertion that even the strongest remedial options are available for social rights that the Court later would forefront in *Mazibuko* when it summarized its earlier precedents and concluded that its principal obligation was to ensure procedural fairness and democratic accountability.[88]

E. *Khosa*

At first glance, the Court's next foray into social rights seems something of an anomaly.[89] *Khosa* involved an application to confirm a High Court declaration invalidating provisions in social-assistance legislation that categorically excluded noncitizens from the assistance programs.[90] A group of permanent residents – Mozambicans who had emigrated to South Africa in 1980 – challenged their exclusion under both the right to access social security in section 27(1) and the equality provisions in section 9.[91] A majority of the Court held that excluding permanent residents was unjustifiable discrimination under section 9 and an unreasonable legislative measure under section 27(2). Rather than simply striking down the legislation, the Court directly altered the legislation by "reading in" the words "or permanent resident" to each relevant provision.[92]

TAC is frequently cited as the Court's strongest intervention in a social rights case because it ordered specific changes to a social-welfare program, but *Khosa* stands apart even from *TAC* for several reasons.[93] First, both

88 *Mazibuko, supra* note 3, [62], [64] (emphasizing that in *TAC* and *Grootboom* "the Court took care not to draft policies of its own and impose them on government" and that "all the Court did [in TAC] was to render the existing government policy available to all").

89 *Khosa and Others v Minister of Social Development and Others, Mahlaule and Another v Minister of Social Development*, 2004 (6) BCLR 569 (CC) (2004) ("*Khosa*").

90 Section 172(2) of the Constitution requires the Constitutional Court to confirm any lower court order invalidating legislation. S. Afr. Const. 1996 § 172(2). The High Court invalidated provisions of the Social Assistance Act 59 of 1992 and Welfare Laws Amendment Act 106 of 1997. *Khosa, supra* note 89, [7–8].

91 Ibid., [2–5]. The application alleged several other violations, including the children's rights under section 28. The government eventually conceded that it could not exclude children from the program. Ibid., [33].

92 Ibid., [98].

93 E.g., Mark Tushnet, *Weak Courts, Strong Rights: Judicial Review and Social Welfare Rights in Comparative Constitutional Law* (2008), 245; Katherine Young cites *Khosa* as a rare

cases involved court-directed changes, but the national social-assistance program at issue in *Khosa* was much larger in scope than the nevirapine protocol in *TAC*.

Second, in *TAC* the Court emphasized the minimal cost implications of its order while the cost of the changes in *Khosa* was a central issue in the case, and the majority showed little concern for the government's resources arguments. The majority rejected with minimal analysis (and no deference) the government's own analysis that it could not sustain the costs of expanding the program and in the process appeared to impose a fairly high evidentiary burden on the state when it raises resources arguments in social rights cases.

Third, in terms of substance the Court in *Khosa* agreed to address the applicants' broader claim that the exclusion was unconstitutional not only in their case but across the board as applied to all permanent residents. The High Court had ordered the state to extend the programs to an even broader class of all residents of South Africa based on section 27's unqualified language extending social security to "everyone." The Constitutional Court analyzed the case as challenging the exclusion of only permanent residents – a move that required it to develop criteria for distinguishing between permanent and temporary residents under section 27 – but it easily could have limited its analysis to this particular group. In other social rights cases, the Court has frequently cited the context-specific nature of reasonableness review to avoid extending its analysis beyond the specific facts and individuals involved.[94]

Finally, the Court chose to change the legislation directly by reading the words "permanent resident" into the statute. This was the exact opposite of the open-ended declaration in *Grootboom* and contrasted even with the *TAC* order that the Court emphasized it carefully structured to maintain executive discretion.[95]

Interpretive Approach. Citing its prior precedents, the Court once more confirmed that they made "clear" that "section 27(1) and section 27(2) cannot be viewed as separate or discrete rights creating entitlements and

example of the Court exercising what she calls "peremptory" review. Katherine G. Young, *Constituting Economic and Social Rights* (2012) 162–64.

94 This tendency is more pronounced in the second-wave cases. *See* Part II.

95 The Court has applied the "reading-in" remedy in other cases, notably in the equality context to achieve what Justice O'Regan has called "vineyard" (vs. "graveyard") equality. *See* Kate O'Regan, "Fashioning Constitutional Remedies on South Africa: Some Reflections," 42–43, at www.sabar.co.za/law–journals/2011/april/2011–april–vol024–no1-pp41–44.pdf.

obligations independently of one another." This means that "the content of section 27(1) and the ambit of the section 27(1) right can therefore not be determined without reference to the reasonableness of the measures adopted to fulfil [that obligation]."[96] The Court also repeated that reasonableness review does not permit it to consider alternative measures – it starts and stops with the challenged program.[97]

Outside of these rote repetitions of the analytical structure of reasonableness review, however, the analysis abandons even the relatively limited deference in *TAC*. First, the majority viewed the effect of the intersecting rights much differently than it had in *Soobramoney* where it relied on the narrow scope of section 27(3) to reject the application of the broader right to life. Here it adopted the opposite approach: "when the rights to life, dignity and equality are implicated in cases dealing with socioeconomic rights, they have to be taken into account along with the availability of human and financial resources" in determining the reasonableness of the program.[98] The majority emphasized that the reinforcing effect of these intersecting rights was stronger in this case than in its earlier social rights cases because the challenged program raised equality issues as well as implicating the rights to life and dignity.[99] In other words, unfair discrimination could provide an outside constraint on the state's ability to raise resource-limitations arguments.

The majority then noted that the state had advanced the inflexible position "that non-citizens have no legitimate claim of access to social security" rather than justifying its exclusion of noncitizens as a temporary measure to progressively realize the right.[100] This strengthened the equality claim by eliminating the argument that the exclusion was a deliberate policy choice to prioritize one group over another.

Justice Yvonne Mokgoro, writing for the majority, first emphasized that the reasonableness standard was stronger than mere rationality and required the state to show more than that the challenged measure was rationally connected to a legitimate purpose.[101] She then turned to the equality challenge and noted that citizenship is analogous to race – a specified ground of nondiscrimination in section 9. She found that permanent residents eligible for social-assistance grants are a highly vulnerable group and excluding them from these grant programs has a substantial dignity-degrading effect.[102] This meant that their exclusion from the grant

[96] *Khosa*, *supra* note 89, [43]. [97] Ibid., [48]. [98] Ibid., [44] (emphasis added).
[99] Ibid. [100] Ibid., [50]. [101] Ibid., [67]. [102] Ibid., [71–79].

schemes "is discriminatory and unfair and that this unfairness would not be justifiable under section 36 of the Constitution."[103]

Without specifically analyzing the government's financial arguments – arguments which the Court had granted an unusual delay so the government could provide them – Mokgoro found that "the impact upon life and dignity that a denial of such access has, far outweighs the financial and immigration considerations on which the state relies." Those "same reasons" rendered the scheme unreasonable under section 27.[104]

The Government's Case. Justice Mokgoro's analysis is remarkable for its lack of deference to the government's arguments, especially its claim that the cost of extending the social-assistance scheme would be significant and affect its ability to provide other services. Mokgoro summarized these arguments, emphasizing at several points that the state was unable to provide concrete numbers and that its cost estimates were at best speculative.[105] She then roundly rejected the state's own conclusion finding instead that – even accepting its "speculative" estimates – extending the program would result in only a relatively small increased cost when compared with the overall size of the program.[106] Addressing the government's related argument that the exclusion was a reasonable measure to prevent immigrants from becoming financial drains on the state after they are admitted, Mokgoro identified several ways that the state could constitutionally employ to achieve the same thing without categorically excluding permanent residents from the social-assistance programs – precisely the kind of identification of alternative policies the Court says it will not engage in under section 27(2).[107]

An Anomaly? The Court in *Khosa* applied reasonableness review in an almost unrecognizable fashion and also adopted a direct remedy in circumstances where it easily could have allowed the legislature to devise its own solution by suspending its order, as the Court has done in numerous other cases.[108] In the process the Court also established some fairly strong

103 Ibid., [80]. 104 Ibid., [82]. 105 Ibid., [62].

106 Ibid. Justice Ncgobo in his dissent drew precisely the opposite conclusion from the lack of concrete data finding that the state was entitled to deference: "Policymakers have the expertise necessary to present a reasonable prediction about future social conditions. That is precisely the kind of work that policymakers are supposed to do. Unless there is evidence to the contrary, courts should be slow to reject reasonable estimates made by policymakers." Ibid., [128].

107 Ibid., [64–65].

108 Even in equality cases it sometimes has referred the legislation back to Parliament to remedy the unfair discrimination through amendment. *See Minister of Home Affairs and Another v Fourie and Another* 2006 (3) BCLR 355 (CC) (2005) [156].

principles for applying reasonableness review in future cases: reasonableness is a higher standard than rationality; the state bears a substantial burden to provide evidence of any cost-based arguments, and courts are free to independently assess those estimates. Finally, with respect to the intersecting rights, the Court essentially abandoned the *Soobramoney* approach where it treated the more specific language in section 27 as narrowing the relevant inquiry to effectively exclude the broader right to life from having any effect.[109]

The Court's consistently stronger interventions from *Soobramoney* through *Grootboom*, *TAC*, and *Khosa* suggest a gradual weakening of the justiciability concerns and an emerging confidence in its ability to intervene in social rights cases even where those concerns are present. The final set of first-wave cases – each dealing with section 26 – fit the same trend. The sharp turn toward proceduralization in the second-wave cases is particularly remarkable given this trend. Why would the Court reverse this trend and shift decidedly into a more procedural role?

Chapter 7 argues that, rather than a reversal, the second-wave cases illustrate the largely consistent influence of the justiciability concerns in each case. Mapping the extent of those concerns helps explain the relative strength of the Court's role. On this view, the first-wave sequence demonstrates not the Court's increasing confidence in addressing the justiciability concerns but instead the persistence of those concerns as a consistent constraint. The second-wave cases mark a more explicit shift toward a procedural role as a way to consistently avoid those concerns and so diminish the potential for a more substantive role evident in some of the first-wave cases. Nonetheless, the overall patterns in the cases are largely consistent.

Many analyses of *Khosa* attribute the Court's stronger approach to the section 9 equality issue in the case.[110] The majority's reliance on the exact same reasoning to find violations of both section 9 and section 27 – the exclusion degrades the dignity and threatens the lives of a vulnerable group to whom the Constitution expressly extends the right to access social security – supports that reading. Others emphasize the intersection of rights in *Khosa* and view it as an example of other rights ratcheting up the Court's approach to reasonableness review.[111]

[109] *See* Liebenberg, *supra* note 2, 142–43.

[110] E.g., Jackie Dugard, "Courts and the Poor in South Africa: A Critique of Systemic Judicial Failures to Advance Transformative Justice," 24 *S. Afr. J. Hum. Rts.* 214, 235 (2009) (characterizing *Khosa* as an equality decision).

[111] Liebenberg, *supra* note 2, 161 ("The stringent standard of review applied in this case should be understood in the context of the denial of a basic social benefit to a vulnerable

On these readings, rather than a distinct anomaly, *Khosa* highlights first that the Court treats the justiciability concerns quite differently when faced with issues that place it in a more traditional judicial role. Here the Court forefronted the equality arguments and, despite formally applying reasonableness review, collapsed the analyses in a way that essentially transformed it into a section 9 case.

Focusing on the equality issue – especially the sharp-edged question whether the state constitutionally could categorically exclude permanent residents – also allowed the Court to frame the case in a way that eliminated the justiciability concerns. Rather than a case about the wisdom of competing policy priorities and limited budgets, *Khosa* turned into the much simpler question of whether the state could discriminate across the board against noncitizens.

Khosa also illustrates the Court's greater willingness to adopt a stronger role when faced with strong evidence the state is ignoring or deliberately violating its social rights obligations. The state's argument it could categorically exclude permanent residents raised that concern directly. In addition, the government's failure to file papers timely with the Court pointed toward a failure to take these claims seriously.

F. *Port Elizabeth, Jaftha,* and *Modderklip*

Chronologically *Khosa* is bookended by three significant housing-rights decisions: *Port Elizabeth* in 2003, *Jaftha* in 2004 and *Modderklip* in 2005.[112] All three cases dealt with evictions – a subject the Court emphasized in *Grootboom* has a strong connection to the legal construction of apartheid. *Port Elizabeth* and *Modderklip* considered the application of the Prevention of Illegal Eviction from and Unlawful Occupation of Land Act 19 of 1998 (PIE), legislation adopted specifically to implement section 26 by prohibiting eviction of illegal occupiers except by a court order.[113] PIE creates substantial procedural protections and establishes a multifactor, equitable framework for courts to assess eviction applications. *Jaftha* involved a section 26(1) challenge to two sections of the Magistrates'

group and the intersecting breaches of a socio-economic right and the right against unfair discrimination").

112 *Port Elizabeth Municipality v Various Occupiers* 2004 (12) BCLR 1268 (CC) (2004) ("*Port Elizabeth*"); *Jaftha v Schoeman and Others, Van Rooyen v Stoltz and Others* 2005 (1) BCLR 78 (CC) (2004) ("*Jaftha*"); *President of the Republic of South Africa and Another v Modderklip Boerdery (Pty) Ltd.* 2005 (8) BCLR 786 (CC) (2005) ("*Modderklip*").

113 *Port Elizabeth, supra* note 112, [24] (PIE's preamble "makes clear that it was enacted to" enforce section 26(3)).

Courts Act 32 of 1944 that permitted a creditor to force sale of a person's home to satisfy a judgment debt regardless of the amount of that debt.[114]

Port Elizabeth and *Jaftha* share the distinctive feature of a relatively substantive analysis of section 26 with only limited references to the justiciability concerns that the Court consistently highlighted in its cases through *TAC*. Unique among the social rights cases to date, *Jaftha* interpreted what the Court characterized as the "negative" dimension of section 26(1) without considering the internal limitations in section 26(2). Despite these departures from earlier decisions, both decisions still applied a context-specific enforcement approach to section 26 that limited the scope of the substantive analysis. Each case establishes considerable authority for courts to protect individual housing rights, but the highly fact-specific nature of the inquiries reduces their precedential effects. The strong but case-specific authority is the core of what Chapter 9 calls the eviction model that has emerged in the second-wave eviction cases.

Modderklip presaged the Court's retreat from substantive interpretations in favor of procedural approaches that would emerge as a central feature of the second-wave cases. The Court upheld an innovative remedy issued by the Supreme Court of Appeal (SCA) that balanced the private property rights of a landowner with the section 26 rights of a large community of people who illegally occupied its land. The Court, however, explicitly avoided the SCA's interpretation of sections 25 and 26 – including its finding that section 26 applied horizontally – and instead upheld the remedy on the largely procedural right to access to courts in section 34.

1. *Port Elizabeth*

This case involved a challenge to the Port Elizabeth Municipality's application to evict a small number of people unlawfully occupying vacant, private land. Justice Albie Sachs drafted a unanimous opinion for the Court affirming the SCA's order rejecting the City's application under PIE. As Sachs explained in detail, PIE "was adopted with the manifest objective of overcoming the above abuses [under apartheid] and ensuring that evictions in future took place in a manner consistent with the values of the new constitutional dispensation."[115] PIE was designed to implement the balance the Constitution struck between protecting property rights under section 25 and the right to access housing in section 26

[114] Magistrates' Courts Act 32 of 1944 §§ 66(1)(a), 67.

[115] *Port Elizabeth*, *supra* note 112, [11].

and related rights. PIE does this by permitting eviction of illegal occupiers only through a court order and requiring courts to assess a range of factors in determining whether eviction is "just and equitable . . . considering all relevant circumstances."[116]

Whereas *Grootboom* addressed section 26 directly in the context of an eviction request, *Port Elizabeth* was the Court's first case interpreting PIE's legislative framework implementing section 26(3). These two cases together were the start of an evictions-related jurisprudence that included more than fifteen decisions through the end of 2014. As Chapter 6 explains, however, *Port Elizabeth*'s statutory-focused analytical model would emerge as the Court's dominant framework in these decisions rather than *Grootboom*'s direct engagement with section 26.

Port Elizabeth also was the Court's first sustained foray into the procedural obligations social rights impose on the government – in particular the role that informal dispute-resolution mechanisms should play in resolving social rights disputes and the related obligation to consult with individuals before taking action that implicates those rights.[117] This laid the groundwork for the meaningful engagement requirement that *Olivia Road* identified as an independent constitutional requirement.[118] The Court frequently cites this procedural aspect of *Port Elizabeth* but, despite its substantial evictions jurisprudence, only rarely has the Court elaborated the "constitutional matrix" of PIE.

Sachs explained that PIE inverted the apartheid legal framework in several ways. First, it decriminalized squatting and subjected the eviction process "to a number of requirements, some necessary to comply with certain demands of the Bill of Rights."[119] Second, it reversed the relationship between private and public law. Rather than relying on the common law to normalize the political objectives of apartheid, PIE "temper[s]" common law remedies with "strong substantive and procedural protections" to acknowledge the constitutional imperative to provide homes for victims of apartheid and to treat them with dignity and respect in the interim.[120]

PIE also defines how courts should balance the complex constitutional principles that evictions raise: "rescuing the courts from their invidious

116 Ibid., [25] (quoting PIE section 6).

117 In *Grootboom*, the Court made passing reference to these obligations. *Grootboom, supra* note 28.

118 *Occupiers of 51 Olivia Road, Berea Township and 197 Main Street Johannesburg v City of Johannesburg and Others* 2008 (5) BCLR 475 (CC) (2008).

119 *Port Elizabeth*, supra note 112 [12].

120 Ibid.

role as instruments directed by statute to effect callous removals, the new law guided them as to how they should fulfil their new complex and constitutionally ordained function: when evictions were being sought, the courts were to ensure that justice and equity prevailed in relation to all concerned."[121] PIE effects neither a straightforward "restoration" of common law property and contract rights nor is it simply an opportunity for "judicial philanthropy" for potential evictees.[122] Instead, "PIE has to be understood, and its governing concepts of justice and equity have to be applied, within a defined and carefully calibrated constitutional matrix" that balances sections 25 and 26.[123]

Sachs identified several key principles in this matrix. On one side of the ledger, section 25 recognizes the need to provide some measure of tenure security to people living in informal settlements.[124] There are "three salient features of the way the Constitution approaches the interrelationship between land hunger, homelessness and respect for property rights."[125] The first of these applies the limiting principles the Court adopted in its earlier cases that these rights "are not delineated unqualified terms" or "intended to be immediately self-enforcing" and the primacy of political enforcement: "they presuppose the adoption of legislative and other measures" for fulfillment.[126] Although Sachs was describing section 26 as a whole – as well is the interaction of section 25 – this arguably extends at least indirectly the political control over substance in 26(2) to section 26(3).

The second feature starkly recognizes that 26(3) is not an absolute bar to eviction and instead "expressly acknowledge[s] that eviction of people living in informal settlements may take place, even if it results in loss of a home."[127] The third feature is a corollary of this flexible standard: section 26(3) emphasizes "the need to seek concrete and case-specific solutions to the difficult problems that arise."[128] This reflects an intentional constitutional strategy. The mandate to take all relevant factors into account "is there precisely to underline how non-prescriptive the provision is intended to be" and to leave the judicial task "as wide open as constitutional language could achieve."[129] The upshot is a "judicial function" not designed to "establish a hierarchical" analysis of interests and rights "in an abstract and mechanical way" but instead to effect a flexible, equitable balancing that depends "on the specific factors relevant in each case."[130]

121 Ibid., [13]. 122 Ibid., [14]. 123 Ibid. 124 Ibid., [19]. 125 Ibid., [20].
126 Ibid. 127 Ibid., [21]. 128 Ibid. 129 Ibid., [22]. 130 Ibid., [23].

After setting up this constitutional background, Sachs applied it in a twenty-three-paragraph analysis of PIE's specific requirements. In terms of substance, PIE is almost as nonprescriptive as the constitution. Although PIE provides "legislative guidance" for courts to implement the equitable balance in the form of a set of prescribed factors, it still replicates the context-specific emphasis of the constitution: "PIE treats [the constitutional] values as interactive, complementary and mutually enforcing" that requires "a close analysis of the actual specifics of each case."[131] Thus, the court's role is not to identify abstract principles governing evictions across cases, but to ascertain only what justice requires under specific circumstances: "the phrase 'just and equitable' makes it plain that the criteria to be applied are not purely of the technical kind that flow ordinarily from the provisions of land law."[132]

Lurking behind this flexible framework, however, is a hard principle linked to *Grootboom*'s holding that the state can't ignore the needs of people facing homelessness. In *Grootboom* this translated into a policy gap that Parliament was required to fill. In *Port Elizabeth*, Sachs identifies it as a strong presumption against eviction that shapes a court's application of the PIE factors: "a court should be reluctant to grant an eviction against relatively settled occupiers unless it is satisfied that a reasonable alternative is available, even if only as an interim measure pending ultimate access to housing in the formal housing programme."[133]

This presumption comes from a single factor within PIE's equitable balancing framework: a court must consider the availability of alternative accommodation or land for people in occupation six months or longer. PIE contains no textual indication that courts should give this factor any more weight than the others and certainly doesn't set it up as a presumption. Sachs instead relied on the broader constitutional principles at play in evictions: "the Constitution requires that everyone must be treated with care and concern; if the measures though statistically successful, fail to respond to the needs of the most desperate, they may not pass the test."[134]

Sachs never cites *Grootboom* directly in this discussion but his reference to "the needs of the most desperate" applies the core principle *Grootboom* established. Sachs also repeats *Grootboom*'s emphasis on reasonable implementation and arguably extends it. Whereas *Grootboom* held that reasonable implementation requires policies that "plan, budget and monitor the fulfillment of immediate needs" so that "a significant number"

[131] Ibid., [35]. [132] Ibid. [133] Ibid., [28]. [134] Ibid., [29].

receive accommodation, it also recognized that "not all of them need receive it immediately."[135] Sachs said that even an ideal policy "designed to house the maximum number of homeless people over the shortest period of time in the most effective way" does not exhaust the obligations section 26 imposes. Such a plan is strong evidence supporting an eviction order under PIE; it "falls short, however, from being determinative of whether and under what circumstances an actual eviction order should be made in a particular case."[136]

Sachs's reading of PIE dramatically expands judicial authority and seems to guarantee future clashes between courts and the state in eviction cases. Even an ideal housing policy is subject to challenge as applied to any individual or group that might end up homeless if evicted under it. This cuts back the broad discretion over housing policy that *Grootboom*'s weak remedy yielded to the political branches and restores power to courts to enforce section 26. Why would the Court resurrect the justiciability concerns that *Grootboom*'s declaration seemed so cleverly to put to rest and reinsert itself in what clearly promised to be repeated engagements with those concerns?

Sachs's description of the Court's role in applying PIE's test provides part of the answer. It turns out that courts aren't going to second-guess substantive policies under PIE but instead will rely on nontraditional mechanisms like mediation to prod the parties themselves to find a solution. PIE requires a court to go "beyond its normal functions" and involves "active judicial management according to equitable principles of an ongoing, stressful and law-governed social process."[137] This nontraditional role in managing disputes to achieve justice "has major implications" for all aspects of judging from the issues the court addresses, "questions of evidence, the procedures it may adopt, [to] the way in which it exercises its powers and the orders it might make."[138] Sachs also emphasized that although courts lack the capacity to "correct all of the systemic unfairness to be found in our society," they "can at least soften and minimize the degree of injustice and inequity" in the eviction process.[139] This foreshadowed the emphasis on procedural responses to the justiciability concerns that the Court would later increasingly emphasize.

In a separate sub-section titled "Mediation," Sachs explained that informal dispute-resolution processes like mediation represent "one

[135] *Grootboom, supra* note 28, [68]. [136] *Port Elizabeth, supra* note 112, [29].
[137] Ibid., [36]. [138] Ibid. [139] Ibid., [38].

potentially dignified and effective mode" to resolve the competing constitutional principles and individual interests.[140] He went on to describe in detail how informal processes not only avoid the combativeness of litigation but also promote respect for human dignity and develop pragmatic solutions to "the intensely emotional and historically charged problems" of eviction and land rights.[141] In a clever move that translated PIE's flexible substantive test into a hard procedural requirement, Sachs concluded that "it would not ordinarily be just and equitable to order eviction" under PIE "if proper discussions, and where appropriate, mediation, have not been attempted."[142]

In *Port Elizabeth*, Sachs grounded this nontraditional and procedurally innovative judicial role in PIE's own requirements – especially the emphasis PIE places on informal resolution of eviction disputes through mediation. In *Olivia Road* the Court would transform these into a set of free-standing techniques available in any social rights case either because the parties dispute whether consultation was sufficient or because a court identifies on its own that further process might resolve the case.

2. Jaftha

Jaftha involved a section 26–based challenge to provisions of a 1944 law regulating court procedure that permitted sale of a person's home to satisfy judgment for a debt.[143] The homeowners challenging the law each had received their homes through a state-subsidized program and incurred a relatively small debt – less than approximately thirty US dollars – that they could not repay. Their debtors sought to enforce judgments for those debts by forcing sale of their homes. The sale of their homes would render the owners homeless and also disqualify them from future state housing subsidies, thus implicating section 26(1).[144]

The homeowners argued that the forced sale of their homes violated only what they characterized as the "negative" dimension of section 26(1). Relying on the negative dimension had two important consequences, they argued. First, it required the state to protect their existing access to housing against interference both by the state itself and private individuals. Second, it was not limited by section 26(2) because it did not involve the state's positive duty to provide housing. The High Court had rejected this argument relying on the Court's statements in *TAC* that social rights

[140] Ibid., [39]. [141] Ibid., [39–43]. [142] Ibid., [43].
[143] *Jaftha*, *supra* note 112, [2]. [144] Ibid., [1–7].

do not give rise to any free-standing right separate from the qualified legislative obligations in sections 26(2) and 27(2).[145]

The Court, in a decision written by Justice Yvonne Mokgoro, largely agreed with the homeowners and interpreted section 26(1) to include a negative dimension that is not limited by section 26(2).[146] The Court declined to reach the argument that this negative right applies directly to private individuals, and it also held that the general limitations clause in section 36 applied, thus limiting the scope of the right to some extent.[147] Nonetheless, it held the challenged provisions unjustifiably infringed section 26(1) in some circumstances. Remedying this infringement required reading in a requirement that courts oversee the execution process and consider "all relevant circumstances to determine if there is good cause for the execution" in each case.[148] The Court also spent considerable time elaborating the substantive factors that should guide that oversight.[149]

The government defended the Act under section 36, arguing it was necessary and reasonable to ensure that debts could be collected and that requiring judicial oversight in every case would hamper the ability of poor people to use their homes as collateral to secure loans. The Court accepted these purposes were important enough to warrant some degree of limitation but, in an analysis that accorded little deference to the government, concluded that the facts of these homeowners demonstrated that the challenged provisions emphasized that the limitation in these particular cases were severe both because of the "trifling" size of each debt and the severe consequences of the sale on each homeowner.[150] Liebenberg argues that the Court's analysis "demonstrated considerable sensitivity to the real-life constraints" faced by poor people – a sensitivity that is notably lacking in several of the second-wave cases.[151] The analysis also reveals considerable confidence and a striking absence of any reference to the justiciability concerns.

145 Ibid., [30–32]. 146 Ibid., [33–34].

147 Ibid. Section 36 is referred to as a "general limitations" provision because it permits legislation to limit any constitutional right "to the extent that the limitation is reasonable and justifiable in an open and democratic society based on human dignity, equality and freedom" and "taking into account all relevant factors including – (a) the nature of the right; (b) the importance of the purpose of the limitation (c) the nature and extent of the limitation (d) the relation between the limitation and its purpose; and (e) less restrictive means to achieve the purpose."). S. Afr. Const. 1996 § 36(1).

148 *Jaftha, supra* note 112, [55]. 149 Ibid., [56–60].

150 *Port Elizabeth, supra* note 112, [39–42]. 151 Liebenberg, *supra* note 2, 216.

This confidence is due in large part to the remedy the Court adopted. The Court's remedy transforms this potentially strong substantive right against negative infringements into a largely procedural right to expanded judicial process that looks remarkable similar to the role it established in *Port Elizabeth.* It is no accident that the Court inserted language that tracks PIE. The balancing test the Court adopted boils down to the core requirement of PIE's equitable test that courts consider all relevant circumstances in eviction cases. The key difference is that *Jaftha* pushes that analysis back and applies it to the procedurally prior question of whether an execution should be permitted at all. This is an important distinction because it directly enforces section 26(1), but where successful, the substantive result is largely the same in each instance: access to existing housing is preserved.

More troubling, both analyses explicitly allow for the possibility that a person can be deprived of that access under the right circumstances. *Jaftha* rejected the homeowner's argument for a blanket prohibition against sales in execution for debts below a set amount.[152] *Jaftha* also emphasized that a sale in execution "should ordinarily be permitted" in cases where the debtor "willingly put his or her house up in some or other manner as security for the debt" absent some abuse of court procedure.[153]

3. Modderklip

The Court's final first-wave case, *Modderklip*, is significant for two reasons. First, it presages the pronounced shift to procedure in the second-wave cases and the creativity the Court frequently employs in reframing the issues to avoid the justiciability concerns when enforcing social rights. Second, it reinforces the pattern started in *Port Elizabeth* where *Grootboom*'s abstract principle is transformed into a de facto bar on eviction in individual cases where the state cannot provide alternative accommodation that Chapter 6 analyzes.

In *Modderklip* the Court affirmed an order of the SCA awarding damages against a local government for its failure to enforce an eviction order against the approximately 40 000 residents of an informal settlement that had developed on a private landowner's property. Although both lower courts based their holdings in part on findings that the local government

152 *Jaftha, supra* note 112, [51]. 153 Ibid., [58].

violated section 26(2) by failing to provide alternative temporary housing for the illegal occupiers as required by *Grootboom*, the Constitutional Court declined to reach the section 26(2) question and affirmed the SCA's order on other grounds. By eliminating section 26(2) from its analysis, the Court left open the question whether the SCA's more aggressive remedy for a section 26(2) violation was an appropriate extension of the relatively restrained remedies the Court appeared to favor thus far. Significantly, however, the Court found that a declaratory order, like the one it issued in *Grootboom*, was insufficient in this case.[154]

Modderklip (Pty) Ltd ("Modderklip") was part owner of land upon which some 40 000 squatters had occupied in a township outside of Johannesburg. The owners sued the occupiers for trespass but the individuals convicted were given warnings and simply returned to the settlement upon release.[155] Modderklip unsuccessfully sought assistance from the local authorities to deal with the problem and even offered to sell the land to the local municipality.[156]

Modderklip eventually obtained an order from the Johannesburg High Court evicting the occupiers and requiring the local sheriff to assist in the eviction. The sheriff, however, insisted that Modderklip post a security of 1.8 million rand to cover the costs of the eviction. After additional unsuccessful attempts to gain support from local and national government entities, Modderklip then brought suit in the Pretoria High Court seeking an order to compel the state to remove the occupiers and alleging violations of its rights under section 25(1) of the Constitution, which prohibits arbitrary deprivations of property, its equality rights under section 9, and the rights of the occupiers under section 26(2).[157]

The Pretoria High Court found that the illegal occupation violated Modderklip's property rights under section 25(1) and that this violation was the result of the state's failure to fulfill its obligations under sections 26(1) and 26(2) to provide adequate housing to the occupiers.[158] On the basis of these and additional findings, the court imposed a structural injunction requiring the state to present a plan for remedying these violations.[159]

154 *Modderklip, supra* note 112, [60]. 155 Ibid., [5]. 156 Ibid., [6].

157 Ibid., [11]. Modderklip also alleged that the state violated its duty under section 7 of the Constitution to "protect, promote and fulfil the rights in the Bill of Rights." Ibid.

158 Ibid., [15]. The High Court also found that the state's refusal to assist in the eviction infringed Modderklip's section 9 equality rights. Ibid.

159 Ibid., [16].

The state appealed to the SCA, which largely upheld the High Court's findings but replaced the injunction with an award of damages to Modderklip and a declaration that the occupiers are entitled to continue to occupy the settlement until the state provides alternative housing.[160] Two aspects of the SCA's judgment deserve particular attention. First, the SCA found that the illegal occupation was the result, in part, of the state's lack of any plan "for the immediate amelioration of the circumstances of those in crisis," as required by *Grootboom.*[161] Thus, like the High Court, the SCA found that *Grootboom*'s interpretation of section 26(2) imposed an immediate and concrete duty on the state to provide housing in certain extreme circumstances.

Second, the SCA found that the injunction imposed by the High Court violated the separation-of-powers principle by impermissibly invading the policy-making province of the executive and legislative branches. As the SCA stated it, "[such interdicts] tend to deal with policy matters and not with the enforcement of particular rights. . . . Then there is the problem of sensible enforcement: the state must be able to comply with the order within the limits of its capabilities, financial or otherwise."[162] Specifically, the High Court's order "encroached on policy matters by requiring a prioritisation of the [existing settlement] while there is no evidence that these people are entitled to it."[163]

To avoid these issues, the SCA found that the "only appropriate relief" was an award of "constitutional damages" based on the value of the property. This temporarily protected the occupiers' rights while permitting the state to determine whether to ultimately expropriate the land or find alternative housing for its residents.[164]

The Constitutional Court affirmed the SCA's judgment and remedy but found that it was unnecessary to determine whether the occupiers' section 26(2) rights were violated.[165] Instead, the Court held that the state's failure to assist Modderklip in evicting the occupiers was principally a violation of Modderklip's right to have access to the courts to resolve disputes under section 34 of the Constitution.[166]

[160] *Modderfontein Squatters, Greater Benoni City Council v Modderklip Boerdery (Pty) Ltd; President of the Republic of South Africa and Others v Modderklip Boerdery (Pty) Ltd,* (2004) (6) SA 40 (SCA), [52].

[161] Modderklip, *supra* note 112, [21] (quoting *Grootboom, supra* note 28, [64]).

[162] Ibid., [38–39]. [163] Ibid., [40]. [164] Ibid., [43]. [165] Ibid., [26].

[166] Ibid., [39–48]. Section 34 provides that "everyone has the right to have any dispute that can be resolved by the application of law decided in a fair public hearing before a court or,

The Court's interpretation of section 34 reinforces the emphasis in *Port Elizabeth* and the later eviction cases on judicial management of the effect of eviction orders as well as the principle that the state is required to provide accommodation in all eviction cases both public and private. Specifically, the Court held that section 34 imposes an obligation on the state to enforce court orders and also "to take reasonable steps, where possible, to ensure that large-scale disruptions in the social fabric do not occur in the wake of the execution of court orders, thus undermining the rule of law."[167] In Modderklip's case, this meant that the state was required to do more than rely on existing mechanisms to enforce the eviction order because the eviction of this number of people "would cause unimaginable social chaos and misery and untold disruption."[168]

The Court found that the damages remedy imposed by the SCA was therefore appropriate because it compensated Modderklip while leaving the state with the ultimate responsibility for providing accommodations for the occupiers.[169] In doing so, the Court rejected the state's contentions that declaratory relief was sufficient. Noting the "long history of Modderklip's efforts to relieve its property from unlawful occupation," the Court determined that the situation had reached a stage that required "something more effective than the suggested clarification of [Modderklip's] rights."[170]

The Court's shift from section 26(2) to section 34 as the basis for the constitutional damages remedy also previewed its reluctance to ground a substantive housing-rights jurisprudence on *Grootboom*, and its corresponding preference for finding alternative procedural grounds – even grounds not raised by the parties – for indirectly enforcing section 26 on a case-by-case basis. As Roux explains, the case as framed by the parties posed two potentially far-reaching substantive questions: (1) whether the illegal occupation violated the owner's property rights under section 25(1) and (2) whether the state's inaction both in refusing to evict the occupiers and to provide alternative accommodation violated both the occupiers' section 26 rights and the owners section 25 rights.[171] By shifting to section 34 to uphold the SCA's remedy, the Court avoided both

where appropriate, another independent and impartial hearing or forum." S. Afr. Const. 1996 § 34.

167 *Modderklip*, *supra* note 112, [42]. 168 Ibid., [46]. 169 Ibid., [59].

170 Ibid. 171 Roux, *supra* note 1, 328–29.

questions and still limited *Modderklip*'s precedential effect by finding that the case involved "extraordinary circumstances" not present in the typical eviction.[172] In later cases, in particular *Blue Moonlight*, the Court would reach both of these substantive questions but rely on PIE's equitable balancing test to limit the scope of its analysis in similarly limited fashion.[173]

G. Conclusion

This chapter analyzed the Court's first wave of social rights decisions and traced the continued influence of the justiciability concerns. Those concerns manifested in a relatively consistent set of constraints on the Court's role, including a reluctance to adopt a strong interpretive role and an emphasis on context-specific, case-by-case analysis of social rights. The Court's famous reasonableness review standard, including its analytical marching order that reads the substantive rights provisions in sections 26 and 27 with the internal limitations embodies these constraints. *Grootboom*'s careful declaration reflected those same constraints but also appeared to presage a weak-form compromise that would allow for a limited, incremental substantive role in later cases.

In *TAC* and *Khosa*, however, the Court applied reasonableness review with much less deference and issued direct remedies. These decisions seemed to signal greater confidence in dealing with the separation-of-powers and democratic-legitimacy concerns that constrained the Court in its first several cases and set up a possible shift toward a stronger role. The later eviction-related decisions featured a similarly confident Court, and *Jaftha* in particular suggested the Court might selectively adopt a stronger interpretive role at least with respect to the negative dimensions of the social rights.

The next chapter discusses the debate that emerged over these early cases. On one side, critics of the Court's self-imposed restraints argued that – *TAC* and *Khosa* notwithstanding – the structure of reasonableness review and the Court's insistence on a case-by-case approach fundamentally undermined the power of social rights to effect transformation and hold the state accountable. On the other, commentators – many from

172 *Modderklip, supra* note 112, [47]. 173 *See* Ch. 6.

outside of South Africa – identified reasonableness review and *Grootboom*'s careful compromise as a promising enforcement model that provided a legitimate and pragmatic solution to the dilemmas posed by the justiciability concerns.

4

A "curious divergence"

This chapter assesses the "curious divergence" of opinion over the Court's first-wave social rights decisions.[1] Outside of South Africa several commentators hailed the Court's decisions in *Grootboom* and *TAC* as carefully calibrated interventions that managed to create an appropriately limited role for judicial enforcement without involving courts in the details of social-welfare policy.[2] Within South Africa, however, many argued the Court had adopted an unduly limited interpretive framework for the social rights. In particular, critics cited the Court's apparent rejection of a minimum-core standard in favor of the substantively weak reasonableness review and a remedial approach that defers to state decisions on policy details.[3]

Both sides of this debate recognized that the Court had moved away from the strongly deferential review of *Soobramoney* and that subsequent decisions demonstrated a willingness to use social rights to scrutinize

[1] Theunis Roux, *The Politics of Principle: The First South African Constitutional Court, 1995–2005* (2013) 262.

[2] *See* Cass Sunstein, *Designing Democracy: What Constitutions Do* (2001) 234; Mark Tushnet, *Weak Courts, Strong Rights: Judicial Review and Social Welfare Rights in Comparative Constitutional Law* (2008) 243–47; Mark Kende, *Constitutional Rights in Two Worlds, South Africa and the United States* (2009) 248; Frank I. Michelman, "The Constitution, Social Rights, and Liberal Political Justification," 1 *Int'l J. Const. L.* 13 (2003); Rosalind Dixon, "Creating Dialogue about Socio-economic rights: Strong-Form versus Weak-Form Judicial Review Revisited," 5 *Int'l J. Const. L.* 391 (2007).

[3] Roux, *supra* note 1, 262–65. Prominent critiques include: David Bilchitz, "Giving Socio-Economic Rights Teeth: The Minimum Core and Its Importance," 117 *S. Afr. L. J.* 484 (2002); Marius Pieterse, "Possibilities and Pitfalls in the Domestic Enforcement of Social Rights: Contemplating the South African Experience," 26 *Hum. Rts Q.* 882, 885 (2004); Danie Brand, "The Proceduralisation of South African Socioeconomic Rights Jurisprudence, or 'What Are Socioeconomic Rights For?,'" in Henk Botha *et al.* (eds.), *Rights and Democracy in a Transformative Constitution* (2003); Sandra Liebenberg, "South Africa's Evolving Jurisprudence on Socio-Economic Rights: An Effective Tool in Challenging Poverty?," 6 *L. Dem. and Dev.* 159 (2002).

government programs to some extent.[4] But the critics argued that the Court's context-specific application of reasonableness review resulted in limited substantive interpretations and established an interpretive framework that easily could devolve back into deference. Danie Brand coined the term "proceduralization" to describe this set of critiques.[5]

Others, however, saw in those same limitations the broad outlines of an enforcement approach that could develop into a judicial–political dialogue capable of gradually generating flexible but increasingly substantive principles. The very same features that proceduralized the Court's approach also rendered it an exemplar of "weak-form" or "dialogic" review that could allow the Court to avoid the twin dangers of democratic usurpation or outright abdication while still maintaining a meaningful interpretive and enforcement role.[6]

A. Weak-form dialogue

Grootboom's nuanced application of reasonableness review and carefully limited declaration that the South African government's failure to address the emergency needs of people facing imminent homelessness violated section 26(1) has made it a canonical case in the weak-form literature.[7] *TAC* is the Court's other decision frequently cited as an example of a dialogic approach that is sensitive to separation-of-powers concerns.[8] The heightened scrutiny and direct remedy in *TAC* make it a much stronger intervention on Tushnet's weak–strong continuum.[9]

[4] Murray Wesson, "Grootboom and Beyond: Reassessing the Socio-Economic Jurisprudence of the South African Constitutional Court," 20 *S. Afr. J. Hum. Rts* 284, 285 (2004).

[5] Brand, *supra* note 3.

[6] *See* Tushnet, *supra* note 2; Sunstein, *supra* note 2; Frank I. Michelman, "The Constitution, Social Rights, and Liberal Political Justification," 1 *Int'l J. Const. L.* 13, 27 (2003). *See, generally*, David Landau, "The Reality of Social Rights Enforcement," 53 *Harv. Int'l L. J.* 190, 196 (2012) (critically assessing the Court's "weak-form" model).

[7] *See* Heinz Klug, "*Grootboom* at Home and Abroad: Adventures in the Construction of a Global Constitutional Canon" (2012), available at www.digitalcommons.law.umaryland.edu/schmooze_papers/150/; David Landau, "*Grootboom* the One-Case (or Country?) Canon on Social Rights" (2012), available at http://digitalcommons.law.umaryland.edu/schmooze_papers/142/.

[8] Katherine G. Young, *Constituting Economic and Social Rights* (2012) 149–50 (describing *TAC*'s delayed remedy as an example of "conversational" review); Roux, *supra* note 1, 303 (arguing the Court's remedy in *TAC* was driven by concern for "its longer term relationship with the ANC and the need . . . to engage the political branches as partners in the constitutional project").

[9] Tushnet, *supra* note 2, 245 (characterizing *TAC* as a strong-rights decision).

But the decision still reflects aspects of weak-form review, including a limited interpretation of section 27 and some remedial flexibility. The Court explicitly premised its intervention on the absence of strong justiciability concerns. It also incorporated weaker features where those concerns resurfaced by refusing to retain jurisdiction and creating discretion in its order for the executive to adopt alternatives.

TAC also has been identified as a model of judicial dialogue with non-state actors and as an example of social rights litigation supporting political mobilization to effect social and political change through democratic as well as legal channels.[10] These aspects show continuity with *Grootboom* and illustrate how the Court's context-specific approach appears to invite democratic dialogue even where it scrutinizes challenged programs more closely.

These two cases form the core of the Court's international reputation as a leader in developing weak-form or dialogic enforcement approaches with the potential to instigate broader enforcement of social rights through democratic processes.[11] William Forbath's description of the Court's "judicial collaboration with civil society and reform-minded state actors" in his analysis of the *TAC* case is representative of this assessment. For Forbath, the Court's social rights decisions exemplify a judicial model that "prefers to help and rely upon civil society organizations and reform-minded political actors to develop the political and institutional contexts that make relatively modest, episodic, and iterative judicial interventions yield maximal effects."[12] The key features of this model are an indirect (usually weak-form) judicial role, an emphasis on democratic enforcement processes and incremental (and generally contingent) substantive development of social rights over time usually through some form of dialogue among courts, the political branches and civil society. The largely critical domestic response to these decisions focuses on those same features.

[10] William Forbath, "Cultural Transformation, Deep Institutional Reform and ESR Practice: South Africa's Treatment Action Campaign," in Lucie E. White and Jeremy Perelman (eds.), *Stones of Hope: How African Activists Reclaim Human Rights to Challenge Global Poverty* (2011) 52.

[11] *See* Cesar Rodriguez-Garavito, "Beyond the Courtroom: The Impact of Judicial Activism on Socioeconomic Rights in Latin America," 89 *Tex. L. Rev.* 1670, 1692 (2009); 1692; Landau, *supra* note 6, 195; Roux, *supra* note 1, 38–45.

[12] Forbath, *supra* note 10, 88.

B. Proceduralization

Writing in 2004, Murray Wesson argued that "[t]he approach in *Soobramoney* seems now to have been largely abandoned" in favor of *Grootboom*'s more muscular application of reasonableness review that set the stage for the Court's interventions in both *TAC* and *Khosa*."[13] Despite this, the domestic reaction to the first-wave cases moved from initial "cautious approval" quickly "into searing criticism and general disgruntlement."[14]

Theunis Roux identifies this same "curious divergence of opinion in the academic literature" between foreign and domestic commentary on the first-wave cases.[15] He describes the domestic critique as focused principally on the Court's rejection of the minimum-core framework in favor of a highly proceduralized approach that systematically avoids strong substantive interpretations.[16] As Roux notes, he was among the early critics of *Grootboom* and responded directly to Sunstein's approving assessment by pointing out the now familiar critique that the Court's failure to retain jurisdiction caused substantial delays in implementation of the order.[17]

In an essay written after the Court decided *TAC* but before *Khosa*, *Jaftha*, or *Port Elizabeth*, Danie Brand coined the term "proceduralization" that has become short-hand for the central themes in this critique.[18] Brand argues that the Court's approach to reasonableness review focuses on "structural rather than concrete guiding values and ends: structural good-governance standards such as legality (rationality and nonarbitrariness), coherence, coordination and inclusivity in government policy formulation and decision-making."[19] This procedural approach risks discouraging future social rights litigation, limits the guidance the decisions provide to both policymakers and judges in future cases and is theoretically disappointing because it fails to identify any "substantive political philosophy" underlying the social rights.[20]

[13] Wesson, *supra* note 4, 285. [14] Ibid. [15] Roux, *supra* note 1, 262. [16] Ibid.

[17] Theunis Roux, "Understanding Grootboom – A Response to Cass Sunstein," 12 *For. Constitut.* 41, 42 (2002).

[18] Brand summarizes key arguments made by other domestic critics of the early cases, including David Bilchitz, Dennis Davis, Sandra Liebenberg, Marius Pieterse, and Theunis Roux. Brand, *supra* note 2.

[19] Brand, *supra* note 1, 36. Brand based his argument on *Soobramoney*, *Grootboom*, and *TAC*. He later extended it to other cases. E.g., Danie Brand, "Judicial Deference and Democracy in Socio-Economic Rights Cases in South Africa," 3 *Stell. L. Rev.* 615, 616 (2011).

[20] Brand, *supra* note 2, 37.

Brand acknowledges that the Court applied the reasonableness standard with greater scrutiny in both *Grootboom* and *TAC* than in *Soobramoney* and that it exerted stronger remedial control in *TAC* by directing the government to adopt the nevirapine program.[21] Brand nonetheless finds that the Court's failure to independently develop a substantive standard against which to test the challenged programs in each case still proceduralized the rights because the inquiry is reduced to "whether [the challenged] policies are reasonable in the sense that they are rational, coherent, comprehensive, inclusive and so on and so forth."[22]

For Brand all three decisions reflect the strong influence of this procedural "good-governance" standard. *Soobramoney* limited itself to simple rationality review. *Grootboom*, while incorporating a core substantive interpretation, essentially focused on the obvious "structural" gap in a housing policy that completely excluded the desperately poor. Even *TAC* rested on the clear irrationality of the government refusing to extend a largely cost-free, potentially life-saving protocol that it already approved as safe and effective.[23]

More troubling to Brand, the overall interpretive approach – especially the Court's rejection of the minimum core and incorporation of the internal limitations provision into the content of each right – prevent the Court from engaging in a substantive analysis in future cases.[24] These aspects of proceduralization, he argues, would make it impossible for the Court to address challenges to more complex policies with cost implications and where the arguments are over the relative adequacy of service provision rather than irrational exclusions. This lack of substantive analysis also limits "the wider political impact that socio-economic rights can have on policy formulation and social activism to effect policy change" because it leaves civil society without any leverage to push for substantive changes in legislative and policy debates.[25]

Several critics of the first-wave cases trace these proceduralizing features of reasonableness review to the persistent influence of a judicial culture steeped in a liberal democratic tradition with a history of strong parliamentary sovereignty that reflexively accepts the justiciability objections. Pieterse observes there are "distinctive discursive similarities between the Court's objections to recognizing minimum core obligations" and conventional objections to constitutionalization of social

[21] Ibid., 41–43. [22] Ibid., 49. [23] Ibid., 49–50. [24] Ibid., 46–47. [25] Ibid., 53.

rights.[26] He cites the same features as Brand and adds that the Court's limited interpretations of even the unqualified rights in sections 28, 26(3) and 27(3) reflect "a lingering sense of institutional unease" over "engaging with the explicit prioritization" social rights establish.[27] Pieterse attributes this unease to the reinforcing effects of "'traditional' liberal objections to social rights" including "the associated perceived differences between social and civil rights" and the "conservative, formal, rule-bound and overwhelmingly positive" features of traditional, legal, and judicial culture in South Africa.[28] The cultural roots of these concerns in Pieterse's view make it unlikely the Court will "transcend the imagined boundaries" evident in these cases.[29]

C. Assessing the divergence

What should we make of this curious divergence of views and what does it suggest about the constrained-court thesis and the viability of weak-form review as a response? On one hand, the shared assumption on both sides of the debate is that the Court has developed an institutionally weak approach. Both sides agree that the Court has applied reasonableness review in flexible and substantively limited ways and shown a general propensity for limited remedies that rely heavily on political enforcement either directly through political-branch compliance or through civil society and social-movement pressure.

This descriptive consensus suggests that there's relatively little disagreement over the general shape and key features of the Court's interpretive and enforcement approach in the first wave. These competing accounts diverge instead over the legitimacy and likely effectiveness of this limited and institutionally weaker role. The weak-form view sees the Court's approach as justified because it pays due attention to separation of powers and institutional limits. On this view, attending to those limits may work better over the long term by developing political-branch commitment to the social rights (as well as technically superior programs) that outweigh the short-term costs of delayed remedies and softer constitutional principles. The proceduralization critique views the democratic benefits

[26] Pieterse, *supra* note 2, 899; Stuart Wilson and Jackie Dugard, "Constitutional Jurisprudence: The First and Second Waves," in Langford *et al.* (eds.), *Socio-Economic Rights in South Africa: Symbols or Substance?* (2014) 38.

[27] Pieterse, *supra* note 26, 902–5. [28] Ibid.

[29] Ibid., 905. *See, generally*, Roux, *supra* note 1, Ch. 5.

as likely illusory and, even if genuine, achieved at significant cost to the capacity of the social rights to transform South African society.

1. *Weak-form review without dialogue*

The *Soobramoney/Grootboom/TAC* trilogy is the main focus of this assessment and, especially outside of South Africa, these three cases have received the most attention. The later first-wave decisions – *Port Elizabeth, Jaftha, Khosa*, and *Modderklip* – have received relatively less scrutiny. Yet in each of these cases the Court adopted a relatively stronger role, and with the possible exception of *Port Elizabeth*'s discussion of a managerial role for courts, none of these cases contain weak-form elements. When we connect these cases to the second-wave decisions, it becomes increasingly clear that the Court has not established a generally weak-form approach or tried to structure its decisions to establish a sustained dialogue with the political branches over the substantive scope of the social rights.

Instead, mapping the justiciability concerns on these cases shows the Court generally calibrates its interventions inversely to the strength of those concerns. Although it does not account for all of the variations among the first-wave decisions, focusing on this relationship helps explain to a large extent the range from complete deference in *Soobramoney* to the stricter scrutiny and direct remedy in *Khosa*.

Port Elizabeth, Jaftha, and *Modderklip* are closely linked to *Grootboom* because all four address the politically sensitive question of evictions – an area that would come to dominate the Court's social rights docket beginning in 2011. The literature's focus on *Grootboom*'s famous weak remedy overshadows what has turned out to be the strong, if fairly limited, substantive principle later decisions beginning with *Port Elizabeth* have relied on *Grootboom* to establish: courts can intervene directly to prevent evictions whenever the state does not provide alternative accommodation. Chapter 6 shows that *Grootboom* has not generated a robust democratic dialogue between the Court and the political branches that gradually elaborates what section 26 means for housing policy. Instead the decision's real legacy is a largely procedural, strong-form judicial control over the eviction process in individual cases that follows the model established in *Port Elizabeth.*

Port Elizabeth interpreted PIE as an extension of *Grootboom*'s principle to reassert judicial authority over evictions. In a series of later cases, the Court has steadily hardened *Port Elizabeth*'s presumption against evicting people likely to become homeless into a defacto bar and now routinely issues injunctions in eviction cases. The role the Court plays in these cases doesn't fit the weak-form model both because the Court frequently issues temporary but strong remedies and because the analysis isn't structured to generate dialogue about either housing policy or section 26. These cases focus narrowly on the eviction process itself often with only a limited analysis of the PIE factors and generally without any direct constitutional analysis. This is, of course, the role Sachs described when he asserted that courts could refuse to order eviction even in the face of an ideal housing policy and should deploy nontraditional forms of judicial control to attempt to resolve disputes.

Likewise *Jaftha* expanded *Grootboom* to create mandatory jurisdiction and a new process for courts to balance property and housing rights. The Court articulated an apparently strong substantive principle that negative infringements of section 26 (and by implication section 27) are not subject to the progressive-realization and resources qualifiers. But it translated that principle in largely procedural terms by creating a flexible equitable standard for courts to apply in the same kind of context-dependent, case-by-case fashion that *Port Elizabeth* mandates for evictions under PIE. *Modderklip* is yet another variation of *Port Elizabeth*'s case-management model, although it adds the new remedy of constitutional damages to the judicial arsenal in that role.

Khosa and *TAC* are less closely related than the eviction decisions. Both decisions applied section 27 but in factually and politically different situations. Those very differences, however, put *TAC* in a different light. The stronger role the Court adopted in *TAC* generally is attributed to the Treatment Action Campaign's effective organization and skillful tactics combined with the extraordinary political circumstances of the case.[30] *Khosa* featured none of those things, and yet the Court adopted an arguably stronger standard of review and an even more intrusive and expensive remedy. In both *TAC* and *Khosa*, however, the Court was able to frame the issues in ways that minimized the justiciability concerns and to limit its role as a result. In *TAC*, the narrow issue and the government's inconsistent stance with respect to the scientific questions significantly limited those concerns. Likewise, the government's argument that section 27 excludes noncitizens across the board turned a potentially complex set of issues into a straightforward equality question.

[30] E.g., Young, *supra* note 10; Forbath, *supra* note 11; Mark Heywood, "Preventing Mother-to-Child HIV Transmission in South Africa," 19 *S. Afr. J. Hum. Rts.* 278 (2003).

Taken together the first-wave cases call into question the view that the Court is developing a largely democratic, dialogic approach to enforcement. Sometimes the Court employs weaker interpretations and/or remedies that create the possibility for dialogue – as in *Grootboom* – but a true dialogue in the sense of a series of inter-branch interactions over the same or related substantive issues has not yet developed. More importantly, there's little evidence that the Court's interventions are really aimed at that kind of sustained, iterative substantive exchange. The Court frequently has ignored – and in the eviction cases gone out of its way to avoid – obvious opportunities for inter-branch interaction.

2. *Proceduralization without deference*

Although the Court does not appear to be establishing the kind of political dialogue that is the hallmark of weak-form review, its consistent preoccupation with the justiciability concerns and strong preference for procedural rights and remedies has similar effects and often results in a role that has weak-form characteristics. The Court consistently justifies the core features of reasonableness review and the remedies it employs by reference to the separation-of-powers and institutional-competence issues in each case.[31] This preoccupation also frequently results in a relatively formal, positivist approach to separation of powers and greater deference to the state. In combination the justiciability concerns and this traditional role push the Court away from issues that require assessments of the adequacy or relative merits of particular actions or policies.

Conversely, the Court has been more willing to scrutinize challenged policies closely in cases that raise issues that seem judicially manageable. It also frequently defined the issues it addressed and crafted its interventions to make them fit within a more traditional judicial role. For example, in *TAC* the Court identified the absence of cost considerations as one reason for its stronger intervention and limited its remedy to avoid having to manage the rollout process.[32] In *Khosa* it eliminated potentially complicated resource and priority issues by framing the case as a straightforward

[31] Others have identified these same constraints including the link between them and background cultural and professional expectations that I identify later. *See* Wilson and Dugard, *supra* note 26; Marius Pieterse, "Eating Socioeconomic Rights: The Usefulness of Rights Talk in Alleviating Social Hardship Revisited," 29 *Hum. Rts. Q.* 796 (2007).

[32] *Minister of Health and Others v Treatment Action Campaign and Others*, 2002 (10) BCLR 1033 (2002) ("*TAC*").

textual interpretation of section 27 and clear-cut application of the equality provisions in section 9. *Port Elizabeth* reasserted judicial authority over evictions but shifted the focus of *Grootboom* away from the broader housing policies driving those evictions to the much narrower issues of whether and how a specific eviction can be made more humane. *Jaftha* created an important test for limiting private property rights but one that adopts the *Port Elizabeth* model of case-by-case procedural control and avoids direct involvement in real estate and financial services.

The Court's repeated emphasis that the state plays the lead role in enforcing social rights has a similar dual effect. This generally results in a strong reluctance by the Court to closely scrutinize or overturn policies or programs that reflect a genuine effort by the government to fulfill the social rights. Recall the ANC's concern over judicial rights enforcement becoming a conservative obstacle to meaningful social and economic reforms played a role in the drafting debates. By emphasizing its role as a partner – and a junior partner at that – the Court responds to this concern but also positions itself for deference to government decisions, especially where there's no evidence the government is actively avoiding its responsibilities under the social rights. *Soobramoney* is a straightforward example of this deferential effect, but the weak remedy in *Grootboom* also arguably was driven by this same concern with maintaining a secondary, supportive role.

Conversely, where the Court can characterize its role as facilitating democratic control especially where it implements legislative mandates, it is generally willing to intervene in stronger ways. One example of this is the Court's pattern of proactively interpreting constitution-enforcing legislation. The expansive interpretation of PIE in *Port Elizabeth* and even the Court's emphasis in *TAC* that it was merely implementing the government's own policy reflect this.[33] Also where there's clear evidence that the government has failed to take seriously the social rights' promise of economic and social transformation, the Court also typically finds ways to intervene. *TAC*'s combination of close scrutiny in reaction to the government's pretextual arguments combined with a flexible remedy is a carefully calibrated upward ratchet that arguably reflects

[33] Wilson and Dugard, *supra* note 26, 11 (arguing that "the Court often chose to reach its desired outcome by enforcing procedural rights through directing the implementation of pre-existing policy and through directing the state to keep promises it was alleged to have made to the claimants in a particular case. Where it can, the Court has also relied on applicable legislation and policy to give content to rights").

this aspect. Likewise, *Khosa*'s characterization of the government's position as extreme and inflexible created a direct conflict with section 27's text and a straightforward equality violation that justified the strong remedy of reading in changes to the statute to cover all permanent residents. That broader interpretation of section 27 also eliminated the possibility of follow-up litigation by extending benefits to a clearly defined class rather than applying a fact-specific analysis to extend them only to the plaintiffs.

3. *Proceduralization and politics*

We can trace the weaker elements of the Court's approach in the prominent role the justiciability concerns played in the constitutional drafting history and also to the conservative legal culture that is both a reaction to those concerns and a legacy of the apartheid era. In cases that minimize those concerns and in which the Court can adopt a more traditional role, it is more likely to employ closer scrutiny and/or issue stronger remedies. The Court's critics argue, however, that even those cases are problematic because the Court maintains the structurally flawed reasonableness standard that avoids establishing any substantive principles even where it applies that standard in markedly stronger ways.[34]

Those arguments have force, and the Court has consistently avoided a strong interpretive role. But focusing on the interpretive weakness of reasonableness review obscures the genuinely progressive effects of these decisions and the surprisingly strong role the Court adopted in several cases. A Court solely or even primarily driven by the justiciability concerns and operating within a traditional judicial paradigm would have maintained the strongly deferential version of reasonableness review in *Soobramoney*.

Theunis Roux's analysis of the complex mix of external political, social, and historical that have influenced the Court provides an alternative framework for reconciling both aspects of the Court's approach. Roux identifies the first-wave social rights cases as clear examples of an overall judicial strategy that adeptly exploits external factors to preserve institutional independence.[35] The analysis here focuses more narrowly on the adjudicative strategies in the decisions themselves and the patterns they reveal. I don't attempt to account for the broad range of influences

[34] Wilson and Dugard, *supra* note 26, 226. [35] Roux, *supra* note 1.

that Roux investigates, but the features of the Court's approach I identify largely are consistent with Roux's account.

Roux argues that the limiting features of reasonableness review are part of a deliberate strategy by Court to protect its institutional independence within a political climate that featured an increasing risk of political attack by the ANC while still developing legal standards that were consistent with both the Constitution's text and a set of mostly domestic but partly international legal-professional norms.[36]

The context-dependent reasonableness standard and rejection of potentially inflexible substantive principles like the minimum core that are at the center of the debate over the first-wave cases Roux says reflect these competing pressures. Flexibility is the hallmark of these cases for Roux. The Court's consistent refusal to establish strong normative principles allows it when necessary to adopt a deferential approach. At the same time the Court can ratchet up its standard of review, the remedy, or both in other cases where the "micro-politics" allow for a stronger role.[37] The net result is that the Court is able to operate in a way that both demonstrates its fidelity to constitutional principles while still avoiding unsustainable conflict with either the ANC or the general public.[38]

The external constraints Roux identifies as part of the micro-politics in these cases include aspects of the conservative legal culture that the Court's critics argue reflect the justiciability concerns but also the more progressive legacy of the antiapartheid movement and the expectation that the social rights should play a meaningful role in contributing to social and economic transformation. This includes the personal history of several of the judges who were involved in law-based efforts to resist apartheid.[39] These countervailing influences help explain the cases where the Court adopted a stronger role despite the justiciability concerns as well as the Court's persistent interpretive and remedial creativity.

Taking into account the external political constraints Roux identifies helps to explain the different approaches the Court adopted in the first-wave cases. The Court's inconsistent application of reasonableness review reflects it tacking between the twin pressures of avoiding institutionally unsustainable conflict with the ANC and operating within the boundaries of a traditional judicial role while still living up to the expectations of

[36] Ibid., Ch. 4 and 5. [37] Ibid., 291–92.

[38] Roux uses this model to explain the Chaskalson Court's success in establishing a strong domestic and international reputation across a range of cases. Ibid.

[39] Ibid., 219–31.

constitutional transformation by giving social rights some meaningful effect. In cases where the Court can do both things at once – enforce these rights to some extent while still minimizing justiciability problems and avoiding unsustainable political conflict – its interventions are stronger.

The effects of the justiciability concerns and the conservative legal culture overlap to a large degree with Roux's political account of the first-wave cases. The focus on the internal dynamics of each case in my analysis, however, suggests that there is less consistency to these patterns than Roux's broader focus identifies. Examining Roux's analysis of the more prominent first-wave decisions helps illustrate this difference.

Roux reads *Soobramoney* as a strategic choice by the Court to take a factually and politically uncontroversial case so that it could establish a principled but flexible interpretive framework that allowed it to avoid institutionally damaging decisions in more difficult cases.[40] He points out that the Court went out of its way both to take the case, which it could have declined as lacking sufficient prospects for success, and to analyze sections 27(1) and 27(2), which the plaintiff did not raise. It then proceeded to analyze 27(1) and 27(2) and describe a broad range of institutional limitations not required to resolve the case. Both the Court's decision to reach this largely unbriefed issue and the breadth of the analysis, Roux argues, ran contrary to prudential considerations it has articulated in other cases. It was this superfluous analysis that set the precedent for both the later rejection of the minimum core and the formal integration of the limitations clause into the substance of 27(1).[41]

Grootboom is an application of the flexible strategy the Court set up in *Soobramoney* in a case that presented more difficult legal and political issues. The much-criticized features of reasonableness the Court articulated, Roux argues, reflect a savvy strategy that allowed the Court to adopt a legally defensible interpretive approach that "enlist[s] the ANC as a partner, knowing that the realisation of social rights ultimately lay in its hands."[42]

TAC, for Roux, shows the political genius of this approach but also how a well-resourced social movement can exploit the framework. Roux argues that *TAC* presented a potentially combustible combination of entrenched, public opposition by the ANC grounded in constitutionally unsustainable reasons. The Treatment Action Campaign maneuvered the political environment through a successful organizing, lobbying, and protest campaign that forced the government to take the steps that made the scientific

[40] Ibid., 275–80. [41] Ibid., 275–78. [42] Ibid., 290.

and legal objections untenable and eliminated cost objections. This set up legal arguments that framed the constitutional question as "a simple case of unequal treatment" rather than an exercise in judicial second-guessing of technically complex policy decisions or one that required substantial resources.[43] The public pressure TAC's organizing campaign generated also succeeded in forcing the national government to abandon its opposition before the Court issued its final decision, thus transforming the case into one where a decision in TAC's favor "was President Mbeki's best hope of political salvation" because it would provide a principled excuse for changing course.[44]

Roux concludes that the range of approaches the Court adopted in each of these decisions demonstrates that reasonableness review is a deliberately "shrewd development" that "allows the level of scrutiny to be adjusted to the micro-politics of particular cases."[45] The Court strategically responds to those micro-politics by deliberately calibrating the scrutiny it applies and the remedies it selects in each case.

The account developed here, although less comprehensive in its largely internal focus, generally is consistent with Roux's but suggests that the Court exercises less deliberate strategic control in individual decisions and is more responsive to the particular mix of external and internal factors present in each case. Rather than consistently maneuvering with long-term political consequences in mind, the Court instead is influenced more by the configuration of each case.

On one hand, the conservative effect of the justiciability concerns means the Court is more constrained in its capacity to radically change its approach to exploit the micro-politics of a single case. Where Roux analyzes the Court's consistently "contentless" application of reasonableness review as a tactical maneuver to preserve strategic opportunities, this analysis views them as a reflection of the institutional limits created by the justiciability concerns and conservative conception of the judicial role.[46] As Chapter 7 explains, this makes it unlikely the Court will begin to develop a significantly more substantive interpretive approach to the social rights.

At the same time, the progressive aspects of this mix of influences sometime pushes the Court to reach results in an individual case that set up the possibility of future political conflict but only where it can characterize itself as operating within a more traditional judicial role that

[43] Ibid., 295–96. [44] Ibid., 299. [45] Ibid., 292. [46] Ibid.

does not implicate the justiciability concerns. This opens the door to potentially stronger interventions within those limits even where doing so comes with the risk of political confrontation. The individual politics of each case as well as the Court's long-term institutional survival clearly will play a role in the strength and nature of those interventions, but the first-wave cases show that political considerations aren't the only or even the overriding concern in each case.

This explanation of the decisions tracks Roux's overall analysis and is reinforced by his account of the external factors influencing the Court. But it views the Court as more reactive and less deliberate in its decisions. It also identifies a greater range of complexity in the ways the external and internal influences combine to reach results in single cases that are not always consistent with institutional preservation.

Roux's analysis also reinforces the conclusion that the Court in the first-wave cases was not setting up a long-term dialogue with the legislature and executive over social rights. The weak-form model hypothesizes the possibility for a legislative-judicial exchange and is driven by the perceived democratic benefits of breaking up a judicial monopoly over constitutional interpretation and enforcement while still maintaining traditional constitutional constraints on political power. The constitutional drafting history shows that social rights start from the opposite premise that the Constitution would provide a framework to facilitate political enforcement by an ANC-dominated government that was the natural ally of the social and economic transformation the social rights promise. The partnership that some of these cases discuss is framed as judicial implementation of legislative enforcement measures rather than substantive dialogue over their interpretation.

The broad implications of both an analysis focused on the influence of the justiciability concerns and Roux's emphasis on the Court's institutional security are the same: the Court has shaped its approach in relatively consistent ways in response to an identifiable set of legal, social, and political factors. That consistency, however, is identifiable within each decision and not always across them. Decisions like *Khosa*, *Jaftha*, and *Port Elizabeth* – as well as the strong evictions jurisprudence in the second wave – show that the Court sometimes is influenced by the specific mix of factors in a case to take inflexible stances that it might later have to retreat from to avoid political confrontations despite potential reputational costs in legal-professional terms. This shift in emphasis doesn't diminish the force of Roux's general claim that institutional-security concerns played a substantial role in these cases, but it complicates the picture somewhat by allowing for the possibility that countervailing influences sometimes trump those needs in the short term.

Roux's emphasis on strategic positioning suggests that the Court will seek to maximize flexibility in all cases. This leaves room for stronger interventions like *TAC*, but those interventions should, as *TAC* does, feature "contentless" interpretations that don't commit the Court to strong interventions in later cases. Emphasizing the internal patterns in the Court's approach and their connection to the justiciability concerns shows that the Court sometimes sacrifices flexibility in favor of stronger interventions that demonstrate its commitment to progressive expectations but only where it can characterize those interventions as consistent with a more traditional judicial role.

Roux's reading of *Soobramoney* illustrates both the substantial overlap and key differences in our analyses. Roux cites the fact that the Court easily could have declined jurisdiction on the procedural ground that the case lacked prospect for success and its technically unnecessary analysis of section 27(1) as evidence of the Court's calculated development of reasonableness review.[47]

Roux is correct on both counts: the Court could have avoided taking the case altogether and stopped its analysis with section 27(3). The alternative explanation that Roux raises for these moves, however, is more convincing than the conclusion he draws that they demonstrate a calculated decision to position the Court in later cases.

Roux acknowledges both decisions could have been driven by Mr. Soobramoney's "tragic circumstances" and the potential for adverse publicity if the Court rejected Mr. Soobramoney's claims on narrow section 27(3) grounds without considering section 27(1).[48] The expectations of domestic social rights advocates as well as the substantial international interest in the 1996 Constitution's social rights support this alternative explanation.[49] Refusing on technical procedural grounds the very first case to raise a substantive social rights challenge might have signaled a troublingly narrow approach to jurisdiction generally in social rights cases that arguably would have provoked an even stronger reaction than handing down a disappointing decision in a single case.

47 Roux, *supra* note 1, 276–77. 48 Ibid.

49 It also significant that the Court's docket at this time was still limited by the relatively small number of applications it received, and thus it only rarely refused to hear an application that raised constitutional issues.

The significant justiciability concerns created by the technical and resource-allocation issues intensified by the nature of the services – life-extending versus life-saving in Sachs's characterization – triggered the countervailing pressure to interpret section 27(1) and 27(2) in a way that prevented the Court from intervening. Doing so also would have opened the door to numerous individual challenges for denial of services under each of the social rights that would raise these same justiciability concerns. On this reading, the apparent contradiction in the Court's decision to accept the case only to apply a narrow interpretive approach is more likely a reaction to these countervailing pressures than a deliberate attempt to position itself in later social rights cases.

Khosa, *Jaftha*, and *Port Elizabeth* provide some evidence for this reading. All three cases are difficult to explain if minimizing conflict in individual cases is the overarching principle. *Khosa* rejected the government's argument for resolving the case on its specific facts in favor of establishing an inflexible principle extending social-assistance benefits to all permanent residents despite the government's objection that doing so would create significant resources pressures. The Court also directly altered the legislation rather than stating a general principle and leaving it to Parliament to determine how to comply.

Jaftha abandoned the cornerstone of reasonableness review's flexibility by holding that the internal limitations provisions doesn't apply to enforcement of the negative dimension of section 26(1) and created a new form of expansive jurisdiction for courts in foreclosure cases where homelessness could result. *Port Elizabeth* likewise interpreted PIE to reassert judicial control over evictions even where the underlying housing policy is constitutionally unimpeachable.

Khosa best illustrates the relationship between the justiciability concerns and the strength of the Court's role. The case looks like it should fail on this metric because it required the Court both to change legislation and ignore resource arguments. But the Court made two moves that allowed it to characterize the case as an easy one. First it essentially reframed the issue as an equality question. This put the case firmly within the "traditional" scope of judicial authority and substantially raised the threshold for justification under either section 27(2) or 36. Second, it read the government as arguing for permanent, categorical exclusion of permanent residents. This set up a straightforward textual conflict establishing a clear violation of section 27 and eliminated the argument that this was a temporary prioritization decision justified by limited resources. Paradoxically this highly inflexible legal standard that completely preempted democratic choice solved the democratic-legitimacy problem by narrowing the range of constitutionally permissible options.

These same interpretive moves also eliminated the institutional-competence concerns that the potentially complicated technical and budget questions could have triggered under a serious application of the resources-limitation analysis. They transformed what could have been essentially a series of difficult judgment calls over how much to spend on social assistance and which groups to prioritize into a nearly black-and-white question of whether the government could discriminate across the board against permanent residents in clear violation of section 27's text.

By reading the government's position in this way, the Court made its conclusion inevitable. Equally significant, developing this strong and inflexible interpretation did not set up the prospect of continued interventions that might raise greater justiciability problems in future cases. The hard-and-fast rule that permanent residents are entitled to social assistance is simple and raises no complicated interpretive questions. This explains the Court's decision to frame the case in these broad terms instead of relying on the opportunity to deal with the case strictly on the facts of this group or accepting the proposed settlement. Although adopting a narrower, fact-bound approach would have minimized the justiciability concerns in this case, it would have set up the Court to deal with those same issues later on a case-by-case basis and thus increase the chance of those concerns arising over time.

This also explains the Court's somewhat awkward distinction between permanent residents and temporary residents. Section 27 on its face doesn't make that distinction, but, as the Court acknowledged, extending social assistance to literally everyone would necessarily implicate the resources balancing that the Court so clearly wanted to avoid and managed to avoid here by setting the constitutional bar so high.

This same analysis fits Roux's explanation of *TAC*. The Treatment Action Campaign in *TAC* laid the political groundwork so it could frame the legal question in simple equality terms that effectively raised the constitutional bar for the scientific and policy arguments. The Court in *Khosa* framed the issue as whether section 27 permits a categorical exclusion of permanent residents that allowed it to closely scrutinize the cost arguments. Approaching the analysis in both cases in terms of judicially manageable standards like "equality" and "rationality" allowed "the Court to enforce significant changes to social policies without appearing to set the Government's priorities for it."[50] In *TAC*, that resulted in applying reasonableness review to create flexibility in future cases. In *Khosa*, it required the Court to inflexibly interpret section 27 to substantially reduce the possibility of future challenges.

In contrast to *TAC* and *Khosa* where the Court assumed different interpretive roles to prevent getting entangled in future similar disputes, *Jaftha* and *Port Elizabeth* show the Court expanding its jurisdiction over classes of cases that will bring it into conflict with government policies or decisions. Although the multifactor tests the Court adopted in each case create the flexibility Roux highlights, they also guarantee a steady flow of cases that require judicial intervention.

D. Conclusion

This chapter explored the curious divergence in the assessments of the first-wave decisions. There is no doubt that the Court has adopted a generally weak interpretive approach and that it tends to operate in a procedural paradigm that limits its role. It's also clear that those limitations are driven by the traditional objections to the justiciability of social rights and connected to South Africa's conservative legal culture. At the same time, the Court has demonstrated remarkable persistence and creativity in finding ways to enforce the social rights while still operating within those limits. Whereas that creativity in some ways appeared to position the Court for a sustained substantive dialogue with the political branches, it also reflects a different kind of judicial–political partnership. Rather than substantive exchanges over the interpretation of the social rights, the Court both implements constitution-enforcing legislation and polices instances of obvious political failure to recognize the obligations social rights impose. Both the limitations in the Court's approach and this more affirmative partnership role largely track Roux's account of the political constraints that have shaped the social rights decisions.

The next several chapters explore how the external constraints Roux identifies and the justiciability concerns together have continued to influence the Court's social rights jurisprudence. This combination of internal and external influences helps explain the Court's shift to a more explicitly procedural approach in the second-wave cases. That shift fulfills the critics' prediction that the Court would continue to apply reasonableness review in a substantively thin way that limits the precedential effect of

[50] Roux, *supra* note 1, 292.

individual cases. At the same time, however, the Court also has developed a set of procedural rights and remedies and applied them in relatively limited but surprisingly strong ways to protect poor people, especially in the eviction context. It also has expanded its partnership role both by finding opportunities to robustly enforce legislative mandates and by developing an explicit account of the connection between social rights and democracy.

PART II

Procedure and the second wave

5

The second-wave cases

Writing in 2009 for a unanimous Court in the water-rights case *Mazibuko v City of Johannesburg*, Justice Kate O'Regan summarized the Court's approach to reasonableness review for social rights claims in procedural terms: "a reasonableness challenge requires government to explain the choices it has made. To do so, it must provide the information it has considered and the process it has followed to determine its policy."[1] Courts can provide "appropriate relief" if "the process followed by government is flawed or the information gathered is obviously inadequate or incomplete."[2] Enforcing the social rights by requiring the government to explain and defend the process it used to reach a challenged decision, O'Regan explained, turns these rights into tools for "the deepening of democracy. They enable citizens to hold government accountable not only through the ballot box but also, in a different way, through litigation."[3]

Mazibuko was the most significant case in what turned out to be an extraordinary term that included no fewer than seven social rights decisions.[4] *Mazibuko* looms largest among this group because social rights advocates perceived the strong procedural emphasis and deliberately secondary judicial role the Court adopted as a distinct and disappointing

[1] *Mazibuko and Others v City of Johannesburg and Others* 2010 BCLR 239 (CC) (2009) [71]. In this case the Court rejected claims by residents of Soweto that the installation of prepaid water meters and the City of Johannesburg's broader water policy violated their right to access to water in section 27 of the Constitution.

[2] Ibid. [3] Ibid.

[4] The other six decisions are as follows: *Machele and Others v Mailula and Others* 2009 (8) BCLR 767 (CC) (2009) ("*Machele*"); *Residents of Joe Slovo Community, Western Cape v Thubelisha Homes and Others* 2009 (9) BCLR 847 (CC) (2009) ("*Joe Slovo*"); *Joseph and Others v City of Johannesburg and Others* 2010 (3) BCLR 212 (CC) (2009) ("*Joseph*"); *Head of Department: Mpumalanga Department of Education and Another v Hoërskool Ermelo and Another* 2010 (3) BCLR 177 (CC) (2009); *Abahlali baseMjondolo Movement SA and Another v Premier of the Province of Kwazulu-Natal and Others* 2010 (2) BCLR 99 (CC) (2009) ("*Abahlali*"); *Nokotyana and Others v Ekurhuleni Metropolitan Municipality and Others* 2010 (4) BCLR 312 (CC) (2009) ("*Nokotyana*").

retrenchment from the more substantive interventions that the Court appeared to be moving toward in the progression from *Grootboom* to *Khosa*.[5] *Mazibuko* has emerged as the poster child for critiques that the Court has decisively abandoned any attempt to develop a more substantive social rights jurisprudence and has reverted to a procedural enforcement model.[6]

This "second wave" of cases came after a close to four-year hiatus.[7] Following *Jaftha* in 2004, the Court did not decide another social rights case until *Olivia Road* in 2008.[8] The six 2009 decisions were followed by a steady stream of eviction-related cases beginning with *Joe Slovo II* in 2011.[9] 2011 also included *Glenister*, a high-profile challenge to legislation disbanding the Scorpions, a specialized anticorruption police unit, where the Court based a constitutional obligation to fight corruption in part on the social rights provisions.[10]

Collectively the second-wave cases reinforce the procedural emphasis of *Mazibuko*.[11] The Court continued to apply reasonableness review with the same features that critics charge prevent it from giving substantive

[5] Pierre deVos captured the contemporary reaction in a blog post shortly after the judgment. "Water is life (but life is cheap)," at www.constitutionallyspeaking.co.za/water-is-life-but-life-is-cheap/. *See, also*, M. Langford, R. Stacey, and D. Chirwa, "The Right to Water," in S. Woolman, M. Bishop, and J. Brickhill (eds.), *Constitutional Law of South Africa* (2011); Sandra Liebenberg, *Socio-Economic Rights: Adjudication under a transformative constitution* (2010) Ch. 9.4; Daria Rothmayr, "Lessons from Mazibuko: Persistent inequality and the commons," 3 *Const. Ct. Rev.* 317 (2010).

[6] Rothmayr, ibid.; Danie Brand, "Judicial Deference and Democracy," in Sandra Liebenberg and Geo Quinot (eds.), *Law and Poverty: Perspectives from South Africa and Beyond* (2012); Marius Pieterse, "Procedural Relief, Constitutional Citizenship and Socio-Economic Rights as Legitimate Expectations," 28 *S. Afr. J. Hum. Rts* 359, 362 (2012).

[7] Stuart Wilson and Jackie Dugard developed the first- and second-wave periodization. Stuart Wilson and Jackie Dugard, "Constitutional Jurisprudence: The First and Second Waves," in Malcolm Langford *et al.* (eds.), *Socio-Economic Rights in South Africa: Symbols or Substance?* (2013).

[8] *Occupiers of 51 Olivia Road, Berea Township and 197 Main Street Johannesburg v City of Johannesburg and Others*, 2008 (5) BCLR 475 (CC) (2008) ("*Olivia Road*").

[9] *Residents of Joe Slovo Community, Western Cape v Thebelisha Homes and Others*, 2011 (7) BCLR 723 (CC) (2011) ("*Joe Slovo II*"). Chapter 6 discusses this and the other eviction-related decisions.

[10] *Glenister v President of the Republic of South Africa and Others* 2011 (7) BCLR 651 (CC) (2011) ("*Glenister*"). *Glenister* generally is not viewed as a social-rights case, but the majority decision identified the social rights as one source of a general constitutional requirement that the state establish mechanisms to battle corruption. This adds another largely procedural dimension to the social rights that is consistent with the other second-wave cases.

[11] E.g., Paul O'Connell, "The Death of Socio-Economic Rights," 74 *Mod. L. Rev.* 532, 552 (2011) (arguing *Mazibuko* represents a "hyperproceduralized" approach to social rights); Pieterse, *supra* note 6, 362–63 (the other second-wave cases reflect the same "administrative

content to the social rights.[12] The Court also developed creative procedural remedies like meaningful engagement, sometimes stretching its own procedures to create them and to avoid more substantive measures. Several cases show similar creativity in applying context-specific legislative balancing tests to extend procedural protections to poor litigants. A consistent theme throughout is the connection between social rights and democracy – what the Court often calls "participatory democracy" – and a corresponding emphasis on the primacy of the democratic process in enforcement.[13]

The second-wave cases also shed a different light on the first-wave debate over the Court's approach and especially the potential for that approach to ground a productive dialogue with the political branches over substantive interpretation of social rights. These cases to a large extent fulfill the critics' prediction that the Court would continue to rely on context-specific analyses that largely avoid independent substantive principles. This is most evident in the remarkable string of pro-poor eviction decisions beginning with *Blue Moonlight* in 2011.[14] These decisions don't feature the kind of iterative substantive development through a judicial-government partnership that many predicted *Grootboom*'s famous weak-form declaration could prompt. Indeed the Court has gone to great lengths to avoid applying *Grootboom* in ways that require more specific elaboration of section 26. Instead, the Court has channeled its energies into applying and extending the procedural control it first identified in *Port Elizabeth* to prevent evictions and manage eviction processes. Chapter 6 identifies some modest potential in these cases for incremental substantive development primarily where the Court can rely on constitution-enforcing legislation, but they nonetheless are consistent with this overall shift toward procedure.

Whereas the second-wave cases confirm fears that the Court would adopt a weak interpretive role that focuses on the procedural dimensions of the social rights, they also show a Court much more confident – at times even aggressive – when operating within this procedural role. Rather

law sensibilities" as *Mazibuko* and "predominantly procedural remedies" although several depart from or supplement *Mazibuko*'s framework).

12 E.g., Wilson and Dugard, *supra* note 7.

13 Chapter 9 discusses the Court's democratic rights decisions that more fully develop the concept of participatory democracy. *See Doctors for Life International v Speaker of the Assembly* 2006 (12) BCLR 1399 (CC) (2006), and *Matatiele Municipality v President of the Republic of South Africa* 2006 (5) BCLR 622 (CC) (2006).

14 *City of Johannesburg Metropolitan Municipality v Blue Moonlight Properties 39 (Pty) Ltd and Another* 2012 (2) BCLR 150 (CC) (2011).

than simply deferring to the other branches, which *Mazibuko* seemed to require, the Court has found ways to use social rights to protect poor people's interests using through largely procedural mechanisms that directly or indirectly prompt changes in government policy.[15]

This configuration does not fit completely into either the critics' or the weak-form or dialogue accounts of the Court's approach. It pairs a willingness both to develop creative procedural mechanisms and to apply those mechanisms in ways that assert relatively strong institutional authority with limited substantive elaboration of the rights at issue that diminishes the Court's interpretive control over the social rights. The result is a form of procedural authority that at least temporarily asserts judicial control over government (usually executive) action and sometimes prompts revision of the underlying policy but without direct substantive guidance from the Court. As the critics point out, this approach generally fails to establish clear interpretations – even the kind of contingent interpretations envisioned by weak-form review – that could guide policymakers and legislators or that poor people could use as precedent in future litigation. But the direct procedural control and the corresponding leverage to force the government to change policy it creates goes beyond a simple administrative-law model.

These two aspects of the second-wave cases – the turn to proceduralization and consequent emphasis on indirect enforcement through democratic processes and the strong procedural control evident in the eviction cases – track the set of constraints Chapter 4 identified. They reflect the continued and frequently conflicting influences of the Court's desire to avoid the justiciability concerns while still applying the social rights to create some measure of social and economic transformation. On one hand, these constraints push the Court to limit the formal scope of its interpretive power and to avoid remedies that require large-scale systemic changes. On the other hand, they prompt the Court to find creative ways within the confines of a traditional judicial role to give poor people some relief against the state where it completely fails to meet its obligations and also to give poor people increased access to and leverage in the policy-making process.

This conflict crystallizes in the second-wave cases in three ways. First, these decisions solidify the shift away from substantive interpretations toward a focus on procedural protections and evidence of obvious bad faith or intransigence. The Court consistently shies away from any

[15] *See* Pieterse, *supra* note 6, 362–63.

consideration of the relative adequacy of challenged programs and generally limits its interventions to enforce or establish new opportunities for poor people to have some voice in the policy-making process. Where the challenged program is a legitimate attempt to fulfill the social rights – even one that suffers from significant and well-documented implementation problems – the Court also generally defers to government choices and refuses to assess the substance of the program or directly to intervene in its implementation.

At the same time that the Court has limited the scope of its interventions, however, it also has demonstrated a greater willingness to intervene in stronger ways when it operates within those limits. This confidence includes relatively strong and sometimes intrusive measures to enforce procedural protections either through expanding existing procedural protections or by creating new procedures itself. Several of these procedural victories have resulted in de facto substantive developments, which, although more precarious and contingent than the formal development critics have called for, nonetheless create significant tools for enforcing social rights.

This confidence is enhanced first where the Court applies legislation that enforces the social rights and often manifests in progressive interpretations of such legislation. The Court also is more willing to intervene where there is clear evidence that the state party has completely failed or deliberately refused to consider the obligations the social rights create, although even in those cases, it typically relies on largely procedural interventions.

A. Evictions and meaningful engagement

In its first three second-wave decisions, the Court returned to the question of evictions.[16] Two of these cases involved challenges to state-initiated evictions that were part of large redevelopment projects. These two cases also implicated new housing legislation and policies developed specifically in response to *Grootboom*. In *Olivia Road*, the City of Johannesburg's inner-city regeneration program arguably conflicted with the obligations the National Housing Act imposed on municipalities to assess and plan for emergency housing needs. In *Joe Slovo*, the evictions were part of a new housing development specifically created to implement a new national

[16] These are *Olivia Road*, *supra* note 8; *Machele* and *Joe Slovo*, *supra* note 4. Chapter 6 discusses *Machele* as part of the later evictions cases.

housing policy. Both cases thus presented the Court with the opportunity to elaborate and expand *Grootboom*'s interpretation of section 26 and assess whether and how these responses satisfied the requirement that the state develop policies to address emergency housing needs.

The Court declined that opportunity and instead focused on a new procedural requirement that it called meaningful engagement. Engagement is rooted in *Grootboom*'s interpretation of section 26, and as we'll see, it creates a significant and powerful tool for courts to limit state power and manage eviction processes in rights-protective ways. But the Court's decision to ignore the broader substantive questions in each case and focus on this new procedure as a tool to exercise some limited control over the effects rather than the substance of housing policies represents the triumph of *Port Elizabeth*'s model of managerial judging over the abstract substantive approach that *Grootboom* seemed to presage. The later eviction cases discussed in Chapter 6 confirm that shift.

The third eviction-related case, *Abahlali*, involved a challenge by a Durban-area shack-dweller's rights movement to a provision in provincial legislation that gave provincial authorities the power to require landowners and municipalities to initiate eviction proceedings in areas deemed "slums."[17] The Court relied in part on the new meaningful engagement requirement to strike down the provision finding that it effectively precluded meaningful engagement over the decision whether to seek an eviction in violation of section 26(2) and PIE.

All three decisions feature the characteristics of the second wave. *Olivia Road* involved a fairly obvious example of a municipality actively violating the rights of poor people and a policy that almost completely ignored the right to housing. The legislation in *Abahlali* was designed to fulfill the right to housing but the challenged provision's sole purpose was to inflexibly force evictions in direct conflict with *Grootboom* and *Port Elizabeth*. In each case the Court found ways to intervene that remedied the most egregious violations without reaching the broader issues at play.

The interventions in these cases also were primarily procedural. *Abahlali* essentially restored what the Court described as the "dignified framework" for evictions established by its decisions and national housing policy.[18] In *Olivia Road*, however, the Court was forced to invent meaningful engagement so that it could sidestep the main issue the parties contested: whether the City of Johannesburg had a *Grootboom*-compliant housing program.

[17] *Abahlali, supra* note 4. [18] Ibid., [122].

Joe Slovo involved an arguably misconceived and mismanaged policy designed in good faith to meet the government's obligations under section 26. Providing direct relief to the residents in that case would have required the Court to second-guess core policy choices. Citing *Olivia Road*, the residents argued that the government's engagement efforts were inadequate, but at that point resorting to even the procedural alternative of ordering further engagement over the decision to relocate would have disrupted a large-scale program that was well advanced.

1. Olivia Road

"Between 2002 and 2006, mass evictions in the inner city of Johannesburg became a regular occurrence."[19] *Olivia Road* involved a class action brought by more than 400 residents of two buildings in the City of Johannesburg to challenge both their eviction and the City's mass-eviction program.[20] This program started shortly after *Grootboom*'s order that the state develop policies to deal with the emergency housing needs of people facing eviction and overlapped *Port Elizabeth*'s subsequent insistence that courts have the power and obligation to stop evictions that threaten human dignity. How was it possible for South Africa's largest and richest municipality to adopt such a massive eviction program in the face of these decisions?

Evictions were a core component of the City's inner-city regeneration strategy. In its 2004 version of the plan the City described a steady decline of the city center that manifested "in bad buildings, increase in slums, increase in crime and shoddy urban environment" propelling "disinvestment and flight to the suburbs."[21] Clearing these "bad" buildings – twenty-five buildings housing some 25 000 people – was the first step in restoring the city center and restoring Johannesburg to an "African World Class City."[22] Notably absent in the fifty-three-page plan outlining this strategy is any discussion of what would happen to the people "cleared"

[19] Stuart Wilson, "Litigating Housing Rights in Johannesburg's Inner City: 2004–2008," 27 *S. Afr. J. Hum. Rts* 127, 135 (2011).

[20] *Olivia Road, supra* note 8, [1].

[21] Johannesburg Inner City Regeneration Strategy Business Plan, March 10, 2004, 6 at www.slideshare.net/Alistercrowe/johannesburg-inner-city-regeneration-strategy-business-plan ("Regeneration Plan").

[22] Centre on Housing Rights and Evictions, *Any Room for the Poor? Forced Evictions in Johannesburg, South Africa*, (2005) 41–46, 60–64, at www.sheltercentre.org/sites/default/files/COHRE_ForcedEvictionsInJohannesburg.pdf; Regeneration Plan, *supra* note 21, 8.

from these buildings or the effects of section 26 and *Grootboom*. Instead the plan focused primarily on attracting private investment and strict enforcement of existing laws and policies to increase property values. Only two of its detailed "programs and activities" addressed housing at all, and one of those prioritizes "building conversion and the construction, sale and letting of middle to upper income residential units."[23] Homelessness appeared solely as one of several examples in the general "strategy and programme to address issues of poverty reduction and social exclusion within inner city activities (including homelessness, street children, drug abuse, etc)."

In addition to ignoring the obvious displacement and increase in homelessness that this mass-eviction program would create, the plan focused on identifying "additional, revised or new powers to allow for faster and more effective legal interventions" as a strategy. In other words, the City sought not only to evict large numbers of people but also to streamline the legal process to make eviction "faster and more effective."

Consistent with this objective, the City ignored the cumbersome requirements of PIE and relied instead on an apartheid-era law, the National Building Standards and Buildings Regulation Act, that permitted a municipality to order summary eviction of buildings declared unsafe for occupation.[24] These "faster" evictions were also more "effective" because they minimized the possibility of opposition by poor residents who lacked the knowledge or resources to muster legal representation.

The plan's specific targeting of poor people and deliberate indifference to the devastating effects of these evictions made the City's mass-eviction policy a ripe target for litigation that could build on both *Grootboom*'s general principle as well as *Jaftha*'s analysis of the negative dimension of section 26. Stuart Wilson – who was closely involved in the *Olivia Road* litigation – explains that the legal framework for challenging the policy crystallized in 2003 through the interaction between a community-based organization, the Inner City Resources Centre (ICRC), and several legal organizations, the Wits Law Clinic, the Centre for Applied Legal Studies (CALS), and the Johannesburg Bar. Together these organizations identified five core arguments that could be used to challenge the City's eviction policy: (1) the decision to clear a bad building triggers procedural protections under administrative law that the City doesn't provide; (2) the expedited eviction process the Act creates violates section 26(3) because

[23] Regeneration Plan, *supra* note 21, 28. [24] Wilson, *supra* note 19, 136.

it does not require a court order; (3) most residents of bad buildings are illegal occupiers, thus triggering the protections of PIE, not the Act, and the City's policy of evicting with providing alternative accommodation violates PIE; (4) the City's failure to provide alternative accommodation or to create a plan for providing such accommodation to residents of 'bad' buildings violates *Grootboom*; and (5) the City's selective use of its health and safety powers to implement inner-city economic redevelopment objectives and complete failure to use those powers in informal settlements elsewhere demonstrates health and safety is merely a pretext for discriminating against the inner-city poor.[25]

After successfully deploying these arguments in several individual cases, the ICRC and CALS collaborated with the Centre for Housing Rights and Evictions (COHRE) – a Geneva-based international nongovernmental organization – to develop research that could lay the groundwork for a broader legal challenge. The COHRE's report presented a counternarrative that exposed the hypocrisy in the City's justification for the evictions as a necessary response to genuine health and safety concerns and the complete failure of its regeneration strategy to address the needs of the people it was displacing.

The report carefully analyzed *Grootboom*'s requirements and new national housing legislation to show that neither adequately addressed the needs of the inner-city poor. The inner city is the economic hub of both the informal and formal economy and people needed to live close to their jobs because transportation is too expensive. The COHRE report was used to generate press coverage critical of evictions and to shift public perceptions of the regeneration program. The *Olivia Road* case was the culmination of this careful, multi-pronged campaign.

High Court. The High Court judgment included everything these groups had hoped. Weaving together *Grootboom*, *Port Elizabeth*, *Jaftha*, and the SCA judgment in *Modderklip*, the court first held that the City was not entitled to evict simply on the basis that a building poses health or safety risks. It quoted *Port Elizabeth*'s constitutional matrix at length to find that section 26(3) on its own – irrespective of whether PIE applies – requires a court "to balance out and reconcile the opposing claims in a just manner, taking account of all interests involved and the specific factors relevant in each case."[26]

[25] Ibid., 140–41.

[26] *City of Johannesburg v Rand Properties (Pty) Ltd.* (City of Johannesburg High Ct.) 2006, Case No. 04/10330, ¶ 2 (HC, Witwatersrand Local Div.) (S. Afr.) [38].

Moving to the National Housing Act, which it noted was passed to comply with *Grootboom*, the court found that the City lacked any program to assess and "plan proactively" for emergency housing needs or to access funds to provide emergency services as required by the Act. The City's failure to implement its obligations under the Act violated *Grootboom*'s interpretation of section 26. Notably, the court accepted the argument set up by COHRE's research that the right to housing for these people meant not just housing somewhere but specifically "access to adequate housing in the inner city."[27]

The court issued a declaratory order modeled on *Grootboom* declaring the City's failure to "give adequate priority and resources to people in the inner city" violated both section 26 and the Housing Act and requiring the City "to devise and implement" a new program that addressed the needs of the inner city poor.[28] While closely tracking *Grootboom*'s structure, this part of the order clearly extends *Grootboom* by establishing first that municipalities have independent obligations to fulfill section 26 including to create housing opportunities specifically in the inner city. The court went further, however, and enjoined the City from evicting the residents until it developed this new housing plan.[29]

The High Court's order looks much like the kind of dialogic development that weak-form review anticipates. It's a substantive but still flexible judicial follow-up to the legislative response to *Grootboom*'s broad declaration. It builds on *Grootboom* by specifying how the broad principle applies to the inner-city poor and how it affects municipal planning. It also draws on the National Housing Act by interpreting it to both reinforce this new principle by requiring municipalities to assess and plan for emergency housing needs in the inner city as well as to provide a mechanism for fulfilling those needs by permitting municipalities to seek funding from the provincial government. The result is a modest substantive expansion of section 26 grounded in national implementing legislation.

The remedy replicates *Grootboom*'s weak declaration, giving the City flexibility to set the policy details thus preserving its dialogic character. But the order includes both more specific guidance and also a procedurally stronger incentive because the City is prevented from moving forward with this eviction – and likely other evictions of similarly situate residents – until it develops a new eviction policy.

Constitutional Court. The Constitutional Court's judgment is markedly different. Rather than developing *Grootboom* or addressing the effect of

[27] Ibid., [66]. [28] Ibid., Order. [29] Ibid., [67].

the legislative response to it, the Court went out of its way to avoid continuing down the substantive path set up by *Grootboom.* Instead the Court pivoted toward the procedural role *Port Elizabeth* described by establishing what it called "meaningful engagement" as a stand-alone constitutional requirement. Meaningful engagement shares some characteristics with experimentalist review and creates a mechanism that courts could use to develop the kind of broad participatory constitutional development Sabel and Simon describe. Engagement also is a tool for courts to exert the strong procedural control to manage and mitigate the unconstitutional effects of government policies that the Court first established in *Port Elizabeth.* In later eviction-related cases, the Court has focused on this aspect of engagement, applying it as a tool to pressure the government to change policy without specifying any substantive constitutional principles.

The City appealed the High Court's order to the SCA. The SCA lifted the injunction against evicting the residents but ordered the City to find alternative accommodation without specifying precisely the legal basis of that order.

The residents appealed the SCA's order to the Constitutional Court, which accepted the application in May 2007.[30] The Court heard oral argument on August 28, 2007, and two days later issued its first "engagement" order requiring the parties to "engage with each other meaningfully . . . in an effort to resolve the differences and difficulties aired in this application in light of the values of the Constitution, the constitutional and statutory duties of the municipality and the rights and duties of the citizens concerned."[31] The Court also ordered the parties to file affidavits reporting the results of the negotiations with the Court approximately one month later.[32]

After engaging over several months, the parties eventually reached a partial settlement that largely granted the residents the terms they had sought and won at the High Court and also incorporated provisions for broader change in the City's inner-city housing policy. Among other things, the City agreed not to evict the residents in the case and to take specific measures to make the existing buildings safer and more habitable by cleaning the buildings, providing sanitation services, access to water,

[30] *See* Constitutional Court Interim Order, August 30, 2007, in *Occupiers of 51 Olivia Road, Berea Township and 197 Main Street Johannesburg v City of Johannesburg,* CCT 24/07, available at www.constitutionalcourt.org.za.

[31] Ibid., [1]. [32] Ibid., [3].

and functioning toilets.[33] Before relocating the residents from the buildings designated for redevelopment, the City agreed to refurbish several other buildings in inner-city Johannesburg and to provide essential services at reasonable cost. Finally, the City agreed to continue to engage on longer-term solutions to the housing crisis.[34]

The parties returned to the Court seeking not only approval of the specific terms of the settlement but also a decision on the larger issue central to the case: whether the City had a plan that complied with *Grootboom*'s requirements. Whereas the settlement largely remedied the individual residents' concerns, the *Grootboom* issue was key to whether the litigation would have effect beyond these specific individuals. At this point, both sides viewed the settlement as important but subsidiary to the plan issue, and many expected the Court to use this decision as an opportunity to begin fleshing out *Grootboom*'s interpretation of section 26.[35] The City argued that a revised housing plan it had developed as the litigation progressed was adequate, and the Court should approve it. The residents argued that the City failed to consult them or others on this new plan and that the Court should order further briefing on the issue.[36]

To the surprise of both sides, in its final opinion and order issued several weeks later, the Court refused to address the *Grootboom* issue.[37] Instead the Court formalized the engagement process into a constitutional requirement for all future cases where eviction is a possibility. The Court first located engagement within several constitutional provisions, including the state's obligation to "encourage the involvement of communities and community organizations in local government," as well as the rights to human dignity and life.[38] The Court then described in more specific terms what engagement should entail.

First, the Court connected engagement to reasonableness review and emphasized the context-specific nature and flexibility of that standard. Sometimes reasonableness requires "making permanent housing available

[33] Settlement agreement between City of Johannesburg and the Occupiers of 51 Olivia Road, Berea Township and 197 Main Street, Johannesburg dated October 29, 2007 [2–4] (copy on file with the author).

[34] Ibid., [18].

[35] *See* Brian Ray, "Extending the Shadow of the Law: Using Hybrid Mechanism to Develop Constitutional Norms in Socioeconomic Rights Cases," 2009 *Utah L. Rev.* 797 (2009).

[36] *See* Karen Brit Affidavit in *Occupiers of 51 Olivia Road Berea Township and 197 Main Street Johannesburg v City of Johannesburg*, at www.constitutionalcourt.org.za.

[37] *Olivia Road, supra* note 8.

[38] Ibid., [16].

while in others, to provide no housing at all. The possibilities between these extremes are almost endless."[39]

Second, in most cases, and in particular where a large-scale program is involved, engagement cannot be "ad hoc."[40] Here the Court took the City to task for ignoring the clear consequences for poor residents in its otherwise detailed and extensive regeneration plan. It said that anytime a municipality begins a planning process like the regeneration plan it is required to consider the effects of that process and build engagement into it from the beginning. The Court recognized that this will require developing bureaucratic and administrative capacity, including a cadre of "competent sensitive council workers skilled in engagement."[41] The government has an obligation to use those resources to engage well before litigation is even a possibility.

Third, the Court acknowledged the vulnerability of citizens facing evictions and the need for skilled representation.[42] To deal with this power imbalance, the Court specifically recognized that civil society groups have a constitutional role to play: "civil society organizations that support the peoples' claims should preferably facilitate the engagement process in every possible way."[43]

Finally, the Court required the government to develop and maintain a public record of each engagement so that courts can later review not only the outcome but also the engagement process. Emphasizing that "secrecy is counter-productive to the process of engagement," the Court stated "the provision of a complete and accurate account of the process of engagement including at least the reasonable efforts of the municipality with that process would ordinarily be essential."[44] Courts are then empowered to review "[w]hether there had been meaningful engagement between a city and the resident about to be rendered homeless."[45] The Court added that failure to meaningfully engage can by itself – and irrespective of the substantive merits of the policy requiring eviction – be the basis for a court to deny an eviction request: "the absence of engagement or the unreasonable response of a municipality in the engagement process would ordinarily be a weighty consideration against the grant of an eviction order."[46]

What prompted the Court to ignore the opportunity to follow up on *Grootboom* and instead focus its judgment on an issue it acknowledged

[39] Ibid., [18]. [40] Ibid., [19]. [41] Ibid., [18]. [42] Ibid., [15].
[43] Ibid., [20]. [44] Ibid., [21]. [45] Ibid., [22]. [46] Ibid., [21].

the parties did not even raise directly and to provide a remedy that neither party sought?[47] One obvious answer is that the extraordinary settlement made it easy to duck the substantive issues in the case. Wilson explains that the settlement represented a nearly complete capitulation by the government, including both extensive services for these specific residents and a commitment to develop policies to address the medium and long-term housing needs of poor inner-city residents.[48]

This likely played an important role in the Court's decision to ignore the parties' arguments over the adequacy of the City's new housing plan. But it doesn't explain the Court's creation of meaningful engagement – a new free-floating, specifically procedural constitutional right. The Court easily could have confirmed the settlement and simply ended the case. Instead it wrote a detailed opinion elaborating this new procedural right.

Viewed in isolation, *Olivia Road* could be explained as largely driven by the successful settlement and the elaboration of meaningful engagement as merely a by-product of that remarkable success. The Court didn't need to reach the substantive issues because the settlement provided these specific plaintiffs with all the relief they sought. Elevating meaningful engagement to constitutional status simply reinforced the message that the City should have conducted these evictions much more humanely and institutionalized the process that prompted it to do so here. When we connect *Olivia Road* to *Joe Slovo*, however, it's much clearer that this shift toward procedure is part of a broader reconfiguration in the Court's general approach broadly consistent with *Mazibuko* and the other two basic-services cases in the 2009 term. The eviction-related cases beginning with *Blue Moonlight* in 2011 confirm this shift away from a strong substantive role but also illustrate ways that the Court can still exercise relatively greater authority while principally relying on procedural mechanisms like engagement.

2. Joe Slovo

In its next decision, *Joe Slovo*, the Court once again declined the opportunity to elaborate *Grootboom*'s interpretation of section 26 and instead revisited meaningful engagement. This time the Court deployed this new

[47] Ibid., [9]. In *Maphango* the Court would cite *Olivia Road* for the authority to issue a remedy neither party sought. *Maphango and Others v Aengus Lifestyle Properties (Pty) Ltd* 2012 (5) BCLR 449 (CC) (2012) n. 121.

[48] Wilson, *supra* note 19, 147–48.

procedural requirement to return some measure of control to the more than 20 000 residents whose eviction it approved as part of a large-scale housing project along the N2 highway – the major east–west artery in the Western Cape.[49] Despite finding that the City of Cape Town had meaningfully engaged with the residents when developing this policy, the Court issued a detailed order and agenda requiring the City to engage further over the timing and details of the eviction process – a requirement that ultimately led to the City's decision to postpone the eviction plans and reconsider the on-site upgrade the residents originally sought in the litigation.[50]

Both *Olivia Road* and *Joe Slovo* involved challenges to government-initiated evictions that were integral to large-scale redevelopment projects, but the stakes were much higher in *Joe Slovo* and the nature of the program was much different. The project in *Joe Slovo* – called the "N2 Gateway" project – was the lead pilot project of the "Breaking New Ground" or BNG plan adopted by South Africa's Cabinet in 2004 as a new framework for housing delivery partially in response to *Grootboom*.[51] The N2 Gateway Project from the start "was steeped in controversy and riddled with problems of both planning and implementation" exacerbated by political conflict between the ANC, which at that time controlled the Western Cape Provincial Government and the leading opposition party the Democratic Alliance, which controlled the City of Cape Town.[52] These problems were widely reported and largely confirmed by a highly critical auditor's report concluded in June 2008.[53]

Many of the Joe Slovo residents originally embraced the plan, in part because the City and the parastatal developer, Thubelisha Homes, promised that most of them would be entitled to return to the new development and acquire new low-cost rental housing.[54] But when the first of the three phases of the project was complete, none of the houses were allocated to the lowest rental range the residents say they were promised.

49 *Joe Slovo, supra* note 4.

50 The government's decision to postpone and reconsider was reported by Anna Majavu, "Evictions Suspended – Shack Dwellers Reprieved," *Sowetan* (September 4, 2009), at www.abahlali.org/node/5665/).

51 Centre on Housing Rights and Evictions, "N2 Gateway Project: Housing Rights Violations as 'Development' in South Africa," 1–2 (2009).

52 Ibid.

53 *See* Ella Smook, "Report Slams Running of N2 Gateway Project," *IOLnews* (May 1, 2009), at www.iol.co.za/news/politics/report-slams-running-of-n2-gateway-project-1.441984#.VKGfyMAAA.

54 *Joe Slovo, supra* note 4, [327] and [30–33].

In addition, phase 2 included no housing for low-income residents, only "bonded housing," that is, market-rate housing for purchase through a mortgage.[55]

Upset at what they called the "broken promises" of the first two phases, the residents began to organize both formal and informal protests against the development.[56] The government brought an emergency application in the Cape High Court seeking an injunction ordering the eviction of the residents under the PIE act.[57]

The High Court ordered the relocations to proceed and denied the residents relief shortly after the Constitutional Court decided *Olivia Road.* The judge made only passing reference to the engagement requirement and found that the numerous meetings the City Council held with residents indicated that there was a sufficient engagement.[58]

The residents – now represented by the Legal Resources Centre appealed directly to the Constitutional Court.[59] The Community Law Centre based at the University of the Western Cape and COHRE represented by CALS – organizations all involved in *Olivia Road* – submitted *amicus curiae* briefs in which they argued specifically that the City of Cape Town failed to adequately engage with the residents.[60] COHRE issued a report following the High Court's judgment describing in detail the widespread problems implementing the N2 project and arguing that relocating the residents to Delft violated the residents' section 26 rights. The case thus raised a set of issues similar to those in *Olivia Road* and also presented another opportunity for the Court to follow-up on *Grootboom* by analyzing the BNG policy and/or its application in the N2 project to further elaborate what section 26 requires.

In contrast to the inner-city regeneration plan in *Olivia Road* that ignored section 26, however, the evictions in *Joe Slovo* were part of legislation and policy specifically intended to fulfill the right to access to adequate housing. Equally significant, the evictions did not leave the residents homeless but instead provided temporary housing, albeit at a

[55] Ibid., [31] and [374]. [56] Ibid., [33] and [327, 376–78].

[57] Ibid., [13]. [58] Ibid., [13-15], [116].

[59] *See* Pearlie Joubert, "It's Our Duty Not to Be Silent," *Mail and Guardian* (August 24, 2008) ("In a surprise move, the Constitutional Court gave the community permission to challenge the ruling and approach it without going through the Supreme Court of Appeal").

[60] Ibid. ("the community law centre of the University of the Western Cape and the Centre for Housing Rights and Evictions were admitted as friends of the court, in support of the residents right to be properly consulted before being evicted").

location much farther from the city center. The Court thus was dealing with challenges to the adequacy, wisdom, and execution of legislative and executive decisions over how best to fulfill the right to housing. The Court's decision to uphold the evictions evinced the same deep reluctance to implicate the justiciability concerns that characterized the first-wave cases.

Following the *Port Elizabeth* model, however, the Court was willing to scrutinize the execution of these decisions closely and to mitigate the impact on individuals facing eviction. Although the Court affirmed the government's overall policy and decision to relocate these residents, it still intervened to protect the residents by using the newly established meaningful engagement requirement to control the details of the eviction process and indirectly to apply pressure on the City of Cape Town to reconsider its decision to relocate the community.

The decision consists of five different opinions spanning 221 pages. All five opinions concur in the final order that prescribes a structured eviction process requiring engagement with the residents to determine most of the significant details for eviction and relocation.[61] In addition to the unanimous order, all of the justices rejected – but for substantially different reasons – the residents' core contention that the length of their occupation combined with the City of Cape Town's periodic provision of services and efforts to improve the living conditions in the settlement constituted uninterrupted consent for their occupation of the land. Justice Yacoob, joined by Justices Langa and Van der Westhuizen, agreed with the City that it had never consented to the occupation. But Justices Ngcobo, Moseneke, O'Regan, and Sachs each wrote separately to emphasize that, as Justice Sachs describes it, "the community lawfully occupied the land with the knowledge, acquiescence and support of the [City] Council, but on the understanding that their occupation would be of a temporary nature pending the provision of adequate housing."[62]

Several of the judgments express deep reluctance at allowing these evictions to go forward. Echoing *Port Elizabeth*'s insistence that even constitutionally compliant policies could have unconstitutional consequences for individuals, Justice Moseneke cautioned that courts "must remain vigilant to ensure that when the government seeks to evict a community in pursuit of commendable housing plans, the plans must include the guarantee that those who are evicted and relocated have a reasonable opportunity of accessing adequate housing within a reasonable time in

[61] *Joe Slovo, supra* note 4, [4–5]. [62] Ibid., [329].

relation to the housing projects concerned." For him the government's concession that the majority of the new homes would be reserved for evicted residents was key to "assuaging the immediate melancholy associated with relocation by offering a rock hard promise of adequate housing and restored human dignity."[63]

All of the opinions agreed on two key points. First, each emphasized the failure of state authorities to adequately communicate with the residents as the project moved forward. Justice Sachs was the most forceful on this point: "there can be no doubt that there were major failures of communication on the part of the authorities. The evidence suggests a frequent top-down approach where the purpose of reporting back to the community was seen as being to pass on information about decisions already taken rather than to involve the residents as partners in the process of decision-making itself."[64] Justice Ngcobo found that the state attempted to engage at various points with the residents but the lack of coordination by the entities involved confused the residents causing "mistrust [that] has prevented any meaningful engagement on relocation from taking place without the intervention of this Court."[65] And Justice O'Regan observed that "much of the heat that has been generated in this case has been generated because the respondents did not engage fully and meaningfully with the applicants and the other communities who have an interest in the housing project."[66]

Second, all of the opinions agreed that the High Court's order completely failed to address this communication breakdown, and that the Constitution required a much more structured order that included consultation with the residents on the details of the relocation process. On this point each of the judgments – and the unanimous order – highlighted the engagement process the Court established in *Olivia Road* as a critical requirement. Justice Moseneke concluded that the eviction order was just and equitable only because it was paired "with a further order guaranteeing that the applicants shall be allocated the specified proportion of new houses . . . within a process of meaningful engagement with the people who are subject of the eviction and relocation order."[67] Justice Ngcobo similarly identified engagement as "crucial" to a relocation process "that is fair to the residents and that has regard to the Constitution."[68] Thus, the Court viewed the procedural control that the engagement order created

[63] Ibid., [172]. [64] Ibid., [378]. [65] Ibid., [246]. [66] Ibid., [301].
[67] Ibid., [174]. [68] Ibid., [261].

as essential to curing the constitutional problems both with the evictions themselves and the underlying redevelopment plan.

The unanimous order reflected this consensus that the evictions would be constitutional only if the process included meaningful engagement with the residents. The Court highlighted three principal differences between its order and the High Court's. First, it required the City to allocate at least 70 percent of the new homes to the displaced residents. Second, it specified the quality of the temporary housing in Delft. Finally, the Court required "an ongoing process of engagement between the residents and the respondents concerning the relocation process."[69]

In contrast to its earlier engagement orders, which did not include detailed instructions for the engagement process itself, here the Court imposed a relatively specific structure. First, the Court ordered engagement on three broad issues: the date the relocation would begin, the timetable for the process, and "any other relevant matter."[70] The Court then established an even more specific agenda of seven issues for the engagement. These include details such as "the exact time, manner and conditions" of each relocation and "the precise temporary residential accommodation units" allocated to each resident.[71] Finally, the Court retained jurisdiction over the case, requiring the parties to report the results of these engagements and also granting explicit permission for any party to seek relief directly from the Court "[s]hould this order not be complied with by any party, or should the order give rise to unforeseen difficulties."[72]

Early reaction to *Joe Slovo* was highly critical. Kate Tissington, then a researcher at CALS, wrote a scathing critique of the judgment, describing the Court as "completely naïve and out of touch with reality, failing at its duty to adjudicate on socio-economic rights compromised by bad implementation of wrongly interpreted government policy."[73] The Legal Resources Centre issued a press release describing the result as mixed but highlighting the fact that it was "the largest judicially sanctioned eviction of a community in post-apartheid South Africa."[74] Pierre de Vos, while acknowledging that "the judgment shows a genuine concern for the plight of the Joe Slovo residents," criticized the Court for failing to

69 Ibid., [5]. 70 Ibid., [7]. 71 Ibid. 72 Ibid.

73 Kate Tissington, "South Africa: Joe Slovo Residents Let Down by Court" (June 26, 2009), at http://allafrica.com/stories/printable/200906260735.html.

74 Legal Resources Centre, "Residents of Joe Slovo Lose and Win in the Constitutional Court" (June 16, 2009), at www.lrc.org.za/press-releases/1008–2009–06–16-residents-of-joe-slovo-lose-and-win-in-the-constitutional-court-lrc.

expect "the state to act in an honest manner and to cater also for the most vulnerable and poor members of a well-established community whose area is to be upgraded."[75] Sandra Liebenberg expressed similar concerns in an editorial on the decision. After noting that the detailed requirements of the Court's order was a marked improvement over the High Court's order, Liebenberg said that "the willingness to effectively condone the inadequate consultation process raises serious concerns."[76]

The ambivalence in some of these critiques illustrates the conflicting influences I described earlier. On one hand, *Joe Slovo* shows the Court moving more definitively away from interpreting social rights to establish independent standards and to evaluate policies and decisions against those standards. As Tissington points out, the Court accepted with some reluctance but no real scrutiny the government's decision to go forward with the N2 Gateway Project, and its determination that relocation of the residents rather than on-site upgrade was the only feasible way to accomplish the project's goals. The Court also was unwilling – despite clear recognition of the government's failure to negotiate meaningfully with the residents – to halt a government project of this magnitude to rectify the serious procedural defects in the planning process.[77] Both aspects of the decision highlight the Court's reluctance to use these rights – either the substantive or procedural dimensions – to alter in any significant manner a policy or program that is well under way.

At the same time, the Court deployed meaningful engagement in a much more muscular manner that included both substantive and procedural interventions. In *Olivia Road*, the court ordered engagement over the eviction order at a point where the government was already considering adopting a revised plan for inner-city development and had stopped pursuing the challenged eviction policy. This set the stage for the successful negotiation that ultimately resulted. In that context, the very general engagement order combined with an obligation to report back to the Court was sufficient by itself to trigger reconsideration of the challenged

[75] Pierre deVos, "Joe Slovo Case: The Good, the Bad and the (Mostly) Unstated," *Constitutionally Speaking* (June 14, 2009), at http://constitutionallyspeaking.co.za/joe-slovo-case-the-good-the-bad-and-the-mostly-unstated/.

[76] Sandra Liebenberg, "Joe Slovo Eviction: Vulnerable Community Feels the Law from the Top Down," *Business Day* (June 22, 2009), at www.businessday.co.za/articles/Content.aspx?id=73812.

[77] Ibid. ("a few of the judges held that the laudable objectives and greater good of the N2 Gateway project outweighed the defects in the consultation process. It would be too burdensome to expect higher standards from the State in these circumstances").

policy and good-faith negotiation over how to develop a revised policy consistent with the obligations section 26 imposes. But, following a disastrously ineffective engagement order in another case,[78] the Court in *Joe Slovo* recognized the need to structure the engagement order in ways that enhanced the accountability of the parties to the negotiation.

The Court's order adopts several innovations that could be adapted in future cases to improve the effectiveness of this novel remedy, including a detailed agenda for the engagement, a baseline substantive interpretation, and more direct court oversight of the process. Increasing control over the details of the negotiation agenda accomplishes two things: first, it establishes a substantive framework for the negotiation that forces the parties to bargain over key aspects of the challenged policy. Rather than leaving it to the parties to develop their own agenda, the Court decides which issues are most important and subject to potential concessions. Most critically in the *Joe Slovo* case the government was required to negotiate the overall timetable for the relocation and the precise terms of the relocation for each individual and family. This created considerable leverage for the residents to negotiate a process that is attentive to their constitutional rights on both a group and individual level.

Greater transparency also is possible with a more detailed agenda. This is particularly important if the negotiations break down and the parties return to the court for resolution. The public-record requirement the Court established in *Olivia Road* already requires the state to keep detailed records of the process. An order that includes a detailed list of negotiation items will require a detailed account of precise negotiations over each individual item. This will create an even more robust record on which a court faced with a negotiation impasse can determine whether to order further engagement – possibly with a revised agenda – or to order substantive relief on the basis of the information disclosed during the structured negotiation.

The Court's substantive decision that the project must reserve at least 70 percent of the new housing stock for the displaced residents is also a significant innovation. In its earlier uses of the remedy the Court ordered engagement before addressing any issue on the merits. Here the Court

[78] *Mamba v Minister of Social Development*, CCT 65/08 (2008). In *Mamba*, the Court ordered the Gauteng government to engage with a group of foreign national refugees displaced by the xenophobic violence that swept through parts of South Africa in spring 2007 over closure of the camps where they were housed. The government effectively ignored the order and treated it as requiring it to merely report to the residents and others the progress of its closure plans.

effectively determined that the parties' own negotiations resulted in a commitment to reserve 70 percent of the housing stock for the displaced residents, and that the government failed to fulfill it in the first two phases of the project. By taking this aspect of the policy off the table in the engagement, the Court both resolved a key issue in the case and also enhanced the bargaining position of the residents by requiring the government to take seriously their demands over the relocation process.

Several weeks after issuing its decision in *Joe Slovo*, the Court quietly suspended its order "until further notice" in response to a report submitted by the Western Cape minister for housing that stated the minister had "grave concerns" that the relocation plan might be more expensive than an on-site upgrade of the Joe Slovo settlement.[79] In a news report on the suspension order, a special adviser to the national Human Settlements Minister said that he "thought it best that the evictions be postponed to allow the government time to consult with residents."[80] The government had reversed course and decided not to go through with the eviction and relocation plan. Eventually, it formally decided to pursue on-site upgrading – precisely the route the residents sought – as an alternative.[81] In the end, then, the engagement order accomplished indirectly what the Court was unwilling to do directly.[82]

3. Abahlali

In *Abahlali*, a Durban-based shack-dweller's movement challenged the constitutionality of the KwaZulu-Natal Elimination and Prevention of Re-emergence of Slums Act 6 of 2007 (the "Slums Act") arguing that the Act regulated land, an area reserved to the national government, and was inconsistent with the National Housing Act and PIE.[83] The residents also argued that section 16 of the Act violated the right to adequate housing, in particular the newly established engagement requirement, by allowing provincial authorities to require eviction of areas deemed slums

79 Anna Majavu, "Evictions Suspended – Shack Dwellers Reprieved," *Sowetan* (September 4, 2009), at http://abahlali.org/node/5665/.

80 Ibid.

81 *See* Kirsty McLean, "Meaningful Engagement: One Step Forward or Two Back?," 3 *Const. Ct. Rev.* 223, 231–32 (2010).

82 Malcolm Langford and Jackie Dugard, "Art or Science? Synthesizing Lessons from Public Interest Litigation and the Dangers of Legal Determinism," 27 *S. Afr. J. Hum. Rts.* 39 (2011).

83 *Abahlali, supra* note 4, [2–3], [9].

without consideration of possible on-site upgrading or consultation with residents.[84]

A majority of the Court in a decision by Justice Moseneke rejected the residents' broader challenge to provincial authority to pass the Act holding it regulated housing, an area of concurrent national and provincial regulatory authority, but struck down section 16 for its failure to "ensure that [residents'] housing rights are not violated without proper notice and consideration of other alternatives."[85]

Two aspects of the majority decision are significant. First, the majority's narrow focus on section 16 and its inconsistency with the procedural protections provided by PIE and the National Housing Act are consistent with the overall shift away from substance in the second-wave cases. Second, the relative ease with which the majority struck down section 16 shows the Court's increasing confidence when enforcing procedural protections and diminished concern with the justiciability objections that characterized the first-wave cases.

Abahlali did not present the Court as clear an opportunity to develop *Grootboom* in light of the national legislative and policy responses as either *Olivia Road* or *Joe Slovo*. But the residents' arguments and evidence that the Court rejected provided fodder for a much more substantive approach than the Court's tight focus on what Justice Moseneke described as the "narrow . . . mainly interpretive" exercise of evaluating section 16.[86] By rejecting the broader challenge to the Slums Act and refusing to permit into evidence a detailed report by COHRE describing the complete failure of the provincial and municipal governments to implement the National Housing Act and the contradictions between national housing policy and the Slums Act, the Court once more avoided an opportunity to develop section 26 in light of the national legislative and policy response to *Grootboom*.

Although meaningful engagement and the obvious procedural defects in section 16 were important issues in the case, the residents framed their arguments in much larger terms as a failure by the provincial and municipal governments' to take seriously their obligations under section 26 and the national housing legislation and policy adopted after *Grootboom*.[87] The COHRE report both documented this state of affairs generally and provided specific evidence that the Slums Act was conceived and being

[84] Ibid. [85] Ibid., [122]. The discussion of meaningful engagement is at [113–17].
[86] Ibid., [95]. [87] Applicants' Heads of Argument, *Abahlali*, *supra* note 4, at [1–85].

implemented in patently unconstitutional ways that were clearly at odds with national housing policy.

The Court's focus on the "clearly irrational and overbroad" eviction provisions in section 16 addressed only the lack of procedural protections for people being evicted under the Slums Act.[88] Justice Moseneke reinforced this shift away from the substantive issues by rejecting the COHRE report as irrelevant to the narrow interpretive exercise he identified as the only issue necessary to resolve the case.[89] The result provides further evidence of the Court's move away from the *Grootboom* model and toward the managerial role *Port Elizabeth* describes, reflected in both *Olivia Road* and *Joe Slovo*.

At the same time that *Abahlali* confirms the Court's flight from substance, the Court's willingness to strike down a legislative provision directly – with little angst over separation-of-powers or judicial competence issues – illustrates the possible substantive effects of procedural protections and demonstrates the Court may be more willing to reach results that have substantive reverberations when enforcing those protections. Here protecting the residents' procedural rights effectively trumped the legislative decision that expedited slum eradication was an important tool to provide adequate housing in the long term. To reach that result the Court had to explicitly confirm some of the substantive implications of its earlier decisions finding that, together with the provisions of the National Housing Act and National Housing Code, there was an established set of substantive limits – a "dignified framework" – governing all evictions. Under this framework eviction should be a "last resort" considered only after adequate engagement with residents and authorities should first consider on-site upgrading over relocation.[90]

By framing it as a simple interpretive exercise and focusing on the procedural defects of section 16, however, Moseneke was able to avoid acknowledging that the decision in effect selected one policy approach to enforcing the right to housing – the robust procedural protections identified in national legislation and policy and shaped by the Court's own decisions – over another – the Slums Act's focus on long-term development. Equally significant, the principles the Court identified as the components of the dignified framework for evictions – with the possible exception of the requirement to consider on-site upgrading – track the *Port Elizabeth* model by asserting the power of courts to manage eviction

[88] *Abahlali*, *supra* note 4, [118]. [89] Ibid., [95].
[90] Wilson and Dugard, *supra* note 7, 53–54.

processes rather than to scrutinize the underlying housing policies that lead to eviction. The later eviction cases follow a similar pattern and show the Court asserting increasingly direct control over evictions that have correspondingly greater, if still indirect effects on underlying policies.

B. Basic services and proceduralization's triumph

The three basic-services cases the Court decided in 2009 – *Mazibuko*, *Joseph*, and *Nokotyana* – follow patterns similar to the eviction decisions. The Court largely denied relief in *Mazibuko* and *Nokotyana* the two cases that challenged the adequacy of service programs. It upheld a challenge to termination of electricity services in *Joseph* but, in a move reminiscent of *Olivia Road*, developed an entirely new, largely procedural right to receive municipal services to avoid a ruling that expanded the substantive scope of section 26.

1. Joseph

When the City of Johannesburg cut off electricity service to a privately owned building in inner-city Johannesburg, tenants of the building challenged the City's policy on several grounds including section 26 and the Promotion of Administrative Justice Act (PAJA).[91] The Court rejected the residents' principal argument that the right to access adequate housing in section 26 included an implied right to receive basic services, including electricity. Instead, it developed a free-standing right to receive municipal services but strictly limited the scope of that right to triggering the procedural requirements of PAJA.

Joseph presented a similar situation as *Mazibuko* in many respects. Both cases addressed the complex challenges faced by municipalities in delivering basic services and the difficulty balancing cost-recovery schemes to make delivery sustainable against the social rights of poor residents to receive access to those services. Both cases also presented substantive and procedural grounds for challenging these policies under the social rights and related legislation.

CALS also provided representation in both cases and considered *Joseph* a much riskier litigation than *Mazibuko*.[92] Two significant hurdles faced

[91] *Joseph*, *supra* note 4. PAJA provides the right to "lawful, reasonable and procedurally fair," administrative action and imposes a set of procedural requirements on state entities. Act No. 3, 2000.

[92] Langford and Dugard, *supra* note 82, 42.

the tenants. First, no textually specific constitutional right protected their claim to access to electricity. Instead they argued the right to receive electricity derived implicitly from section 26 and the Court's expansive interpretation of its negative dimensions in *Jaftha* and also their right to human dignity. Second, the traditional common law of contract did not confer any rights on the tenants against the City that would trigger PAJA's procedural requirements. The tenants paid electricity fees directly to the landlord as part of their monthly rent. It was the landlord who incurred the arrears triggering the cutoffs, and the City provided the landlord, but not the tenants, with prior notice.[93] Thus even the tenants' procedural arguments seemed to depend on the Court either expanding section 26 or changing the common law. Either route involved potentially significant substantive development either of the Constitution or the common law.

The Court – in a unanimous judgment by Justice Thembile Skweyiya – found a different basis for applying PAJA's procedural protections to the tenants. Rather than expand section 26 or develop the common law, the Court recognized an independent and potentially broad-reaching right to receive municipal services based on what it called "the broader constitutional relationship" between "public service providers and members of the local community" and the duties imposed on municipalities by the Constitution and national legislation.[94]

Significantly, the Court adopted this broad right as an alternative to the residents' substantive arguments.[95] Justice Skweyiya analyzed this new right only as a trigger for PAJA's procedural protections. Beyond recognizing that the right to receive services established a relationship between the City and the tenants sufficient to invoke PAJA, he said nothing more about its scope or content.

Skweyiya began his analysis quoting Justice Sachs's concurrence in *Joe Slovo* that identified a "'special cluster of relationships' that exist between a municipality and citizens" and finding that "administrative law principles operate to govern these relations beyond the law of contract."[96] He emphasized that the "provision of basic municipal is a cardinal function, if not the most important function, of every municipal government."[97]

93 *See* David Bilchitz, "Citizenship and Community: Exploring the Right to Receive Municipal Services in Joseph," 2010 *Const. Ct. Rev.* 45 (2010); Geo Quinot, "Substantive Reasoning in Administrative-Law Adjudication," 2010 *Const. Ct. Rev.* 111, 119–24 (2010).

94 *Joseph*, *supra* note 4, [33–40].

95 Ibid., [32]. 96 Ibid., [24]. 97 Ibid., [34].

Quoting an earlier decision with emphasis he found that this means "municipalities are *obliged* to provide water and *electricity* to the residents in their area *as a matter of public duty*."[98]

Section 152 of the Constitution establishes these municipal obligations, and several laws give "legislative content to the various constitutional duties of local government."[99] These include the Municipal Systems Act 32 of 2000 and the Housing Act 107 of 1997. "Taken together, these provisions impose constitutional and statutory obligations on local government to provide basic municipal services, including electricity."[100]

This extended discussion of the constitutional and statutory framework turned out to be only a predicate for applying the "procedural fairness" requirements of PAJA.[101] The remainder of the decision focused almost exclusively on whether these obligations triggered PAJA and what procedural protections PAJA imposes prior to service disconnection.

Skweyiya first connected PAJA to the founding values in section 1 of the Constitution, "namely that South Africa is founded on the rule of law and on principles of democratic government to ensure accountability, responsiveness and openness."[102] He explained that it is "crucial" for local government to act in procedurally fair ways "not only for the protection of citizen's rights but also to facilitate trust in public administration and in our participatory democracy."[103]

Skweyiya then carefully limited the issue in the case to the specific question of the tenants' procedural rights rather than the substance of the disconnection policy. The tenants did not directly question whether the policy of disconnecting electricity to collect a landlord's debt is illegal, in his view, "but more narrowly, whether users of municipal services are entitled to procedural fairness" before their service is disconnected.[104] He concluded that PAJA extends to service recipients, and that the City's failure to provide notice to the tenants violated their PAJA rights.[105]

This reading significantly expanded PAJA's scope. Geo Quinot argues that *Joseph*'s interpretation broke away from the strong formalism that traditionally characterized South African administrative law by focusing more on the underlying substantive implications of the administrative action rather than the technical requirements of PAJA that the High Court

[98] Ibid. (quoting *Mkontwana v Nelson Mandela Metropolitan Municipality and Another* 2005 (2) BCLR 150 (CC) (2004)).
[99] Ibid., [37]. [100] Ibid., [39]. [101] Ibid. [102] Ibid., [42].
[103] Ibid., [45]. [104] Ibid., [55]. [105] Ibid., [76].

found clearly barred the tenants' claims.[106] It is no accident, however, that the result of the Court's broad interpretation was the expansion of procedural protections for tenants. Equally important, that expansion was an alternative to the argument that section 26 itself should be interpreted broadly to trigger those same procedural protections.

Although the Court expanded PAJA's reach both by recognizing the right to receive services and defining the scope of administrative action broadly, it used that same flexible interpretive approach to read into PAJA's requirements considerable judicial discretion over whether and when the full panoply of PAJA's protections apply. PAJA requires administrators to provide not only notice but also the opportunity to make representations before taking action. Justice Skweyiya noted that all of PAJA's listed requirements are mandatory under "a literal reading" of the Act,[107] but found that this "literal approach" would "hamstring the courts" and instead read the requirements as creating judicial discretion to decide what protections apply in each case. Exercising that discretion here, he found that PAJA required only notice to the tenants because allowing representations would put too great a strain on the City's resources and administrative capacity.[108]

Skweyiya then identified two additional limits on the City's ability to disconnect services. First, where a service recipient raises a valid objection following notice "it must be presumed that City Power, acting in good faith, would not proceed" to disconnect. Second, some kind of engagement by the government with residents, like the engagement the City committed to in this case, is "consistent with what would be required" in similar situations.[109]

Finally, turning to the City's bylaws, he rejected the tenants' argument that the Court should interpret the term "customer" broadly "to include customers of a service who have no contractual relationship with the service provider."[110] He found it was "not necessary to expand that definition" because the Court's extension of PAJA "to require that pre-termination *must* be sent to all persons" materially affected provided practical protection to "the rights of affected persons, without obstructing the City's credit-control and debt-collection policies."[111] This

[106] Quinot, *supra* note 93, 122–23. Quinot contrasts this with the "overly conceptual formalistic reasoning" the the Court reverted to in *Mazibuko* to reject the residents arguments that the pre-paid water meters violated PAJA. Ibid., 135 (citing *Mazibuko, supra* note 1, [131]).

[107] *Joseph, supra* note 4, [56–57]. [108] Ibid., [59]. [109] Ibid., [63–64].

[110] Ibid., [74]. [111] Ibid., [75].

interpretive move also allowed the Court to avoid potentially changing traditional common law contract principles and thus to limit the potential substantive reverberations of its holding in that area in the same way it avoided expanding the substance of section 26.

Dugard and Langford note that *Joseph*'s success and *Mazibuko*'s failure confound analyses that suggest deep support structures and careful planning are necessary for social rights litigation to succeed.[112] *Mazibuko* was a carefully orchestrated case based on the explicit textual right to water in section 27. The litigation was supported by a broader political mobilization effort lead by the Anti-Privatisation Campaign, a well-organized social movement that had worked extensively to protest the implementation of water meters before bringing the case. By contrast, *Joseph* was an ad hoc case based on an implied right to receive electricity. The litigation was unsupported by any broader social movement and brought by relatively better-resourced plaintiffs than those in *Mazibuko*.[113]

What explains this counterintuitive result? The answer seems to be that the Court found a procedural route to resolve both *Joseph* and *Olivia Road* but not *Mazibuko*. The similarities between meaningful engagement and the new right to receive municipal services and the lengths the Court went to invent them rather than rely on the parties' arguments are remarkable. Chapter 7 explores these moves in more detail and argues they reflect a consistent pattern in the second-wave cases.

But *Mazibuko* also presented several procedural arguments that the Court could have relied on to resolve the case in favor of the residents. The Court's refusal to take those up is more difficult to explain. Chapter 7 returns to this question. Here, I'll briefly note that *Joseph* shares two key characteristics with *Olivia Road* that distinguish both decisions from *Mazibuko* – or at least from the way the Court characterized *Mazibuko*.[114] First, both *Joseph* and *Olivia Road* involved relatively small-scale situations where providing direct relief would not directly change – or even significantly disrupt – any large-scale program. Second, the challenged practices in both cases involved government action that either directly conflicted with the social rights or ignored the significant implications

[112] Langford and Dugard, *supra* note 82, 52–55. [113] Ibid.

[114] Langford and Dugard argue that, despite the litigants' careful framing of the issues "as a negative violation of both administrative justice and equality," the Court "(re)characterized *Mazibuko* predominantly as a positive-rights claim" and as an attempt to reopen the minimum-core approach. It likewise reframed the positive-rights claim in *Joseph* "as a case about the negative infringement of administrative justice principles in relation to municipal services." Langford and Dugard, *supra* note 82, 51.

the policy had on those rights. *Mazibuko*, by contrast, involved a direct challenge to a large-scale program that the government argued was necessary to fulfill its social rights obligations by managing a scarce resource. Those differences arguably heightened the democratic-legitimacy and institutional-competence concerns in the Court's view.

2. Mazibuko

Mazibuko involved a challenges by five residents in Phiri, one of the poorest suburbs of Soweto, to the City of Johannesburg's new water policy designed to reduce unaccounted-for water and increase the revenue from water services by installing prepaid water meters in each household. These prepaid meters automatically disconnect water supplies once a set amount of free water is used unless the household purchases credit. The new policy replaced a system of "deemed consumption" established under apartheid in which each household had access to unlimited water supplies and were charged a set rate regardless of actual use.[115] The City's new policy targeted poor, black areas of the City and did not encompass wealthier suburbs, which were given access to unlimited water on credit subject to potential disconnection for nonpayment.[116]

This policy was part of a complicated web of constitutional and statutory provisions, including the right to water under section 27, the national Water Services Act (WSA), which implemented section 27, regulations issued under that Act and the City's Free Basic Water Policy.[117] The WSA defined "basic water supply" in qualitative terms as the minimum necessary for "households, including informal households, to support life and personal hygiene."[118] The national implementing regulations specified that this requires a minimum of twenty-five liters daily per person or six kiloliters monthly per household.[119] The City's Free Basic Water Policy sought to fulfill the municipal obligations under this regulation by providing six kiloliters of free water per household each month regardless of the number of people residing in the household.[120]

The inflexibility and inadequacy of the City's policy – which the residents argued violated both section 27 and the qualitative standard in the WSA by providing only the minimum amount of water prescribed by the national regulations for every household regardless of the number

[115] *Mazibuko, supra* note 1, [10–15]. [116] Ibid., [80], [145–46].
[117] Act No. 108 of 1997. [118] *Mazibuko, supra* note 1, [22] (quoting WSA § 1).
[119] Ibid., [23]. [120] Ibid., [78] (describing the City's policy).

of people and their actual water needs – was central to the case. But the residents deliberately framed the issues more broadly to fit themes that had resonated with the Court in its earlier cases, including the lack of consultation with residents, the procedural unfairness of automatic disconnection and the unfair discrimination in targeting black communities for prepaid meters.[121]

Both the High Court and the SCA upheld the residents' challenge and ordered the City to change its policy.[122] The lower-court judgments each adopted versions of the incrementally substantive approach that the Constitutional Court began to develop in the first-wave cases. Both judgments relied principally on the legislative and executive measures that enforced the right to water to establish substantive requirements and also interpreted administrative-law principles and the right to equality to create strong procedural protections that reinforce those requirements. The SCA judgment also followed *Grootboom*'s weak-form model by suspending its order to give the City time to develop a revised policy.

The High Court sided with the residents in nearly all respects and issued a sweeping opinion that focused on the substantive inadequacy of the City's policy and required the City to provide fifty liters of free water per month to each Phiri resident. It found that the City's own bylaws did not permit installation of prepaid meters; the City's implementation of the program lacked meaningful consultation and violated administrative-law principles; the prepaid meter program's focus on poor-black areas constituted unjustifiable discrimination; and the City's inflexible six-liter-per-household limit was irrational and unreasonable.[123]

Although striking in its result, on close inspection the High Court's analysis of most of the issues is relatively restrained. The Court relied on progressive interpretations of the legislative framework, the City's own policies, and factual concessions the City made in the case to resolve the most contentious issues. Notably, the High Court's determination that the City was legally obligated to provide fifty liters of water per person, per day was not based on a direct interpretation of section 27 or resolution of the competing expert evidence. Instead the court relied on what it described as "common cause" that the average Phiri household consisted of sixteen

[121] Langford and Dugard, *supra* note 82, 51.

[122] *Mazibuko and Others v City of Johannesburg and Others* [2008] 4 All SA 471 (W) ("*Mazibuko* High Ct."); *City of Johannesburg and Others v Mazibuko and Others* 2009 (8) BCLR 791 (SCA) (2009) ("*Mazibuko* SCA").

[123] *Mazibuko*, *supra* note 1, [25].

residents – double the eight-person household on which the twenty-five-liter-per-day requirement in the WSA regulations was based.[124]

The SCA reversed the High Court but still found both the prepaid meter policy and the twenty-five-liter-per-day restriction unlawful. Unlike the High Court, the SCA evaluated the competing expert evidence and held that section 27 requires a minimum of forty-two liters per person, per day. The court suspended its order for two years to allow the City to develop a revised program.[125]

The case thus reached the Constitutional Court following two strongly pro-plaintiff decisions that mapped out a range of grounds on which the Court could reject the prepaid meter program, the limitations on free water, or both without expansively interpreting section 27. The residents appealed the SCA's judgment hoping to reinstate the more favorable High Court order, and the City initially failed even to file a cross-appeal, suggesting that both sides viewed the issues in the Constitutional Court as likely limited to the differences between the two lower-court judgments. In a "shock" decision, the Constitutional Court instead upheld the City's water policy as it had evolved during the litigation and also broadly recast its overall approach to positive social rights claims in deferential and largely procedural terms.[126]

Several aspects of the decision are significant: (1) the Court found that social rights raise unique concerns that can justify departures from normal appellate procedural rules; (2) it conservatively reinterpreted the first-wave cases to emphasize the lack of independent substantive development and importance of the justiciability concerns; (3) for the first time it formally articulated the full scope of the judicial enforcement role and did so in strongly procedural terms; and (4) it described the social rights as aspects of the Constitution's protection of democratic elections and social rights litigation as primarily a mechanism for promoting open, transparent, and accountable government.

The Court first addressed three preliminary questions: whether to grant leave to appeal, to permit the government's tardy cross-appeal, and to consider the City's revised water policy even though it constituted new evidence, which the normal rules of appellate procedure prohibited. The

[124] *Mazibuko* High Court, *supra* note 122, [166–69].
[125] *Mazibuko* SCA, *supra* note 122, [24], [38], [62].
[126] Jackie Dugard, "Civic Action and the Legal Mobilization: The Phiri Water Meters Case," in Jeff Handmaker and Remko Berkhout (eds.), *Mobilising Social Justice in South Africa: Perspectives from Researchers and Practitioners* (2010) 71, 75.

Court agreed to consider both the appeal and the cross-appeal, emphasizing the novel and important constitutional questions raised by both.

The Court rejected the City's bid to introduce evidence of its revised policy but only after concluding that social rights claims often would justify departures from normal procedural rules. Justice O'Regan identified two reasons "both of which flow from the fact that this case concerns the state's obligations in respect of a social right" for permitting new evidence on appeal in social rights cases. First, the nature of progressive realization requires courts to consider evidence that the government has revised its policies to meet its obligations. Second, new evidence of revised policies can assist courts to fashion effective relief in social rights cases.[127] This characterization echoed the First Certification judgment's cautious assessment and set the stage for the later conservative description of the Court's enforcement role.

Why would the Court here say that social rights raise unique concerns that could justify relaxation of its own procedural rules when days later in *Abahlali* it would refuse to consider the COHRE report, in part because it reflected new circumstances and then in *Nokotyana* it would reject similar evidence both sides submitted, noting that it "has expressed itself strongly" against new evidence on appeal with no reference to *Mazibuko*'s determination that social rights are an exception?[128] Arguably the Court in all three cases adapted its approach to minimize the justiciability concerns. In *Abahlali* rejecting the new evidence both facilitated and was a consequence of the narrow focus on the procedural defects in section 16. Rejecting the evidence in *Nokotyana* served the same function of narrowing the issues. Here, although the Court ultimately declined to consider the new evidence, acknowledging that social rights are sufficiently different from other rights softened its rejection of the City's evidence and set up the deferential analysis that followed.

Before turning to the issues in the case itself, in a twenty-nine-paragraph section titled "The role of courts in determining the content of social and economic rights: the proper interpretation 27(1)(b) and 27(2) of the Constitution," Justice O'Regan surveyed the first-wave cases and articulated the most comprehensive description of the Court's role to date.[129] O'Regan first identified the case as dealing with the positive obligations of section 27(1) and governed by *Grootboom* and *TAC*. She

[127] *Mazibuko, supra* note 1, [38–43].

[128] *Abahlali, supra* note 4, [95]; *Nokotyana, supra* note 4, [19].

[129] *Mazibuko, supra* note 1, [48].

then rejected the residents' argument that the Court should "quantify" the amount of water necessary for a dignified life under section 27(1) as a version of the "minimum core" approach of the ICESCR. Quoting both *Grootboom* and *TAC* at length, O'Regan said both cases definitively rejected the minimum-core approach. O'Regan quoted key passages from each case describing the justiciability concerns and emphasized that *TAC*'s acknowledgment that the minimum core "might possibly be relevant" was followed by the Court's recognition that it is "ill-suited to adjudicate" issues raising complex social and economic consequences and requires "a restrained and focused role for" the Court.[130]

She concluded that the Court could not adopt the minimum-core approach for two reasons. First, the language of progressive-realization and the resources qualifier mean that individuals cannot claim these rights immediately from the state. Instead, they "enable citizens to hold government to account for the manner in which it seeks to pursue the achievement of social and economic rights."[131]

Second, "ordinarily it is institutionally inappropriate for a court to determine" what social rights require or even what steps government should take to fulfill those requirements. The legislature and executive are "best placed to investigate" the social conditions and budget constraints, and "it is desirable as a matter of democratic accountability" that they make these decisions.[132]

O'Regan then described the Court's interventions in *Grootboom* and *TAC* as fully consistent with these constraints. In each case, according to O'Regan, "the Court identified deficiencies" and "took care not to draft policies of its own and impose them on government." O'Regan acknowledged that, unlike *Grootboom*'s declaration, the *TAC* order did require the government to provide nevirapine. But she explained that "[i]n a sense, then, all the Court did was to render the existing government policy available to all" and emphasized that the order gave the executive discretion to change the policy if necessary.[133] She concluded that the orders in both cases "illustrate the Court's institutional respect for the policy-making function of the other two arms of government" because the "Court did not seek to draft policy or determine its content."[134]

After surveying these decisions, O'Regan developed a comprehensive description of the Court's enforcement role. First, she reemphasized that "the Constitution envisages that legislative and other measures will be the

130 Ibid., [55]. 131 Ibid., [57–59]. 132 Ibid., [60].
133 Ibid., [63–64]. 134 Ibid., [65].

primary instrument for the achievement of social and economic rights" and social rights "acquire content" when the state passes legislation and creates policies. Courts do not develop the content of social rights but instead review legislation and policy for reasonableness in "at least" three ways. First, where "the government takes no steps to realise the rights, the courts will require government to take steps." Second, courts will review existing measures to determine if they are unreasonable. Unreasonable "limitations or exclusions" of particular classes like those in *Grootboom* and *TAC* are the paradigmatic examples. Third, the government has a duty "to continually review its policies to ensure that the achievement of the right is progressively realised."[135]

O'Regan then found that the lower courts "overlooked" this enforcement model by instead independently quantifying "the content of the right" to water "without first considering the content of the obligation" section 27 imposes on the state. Their approach "erred," and consequently the residents' argument that the Court should set fifty liters as the daily per-person minimum failed.[136]

Turning to the WSA regulations, O'Regan spent several paragraphs describing in greater detail the reasonableness analysis in procedural terms that emphasized the connection between social rights and democratic accountability. O'Regan began by saying "National government should set the targets it wishes to achieve in respect of social and economic rights clearly."[137] Clear targets aren't necessary primarily for judicial review, but so that citizens can "monitor government's performance and to hold it accountable *politically* if the standard is not achieved."[138]

Legal challenges to the reasonableness of a standard also are possible, but court review of the standard focuses not on its substance but the process used to reach it. Government is required "to explain the choices it has made" including the information it considered and the process it followed in setting the standard. "Appropriate relief may be sought" principally where "the process followed by the government is flawed or the information is obviously inadequate or incomplete." This is because the role of social rights is primarily to "deepen[] democracy." Litigation to enforce these rights enables "citizens to hold government accountable not only through the ballot box but also, in a different way, through litigation."[139]

[135] Ibid., [67]. [136] Ibid., [68]. [137] Ibid., [70].
[138] Ibid. (emphasis added). [139] Ibid., [71].

O'Regan then questioned whether the residents' failure to persist in challenging the constitutionality of the twenty-five-liter daily minimum set by the national regulations barred their challenge to the City's policy, which merely implemented that standard. She ultimately avoided the question by noting that the City's policy was reasonable in any case but concluded that challenges to provincial and municipal policies that meet national minimums face a high bar in the absence of a challenge to the national legislation or policy they implement. Any policy that first tries to provide the nationally prescribed minimum before doing more is presumptively reasonable.[140]

This discussion recasts the Court's role in strongly procedural terms that backs away from the more substantive potential the Court seemed to be moving toward in the later first-wave cases. Although all of the first-wave cases featured aspects of this procedural emphasis, *Mazibuko*'s extensive analysis and specific articulation of the limits of the Court's role explicitly embrace that framework. This is evident first in the Court's definitive rejection of the minimum core and conclusion that the lower courts clearly erred by quantifying the right to water cuts off any possibility for courts to set independent quantitative standards, even as aspirational targets. The Court's related insistence that social rights gain substance only through legislation and policy suggests further courts might be limited in setting even nonquantitative substantive standards.

The procedural emphasis is reinforced by O'Regan's significantly limited reading of the Court's interventions in both *Grootboom* and especially *TAC* as merely filling gaps in policies already adopted by the government. Her interpretations of these cases significantly downplay the strongly independent role the Court adopted to closely scrutinize the government's evidence in *TAC* as well as the substantive interpretive authority the Court exercised in *Grootboom* to conclude that section 26 required the government to address emergency housing needs.[141] These readings also suggest the need for much greater deference to legislative and executive decisions that the Court went on to apply in its analysis of the specific issues.

O'Regan's failure to distinguish between the SCA's and the High Court's analyses for determining the amount of free water the City was obligated

[140] Ibid., [76].

[141] *See* Quinot, *supra* note 93, 185–86 (discussing *Mazibuko*'s narrow reading of earlier decisions).

to provide adopts a narrow application even of this more procedurally focused role. Whereas the SCA established the forty-two-liter minimum based directly on section 27, the High Court's analysis relied principally on the government's own standard and a factual determination that the average household size in Phiri was double the number on which the government based the twenty-five-liter minimum. The High Court's approach arguably fit within the confines of the enforcement role O'Regan described, although it involved more independent scrutiny of the effects of government policy. The High Court did not independently quantify the right to water but instead enforced the national standard in the context-specific way that the Court has consistently said reasonableness review requires.

The Court's characterization of the violations here as related only to the positive aspect of section 27 also eliminated the possibility for further developing *Jaftha*'s recognition that the negative content of each right is unlimited by progressive-realization or resource constraints. Finally, the discussion omitted any reference to *Khosa* implicitly excluding it as a positive-rights precedent by citing *Grootboom* and *TAC* as the only previous examples.

The discussion also redefined social rights principally as tools for promoting democratic accountability rather than substantive entitlements. Most telling in this respect is the specific connection O'Regan drew to the "founding values" of section 1, paraphrasing section 1(d)'s reference to accountable, open, and transparent government enforceable through elections. The decision repeatedly identifies social rights as tools to promote democratic accountability, even finding that the litigation here served its purpose by forcing the City to disclose information and possibly to change its policy to provide broader exceptions.[142] This emphasis on democratic access contrasts starkly with the Court's consistent references to the substantive "founding values of human dignity, equality and freedom" in its earlier cases, especially *Khosa*, where it relied on that connection to qualify the resources constraint in section 27(2).[143]

The driving force behind this procedurally focused, deferential description of the Court's own role and strong identification between social rights

[142] *Mazibuko*, *supra* note 1, [95–96].

[143] *Khosa and Others v Minister of Social Development and Others, Mahlaule and Another v Minister of Social Development* 2004 (6) BCLR 569 (CC) (2004) [40–44].

and democratic accountability was in large part driven by the Court's perception that the residents were asking it to reject a complex, carefully developed social policy by independently interpreting section 27 to set an inflexible, quantitative standard based on its own assessment of the expert evidence the parties submitted. In other words to ignore – and in spectacular fashion – the justiciability concerns that it so carefully avoided in the past.

But that was not the only route the parties set up for the Court. The SCA judgment rested largely on the residents' procedural arguments that the City lacked authority under its own bylaws to implement the prepaid water policy and that the automatic cutoff violated the substantial procedural protections in the WSA, including the right to a hearing before automatic disconnection. This argument reflected the same concerns the Court was willing to rely on in *Joseph* and *Abahlali* to protect poor people without directly involving itself in the underlying policies. Yet in *Mazibuko*, the Court rejected even this procedural route and did so through an extraordinarily cramped reading of the legislation.

In a widely criticized analysis, the Court held that the prepaid meter policy merely "suspended" water supply and therefore did not trigger the hearing required under the WSA for "discontinuation."[144] The Court also found that requiring a hearing every time a prepaid meter was about to suspend service is "a result that borders on the absurd" and would establish an "administratively unsustainable" policy.[145] The Court rejected the related argument that the policy violated PAJA's procedural requirements in two short sentences, holding that PAJA did not apply because the policy was an "executive" not "administrative" action.[146]

Like *Joe Slovo*, this aspect of *Mazibuko* seems motivated by the Court's concern with directly disrupting a well-developed policy intended to fulfill the social rights over the long term even where there is clear evidence the policy was poorly conceived or implemented. Both cases suggest that there are limits to the Court's willingness to intervene even to enforce procedural protections in those circumstances. I'll return to this point and consider how applying the emerging eviction model might make a difference in a case like *Mazibuko*. But *Mazibuko* remains a sharp reminder that where the Court perceives a case to raise heightened justiciability concerns, it may be reluctant to enforce even procedural rights like engagement.

[144] *Mazibuko, supra* note 1, [117–19]. [145] Ibid., [121–22]. [146] Ibid., [131].

3. Nokotyana

Nokotyana presented a slightly different set of claims for basic service delivery. Residents of an informal settlement outside the Ekurheleni Municipality in Gauteng Province sued the municipality seeking basic sanitation services and high-mast security lighting under section 26 and national legislation, including the National Housing Code and the WSA.[147] In 2006, before the residents sued, the city had submitted to the province a proposal to upgrade the settlement to a formal township. The province had not acted on that proposal for several years, but the municipality argued the Housing Code required it to wait for a decision on the upgrade before spending money on improved interim services.[148]

The residents' constitutional claims relied on the same theory the tenants in *Joseph* asserted: that the right to housing includes related basic services. They argued that specific provisions of the Housing Code and WSA both recognized that the right to housing extended to basic services and defined in concrete terms the extent to which municipalities were obligated to provide those services. Unlike *Joseph*, however, the claims here were not limited to procedural protections against elimination of basic services.[149] The city was providing some of the services the residents sought and agreed to provide additional services as the litigation progressed. The case, therefore, centered on whether the city was doing enough to satisfy both the requirements of section 26 and implementing legislation and policy.[150]

Consistent with the pattern described previously, the Court in a judgment by Justice Van der Westhuizen refused to directly address the adequacy issues and instead found that the underlying cause of the dispute was the province's failure to act on the pending upgrade application, which would entitle the residents to the services they sought. The Court rejected the residents' claims but ordered the province to act on that application within fourteen months.[151]

In refocusing the case on this procedural question Justice Van der Westhuizen easily found that the Housing Code did not support the residents' claims. He first found that Chapter 12, which was passed to fulfill *Grootboom*'s requirement that housing policy address emergency housing needs, did not apply to the residents. The residents argued that the conditions they lived in – and implicitly by extension the conditions in most, if

[147] *Nokotyana, supra* note 4, [2–3], [21–31]. [148] Ibid., [7–8].
[149] Ibid., [21–31]. [150] Ibid., [33–37]. [151] Ibid., [62].

not all, informal communities – posed immediate and continuing threats to their lives, health, and safety and so constituted a de facto emergency. This set up the possibility for the Court to develop the dialogue that weak-form review contemplates. By clarifying, and possibly extending, what it meant in *Grootboom* through a more specific definition of emergency, the Court could have analyzed the Housing Code's own definition in light of section 26. Instead Van der Westhuizen narrowly interpreted the Code's own provisions to require a formal declaration of emergency by provincial authorities without reference to *Grootboom* or section 26.[152]

He found that Chapter 13 of the Code provided no relief to the residents because the city had complied with the only provision relevant at this point – that it submit an upgrade application. To avoid costly capital investment, Chapter 13 requires the services the residents sought only after the provision decided to upgrade an area.[153]

The residents thus fell in a statutory gap. They were entitled neither to emergency relief nor to the more substantial services that would come with an upgrade. Arguably this was the kind of regulatory omission that *Grootboom* held section 26 required filling. Instead, here the Court relied on a strict application of its own procedural rules to avoid the argument. Van der Westhuizen held that the residents' failure to challenge the constitutionality of the Code foreclosed an argument that the Code itself failed to satisfy section 26 – essentially the argument that succeeded in *Grootboom*. He also said that "it would not be appropriate" for the Court to consider the constitutionality of the City's revised policy because doing so would require the Court to break its rule against considering new evidence – precisely the same rule it said in *Mazibuko* that social rights claims could require relaxing when faced with evidence of the City's revised water policy.[154]

C. Conclusion

The early second-wave decisions surveyed here followed a relatively consistent set of patterns that continue to appear in later cases. *Mazibuko* has dominated discussions and influenced perceptions of the Court's approach to social rights both because of the surprising outcome and the Court's explicit articulation of the limited enforcement role it would play in social rights cases. All the decisions discussed previously generally fit within the constraints of the role *Mazibuko* described and thus they each

152 Ibid., [38–41]. 153 Ibid., [42–44]. 154 Ibid., [46–49].

to a large extent support the critics' fears that the Court would fail to develop a strongly substantive interpretive role.

At the same time, however, these decisions also illustrate the Court's increasing confidence when it operates in that role and a creative willingness to find or invent opportunities to enforce the social rights within those constraints. This dimension of the decisions belies the reflexive association of proceduralization with deference and demonstrates the possibility for the Court to develop a stronger enforcement role even when limited to a largely procedural approach. The next chapter explores the remarkable string of eviction-related decisions that both confirm the limits identified here and further illustrate how that stronger role could emerge.

6

The eviction cases

Beginning in the 2011 term, eviction-related cases began increasingly to dominate the Constitutional Court's social rights docket. In December 2011 four of the Court's five decisions were social rights cases that involved evictions.[1] The Court decided three eviction-related cases in the 2012 term, two in 2013, and two more in 2014.[2] The eviction-related cases that have reached the Court are only the tip of a much larger iceberg of similar cases in the lower courts.

The Court's decisions in these cases each employ and refine aspects of the active, managerial style of judging that *Port Elizabeth* established, in which courts focus on alleviating the unconstitutional effects of an eviction while sometimes incrementally interpreting section 26 usually filtered through legislative balancing tests such as PIE. Following the pattern of both *Olivia Road* and *Joe Slovo*, the Court in most of these cases continued to deliberately avoid direct elaboration of *Grootboom* but nonetheless relied on the core principle of that decision and PIE (or other legislation) to temporarily delay or prevent an eviction and then manage the process toward a more rights-protective outcome. In several cases the Court required a municipality to provide detailed information regarding the

1 *Pheko and Others v Ekurhuleni Metropolitan Municipality* 2012 (4) BCLR 388 (CC) (2011) ("*Pheko*"); *City of Johannesburg Metropolitan Municipality v Blue Moonlight Properties 39 (Pty) Ltd and Another* 2012 (2) BCLR 150 (CC) (2011) ("*Blue Moonlight*"); *Occupiers of Skurweplaas 353 JR v PPC Aggregate Quarries (Pty) Ltd and Others* 2012 (4) BCLR 382 (CC) (2011) ("*PPC Quarries*"); *Occupiers of Portion R25 of the Farm Mooiplaats 355 JR v Golden Thread Ltd and Others* 2012 (4) BCLR 372 (CC) (2011) ("*Golden Thread*").

2 *Maphango and Others v Aengus Lifestyle Properties (Pty) Ltd* (CC) 2012 (5) BCLR 449 (CC) (2012) ("*Maphango*"); *Occupiers of Saratoga Avenue v City of Johannesburg Metropolitan Municipality and Another* 2012 (9) BCLR 951 (CC) (2012) ("*Blue Moonlight II*"); *Schubart Park Residents' Association and Others v City of Tshwane Metropolitan Municipality and Another* 2013 (1) BCLR 68 (CC) (2012)("*Schubart Park*") in 2012; *Motswagae and Others v Rustenburg Local Municipality and Another* 2013 (3) BCLR 271 (CC) (2013) ("*Motswagae*"), and *Hattingh and Others v Juta* 2013 (5) BCLR 509 (CC) (2013) ("*Hattingh*") in 2013; *Zulu and Others v eThekwini Municipality and Others* 2014 (8) BCLR 971 (CC) (2014) ("*Zulu*") and *Malan v City of Cape Town* 2014 (11) BCLR 1265 (CC) (2014) in 2014.

availability of alternative accommodation and its broader planning process so that the lower court could consider all relevant circumstances in determining whether to grant the requested eviction order.

Taken together, these cases turn *Grootboom*'s famously weak programmatic declaration into a strong individually enforceable right to immediate, if temporary, relief under section 26. The Court has avoided articulating this right directly by analyzing each case as part of multifactor legislative balancing tests – usually PIE's but in one case it found an analogue in the Rental Housing Act. Despite its insistence that each result is a case-specific application of multiple factors, the Court has consistently refused to grant an eviction order where alternative accommodation is unavailable across a diverse range of factual contexts. In several cases – most notably the two companions to *Blue Moonlight* – the Court only thinly analyzed the specific PIE factors, further suggesting that where accommodation is unavailable the other factors play at most very minor roles in the analysis.

This is the model of judging Justice Sachs described in *Port Elizabeth* when he called for courts to rely on judicial statecraft to manage eviction processes in humane ways and to rely on the specific facts of a case to resolve conflicting constitutional principles. A court can change the outcome in individual cases to protect the interests of poor people without either specifying precisely what constitutional (or statutory) principles require that protection and without directly ordering changes to government policy.

The Court presaged this shift from *Grootboom*'s abstract substantive analysis to *Port Elizabeth*'s direct procedural model in *Machele*, a 2009 eviction case that dealt with an interlocutory appeal of an interim order by the High Court permitting eviction of close to 300 residents of a block of private apartments in inner-city Johannesburg.[3] In a short opinion by Justice Skweyiya, the Court reversed the High Court's eviction order because it failed to consider the effect of PIE. Quoting *Port Elizabeth*, Justice Skweyiya held that courts are required to apply PIE's multifactor test in every eviction case to ensure that they reach "constitutionally appropriate decisions."[4] Notably, in his analysis of whether the case raised a constitutional issue, Skweyiya connected PIE's mandatory application directly to section 26(1), quoting with emphasis *Jaftha*'s holding that "at the very least, *any measure* which permits a person to be deprived of

[3] *Machele and Others v Mailula and Others* 2009 (8) BCLR 767 (CC) (2009) ("*Machele*").

[4] Ibid., [14].

existing access to adequate housing, limits the rights protected in section 26(1)."[5] He also found that the significant harm the residents faced from eviction clearly outweighed the potential harm to the property owner in part because the eviction threatened the residents' constitutional rights.[6]

The later eviction decisions discussed here present variations on *Machele* and *Port Elizabeth.* They rely on the usually implicit assumption that an eviction cannot proceed unless alternative accommodation is available and develop or refine a set of largely procedural techniques that give courts authority first to temporarily stop an eviction and second to manage the process to provide some concrete relief. By relying on PIE and other constitution-enforcing legislation as the central mechanism for this authority the Court creates a more democratic basis for these procedurally strong interventions but also diminishes or eliminates the constitutional analysis in each case.[7]

This chapter first analyzes the most significant of these cases. I begin with *Blue Moonlight* where the Court employed a robust version of this managerial approach to temporarily prevent eviction of illegal occupiers from private land and to require the City of Johannesburg to change its emergency housing policy to include private evictions generally. I then contrast *Blue Moonlight* with *Maphango*, where the Court went to great lengths to revive a statutory dispute-resolution procedure in landlord–tenant legislation to protect poor tenants from potential eviction.

Both cases arguably enforce section 26 in important ways and create or reinforce principles that give poor people significant leverage to avoid or delay eviction and that refine and strengthen the managerial role *Port Elizabeth* established. *Blue Moonlight* goes further and incorporates a more explicit interpretive role that could be the basis for incrementally developing the substance of section 26 in later cases. The Court's interpretation of the Rental Housing Act in *Maphango* sets up a similar interpretive opportunity through that legislation, but, in contrast to *Blue Moonlight*, the Court reverted to the more purely proceduralized managerial model of *Olivia Road.*

I then turn to two companion cases issued the same day as *Blue Moonlight.* These cases reinforce the principle that courts can stop evictions in

[5] Ibid., [25] (quoting *Jaftha v Schoeman and Others*, 2005 (1) BCLR 78 (CC) (2004), and adding italics).

[6] Ibid., [29–31].

[7] *See* Heinz Klug, "*Grootboom* at Home and Abroad: Adventures in the Construction of the Global Constitutional Canon," 5 (2012), at www.digitalcommons.law.umaryland.edu/schmooze_papers/150/.

every case where alternative accommodation is unavailable and also adopt some important procedural innovations that strengthen judicial power to manage eviction processes. The Court's very thin analyses of PIE in each case, however, raise questions whether it will continue to develop the incremental interpretive role *Blue Moonlight* sets up or revert to the more purely procedural model of *Maphango*.

The chapter concludes with summary analyses of several other eviction-related decisions – including one education-rights case – that develop key aspects of the two-sided model the decisions discussed earlier illustrate: (1) limited substantive interpretations filtered through legislation and (2) application – and sometimes expansion – of procedural tools to reach rights-protective results. These more recent decisions first demonstrate the consistency with which the Court has exercised the stronger authority both sides of this model create for courts. Several cases expansively interpret what constitutes an eviction under section 26(3) and PIE and closely scrutinize attempts to avoid judicial scrutiny and control over eviction processes broadly conceived. Some also refine the use of meaningful engagement as the framework for managing situations like evictions that threaten existing access to goods or services protected by social rights.

A. Rise of managerial judging

This section begins with a close analysis of *Blue Moonlight*, which arguably is the most significant of the recent eviction decisions because the Court engaged in an unusually substantive interpretation of constitution-enforcing legislation including repeated references to section 26. It then contrasts *Blue Moonlight* with *Maphango*, where a majority of the Court changed its normal procedures to revive and expand an informal dispute-settlement process under the Rental Housing Act.

Both decisions illustrate the Court's use of procedural techniques and its preference for flexible balancing tests to intervene to protect against potential evictions that are the hallmarks of the managerial approach the Court first developed in *Port Elizabeth*. Both decisions also laid the groundwork for the Court to develop a more substantive interpretive approach of social rights through incremental development of constitution-enforcing legislation that *Port Elizabeth*'s "constitutional matrix" and extensive analysis of PIE also modeled. Whereas *Blue Moonlight* embraced that substantive role directly and fairly robustly, however, *Maphango* went to great lengths to rely primarily on a statutory procedure. The tight focus on procedure in *Maphango* raises questions whether the Court should develop the substantive side of *Port Elizabeth*'s managerial approach – questions that *Blue Moonlight*'s companion cases reinforce.

1. Blue Moonlight

Justice Van der Westhuizen opened his opinion for a unanimous Court in *Blue Moonlight* acknowledging that South Africa has not yet fulfilled the constitutional promise of a dignified existence or even reached a point where every citizen at least has a roof over his or her head.[8] The facts of the case presented a small subset of that much larger problem. A group of eighty-one adults and five children, the "Occupiers" in the judgment, faced eviction by a private landowner seeking to redevelop the property where they live.[9]

Blue Moonlight involved the combination of several issues: (1) the extent to which section 26 obligates a private landowner to permit people to occupy land where evicting them would undoubtedly result in homelessness; (2) the interactions between section 26 and section 25's protection of private property; (3) the rights of both the Occupiers and the landowner against the municipality where the prospect of homelessness resulted from arguable inadequacies in planning and budgeting; and (4) the obligations of municipal governments generally relative to other levels of government for providing emergency housing to residents evicted from private land.[10]

In framing the questions in the case Van der Westhuizen found that the positive dimension of section 26 was not directly on the table.[11] In a section titled "Constitutional and Legal Framework," he acknowledged that the case raised potentially "compet[ing]" constitutional issues "as well as constitutional allocation of powers" across government.[12] But in the next sentence he emphasized that "[p]olicy has been formulated and statutes enacted to create a scheme for the protection and realisation of these rights."[13] This structure mirrors the constitutional matrix the Court analyzed in *Port Elizabeth* but with a much stronger emphasis on the legislative framework.

8 *Blue Moonlight, supra* note 1, [2]. 9 Ibid., [6]. 10 Ibid., [3–5].

11 Ibid., [5] ("This case does not deal directly with a programme, or measures, to realize progressively the right of access to adequate housing").

12 Ibid., [16] ("The issues to be determined require a consideration of rights enshrined in our Constitution, which may compete in circumstances where homelessness is a likely result of eviction, as well as constitutional allocation of powers and functions to municipalities and the other spheres of government").

13 Ibid.

In fleshing out the constitutional dimensions of the case, the Court acknowledged that the property owner relied on section 25 and noted the Occupiers "anchor their case in section 26." It also cited Chapters 3 and 7 of the Constitution as setting out principles relevant to the City's role in providing housing.[14] But then it quickly moved to the "principal instruments enacted to give effect to the constitutional obligations of the various organs of state in relation to housing," the Housing Act and the National Housing Code.[15]

The Housing Act, the Court explained, "expressly gives effect to the Constitution" and obliges municipalities to take steps to ensure that local residents have access to housing.[16] This mandate intersects with another statute, the Municipal Systems Act, which specifies municipal powers and duties and implements the constitutional distribution of powers in sections 152 and 153 of the Constitution. The Systems Act requires municipalities to work together with other levels of government to progressively realize the rights in sections 25 and 26.[17] Returning to the Housing Code, the Court specifically noted that Chapter 12 "was introduced after the decision of this Court in *Grootboom*" and that the City's housing policy incorporates Chapter 12 by including a program for emergency housing.[18] Finally, the Court put PIE on the table as the statutory framework for assessing evictions and for balancing sections 25 and 26.[19] The Court thus set up an analytical structure in which these statutes largely incorporated the constitutional issues.

The Court devoted most of the rest of its analysis to PIE framing "the critical question" as whether evicting the Occupiers satisfies PIE's equitable, considering-all-circumstances test.[20] This inquiry subsumed virtually every other question in the case. The Court made this clear by explaining that applying the PIE test required it to address five questions: the owner's rights, the City's obligations, the sufficiency of the City's resources to meet those obligations, the constitutionality of the City's emergency housing policy, and "an appropriate order to facilitate justice and equity in the light of the conclusions on the earlier issues."[21] In other words, all of the issues both constitutional and statutory that the parties raised were effectively aspects of the PIE analysis.

In answering these questions the Court touched on the now-subsidiary constitutional issues and also established some significant principles, including that private landowners have a limited obligation to allow occupiers to remain on land where evicting them would cause

[14] Ibid., [17–23]. [15] Ibid., [24]. [16] Ibid. [17] Ibid., [25–26].
[18] Ibid., [27–28]. [19] Ibid., [29]. [20] Ibid., [30]. [21] Ibid., [33].

homelessness and that a municipality cannot rely on lack of resources as a defense where that lack was the result of an incorrect interpretation of its statutory obligations to provide housing. By couching those conclusions as applications of PIE – and interpretations of other statutes filtered through the PIE inquiry – however, the Court was able to rely principally on legislation rather than the Constitution and also to maintain considerable flexibility to reach a different outcome in later cases.

The Court made surprisingly short work of the landowner's argument that it had an unqualified right to evict the Occupiers so long as it followed the applicable legal procedure holding that "[a]n owner's right to use and enjoy property at common law can be limited in the process of the justice and equity enquiry mandated by PIE."[22] Although unlawful occupation is without question "a deprivation of property under section 25(1)," such deprivations may "pass constitutional muster" if they flow from a law of general application and they are not arbitrary.[23] PIE's balancing test meets the criteria for a lawful deprivation because it permits eviction of unlawful occupiers. At the same time, PIE's test protects the section 26 rights of unlawful occupiers by requiring courts to inquire whether and under what circumstances eviction in a particular case is just and equitable.[24]

Under PIE's test, the Court explained, a private landowner, like Blue Moonlight, who purchases land with knowledge of long-standing occupation reasonably should expect "the possibility of having to endure the occupation for some time."[25] The Court did not ground this reasonable expectation in any specific legal source. It is not clearly a function of the Occupiers' offsetting rights under section 26 nor is it a direct limitation on Blue Moonlight's rights under section 25. The analysis stops with PIE and is tied specifically to the facts in this case.

After establishing that PIE could constitutionally limit a landowner's section 25 rights under the appropriate circumstances, the Court then applied PIE's requirement that it consider whether land is or could be made available to house the occupiers. The Court first noted that the

[22] Ibid., [40]. The Court's brief analysis is due in part to the precedent it set in *Modderklip* where it upheld the SCA's grant of constitutional damages to a private landowner who was required to permit temporary occupation of his land because the municipality was unable to provide housing. The Court, however, did not rely directly on section 26 in that case. *President of the Republic of South Africa and Another v Modderklip Boerdery (Pty) Ltd* 2005 (8) BCLR 786 (CC) (2005) ("*Modderklip*").

[23] Ibid., [37]. [24] Ibid., [40]. [25] Ibid.

High Court had rejected the City's motion to join the provincial government and found that "it would generally be preferable for all [levels of government] to be involved in complex legal proceedings regarding eviction and access to housing. Indeed, joinder might often be essential and a failure to join fatal."[26] This establishes a significant procedural power that allows courts to join relevant government entities in all eviction cases under PIE. Doing so extends judicial authority to reach policies and resources at all levels of government and to use individual cases to coordinate broader changes.[27]

The Court then rejected the City's argument that its obligations were limited to implementation of the national and provincial housing schemes and that these require, at most, the City seek emergency funding from the provincial government to provide emergency housing where a private party initiates an eviction. Here, again, the Court relied primarily on the statutory context – in particular Chapter 12 of the Housing Act – to find that "the City has a duty to plan and budget proactively for situations like that of the Occupiers."[28]

The City relied on language in *Grootboom* that it claimed imposed funding obligations on only the national government, restricting local government to implementation of those decisions. In rejecting this argument, the Court expanded its *Grootboom* judgment in an important way. First, the Court quoted *Grootboom* to find that the "duty regarding housing in section 26 of the Constitution falls on all three spheres of government – local, provincial and national – which are obliged to co-operate."[29] This is a key point of the judgment: all levels of government must be proactive in fulfilling section 26. Municipalities cannot hide behind buck-passing arguments as the City tried to do here.[30] The City thus misread *Grootboom* when it determined the scope of its obligations to independently plan for and fund emergency housing.[31]

[26] Ibid., [45].

[27] *See* Gustav Muller and Sandra Liebenberg, "Developing the Law of Joinder in the Context of Evictions of People from Their Homes," 29 *S. Afr. J. Hum. Rts* 554 (2013) (discussing the procedural powers that flow from joining local government in eviction cases).

[28] *Blue Moonlight*, *supra* note 1, [67]. The Court summed up its statutory analysis as follows: "These provisions indicate a legislative purpose that the City ought to plan proactively and to budget for emergency situations in its yearly application of funds." Ibid., [66].

[29] Ibid., [42].

[30] This also is the basis for another important implication of the case: normally complex eviction cases will require joinder of all three levels of government. Ibid., [42–46].

[31] Ibid., [57].

Finding that municipalities have independent obligations to plan and fund emergency housing is a modest but significant clarification and extension of *Grootboom*.[32] It is modest because municipalities only share the obligation *Grootboom* identified to plan and budget for emergency housing needs. It does not create any new obligation under section 26 or even specify in greater detail what the existing obligation requires other than confirming that private as well as state-initiated evictions trigger it. Instead the significance lies in the power this creates for courts to hold municipalities directly responsible for demonstrating they have planned and budgeted for emergency housing whenever an eviction order is sought. This – combined with the power to join municipalities – is a critical predicate for the managerial interventions the Court has employed in later cases where it has started to ask more penetrating questions about the nature and scope of municipal planning and budgeting processes.

The Court applied this seemingly modest refinement of *Grootboom* in remarkable fashion to reject the City's related argument that, even assuming it had an obligation to provide emergency housing in this situation, it lacked sufficient resources to do so. The Court rejected this argument as legally irrelevant because the preceding analysis of the Housing Act demonstrated "the City's budget was the product of its incorrect understanding of Chapter 12."[33] The Housing Act imposes an unqualified obligation on the City to plan and budget for emergency housing for people like the Occupiers and, as the Court bluntly observed, "[h]ad the City prepared its budget on a proper understanding of Chapter 12, it might have made provision for emergency housing."[34]

It's notable that the Court characterized the City's resources argument as an "attack on the factual findings" of the SCA, rather than as an aspect of the section 26 analysis.[35] This avoided a direct constitutional analysis in keeping with the general patterns in the second wave. It also, however,

[32] The Court carefully formulated this principle in the negative as a rejection of the City's argument that it was *prohibited* from expending its own funds: "There is no basis in *Grootboom* for the assertion that local government is not entitled to self-fund, especially in the realm of emergency situations in which it is best situated to react to, engage with and prospectively plan around the needs of local communities." Ibid. This leaves open the question Justice O'Regan posed in *Mazibuko* whether a municipality might have an independent positive obligation to go beyond the requirements of national legislation if it has sufficient resources. *Mazibuko and Others v City of Johannesburg and Others* 2010 BCLR 239 (CC) (2009) [74].

[33] *Blue Moonlight, supra* note 1, [69]. [34] Ibid. [35] Ibid.

eliminated the flexibility that section 26(2) creates and constrained the Court's discretion to find in the government's favor.[36]

Although it found that the City's resources argument technically irrelevant to the question of the Housing Act's requirements, the Court went on to briefly discuss it "because it would be quite inappropriate for a court to order an organ of state to do something that is impossible, the more so in a young constitutional democracy."[37]

In a sharp departure from its usual analysis under 26(2), here the Court placed the burden of proof for the resources argument squarely on the City's shoulders. It found that the City failed to meet that burden because it provided information only on the housing budget, not its overall financials. The housing budget was irrelevant because – as the Court's interpretation of the Housing Act established – the City developed that budget on the mistaken premise that it had no obligation to plan for private evictions.[38]

In concluding this analysis, the Court implicitly shifted from the question of whether the SCA's factual analysis was supportable in an analysis of section 26. The Court noted that the City provided only information specifically related to the housing budget but not its overall budget. It then concluded that this "Court's determination of the reasonableness of measures within available resources cannot be restricted by budgetary and other decisions that may well have resulted from a mistaken understanding of constitutional or statutory obligations." In case there was any doubt, the Court restated the effect of its interpretation: "in other words, it is not good enough for the City to state that it has not budgeted for something, if it should indeed have planned and budgeted for it in the fulfilment of its obligations."[39]

This is an important interpretation of section 26(2) for two reasons. First, it allows courts categorically to reject resource arguments where the claimed shortfall resulted from a flawed budgeting process. Applying this principle arguably requires – or at least permits – courts to interpret the Constitution and relevant statutes in the abstract to make a threshold determination whether to even consider a resources argument. This implicitly establishes the analytical separation of 26(1) and 26(2)

[36] Compare *Port Elizabeth Municipality v Various Occupiers*, 2004 (12) BCLR 1268 (CC) (2004), [7] (rejecting the occupiers' characterization of the case as essentially a challenge to the SCA's factual findings and proceeding to evaluate the claims in expressly constitutional terms).

[37] *Blue Moonlight*, *supra* note 1, [69]. [38] Ibid., [74]. [39] Ibid.

espoused by the Court's critics and that the Court has consistently rejected to avoid imposing unsustainable obligations on the state. A court will have to identify the relevant statutory and constitutional obligations to determine whether a municipality's planning and budgeting process properly included consideration of them.

Second, it appears to impose an evidentiary burden on the government to demonstrate the lack of resources in the context of its entire budget.[40] This not only expands the scope of the resources inquiry but also reinforces the analytical separation of sections 26(1) and 26(2) by making the government responsible for submitting evidence to demonstrate the lack of resources. That evidentiary burden also provides the basis for courts to require municipalities to provide extensive information about their general budgeting and planning processes. The expansive joinder requirement established earlier potentially expands that power to other levels of government and gives courts the authority to scrutinize relevant provincial and national budgeting processes as well.

With the resources argument out of the way, the Court turned to the constitutionality of the policy itself focusing on its differentiation between private and public evictions. The Court applied reasonableness review but explained that it was sufficient in this case to review the City's policy for bare rationality without addressing whether reasonableness requires more.[41] Even under rationality review the Court easily found the policy unconstitutional.[42]

The City's housing policy was a direct response to the *Olivia Road* judgment and at least on its face established a constitutionally sensitive eviction and relocation procedure. The City relied on data to justify prioritizing public-eviction relocation and also included a procedure for addressing emergency housing situations that result from private evictions to further support its policy. In short, it was the kind of policy supported by the kind of justifications that the Court in the past has held falls well within the broad scope of executive authority.[43] Why was a plan as complex as the City's so clearly unconstitutional that it failed even the lowest imaginable standard?

40 Ibid.

41 Ibid., [87] ("Whether a policy which meets the requirements for rationality would necessarily be reasonable does not have to be decided here").

42 Ibid., [95].

43 Two prominent examples are the prepaid meter policy in *Mazibuko*, *supra* note 32, and the housing development plan in *Residents of Joe Slovo Community, Western Cape v Thubelisha Homes and Others* 2009 (9) BCLR 847 (CC) (2009).

The Court simplified the analysis by framing the question as whether the City could categorically exclude people evicted from private land from its emergency housing policy: "the City's housing policy is unconstitutional to the extent that it excludes the Occupiers and others similarly evicted from consideration for temporary accommodation. The exclusion is unreasonable."[44] This narrow inquiry echoes the interpretive framework the Court adopted in *Khosa* and that drove the stronger scrutiny in *TAC*. The question wasn't whether the City was entitled temporarily to prioritize one group over another but whether it could permanently exclude a subset of people. The holding thus does very little to expand the contours of section 26(1) other than confirming that an irrational distinction in a program designed to implement housing obligations will fail, especially where the government lacks a legitimate resources argument.

Blue Moonlight is a remarkable decision that clearly advances the rights of people facing eviction. For the residents themselves it prevented, at least temporarily, a private landowner from evicting unlawful occupiers. In reaching this result, the Court developed some important aspects of sections 25 and 26. It declared that the City's formal policy of excluding potential evictees like the Occupiers from its emergency housing process violates section 26. It held that, although unlawful occupation is a "deprivation" under section 25, the state can constitutionally impose such a deprivation by temporarily delaying an eviction if application of PIE's test makes immediate eviction unjust. Finally the Court modestly expanded *Grootboom* to clarify that section 26, applied through the Housing Act, imposes at least some direct obligation on municipalities to fund emergency housing programs and that sections 152 and 153 likewise impose independent constitutional obligations on municipalities to go beyond mere implementation of national and provincial policies.

On top of this, the Court established several important constitutionally connected legal principles. Most significant among these is that a municipality's resource-limitation arguments are irrelevant where those limitations are the result of its own misinterpretation of statutory or constitutional obligations. In addition, the Court seems to have established a substantial evidentiary burden for municipalities that requires them to demonstrate that resources are unavailable anywhere in the entire budget. For all of these reasons *Blue Moonlight* looks and feels completely different than *Mazibuko* despite its formal reliance on the same analytical framework.

44 *Blue Moonlight, supra* note 1, [95].

Blue Moonlight nonetheless fits the general mold of the second-wave cases for several reasons. First, on one level, this was an easy case. The City of Johannesburg took an extreme position that evinced a complete absence of sensitivity to its constitutional obligations. In essence, the City told the Court that it had no responsibility whatsoever to take an independent role in responding to the needs of people facing homelessness from private evictions. What is more, the City's stance here was part of a long-standing pattern dating back before *Olivia Road.*

The SCA's discussion of the City's long-standing "entrenched" refusal to plan for private evictions is telling.[45] The Court's reliance on bare rationality review to reject the City's arguments demonstrates it viewed its policy as clearly unconstitutional. From this perspective, *Blue Moonlight* is another example of the Court responding to state action clearly in conflict with the social rights' requirements. The requirement at issue here was one already clarified by the Court's earlier eviction cases. Indeed it arguably was simply a variation of *Grootboom*, and so enforcing it resulted in some modest refinements and several significant practical tools. Perhaps most significant is the leverage the Court's analysis of the City's resources argument creates. Any person threatened with homelessness from eviction can now ask a court to scrutinize the relevant municipality's budgeting process for compliance with section 26 and the Housing Act.

But what does that tell us about the substantive content of section 26(1) that can guide either policy development or litigants in future cases? *Blue Moonlight's* reasoning does not provide any guidance on the harder issues that will inevitably arise where a municipality budgets rationally. It simply holds that municipalities are obligated by statute not to completely exclude private evictees from consideration in the budget process. If in the next case, a municipality's argument goes beyond a bare disclaimer of responsibility and instead argues exclusion was the result of competing policy priorities, *Blue Moonlight* doesn't say much about the constitutional standard for assessing those priorities.

The Court also clarified that a private landowner in Blue Moonlight's position who purchases land with known long-standing occupiers may have to expect a reasonable delay in evicting those occupiers if doing so

[45] *City of Johannesburg Metropolitan Municipality v Blue Moonlight Properties 39 (Pty) Ltd and Another* 2011 (4) SA 337 (SCA) (2011) [51] ("The City has for a long time been faced with emergency housing situations of all kinds. It appears to have adopted an entrenched position that excludes persons such as the occupiers from assistance. It is abundantly clear that but for this approach it could have adopted a long-term strategy, which ought to have included financial planning, to deal with such exigencies").

would render them homeless. This too establishes an extremely important tool for protecting poor people. But here again, beyond the principle itself, the opinion provides little guidance on the factors a court should consider in deciding under what circumstances and for how long a private landowner can reasonably be required to delay eviction.

Here we see the obscuring effects of deciding the case primarily through a context-specific test like PIE's without developing the background constitutional principles at play. The Court emphasized that the landowner purchased with knowledge of the occupation and its own housing needs were not at issue.[46] The fact that the Court identified these as relevant considerations provides some guidance for future applications of PIE. But because they aren't specifically connected to section 26 and because they are only part of PIE's multifactor balance, subsequent cases even with those same facts could come out differently. What happens in a case where a city appropriately planned for its obligations to house evictees from private land and the money has run out? What about a landowner with more recent occupiers? The Court leaves these questions open, and although it arguably sets up the possibility those questions could be incrementally resolved through case-specific application of PIE, the main emphasis here is remedying the obvious unconstitutional policy that completely ignores the effects of private evictions.

2. Maphango

Justice Cameron wrote the majority opinion in *Maphango*, a procedurally complicated case that began as a run-of-the-mine landlord–tenant dispute over rent increases in a lease renewal. By the time the case reached the Court, however, as Justice Cameron noted, it raised fundamental questions regarding the relationship between the Constitution and the common law.[47] The case presented the Court with a clear opportunity to clarify that relationship, in particular to develop either the common law of leases or section 26. Instead, in a move remarkably similar to *Olivia Road*, a majority of the Court broke from its normal procedures to revive and expand an informal dispute-resolution mechanism created by the Rental Housing Act. Doing so extended the Act's procedural protections in significant ways but without providing even the modest constitutional and statutory elaboration that *Blue Moonlight* featured.

[46] *Blue Moonlight, supra* note 1, [39].

[47] *Maphango, supra* note 2, [31].

Maphango involved several tenants with long-standing leases containing rent-control provisions who challenged their landlord's attempt to terminate the leases solely to raise the rent. The leases contained a provision limiting rental increases to a set percentage unless the landlord sought permission from the Rental Housing Tribunal – a municipal body created by the Rental Housing Act to resolve landlord–tenant disputes. The leases also included a termination clause that either party could invoke with notice. The landlord argued that the termination provision – supported by long-standing common law – permitted it to terminate the existing leases and offer each tenant a new lease with the same terms but at a higher rental rate.[48]

The tenants, supported by an *amicus curiae* brief, argued that permitting the landlord to circumvent the rent restrictions by terminating the leases violated the tenants' right to security of tenure and access to affordable housing under section 26(1). The Court could recognize this, they argued, by interpreting "unfair practice" in the Act to prohibit termination of these leases solely to increase rent.[49] Alternatively, the Court could develop the common law of contract to provide a constitutionally derived implied term in the lease limiting a landlord's termination rights in leases with protective clauses where termination would result in "disproportionate hardship" to the tenant.[50]

The majority opinion sidestepped each of these arguments by reviving the administrative procedure created by the Rental Housing Act that the tenants had voluntarily abandoned early in the litigation. The Act provides a set of substantive protections for tenants and also establishes an administrative procedure for resolving landlord–tenant disputes under the Act. That procedure is conducted by Rental Housing Tribunals that the Act authorizes each province to establish.[51] The tenants in this case originally proceeded under the Tribunal process but withdrew their claims before that process was complete when the landlord sought an eviction against them in the High Court.[52]

48 Ibid., [3].

49 Ibid., [43–47]. The Inner City Resources Centre laid out this argument in its *amicus curiae* brief. Heads of Argument for Inner City Resources Centre as Amicus Curiae in *Maphango and Others v Aengus Lifestyle Properties (Pty) Ltd* (CC) [6.1–6.5].

50 Ibid., [1.7–1.8.5].

51 *Maphango, supra* note 2, [13], and notes 11–12 (citing and quoting the Act and implementing regulations).

52 Ibid., [14].

The High Court held that landlord had the authority to evict the tenants. The SCA upheld the High Court's judgment focusing primarily on the tenants' constitutional and common law arguments. It also interpreted the Act's "unfair practice" provision to exclude a lease termination on the basis that terminations are single events, not practices.[53]

The Constitutional Court majority reversed the SCA's decision. The majority opinion discussed the tenants' constitutional and common law arguments at length but ultimately relied on an interpretation of the Act that lease terminations could constitute an unfair practice. Rather than taking the next step and determining whether the terminations here were unfair practices, however, the Court issued a procedurally complex order that postponed the appeal to allow either party two weeks to file a complaint with the Housing Tribunal. If that happened, the Court retained jurisdiction to issue further orders based on the outcome of the Tribunal process. If it did not, the appeal would be dismissed, leaving the SCA judgment intact.[54]

The majority revived the Tribunal process in the face of a deeply critical dissent that raised several procedural irregularities and substantive flaws with the order. In addition, as Frank Michelman notes, bringing the Act into play required working through several "seemingly non-trivial" questions about the Act's applicability.[55]

These non-trivial questions were highlighted by Justice Raymond Zondo in a dissent where he took the majority to task for what he viewed as a highly irregular procedural innovation that flouted rule-of-law principles and was deeply unfair to the landowner. Zondo spent several lengthy paragraphs explaining that the applicants had functionally abandoned the Tribunal process and arguing that reviving that process involved a reckless departure from the Court's pleading rules and normal procedure.[56] These arguments underscore the lengths the Court went to find a procedural route for resolving the case and also the remarkable similarities to *Olivia Road.*

The majority explained its decision first by emphasizing the leadership role of the legislature in enforcing the social rights. Justice Cameron

[53] Ibid., [22–23]. [54] Ibid., [70].

[55] Ibid., [48] (observing that "[i]n my view, neither the landlord nor the tenant fully appreciated the force of the Act's provisions in litigating their dispute"). Frank I. Michelman, "Expropriation, Eviction and the Dignity of the Common Law," Harvard Law School Public Law & Legal Theory Working Paper Series Paper No. 12–37 (July 18, 2012), 12–13.

[56] *Maphango, supra* note 2, [133–47].

cited "rule-of-law considerations" to find that "it would be wrong for this Court to take a narrow view of the matter that ignores the importance and impact of the [Rental Housing Act]. That would imply that this Court could allow litigants to ignore legislation that applies to an agreement between them."[57] A short concurrence by Justice Froneman joined by Justice Yacoob restated this same point more directly: "it would be a denial of constitutional responsibility for any court to decide a matter without considering legislation where it was aware of applicable legislation."[58]

Cameron then emphasized the Act's status as "a post-constitutional enactment adopted expressly to give effect to the right of access to adequate housing."[59] This required a broad interpretation of "unfair practice" that potentially extended to the terminations here.[60] Paired with the generic, rule-of-law-driven principle that a court should apply any relevant legislation to a dispute, this seems to suggest a double-ratchet in favor of legislative enforcement techniques in the case of constitutionally driven legislation.

In analyzing the unfair practice provision, Cameron described at length the Act's "complex, nuanced and potentially powerful system for managing disputes between landlords and tenants."[61] The Act "expressly takes account of market forces as well as the need to protect both tenants and landlords" and "is in particular sensitive to the need to afford investors in rental housing a realistic return on their capital."[62] But, "at the same time, the Act does not ignore the need to protect tenants."[63] Indeed, he emphasized, this case focused on the Act's "most potent" provisions in this respect, the power of the Housing Tribunal to prevent a landlord (or tenant) from taking otherwise lawful action if that action constitutes an "unfair practice."[64] Most relevant here, the Act "demands that a ground of termination must always be specified in the lease, but even where it is specified, the Act requires that the ground of termination must not constitute an unfair practice."[65] Cameron went on to unpack not only the Act's definition but also to highlight the provincial regulations promulgated under the Act that give the Tribunal the power to take into account not "only the common law legal rights of a tenant or landlord, but . . . also their statutory interests."[66]

57 Ibid., [48]. 58 Ibid., [152].
59 Ibid., [57]. *See also* ibid., [34] (describing the Act as a "prime instance" of legislative enforcement of section 26).
60 Ibid., [57]. 61 Ibid., [49]. 62 Ibid. 63 Ibid., [50].
64 Ibid. 65 Ibid. 66 Ibid., [53].

The availability of a constitutionally driven, legislatively crafted balancing test for protecting tenants, Cameron found, made it unnecessary to reach the substantive constitutional and common law issues that were the focus of the parties' arguments.[67]

By rejecting the SCA's limited interpretation of unfair practice and finding that the constitutional connection required a broader reading, Cameron's analysis started down the road the amicus and the residents mapped out in their statutory arguments. Indeed, much of the detailed analysis in the majority judgment closely tracks their interpretations and sometimes even the language in their heads of argument. But rather than definitively interpreting unfair practice, the Court stopped short and instead "kick-started" the Tribunal process by, in essence, remanding the case back to that body to determine in light of the powerful balancing mechanism the legislature created whether the terminations here were unfair.[68]

On one hand, this mirrors the similar shift in *Blue Moonlight* from constitutional to statutory analysis. In both cases, focusing on applicable legislation allowed the Court to rely on constitution-enforcing legislation as the vehicle for its substantive analysis. In both cases the primary statutory vehicle established a context-dependent balancing test. In *Blue Moonlight* the Court included analyses of other legislation, including the National Housing Act and also some limited but significant analysis of the background constitutional context. It also applied PIE's balancing test with some specific attention to the relevant factual details. In *Maphango*, however, the Court relied on the Rental Tribunal process in a way that avoided even a limited, case-specific substantive analysis.

As Justice Zondo's dissent illustrates, the majority had to work hard to bring the statutory procedure back into play, including ignoring the issues the parties raised in favor of a resolution not sought by either side. The majority acknowledged in a footnote that reopening the Tribunal procedure required it to craft a remedy that none of the parties sought.

67 Ibid., [55] ("Since in my view this dispute is best approached through the generous and powerful mechanisms the Act offers both sides to the dispute, I express no view on whether the landlord was entitled at common law to cancel the leases, nor on whether, if it was so entitled, the common law should be constitutionally developed to inhibit that power").

68 *See* Michelman, *supra* note 55, 18 (contrasting this result with the alternative of "kick-start[ing]" a common-law revision process). Procedurally this was not a direct remand, but functionally it served the same purpose by giving leave to the parties to file a complaint posing that question.

Tellingly, it cited *Olivia Road* as precedent for creating such a "novel remedy."[69]

Maphango is a significant development in the Court's approach to housing rights. Up to this point, the Court had dealt with the eviction process itself and applied section 26(3) to mitigate the effects of that process. *Maphango* for the first time recognized a legal mechanism that could prevent eviction altogether in some circumstances and so goes beyond the other eviction decisions that provide only temporary protection.[70]

But *Maphango* also is a clear example of the deeper proceduralization and avoidance of substantive interpretation characteristic of the second-wave cases. This is evident not only in the lengths the majority went to revive the Rental Housing Act's procedure but also its celebration of the Act's "complex, nuanced and potentially powerful system" for managing landlord–tenant disputes that is "acutely sensitive to the need to balance the social cost of managing and expanding rental-housing stock without imposing it solely on landlords."[71] This echoes Justice Sachs's description of the creative and flexible role managerial judges can take under PIE to humanely resolve eviction disputes and balance sections 25 and 26 on a case-by-case basis.

Michelman notes that relying consistently on these kind of flexible legislatively crafted balancing measures might "too often tempt courts away from the hard tasks of questioning the compatibility of legislative balances with constitutional requirements and of re-examination of the common law's historically embedded balances to ensure they are in keeping with the Constitution's pro-transformative aims and values."[72]

The lengths the Court went to avoid the substantive issues in *Maphango* illustrate that concern. Although the majority opinion is obviously intent on protecting the tenants' constitutional rights, it deliberately avoided engaging with section 26 or even the Housing Act's implementation. Instead the Act's flexible framework provided an escape hatch for the Court simply to avoid the constitutional and common law issues at play while signaling its preference for a pro-poor outcome without saying much at all – even indirectly through statutory interpretation – about

[69] *Maphango, supra* note 2, n. 121.

[70] Liebenberg's analysis of early SCA decisions that failed to consider the effect of section 26 on the cancellation of lease contracts illustrates a deep-seated reluctance among South African courts to apply the social rights directly to common law issues. Sandra Liebenberg, *Socio-Economic Rights: Adjudication under a Transformative Constitution* (2010), 336–42.

[71] *Maphango, supra* note 2, [49].

[72] Michelman, *supra* note 55, 19.

what those constitutional values are or how they should apply on these facts.

The majority's holding that termination could constitute an unfair practice opens the door to a possible limitation on a landlord's common law rights here and in other complaints that come before a Housing Tribunal. But now, as Cameron emphasized at length, this is a limitation grounded in a set of statutory not constitutional considerations.[73] As an explicitly constitution-enforcing statute, those considerations might – but might not – be constitutionally required.

To be fair, that will typically be the case in a constitutional framework that accepts legislative constitutional enforcement. Constitution-enforcing legislation is unlikely to expressly distinguish between statutory and constitutional dimensions. Nonetheless it does mean that adopting a rule that systematically prefers legislative enforcement is likely to provide less clarity on constitutional questions over time than direct constitutional enforcement or development of the common law. It also puts a premium on courts taking advantage of the substantially reduced opportunities that are likely to arise for identifying specific constitutional norms – opportunities the companion cases to *Blue Moonlight*, discussed later, suggest the Court is not eager to take.

Legislation, like the Rental Housing Act, that creates a multifactor balancing test, compounds the lack of constitutional clarity. Resolving the tenants' claims under its test might begin the process of a legislative-judicial dialogue over what section 26 requires in the rental-housing context but not necessarily. The majority celebrated the even-handed way the test takes into account both market concerns and the need to protect tenants.[74] But that same evenhandedness could swing the result in a particular case in either direction. Whether the specific balance a Tribunal strikes on a given set of facts furthers constitutional values or not is an open question – a question that's impossible to answer because we don't know how section 26 intersects with the common law right to terminate and the majority in *Maphango* doesn't provide any guidance. The Tribunal process itself is unlikely to provide much clarity on that interaction because it's designed specifically to resolve landlord–tenant disputes not to settle legal questions.

[73] *Maphango*, *supra* note 2, [52–53] (emphasizing the difference between "interests" and "rights").

[74] *Maphango*, *supra* note 2, [49].

As *Blue Moonlight* illustrates, where courts interpret constitution-enforcing statutes with consistent and explicit attention to not only general constitutional values but also specific constitutional provisions, it's possible to develop an incremental substantive jurisprudence over time even while maintaining a case-by-case approach. By identifying the aspects of each statute that reflect constitutional norms and how to apply those norms in specific factual situations (including how to weigh them against other statutory factors), courts can play an independent role in elaborating the constitutional dimensions of statutes like PIE and the Rental Housing Act. The majority's refusal to decide whether the terminations in *Maphango* were unfair practices (or even to provide some general guidance by evaluating the statutory factors in light of the constitution) missed that opportunity.

To some extent these problems could relate to timing. This is the first case where the Court addressed the Act's constitution-enforcing function and it did so in the absence of a ruling by the Tribunal. It is reasonable under those circumstances for the majority to leave open some of these questions. And it's possible that the Constitutional Court and lower courts could over time develop both the constitutional dimensions of the statutory framework and the constitutional boundaries of it. This could happen, for example, in appeals from individual cases that reject on explicitly constitutional grounds the particular balance the Tribunal strikes and in direct challenges to the constitutionality of particular factors in the Act or to interpretations of those factors.

But there's no guarantee that kind of incremental constitutional development will happen. Instead of kick-starting a constitutionally infused Tribunal process that will gradually clarify the scope of the Constitution and its effects on the common law, we might end up with a much narrower process that leaves decisions on individual cases predominantly in the hands of the rental tribunals, features few appeals and appeals that limit themselves to straightforward questions of statutory interpretation without any reflection on – much less questioning of – whether and how either the statute itself or the balancing in individual cases meet constitutional muster.

Consider how that risk played out here. The applicants unsurprisingly took up the Court's invitation to file a complaint with the Rental Tribunal. The Tribunal had the authority to determine whether terminating these leases to avoid the rent-increase restrictions in them was an "unfair practice" in terms of the Act. But the first step was for the Tribunal to attempt to mediate the dispute. Here, mediation succeeded, and so the story ends with no opportunity to further develop the Act's substance or its relationship to the Constitution.[75]

Even if that informal resolution had failed and the case returned to the Constitutional Court for review of a decision on the merits, it's relatively easy to imagine a scenario that would have left the constitutional dimensions of the case undeveloped. Following *Maphango*, section 26(1) could operate as a background principle enlarging the potential scope of "unfair practice," and, at least if the Tribunal pays attention to the majority, pushing toward some restriction on the landlord's termination rights with respect to these leases. But (as the majority describes at length) the factors that the Tribunal applies are legislatively defined and the entire process is a legislatively crafted mechanism to implement section 26 in a market-sensitive way. Equally important, the balancing that results under the Act involves factors that extend beyond section 26 and so, even if the Court reviewed the Tribunal's interpretation, it could still avoid saying anything directly about how section 26 affects the Act and instead merely tweak the legislative balance on the specific facts of this case.

The lengths the majority went to bring the Tribunal process back into play here heighten this concern. As Justice Froneman's concurrence notes, the SCA considered the potential effect of the statute and interpreted it directly rather than reviving the procedure the tenants had abandoned. The majority could have done the same thing here and in the process explained the ways in which unfair practice reflected constitutional norms and values and why those required the outcome on these facts.

But the majority not only brought the substantive provisions of the statute into play, it relied on the statutory procedure as well despite the fact that the applicants had voluntarily abandoned that procedure.[76] This involved a potentially pro-poor application of the statute that could result in substantial protections for tenants in the long term. But those gains are channeled through legislation that sets up a procedure designed to avoid legal principles. This is why *Maphango* looks a lot like *Olivia Road*. In both

75 March 9, 2014, e-mail from Stuart Wilson on file with the author.

76 Michelman explains that the Act provided both a substantive route – i.e., interpreting "unfair practice" to prohibit the terminations here – and the procedural route the Court took of delaying judicial action on the eviction case until both parties had "an unhindered opportunity to place the matter before the provincial Rental Housing Tribunal for its disposition (thus allowing the Tribunal to make the primary determinations both of the "unfair practice" question and of any remedial consequence)." Frank I. Michelman, "Expropriation, Eviction and the Gravity of the Common Law" Harvard Public Law Working Paper, No. 12-37 (October 20, 2012, version).

cases the Court found a way to enforce section 26 through a procedure that promotes informal dispute resolution over formal legal resolution.

Maphango applied the Rental Housing Act to create the same kind of procedural control as meaningful engagement over the private landlord–tenant relationship. The key substantive move the Court made was interpreting "unfair practice" to encompass the exercise of a termination clause in a lease. This put the Tribunal *process* to work in potentially pro-poor ways without definitively establishing anything substantive about the Act or the constitutional principles the Act enforces. It's no coincidence that the Tribunal process, like engagement, is structured to resolve disputes informally through party consensus. The result was nearly complete substantive avoidance that contrasts starkly with the specific elaboration of the constitutional context in both *Blue Moonlight* and *Port Elizabeth.*

Both *Maphango* and *Olivia Road* show the considerable power the Court can exercise to shape the outcome of a case even while deliberately avoiding substantive analysis. In each case the Court went out of its way to avoid the parties' substantive arguments by finding a constitution-enforcing procedure that promises the possibility of resolving the dispute in a context-sensitive way. Here that procedure was one Parliament created as part of its obligation to legislatively enforce section 26 and so came with direct democratic credentials. In *Olivia Road*, the procedure was court-crafted but still designed to promote democratic processes through citizen participation in policy making. In both cases, the Court emphasized the democratic aspects of these procedures rather than assessing their substantive dimensions.

One key difference is that engagement is a largely procedural remedy that does not incorporate even statutory standards. The Tribunal process, like PIE, uses a set of statutory criteria that courts could use to incrementally develop substantive principles. But the Tribunals and the Tribunal process – although far more structured than engagement – share similar procedural characteristics and an emphasis on practical resolution of specific disputes over legal development.

The strong emphasis on procedure and clear avoidance of substance in *Maphango* and *Olivia Road* make both cases paradigmatic examples of the second-wave decisions. But the pro-poor outcomes and the confidence the Court displayed in both cases distinguish them from *Mazibuko*'s more deferential approach. Rather than mere deference, the procedural devices the Court relied on in each case provide a different set of possibilities for asserting judicial authority. They put courts in a position to manage specific processes and guide those processes toward constitutionally compliant resolutions. In the case of the Tribunal process this restores judicial authority in a very direct way by giving courts the power directly to balance sections 26 and 25 by resolving individual landlord–tenant cases.

Meaningful engagement is one step removed from that direct implementation and instead gives courts the power first to reject unconstitutional outcomes on procedural grounds and then to influence the subsequent party-directed process for resolving the dispute. Both processes also create opportunities for courts to develop the kind of soft-substantive guidance that incorporates a form of interpretive authority – in the Tribunal process through interpretation of the legislative criteria and under meaningful engagement by setting the agenda and also substantive terms for the parties' consultation or policy-level interventions like the 70 percent set aside in *Joe Slovo.* Chapters 8 and 9 explore how this model of judicial authority could be more fully developed. These cases, along with the more recent decisions discussed later, where the Court employed meaningful engagement are the basis for the expanded version of engagement Chapter 9 develops.

3. Blue Moonlight*'s companion decisions*

The Court issued two companion decisions to *Blue Moonlight* on the same day and featuring nearly cookie-cutter analyses by Justice Yacoob applying *Blue Moonlight*'s broad principle that PIE's analysis can limit private property rights.[77] Both cases involved evictions of people who were unlawfully occupying private land in the City of Tshwane.

In *PPC Quarries*, Yacoob ordered the City to conduct an audit of the occupiers to determine the number of people who would be rendered homeless and to provide alternative accommodation to those people one month before their eviction.[78] In *Golden Thread*, he remanded the case to the High Court for reconsideration and ordered the City to submit a report providing specific information that he held PIE's test required, including the availability of alternative accommodation. The result in each case was a delay in the occupiers' eviction and an order that connected the timing of the evictions to the City's ability to provide alternative accommodation.

[77] *Golden Thread* and *PPC Quarries, supra* note 1.
[78] *PPC Quarries, supra* note 1, [16].

These decisions are important for two reasons. First, they reinforce the reluctance evident in *Maphango* to engage in the more substantively infused application of PIE that *Blue Moonlight* modeled. At the same time, however, the decisions reinforce the de facto strong principle that PIE does not permit eviction without alternative accommodation and also expand the procedural tools available to courts to manage eviction processes in rights-protective ways. These are the heart of what Chapter 8 calls the eviction model and that Chapter 9 argues could be extended through an expansive application of meaningful engagement.

a. *PPC Quarries*

In *PPC Quarries* the Constitutional Court issued a direct order that relied on the general principles in *Blue Moonlight* but without expanding those principles in any easily identifiable way. The case involved an appeal from a High Court order that permitted eviction of a large group of people illegally occupying private land in the Tshwane Municipality but conditioned the eviction on the City auditing the occupiers and providing those without alternative accommodation access to land one day before the eviction.[79] The Constitutional Court set aside that order, holding that the High Court misapplied the PIE analysis as refined by *Blue Moonlight*. Specifically it found that the High Court's order impermissibly permitted the eviction to proceed if the City failed to provide alternative accommodation prior to the eviction.[80]

The Court's own PIE analysis spans three short paragraphs. The first paragraph is a block quote from *Blue Moonlight* stating that PIE may temporarily restrict private property rights.[81] In the second Justice Yacoob identified two facts as relevant: there was no evidence the landowner, PPC Quarries, planned to "use the property gainfully in the foreseeable future" and there was no reason at that point to assume that the City would not "take steps reasonably quickly to provide alternative accommodation" for the occupiers.[82] In the third Yacoob concluded that these facts made it "unjust and inequitable" under PIE to evict the occupiers who risked becoming homeless before the City provided accommodation. The final order required the City first to survey the occupiers to determine who would become homeless and provide accommodation to those people one month before the eviction date the order sets.[83] The only significant difference between this and the High Court's original order was an

[79] Ibid., [4]. [80] Ibid., [10]. [81] Ibid., [11]. [82] Ibid., [12]. [83] Ibid., [16].

extension from one day to one month the time between when the City has to provide accommodation and the eviction.

b. *Golden Thread*

Golden Thread features the same kind of case-specific procedural control as *PPC Quarries*, but the Court delegated that control back to the High Court with a detailed framework for exercising it. The case closely tracked the facts of *PPC Quarries* – an appeal from a High Court order evicting 170 families illegally occupying private land in Tshwane. The families occupying the land had lived there less than six months – a fact the High Court found limited its ability to consider the availability of alternative accommodation under PIE.[84] Justice Yacoob held that the High Court erred by failing to require the City to provide information about alternative accommodation and to investigate the possibility of mediation under PIE.[85]

Reaching that conclusion required an important, somewhat strained, interpretation of PIE. PIE distinguishes between short-term (defined as less than six months) and long-term occupation, and requires courts to investigate the availability of alternative accommodation only for the long term.[86] The High Court noted evidence that the City might be able to provide alternative land for the occupiers and expressed frustration at the City's refusal to participate in the proceedings.[87] It nonetheless concluded that it was powerless to order the City to do more because PIE didn't require it to consider the availability of alternative accommodation.[88]

Yacoob broadly interpreted PIE's general mandate that courts consider all relevant circumstances to include the availability of alternative accommodation in all cases – functionally eliminating the distinction between short- and long-term occupation.[89] This solved the problem in *Golden Thread* by clearly permitting a court to join municipalities in all evictions where PIE applies and to require they provide information on their ability to provide alternative accommodation. This set up the final order that

[84] Ibid., [12–13]. [85] *Golden Thread*, *supra* note 1, [12–13], [19].

[86] PIE requires a court to determine in every case whether ordering an eviction is "just and equitable . . . considering all of the circumstances" but where a person has occupied property for longer than six months, section 4(7) specifies that these circumstances include "whether land has been made available or can reasonably be made available by a municipality or other organ of state or another land owner." Prevention of Illegal Eviction from and Unlawful Occupation of Land Act 19 of 1998.

[87] *Golden Thread Ltd v People who intend invading portion R25 of Farm Mooiplaats 355JR Tshwane, Gauteng and 2 Others* [2010] ZAGPPHC 262 (2010) [11].

[88] Ibid., [12]. [89] *Golden Thread*, *supra* note 1, [15–16].

remanded the case to the High Court for reconsideration and required the City to submit a report identifying several things: the number of families who would be rendered homeless if evicted; the steps the City has taken or plans to take to provide land or accommodation for the occupiers; when the City could provide alternative land or accommodation; the likely effects on the occupiers and surrounding residents if the eviction proceeded without alternative accommodation; and steps the City could take to alleviate the effects of continued occupation on the landowner until it provided alternative accommodation.[90]

Both *Golden Thread* and *PPC Quarries* apply *Blue Moonlight*'s principle that private landowners may have to temporarily delay eviction but do so in a way that looks much more like *Maphango* than *Blue Moonlight* itself. In all four cases, including *Blue Moonlight*, the Court broadly interpreted constitution-enforcing legislation to expand the scope of a multifactor balancing test. But in *Blue Moonlight* the Court connected that interpretation directly to broader constitutional principles and identified specific facts that mattered in the statutory analysis and that could ground further development in later cases. By contrast, in *Maphango*, *PPC Quarries*, and *Golden Thread*, the Court carefully avoided engaging with section 26 and failed to develop the statutory factors in ways that give real guidance on how which facts mattered and why. Indeed, even the significant expansion of PIE to apply the availability of alternative accommodation to all cases simply extends procedural control to a larger set of cases rather than providing concrete guidance on how to resolve them.

The results in both *PPC Quarries* and *Golden Thread* look much like what Sachs called for in *Port Elizabeth*: a court managing a specific eviction process to mitigate its effects rather than to establish broad constitutional principles or to change an underlying policy to comply with those principles. *PPC Quarries* applies *Blue Moonlight*'s core principle that courts can apply PIE to temporarily restrict private property owners' right to evict (and *Golden Thread* clearly expects the High Court will do the same).[91] But the effects of that application are largely limited to the occupiers in each case.

[90] Ibid., [21].

[91] Yacoob observes in *Golden Thread* that it "is possible that the High Court was motivated to some extent by its view that Golden Thread had no obligation toward the applicants" and then notes that *Blue Moonlight* "held that ownership in South Africa is not as unrestricted" followed by a block quote. Ibid., [17]. The limited substantive effect of even this is muted both because Yacoob carefully couches it in hypothetical terms and because he limited his analysis to the High Court's failure to order the City to provide information.

Although these cases reinforce the core principles in *Blue Moonlight* the Court applied those principles primarily to strengthen the flexible management role *Port Elizabeth Municipality* highlights rather than to elaborate those principles. All three cases establish that municipalities are necessary parties in privately initiated evictions. *Golden Thread* provides a template for the range of information a court can require a municipality to provide once it's joined, including the status of the potential evictees as well as its past efforts, future plans, and overall capacity to provide alternative accommodation for any evictees rendered homeless. All three cases also strongly suggest – but stop short from definitively establishing – that a court should order municipalities to provide alternative accommodation when it orders evictions from private land and sequence the orders to prevent homelessness.

The upshot is a set of principles that give courts considerably expanded power to manage evictions. Courts now can convene all the relevant parties in a private eviction. They can obtain extensive information about a municipality's overall housing policies, its total budget, and the planning processes involved. Where appropriate, a court can use that information to craft an order that requires the municipality to provide alternative accommodation and ties the timing of the eviction to provision of that accommodation.[92]

Together with *Blue Moonlight*'s recognition that courts can inquire into municipal budgets and policies these powers form the basis for the extensive procedural authority in the eviction model Chapter 8 elaborates and Chapter 9 expands. Adding the constitutionally attentive analysis that *Blue Moonlight* featured could amplify and extend those tools in important ways that wouldn't unduly strain the limited approach the Court has developed in the second wave. These decisions together with *Maphango*, however, show that the Court may be reluctant to adopt even that modest substantive role.

B. Extending the managerial approach

The Court has continued to employ and refine variations of the strong procedural control it exercised in these cases in several more recent

[92] Wilson has argued that all of these principles are part of the "new normality" in eviction law and that they indicate the possibility for a stronger substantive approach to section 26. *See* Stuart Wilson, "Breaking the Tie: Evictions from Private Land, Homelessness and a New Normality," 126 *S. Afr. L. J.* 270 (2009).

eviction-related decisions. In four decisions the Court broadened the definition of eviction under section 26(3) and PIE to include indirect interference with existing access to housing. These interpretations expand the class of cases where courts can exercise the procedural authority it developed in its earlier eviction decisions.[93] In each of these cases a municipality actively sought to effect evictions without complying with the robust protections the Court's interpretations of section 26(3) and PIE established. The Court's analysis in each case demonstrates it is willing to closely scrutinize any such efforts and to actively guard against interference with existing access to housing.

The most recent of these cases, *Zulu*, is especially important because the Court started down the road toward rejecting a more nuanced set of legal arguments and tactics municipalities are increasingly employing to limit the significant constraints the Court's eviction cases have imposed on forced removals and the de facto rule that alternative accommodation is required in every eviction.[94] *Zulu* is the leading edge of an increasing number of what might be called "third-generation" eviction cases in which municipalities at least formally have accepted the "dignified framework" for evictions the second-wave decisions established but are searching for ways to deal with the growing practical challenges of meeting those obligations.[95] The debate among the three competing opinions in *Zulu* over whether the Court should have gone further down the road extending that dignified framework to address these more refined arguments sets up a future confrontation over its scope and limits.

The final case this chapter considers, *Juma Musjid*, involved eviction of a school from private land and the balance between the right to basic education in section 29 and private property in section 25.[96] *Juma Musjid* is

[93] This interpretive move to extend its authority mirrors *Golden Thread*'s interpretation of PIE to require consideration of the availability of alternative housing in all eviction cases. The effect of both is to give courts some control to manage situations that would fall outside of PIE under narrower readings of the relevant language.

[94] *Zulu*, *supra* note 2.

[95] With *Grootboom* constituting the entire "first" generation that established the substantive basis for the Court's eviction jurisprudence, the decisions from *Port Elizabeth* through *Golden Thread* form the second generation that applied *Grootboom* to manage individual eviction disputes and developed the array of procedural powers just described. *Zulu* and other decisions related to anti-land invasion units represent an extension of both *Grootboom*'s principle and *Port Elizabeth*'s procedural authority to a new set of questions regarding the scope of municipal obligations under section 26 and related legislation.

[96] *Governing Body of the Juma Musjid Primary School & Others v Essay N.O. and Others* 2011 (8) BCLR 761 (CC) (2011) ("*Juma Musjid*").

important because it applies *Port Elizabeth*'s managerial model – including an innovative use of meaningful engagement – outside of the housing context. It also establishes an express constitutional basis for the principle *Blue Moonlight* applied under PIE that private property rights constitutionally can be subordinated at least temporarily to avoid disturbing existing access to goods or services protected by social rights. This allows courts in every case involving potential deprivation of a social right to enforce the negative dimension of the social right in favor of competing privates. Chapter 8 takes up in greater detail this principle as a core feature of the eviction model.

1. *Broadening the definition of "eviction"*

In the following four cases the Court modestly broadened the definition of eviction under section 26(3) and PIE to protect against deprivation of existing access to housing and to reject creative arguments and tactics by municipalities to avoid judicial scrutiny of their actions. In the first of these decisions, *Pheko*, the Court upheld the appeal of several hundred occupiers of an informal settlement whom the Ekurheleni municipality relocated and whose homes it destroyed without a court order, purportedly to protect their safety.[97]

The municipality argued the relocations were part of a lawful emergency "evacuation" under the Disaster Management Act 57 of 2002 (DMA) and so did not implicate section 26.[98] The City based its invocation of the DMA on an engineering study of the land in the area that found it was unsuitable for permanent housing and prone to sinkholes.[99] The Constitutional Court held that the DMA's emergency evacuation provision should be read narrowly in light of section 26(3) and limited to life-threatening situations involving temporary removal. The municipality's reliance on the DMA to remove the occupiers here violated section 26(3) because the condition of the property did not pose an immediate threat to life and the removals were permanent not temporary.[100] The Court ordered the municipality to "engage meaningfully with the occupiers" to identify land closer to their destroyed homes for relocation and

[97] *Pheko, supra* note 1.

[98] Ibid., [8–11]. Section 55 of the DMA grants municipalities the authority to declare a "local state of disaster" and broad authority to take temporary emergency measures, including "the evacuation to temporary shelters of all or part of the population . . . if such action is necessary for the preservation of life." Disaster Management Act 57 of 2002, §55(2)(d).

[99] *Pheko, supra* note 1, [5–7]. [100] Ibid., [37–54].

to report back to the Court by December 2012 on compliance with the order.[101]

In the second case, *Motswagae*, the Rustenberg municipality sought to redevelop land occupied by fifteen homes for a new housing project.[102] The municipality met with representatives of the community several times seeking to negotiate their relocation, but the community could not reach consensus and ultimately rejected the municipality's offer of alternative accommodation. The City proceeded with excavation of the land surrounding the homes despite the residents' refusal to move.[103]

The High Court refused the residents' request to enjoin the City's excavation, finding that the work did not infringe section 26(3) because it took place outside their homes. It also granted the City's cross-application, enjoining the residents from interfering with the excavation.[104] In a short unanimous judgment, Justice Yacoob reversed the High Court and held that the municipality's actions violated section 26(3) because they disturbed the residents' occupation sufficiently to constitute a de facto eviction.[105] Yacoob specifically found that the municipality's actions were an attempted "backdoor" eviction without obtaining a court order.[106]

Schubart Park Resident's Association presented facts that were a mix of *Pheko* and *Olivia Road.*[107] Residents of a block of deteriorating city-owned apartments close to the center of Pretoria engaged in protests several days after the City cut off water and electricity to the apartments.[108] Local police removed residents of one block of apartments, cordoned off the complex, and refused to let other residents return. They later removed all of the roughly 3000–5000 residents without obtaining an eviction order.[109] As in *Pheko*, the City justified removing the residents without a court order in part by arguing it was "evacuating" them for health and safety reasons but without citing any specific statutory authority.[110]

The High Court rejected an emergency application by the residents the evening of their removal, seeking an order allowing them to reoccupy their homes, finding that the buildings were unsafe but ordered the City

[101] Ibid., [53]. [102] *Motswagae, supra* note 2, [1–2].
[103] Ibid., [2–3]. [104] Ibid., [4–5]. [105] Ibid., [13]. [106] Ibid., [16].
[107] *Schubart Park, supra* note 2. The Court cited both *Pheko* and *Olivia Road* as precedents for rejecting "an argument that the immediate removal of residents on grounds of safety and temporary impossibility could result in the permanent lawful deprivation of the occupation of their homes." Ibid., [20].
[108] Ibid., [2–3]. [109] Ibid., [2–3], [8].
[110] The Socio-Economic Rights Institute of South Africa, Heads of Argument on Behalf of Amicus Curiae, [2–6] in *Schubart Park, supra* note 2.

to provide temporary accommodation on terms the City already had offered to the residents.[111] In a later hearing the court issued a final order confirming its dismissal of the residents' application but also requiring the City either to refurbish the apartments and allow the residents to return or to provide alternative permanent accommodation if it determined refurbishment was not feasible.[112]

The Constitutional Court issued a unanimous opinion holding that the High Court's orders could not constitutionally serve as justification for eviction under section 26(3).[113] The Court noted that various legislation, including the DMA, provided for emergency removals but found them inapplicable here. It specifically noted with "concern" the City's attempts to justify the removals as lawful under those statutes, noting it supported the residents' claim that the City was seeking to use the crisis to evict them illegally.[114] The Court then found the High Court should have made clear that its order refusing to require immediate reoccupation was temporary and that the residents had a constitutional right to return to their homes as soon as it was safe.[115]

After rejecting the High Court's order under section 26(3), the Court went on to find that meaningful engagement was appropriate in this situation to ensure the residents' were given a genuine opportunity to influence the City's plans. Quoting *Port Elizabeth* and *Olivia Road* at length concerning the obligation to engage, it found that the City's temporary accommodation offer was "an inadequate basis" for meaningful engagement because it proceeded from a "top-down premise" and gave the residents little opportunity for genuine input. The Court instead issued a detailed order requiring engagement at every stage of the reoccupation process and giving the High Court jurisdiction to supervise the engagement.[116]

All three of these decisions expand the range of situations in which courts can exercise the managerial authority that the Court first identified as part of the "dignified framework" for evictions in *Abahlali*. They are significant first for the consistency they demonstrate in the Court's application of that framework to protect existing access to housing. Second, the Court's broad interpretation of eviction to prevent what it perceived as "back door" evictions in these cases illustrates the strength of that framework and the Court's willingness to closely scrutinize arguments and tactics that undermine it. Finally, the Court's use of meaningful engagement

[111] *Schubart Park*, *supra* note 2, [4–6]. [112] Ibid., [6–7], [12]. [113] Ibid., [29–30].
[114] Ibid., [38–39]. [115] Ibid., [38–41]. [116] Ibid., [42–53].

in some of these cases, as well as in *Juma Musjid* described later, creates a framework for expanding this managerial role to the policy context.

In *Motswagae*, this framework operated in a relatively limited way that simply preserved existing access to housing. Stopping the redevelopment would clearly affect the City's underlying housing policies at least in terms of the challenged project, but the Court's order did not create any mechanism for either the residents or the courts to influence those policies beyond preventing further disturbance to the property around their homes.

The Court's more detailed orders in *Schubart Park* and *Pheko*, by contrast, went one step further by forcing the municipality in each case to remedy its unconstitutional removals by engaging with evicted residents over the obligation to provide alternative accommodation or restore the homes from which they were displaced. These cases thus illustrate that courts can rely on the relatively modest protection against negative infringements of a social right to manage a case to yield positive-rights protections. The engagement order in each of these cases gave the occupiers and their representatives leverage to negotiate themselves for those positive claims rather than relying on a court order. The Court backed up that leverage by using the array of procedural tools it developed in earlier eviction cases, including ordering the government to report back and retaining jurisdiction (either itself or through the High Court) to oversee enforcement.

2. *Anti-land invasions and the third-generation eviction cases*

Zulu is the first Constitutional Court decision addressing a set of emerging legal and tactical responses by municipalities to the increasing constraints on eviction established by this dignified framework and the decisions described earlier. Municipalities in a growing number of cases have used some variant of what are called "anti-land invasion units" purportedly to prevent new illegal construction of homes on public or private land.[117] The legal justification for these units – that the eviction and home-destruction *prevents* illegal occupation – is clearly intended to carve out the power to evict some subset of people illegally occupying land without complying

[117] Sandra Liebenberg describes the central features of this emerging set of tactics and arguments in a recent opinion piece. *See* "What the Law Has to Say about Evictions," *GroundUp* (September 1, 2014), available at www.groundup.org.za/article/what-law-has-say-about-evictions˙2185.

with PIE and the de facto requirement to provide alternative accommodation the Court's cases have established.

In addition to relying on these units and the premise of preventing invasion, municipalities in several instances have sought blanket prospective court orders enjoining invasions against unspecified groups of people and permitting the destruction of recently built homes to prevent future invasions.[118] *Zulu* presented a combination of both tactics. A majority of the Court rejected on narrow grounds an expansive application of those tactics while still leaving room to uphold narrower applications in a later case. Justice Van der Westhuizen concurred but argued the Court should have gone further and expressly rejected those tactics both to prevent further illegal evictions in this case and to resolve the issue for cases pending in lower courts where municipalities used similar tactics. The majority's limited holding leaves open the constitutionality of these tactics – and also the question of how far the Court is willing to extend the dignified framework to protect existing access to shelter.

Zulu involved a suit in the High Court by the KwaZulu-Natal Provincial government seeking an anti-land invasion order of the kind just described. Specifically the government requested the Court authorize the eThekwini Municipality and the South African Police Service to prevent invasions of land slated for housing development. The land in question bordered an existing informal settlement, and the municipality's existing Land Invasion Control Unit had demolished homes built on the land more than twenty-four times. The High Court granted an interim order requested by the Provincial MEC in the case authorizing the police to take "all reasonable and necessary steps" to prevent such invasions, including dismantling houses built on the land. It also prohibited "any persons" from "invading, occupying or constructing any structures" on the land.[119]

The evicted occupiers sought to intervene in the case that would decide whether to confirm the interim order. The High Court dismissed that application, finding that the occupiers' interests were unaffected by the interim order reasoning it operated only prospectively to prevent future illegal occupation.[120] The occupiers appealed that interlocutory order, and

[118] *See* Stuart Wilson, "Evictions: South Africa's Bitter, Year-Round Trauma," *Daily Maverick* (July 15, 2014), at www.dailymaverick.co.za/opinionista/2014–07–15-evictions-south-africas-bitter-year-round-trauma/#.VK1HhmTF-OM (describing recent examples of the use of these tactics); Daneel Knoetze, "Eviction by the Back Door," *GroundUp* (December 1, 2014) (same), at www.groundup.org.za/article/eviction-back-door_2490.

[119] *Zulu, supra* note 2, [9–11].

[120] Ibid., [14–15].

the direct issue on appeal was limited to the procedural question whether they had standing to intervene in the case.[121]

A majority of the Constitutional Court held the occupiers had standing because the interim order encompassed not only future invasions but also continued "occupation." By including people who already occupied homes on the land, the order amounted to an eviction of those occupiers.[122] Rather than reverse the order itself, the Court remanded the case back to the High Court, ordering it to permit the occupiers to intervene and present arguments for overturning the interim order.[123] The majority's analysis thus did not reach the merits of the order itself, including whether municipalities could rely on such orders to remove people like the occupiers here without complying with PIE or section 26.

Justice Van der Westhuizen concurred in the decision but reasoned that the Court should have taken the next logical step and reversed the interim order rather than remanding the case. He specifically noted that the interim order here was similar or identical to orders in several other lower-court cases addressing purported land invasions and that delaying resolution on the constitutionality of such orders created unnecessary uncertainty that threatened the rights of vulnerable people under PIE and section 26(3). He also found that leaving the interim order intact exposed many of the occupiers in this case to potential eviction under it while the case was pending in the High Court.[124]

A second concurring judgment by Justice Moseneke responded to Justice Van der Westuizen's finding that the record demonstrated the parties agreed to extend an interim order by the High Court prohibiting future evictions and demolitions to all of the current residents of the property. This agreement meant that the parties in this case faced no risk of irreparable harm during the course of the following proceedings.[125]

The contrast between Justice Van der Westhuizen's approach and the majority's reflects the consistency between the eviction-related judgments and the other second-wave cases. Van der Westhuizen's approach would have simply recognized the clear import of the Court's earlier cases and the requirements under the dignified framework *Abahlali* identified and applied them both to this case and by extension other cases involving this combination. Even in the context of preventing disruption of existing access to housing, however, a majority of the Court was not willing clearly to establish these principles in a way that makes them broadly applicable

[121] Ibid., [16]. [122] Ibid., [25–27]. [123] Ibid., [38].
[124] Ibid., [50]. [125] Ibid., [75–76].

across cases. Instead, the majority was concerned with leaving options open for the government and preferred to proceed incrementally by temporarily protecting the occupiers from immediate eviction while letting the High Court decide the broader issues.

3. *Managerial judging and other rights*

The decisions discussed previously illustrate the Court's continued development of the *Port Elizabeth* managerial model. They illustrate the Court is consistently willing to assert authority to intervene in cases where deprivation of existing access to housing is threatened and to exert varying degrees of procedural control in ways that seek to manage the situation toward a rights-protective resolution. By relying principally on PIE's flexible, context-specific test for this authority, however, the Court avoided developing clear legal principles applicable across cases either through statutory analysis or interpretation of section 26.

Juma Musjid extends the procedural control the Court has developed in these decisions to a social right other than housing – specifically the right to basic education in section 29 of the Constitution.[126] The decision bears remarkable similarities to the eviction decisions and points to ways the Court could adapt this strong procedural approach to other social rights. The case dealt specifically with the eviction of a public school from private land and so closely paralleled the housing-rights decisions, making it relatively easy for the Court to apply similar procedural authority. Nonetheless, *Juma Musjid* explicitly identified a general constitutional basis for that authority that could be used to apply it in other social rights cases.

Juma Musjid was an appeal from a High Court order evicting a public school from private land following a dispute between the school and the KwaZulu-Natal Minister of Education (MEC) over financing.[127] The High Court held that the landowner was entitled under the common law to evict the school for failure to pay rent and that the schoolchildren's right to basic education was not implicated because it was enforceable solely against the government.[128] The Constitutional Court issued an interim order suspending the eviction and requiring the MEC to meaningfully engage with the landowner and the school's governing body to resolve the dispute, including alternative schooling options for the children. It

[126] *Juma Musjid*, *supra* note 97. [127] Ibid., [1–3]. [128] Ibid., [21–23].

also required the MEC to file a report with the Court describing the engagement process and its results.[129]

After receiving that report, the Court issued a detailed follow-up order requiring the MEC to contact each parent and set up a "dedicated office" to engage with parents on enrolling in new schools, including transportation options, and to report on the results.[130] The Court granted the eviction order in December 2010 after reviewing that second report finding that closure of the school was inevitable and that the government would provide adequate alternative placements for children at the school.[131]

Justice Nkabinde wrote the unanimous opinion explaining the interim orders and decision to grant the eviction. The analytical structure of the opinion tracks *Port Elizabeth* opening with a general discussion of the legal framework focused on the right to basic education in section 29(1). At the outset, Nkabinde emphasized that this right is "immediately realisable" and not subject to the internal limitations that condition the other social rights.[132] The importance of basic education, she noted, is underscored by the South African Schools Act, which makes attendance mandatory and requires the MEC to provide public schools.[133] Nkabinde discussed in some detail the right to education recognized by several international and regional treaties, in particular the International Covenant on Economic, Social and Cultural Rights. She then noted that education was particularly significant "for individual and societal development in our democratic dispensation in light of the legacy of apartheid" and the lasting effects of segregated education.[134]

This background set up the question whether the MEC fulfilled its obligations under section 29. The Court easily found "[t]he answer is clearly in the negative."[135] Over the next seven paragraphs it detailed the multiple failures of the MEC and her unacceptable indifference to the plight of the schoolchildren, emphasizing that the MEC could have avoided the eviction altogether by taking her constitutional and statutory obligations seriously.[136]

Turning to the landowner, the Court then held the High Court's analysis of the scope of the right was too limited and that the landowner had "a negative constitutional obligation not to impair" the right to basic education.[137] This right flows from section 8(2) of the Constitution and

[129] Ibid., [3]. Note 5 reproduces the order.
[130] Ibid., [76–77]. Note 87 reproduces the second order. [131] Ibid., [5].
[132] Ibid., [37]. [133] Ibid., [38–39]. [134] Ibid., [41–42].
[135] Ibid., [45]. [136] Ibid., [45–52] [137] Ibid., [56–60].

the First Certification judgment's recognition that social rights could be enforced negatively against "improper invasion."[138] Here that right was triggered by the landowner's voluntary agreement to provide the land for a public school and its assumption for several years of the "public function of managing, conducting and transacting all affairs" of the school including paying costs normally provided by the state.[139]

The Court nonetheless determined that the sequence of negotiations showed the landowner clearly had fulfilled its limited, secondary obligation not to impair the right to education. The landowner tried for several years to negotiate an agreement with the MEC to take over the school before attempting to evict. The MEC took an "uncompromising attitude" that caused those negotiations to fail, and the landowner's constitutional obligations could not require it to negotiate indefinitely.[140] Under these circumstances, it was not unreasonable for the landowner to seek eviction.

This set up a direct conflict between the schoolchildren's rights and the landowner's, similar to the conflict between sections 26 and 25 in *Blue Moonlight.* Notably the resolution here followed a similar pattern. The Court found that the High Court erred in its analysis first by failing to recognize this clear conflict and second by not requiring the MEC to provide information on how it would provide a basic education to these children. The Court then quoted *Port Elizabeth*'s description of the managerial role courts should adopt to resolve competing constitutional issues, finding them applicable here as well.[141] In a move reminiscent of the sequence in *Olivia Road*, the Court found that the MEC's actions during the appeal under the two engagement orders effectively remedied the conflict here by providing alternative schools in consultation with the parents and largely accommodating their preferences.[142]

Juma Musjid represents something of a hybrid between *Blue Moonlight* and *Olivia Road.* Like *Olivia Road*, the Court here used meaningful engagement as a tool for hands-on resolution of a dispute with clear constitutional implications. The Court deployed engagement in the more muscular fashion it exercised in *Joe Slovo* and also *Pheko* by issuing relatively detailed engagement orders that specified the issues the parties should seek to resolve. Here the Court added a new twist by using a second engagement order that took into account the information following the first failed engagement and managed the situation toward an alternative route for protecting the rights claims of the schoolchildren.

138 Ibid.. [58–60]. 139 Ibid., [59]. 140 Ibid., [63–65].
141 Ibid., [69–71]. 142 Ibid., [77–79].

Juma Musjid resembles *Blue Moonlight* because it involved the same interaction among the state's obligations, the plaintiff's rights and the rights of a private party. As in *Blue Moonlight* the Court engaged in substantive balancing of two constitutional rights – section 29 against section 25. Here the Court paired that substantive analysis alongside the strong procedural management of the case to reach a rights-protective resolution.

Most significant in this respect, the Court explicitly recognized the obligation of private parties to avoid "negative" infringements that disrupt existing access to resources that partially fulfill a social right. Similar to *Blue Moonlight*, that recognition is tied to the specific facts – here the voluntary assumption of state duties by the landowner and the long-standing relationship to the school. In contrast to *Blue Moonlight*, however, where that factual analysis was further weakened because it was filtered through the multifactor PIE analysis, here the Court recognized this private obligation directly under section 29 and in language that plainly extends to each of the social rights. *Juma Musjid* thus provides a clear precedent that where people have secured access to resources protected by a social right, that access – at least temporarily and under certain circumstances – trumps private property rights even where there is no legislation implementing that right. This principle firmly grounds *Blue Moonlight*'s similar analysis of PIE in constitutional territory and it also provides a basis for social rights to temporarily trump private property in other contexts, including service disconnections. Chapter 8 argues that connecting this to *Joseph*'s right to receive municipal services offers an important doctrinal framework for expanding the eviction model to other service-delivery cases.

Juma Musjid also follows *Blue Moonlight*'s framework in that it relied on the potential for the negative aspect of a social right temporarily to trump private property rights as the basis to establish positive obligations on the state to provide an alternative. In both cases rather than mandate the specifics of that alternative, the Court set up a negotiation process that could allow the parties to reach agreement themselves – although notably rejecting in *Blue Moonlight II* the opportunity to use the engagement process to control and oversee the process. In contrast to *Blue Moonlight*, here the Court retained control itself even issuing a second engagement order to redirect resolution in a different direction when the first one failed. Both cases illustrate the close connection between meaningful engagement and the managerial control the Court has developed, but *Juma Musjid* shows the potential effectiveness of adopting a structured process for exerting that control. Chapter 9 picks up on this point and identifies ways courts could expand and structure meaningful engagement orders to have greater substantive effect.

C. Conclusion

The later eviction decisions beginning with *Blue Moonlight* reinforce the limitations of the Court's approach in the second-wave decisions but also illustrate the Court's willingness to work within those self-imposed constraints to manage individual cases to reach rights-protective outcomes and identify a broad array of procedural powers for doing so. These decisions represent the decisive shift away from *Grootboom*'s abstract but more substantive approach to *Port Elizabeth*'s hands-on managerial model. The Court's limited development of substantive constitutional or statutory provisions in *Blue Moonlight* represents a promising elaboration of the more substantive interpretive role *Port Elizabeth* also applied. But *Maphango* and *Blue Moonlight*'s companion cases reverted to a more procedural role.

This shift to a managerial model fits within the role *Mazibuko*'s articulated and in particular its recharacterization of social rights as tools to enforce democratic accountability. Even the rare substantive principles the Court established fit within that recharacterization. For example, *Blue Moonlight*'s significant interpretation that the Housing Act imposes specific responsibilities on municipalities to plan and budget for evictions from private land primarily provides a legal platform to challenge municipal decision-making *procedures* to ensure they properly took into account the obligations social rights and enforcing legislation impose. This is a significant power but it says very little about substantive obligations section 26 or the Housing Act impose. *Juma Musjid*'s interpretation that section 29 imposes obligations in certain circumstances on private parties not to interfere with existing access to goods and services guaranteed by social rights has a slightly different, but similarly procedural effect. It does not elaborate the substantive requirements of section 29; it creates the basis for seeking judicial protection against negative infringements of section 29 (and other social rights).

Despite their substantive limits, however, these principles significantly expand judicial authority to protect poor people and indirectly enforce the positive dimensions of the social rights. Perhaps more important, the remarkable consistency with which the Court has rejected eviction applications where the state is unable to provide alternative accommodation and the authoritative way it has developed the managerial control over eviction processes it first described in *Port Elizabeth*, however, stand in stark contrast to the strongly deferential role it adopted in *Mazibuko*. Chapters 8 and 9 draw on this authoritative approach to identify more specific ways the Court could expand this authority without departing dramatically from the second-wave patterns.

7

Patterns and possibilities in the second wave

The defining characteristics of the second-wave cases – a heavy reliance on procedural remedies and rights, continued avoidance of substantive interpretations and a reframing of social rights as tools for democratic accountability in policy development rather than substantive guarantees – appear to fulfill predictions of the critics in the debate over the first-wave cases that the Constitutional Court would fail to develop a set of strong substantive standards for enforcing the social rights. The fact that the Court has managed to issue multiple rights-protective decisions and establish some significant, if narrowly defined, pro-poor principles while still maintaining a limited interpretive role is an important accomplishment. By operating within this substantively limited role, the Court has avoided the kind of extravagantly antidemocratic occupation of large areas of social policy that was a core objection to entrenching social rights in the new constitution. It also has managed to avoid resolving claims that required it to evaluate and assess institutional-competence-straining issues raising complex technical, scientific or economic arguments.

That success, however, has come at some cost. The Court's critics argue that cost is too high, and that its preoccupation with avoiding the justiciability concerns has unduly limited the social rights and diminished the Court's role under the new Constitution.[1]

These critiques have real force. There is no doubt that the second-wave cases maintain and entrench the Court's reluctance to develop a consistently substantive social rights jurisprudence. For good reason reaction to these decisions has focused on the Court's retreat from any significant

[1] E.g., Danie Brand, "Judicial Deference and Democracy in Socio-Economic Rights Cases in South Africa," in Sandra Liebenberg and Geo Quinot (eds.), *Law and Poverty: Perspectives from South Africa and Beyond* (2012) 172–73; Stuart Wilson and Jackie Dugard, "Constitutional Jurisprudence: The First and Second Waves," in Malcolm Langford *et al.* (eds.), *Socio-Economic Rights in South Africa: Symbols or Substance?* (2013) 35.

interpretive role and insistence that social rights are principally tools for policing democratic accountability.

But this emphasis on the disappointing substantive limits that the Court appears to operate within obscures the relatively strong authority several decisions establish for courts to scrutinize challenged government policies and decisions on procedural grounds. These decisions show that, when operating in a role that it can safely characterize as procedural, especially when faced with a policy that either completely ignores or actively infringes the social rights, the Court has been much more willing to exercise that authority at least to temporarily stop implementation of a challenged policy and sometimes even to change it. The Court has exercised similarly strong authority and confidence in enforcing social rights where it can restrict its interventions to individual cases and rely on the democratic cover of constitution-enforcing legislation.

The stronger authority the Court has exercised in these situations demonstrates that it can enforce social rights using a substantively limited interpretive framework and still avoid the strongly deferential role that *Mazibuko* seemed to require. They also provide a basis for the Court to expand the largely procedural authority it exercises in these situations to further strengthen its enforcement role. This chapter identifies three major patterns in the second-wave cases that highlight the Court's continued reliance on conceptually thin interpretations but also the ways it has avoided deference by creating alternative forms of authority: (1) avoiding abstract interpretations applicable across cases; (2) creatively developing new, and expanding existing, procedural rights and remedies; and (3) managing individual cases to reach rights-protective outcomes without identifying a clear constitutional (or often even statutory) basis for those outcomes.

All three of these patterns reflect the persistent influence of separation-of-powers and institutional-competence concerns, and as a result they share some characteristics with the weak-form review model that many commentators associated with the Court's first-wave decisions, especially *Grootboom*.[2] The Court's consistent reluctance to develop clear substantive principles generally and its specific failure to revisit and

[2] E.g., Mark Tushnet, *Weak Courts, Strong Rights: Judicial Review and Social Welfare Rights in Comparative Constitutional Law* (2008) 227, 264; Rosalind Dixon, "Creating Dialogue about Socio-economic Rights: Strong-Form versus Weak-Form Judicial Review Revisited," 5 *Int'l J. Const. L.* 391 (2007). *See, generally*, David Landau, "The Reality of Social Rights Enforcement," 53 *Harv. Int'l L. J.* 189, (2012) 196-97 (summarizing and critiquing the view).

expand *Grootboom* in its eviction decisions, however, suggests that it is not committed to the iterative substantive dialogue that is the hallmark of weak-form review. The stronger authority in these decisions comes, instead, primarily from the Court's development and application of expanded procedural protections and a greater willingness to intervene at least temporarily in individual cases to prompt the parties themselves to reach solutions that reflect the social rights' requirements.

As a result, the prospects for further strengthening the Court's enforcement role come first from expanding the case-specific authority the Court has exercised in eviction cases and extending that authority to other service-delivery contexts. *Joseph*'s recognition of a general right to service delivery provides one basis for such an expansion.[3] *Juma Musjid*'s application of the model in the education context is another.[4] The strong presumption against deprivation of existing access to essential services the Court identified in its earlier cases and has consistently enforced in each of the later eviction cases and in *Juma Musjid* reinforces that connection.[5]

The second, related, possibility for expanding this authority comes from the Court's creative development of a range of procedural powers, in particular meaningful engagement. The meaningful engagement requirement in particular offers a procedurally focused framework for more authoritative enforcement of the social rights in two ways. First, it creates a doctrinal basis for exercising the procedural powers the Court has developed to protect the interests of poor people in individual cases by ordering, structuring, and managing negotiations to reach rights-protective outcomes. Second, courts could expand the requirement to initiate more complex reforms in policy and decision-making processes by giving poor communities and social rights advocates a structured, long-term role in those processes. This framework is adaptable across a range of substantive contexts and provides a flexible framework for courts to expand their enforcement authority without expanding their interpretive role.

After identifying the patterns in the Court's cases that set up a potentially stronger procedural role, I examine the close parallels between these

[3] *Joseph and Others v City of Johannesburg and Others* 2010 (3) BCLR 212 (CC) (2009) ("*Joseph*").

[4] *Governing Body of the Juma Musjid Primary School & Others v Essay N.O. and Others* 2011 (8) BCLR 761 (CC) (2011) ("*Juma Musjid*").

[5] *See* Ch. 6; *see, also,* Sandra Liebenberg, *Socio-Economic Rights: Adjudication under a Transformative Constitution* (2010) Ch. 4.6 (analyzing the Court's approach to deprivations of existing access).

patterns and Theunis Roux's account of the political constraints that have shaped the Court's early jurisprudence in the postapartheid era.[6] Roux argues that, despite the Court's lack of popular political support and the ANC's domination of South African politics, the Court became a powerful political institution able to enforce constitutional limits against the ANC-dominated government in a range of areas, including the social rights. The Court did so, in large part, by developing a set of flexible adjudicative strategies that allowed it to calibrate its standards of review and remedies to take relatively stronger or weaker roles in individual cases and thus manage its relationship with the ANC to avoid unsustainable conflict.[7] The second-wave decisions reflect a similar set of adjudicative strategies, and the patterns this chapter identifies largely reinforce Roux's account. They also, however, provide a more fine-grained analysis that point to some potential refinements.

This chapter next revisits the "curious divergence" that emerged in the debate over the first-wave decisions in light of the second-wave patterns. I first argue that the second-wave decisions show that the Court has developed a set of approaches that do not fit either administrative-law or weak-form review. The administrative-law label implies a consistently deferential approach that fails to account for the stronger authority the Court has developed in some of these cases. Conversely, weak-form review implies a more consistently substantive judicial–political dialogue over the content of the social rights that the Court has actively avoided.

I then consider more recent analyses of the second-wave decisions that further develop the critique that the Court can and should adopt a more substantive account of the social rights.[8] These critiques point out that the Court's more recent decisions continue to apply reasonableness review in the limited substantive fashion that characterized the first-wave cases and in some instances appear to move toward an even more consistently deferential role. But several commentators also argue that some aspects of the Court's decisions avoid mere deference, and that the Court could engage in stronger substantive analysis with only relatively minor changes to its existing jurisprudence.[9]

[6] Theunis Roux, *The Politics of Principle: The First South African Constitutional Court, 1995–2005* (2013).

[7] Ibid.

[8] E.g., Liebenberg, *supra* note 5, Ch. 4; Stuart Wilson and Jackie Dugard, "Taking Poverty Seriously: The South African Constitutional Court and Socio-Economic Rights," in Sandra Liebenberg and Geo Quinot (eds.), *Law and Poverty: Perspectives from South Africa and Beyond* (2012) 222 (expanding Liebenberg's argument).

[9] *See, especially*, Wilson and Dugard, ibid.

The patterns identified here overlap in many respects with each of these accounts. The stronger procedural roles this chapter outlines and that the next two chapters more extensively develop are based on a shared recognition that the Court's second-wave decisions are not uniformly deferential and that they offer the potential for both stronger substantive development as well as procedural enforcement of social rights. The enforcement mechanisms and overall approach these chapters identify, however, seek to capitalize on the distinctive characteristics of the second-wave cases rather than to change them. In particular, they focus on how expanding procedural rights and remedies could create tools for both the Court and social rights advocates to push for rights-protective policies even in the absence of a more expansive substantive jurisprudence.

There is, no doubt, room for the Court to adopt a more substantive approach to enforcing the social rights even within the bounds of its current jurisprudence and even consistent with *Mazibuko*'s procedurally focused description of the Court's role. This chapter argues, however, that the Court is most likely to develop the substance of the social rights in the context of constitution-enforcing legislation and using case-specific balancing tests that allow it to limit the precedential effects of those principles. Moreover, the Court has been inconsistent at best in establishing clear substantive principles even filtered through legislation or limited to specific cases. The procedural authority the Court has exercised in the second-wave cases, however, creates possibilities for a stronger enforcement role even if it fails to explicitly develop the substance of the social rights.

The chapter closes by examining two models that draw from weak-form review but more accurately capture the procedurally strong aspects of the Court's approach in the second wave. First, it identifies the close connection between the procedural authority and managerial role the Court has used in the second-wave cases and democratic experimentalism. Second, it compares the second-wave patterns with Katherine Young's "catalytic court" model, which itself incorporates aspects of democratic experimentalism.[10] Both democratic experimentalism and the catalytic court model identify adjudicative methods that allow courts to maintain a strong institutional role that also mitigates the democratic-legitimacy and institutional-competence concerns that the Court has consistently emphasized in its social rights decisions.

The apparent tension in the second-wave decisions between the Court's strong aversion to developing the substantive content of the social rights

[10] Katherine G. Young, *Constituting Economic and Social Rights* (2012).

and the strong procedural authority it has exercised reflect important aspects of both of these models, but the combination does not fit neatly within either. Comparing the second-wave patterns to these models, nonetheless, helps identify how the Court could develop a consistently stronger adjudicative role while still respecting the democratic and institutional limits that the second-wave patterns reflect.

A. Patterns in the second-wave cases

1. *Avoiding substance*

The Court's continued avoidance of abstract constitutional interpretations that inflexibly constrain legislative and executive authority or require the Court itself to assess the adequacy of social-welfare policies against an independent constitutional standard is not new. The lack of substance in the Court's approach to reasonableness review is tied to the separation-of-powers and institutional-competence concerns that critics highlighted in the Court's earlier cases. In the second-wave cases, however, the Court developed a more affirmative account of this limited substantive role.

The centerpiece of this affirmative account is the Court's recharacterization of social rights as tools to protect a strongly participatory version of democracy that requires more direct forms of accountability outside of elections. In each of its social rights decisions, the Court has emphasized the connection between social rights and the foundational constitutional values in section 1 of the Constitution. Section 1 declares that South Africa "is one sovereign, democratic state founded on" four values:

(a) human dignity, the achievement of equality, and the advancement of human rights and freedoms
(b) nonracialism and nonsexism
(c) supremacy of the constitution and the rule of law
(d) universal adult suffrage, a national common voters roll, regular elections, and a multiparty system of democratic government, to ensure accountability, responsiveness, and openness[11]

In the first-wave decisions the Court more frequently cited the connection between the social rights and the more substantive section 1(a) values of human dignity, equality and freedom. Although the Court often noted the connection between the social rights and the democratic

[11] S. Afr. Const. 1996 § 1.

values in section 1(d) in the first-wave decisions, those democratic values moved to the forefront in the second wave. Thus in *Grootboom* the Court cited the section 1 rights to human dignity, freedom, and equality when explaining that reasonableness review "must be understood in the context of the Bill of Rights as a whole."[12] In *Mazibuko*, by contrast, the Court did not reference human dignity or freedom anywhere and cited section 1 instead for the "founding values" that "government should be accountable, responsive and open."[13]

When faced with substantive challenges to particular programs in the second-wave cases, the Court frequently relied on this role as democracy's guardian to sidestep the issues the parties presented in favor of a procedural route or simply to defer to the government's decisions. In the first-wave decisions like *Grootboom* and *TAC*, the Court cited the justiciability concerns in largely defensive terms to justify adopting a limited substantive interpretation.[14] In the second wave the Court continued to cite the justiciability concerns, but it began to identify democratic accountability as an affirmative – and defining – objective of the social rights. This has developed into an unapologetic articulation of its largely procedural role as an appropriate means of achieving that objective.[15]

In this revised conception of the social rights, avoiding substantive interpretations in favor of procedural enforcement is not a deviation necessary to minimize the concerns judicial enforcement of the social rights inevitably raise. Instead it is fully consistent with – perhaps even more

[12] *Government of the Republic of South Africa and Others v Grootboom and Others* 2000 (11) BCLR 1169 (2000) [44] ("*Grootboom*").

[13] *Mazibuko and Others v City of Johannesburg and Others* 2010 (3) BCLR 239 (CC) (2009) [70]. The Court discussed equality but only in the context of the residents' argument that the prepaid meter policy selective rollout was discriminatory under section 9. Ibid., [105].

[14] *Grootboom, supra* note 12, [41] ("A court considering reasonableness will not enquire whether other more desirable or favourable measures could have been adopted, or whether public money could have been better spent.... It is necessary to recognise that a wide range of possible measures could be adopted by the state to meet its obligations"); *Minister of Health and Others v Treatment Action Campaign and Others (No 2)* 2002 (10) BCLR 1033 (2002) [38] ("*TAC*") ("Courts are ill-suited to adjudicate upon issues where court orders could have multiple social and economic consequences for the community. The Constitution contemplates rather a restrained and focused role for the courts").

[15] *Mazibuko* is the best example of this contrast. *See Mazibuko, supra* note 13. Compare paragraph 60 ("ordinarily it is institutionally inappropriate for a court to determine precisely what the achievement of any particular social and economic right entails") with paragraph 71 ("A reasonableness challenge requires government to explain the choices it has made [social rights thus] contribute to the deepening of democracy [and] enable citizens to hold government accountable... through litigation").

faithful to – the proper understanding of the social rights and the Court's institutional role relative to the other branches of government. *Mazibuko* explicitly articulated this shift and outlined how it shapes the Court's approach to social rights.[16] It also illustrates the risk that a procedural approach can devolve into deference.

2. *Creative procedure*

The Court's strong preference for procedural rights and remedies is directly connected to its reluctance to develop the substance of the social rights and that pattern, too, is not a new development.[17] The second-wave decisions not only confirmed and deepened the "proceduralization" of the social rights but also frequently featured a remarkable creativity by the Court in developing procedural options for enforcing the social rights. That creativity often seemed motivated by – and resulted in – the Court avoiding a more substantive resolution and so it reinforces the first pattern. At the same time, however, the Court's willingness often to go to great lengths to find a procedural resolution also prevented mere deference to the government and created both direct and indirect leverage for the Court or the parties themselves to press for substantive changes. *Olivia Road*'s conjuring meaningful engagement from a range of constitutional rights remains the model for this kind of creativity. Creating meaningful engagement allowed the Court to simply refuse to address the parties' arguments over the constitutionality of the City of Johannesburg's revised housing plan, but the engagement order resulted in a remarkable substantive victory in that case. Social rights advocates have used that new requirement to great effect in subsequent eviction litigation.[18]

Even decisions where the Court refused to uphold a social rights challenge, like *Nokotyana*, it frequently found a way to provide at least modest procedural relief that indirectly enforced specific social rights by creating some leverage to press the government to change or adjust the policy.[19]

[16] Ibid., [70–71].

[17] E.g., Danie Brand, "The Proceduralisation of South African Socioeconomic Rights Jurisprudence, or 'What are Socioeconomic Rights For?,'" in Henk Botha *et al.* (eds.), *Rights and Democracy in a Transformative Constitution* (2003).

[18] *Occupiers of 51 Olivia Road, Berea Township and 197 Main Street Johannesburg v City of Johannesburg and Others* 2008 (5) BCLR 475 (CC) (2008) ("*Olivia Road*").

[19] *Residents of Joe Slovo Community, Western Cape v Thubelisha Homes and Others* 2009 (9) BCLR 847 (CC) (2009) ("*Joe Slovo*"); *Nokotyana and Others v Ekurhuleni Metropolitan Municipality and Others* 2010 (4) BCLR 312 (CC) (2009) ("*Nokotyana*").

Thus *Nokotyana*'s order required the provincial government to act on the municipality's application to upgrade the informal settlement within a set time frame that, if successful, would begin the process of providing many of the services the residents sought.[20] That order is a fairly mundane but still important use of procedural authority to provide some relief and also to point toward, without requiring, a constitutionally compliant resolution.

The Court's detailed engagement order and decision to retain jurisdiction to enforce that order in *Joe Slovo* is a significant refinement of *Olivia Road.* By requiring the government to fulfill its promise to set aside 70 percent of the units for residents and by setting a detailed engagement agenda and retaining jurisdiction to enforce it, the Court considerably strengthened its role.[21] Housing-rights advocates have used the detailed terms of the engagement order in other cases to argue that municipalities are obligated to engage on the same set of issues whenever they propose to relocate people following eviction.[22] In both cases the Court softened the effects of rejecting the substantive claims by asserting limited control in its order that either gave some direct relief to the plaintiffs or was designed to prompt the government to provide some measure of relief itself.

Abahlali and *Joseph* each illustrate ways the Court has enforced procedural protections to force changes to legislation and policy directly.[23] *Abahlali* relied on the "dignified framework" for evictions established by the Court's decisions and PIE to overturn provincial legislation that required eviction of unlawful occupiers of land in areas designated as "slums."[24] That dignified framework is grounded in section 26 but is fundamentally a procedural framework centered on constitution-enforcing legislation, PIE's equitable balancing test. Moreover, the two principle flaws in the legislation the majority identified were essentially procedural. First, the legislation removed the discretion of landowners and municipalities to evaluate *themselves* whether eviction would be justified under PIE.[25] It did not eliminate PIE's requirement that a court determine whether the eviction was justified. Second, that same

[20] *Nokotyana*, ibid. [21] *Joe Slovo, supra* note 19, [7].

[22] *See* Malcolm Langford. "Housing Rights Litigation", in Langford *et al.* (eds.), *Socio-Economic Rights in South Africa: Symbols or Substance?* (2014) 207 (discussing substantive principles applied in other housing-rights cases).

[23] *Abahlali baseMjondolo Movement SA and Another v Premier of the Province of Kwazulu-Natal and Others* 2010 (2) BCLR 99 (CC) (2009) [122] ("*Abahlali*"); *Joseph, supra* note 3.

[24] *Abahlali*, ibid., [122]. [25] Ibid., [92–95].

requirement eliminated the possibility for meaningful engagement prior to eviction.[26]

In *Joseph*, the Court extended the procedural requirements of the PAJA to tenants facing potential cutoff of electricity services.[27] Like *Olivia Road*, the Court invented a new right – here the right to receive municipal services – to avoid the more substantive arguments the parties asserted.[28] That new right is derived from the obligations and powers of municipalities stated in sections 152 and 153 of the Constitution and legislation implementing those constitutional provisions and so reinforces the Court's related preference to rely on legislation over the Constitution.[29] More importantly, the Court applied the right it created exclusively to trigger the procedures under PAJA.[30] Even limited in that way, however, the right at least temporarily protected the tenants by requiring reconnection of their electricity. It also established a procedural framework for service disconnections that is analogous to the dignified framework governing evictions the Court recognized in *Abahlali.*

3. *Managing individual cases*

The third prominent pattern – managing individual cases to reach rights-protective outcomes – is traceable back to *Port Elizabeth.*[31] Although it was not apparent when *Port Elizabeth* was decided, the Court's approach in that decision represented a break from *Grootboom* and the beginning of the end of the possibility that *Grootboom*'s declaration would be the start of a weak-form substantive dialogue over the right to access to adequate housing. The later eviction decisions confirmed that shift and also developed and refined the two key aspects of *Port Elizabeth*'s model: constitutionally attentive interpretation and enforcement of legislation combined with strong management of individual cases. These decisions apply *Port Elizabeth* either – and in some cases both – to extend that case-management role to new situations or to develop new procedural tools for managing cases where existing access to rights-protected services was threatened.

For example, *Maphango*'s interpretation of the Rental Housing Act established a framework for tenants that is analogous to the dignified

[26] Ibid., [96–98]. [27] *Joseph, supra* note 3. [28] Ibid., [40–48].
[29] Ibid., [35–39]. [30] Ibid., [56–64].
[31] *Port Elizabeth Municipality v Various Occupiers* 2004 (12) BCLR 1268 (CC) (2004) ("*Port Elizabeth*").

protections of PIE.[32] Rental Housing Tribunals now have the same kind of broad authority as courts in eviction cases to manage rental-housing disputes in constitutionally sensitive ways without directly elaborating new statutory or constitutional principles. That interpretation – especially given the procedural developments in the case – featured the same creativity as *Olivia Road*, where the Court went to great lengths to avoid resolving potentially difficult substantive questions regarding the right to housing but created a new set of procedural rights applicable in a broad range of cases.

Blue Moonlight follows a similar pattern and also is the clearest example of the more substantive potential of the managerial approach.[33] *Blue Moonlight* represents a significant application of the procedural authority to temporarily delay an eviction both because it required temporarily subordinating a private landowner's rights under section 25 and also because the Court explicitly rejected a municipal housing policy justified in part by limited resources.[34] But the Court merely stopped the challenged eviction without providing further guidance on how the parties should resolve the impasse and with only a fairly thin analysis of what factors courts should apply to balance section 25 and section 26 in future cases.

Despite these limitations, the decision remains the best example of the Court relying on constitution-enforcing legislation to develop or expand constitutional or statutory principles in incremental ways. The core principle that municipalities have an obligation to house people evicted from private land was essentially established in *Modderklip*, but *Blue Moonlight* both confirmed and expanded it by clarifying that municipalities have a statutory and constitutional obligation to independently plan and budget to fulfill that responsibility.[35] The Court's rejection of the City's resource-limitation arguments because the budget it developed was based on a failure to recognize its statutory and constitutional obligations also is a significant – although arguably still procedural – development that could apply in other, similar situations.

Blue Moonlight's companion cases represent a shift back toward *Olivia Road*'s less substantive approach that relies on the parties themselves to

[32] *Maphango and Others v Aengus Lifestyle Properties (Pty) Ltd* 2012 (5) BCLR 449 (CC) (2012) ("*Maphango*").

[33] *City of Johannesburg Metropolitan Municipality v Blue Moonlight Properties 39 (Pty) Ltd and Another* 2012 (2) BCLR 150 (CC) (2011) ("*Blue Moonlight*").

[34] Ibid., [34], [68–75].

[35] *See President of the Republic of South Africa and Another v Modderklip Boerdery (Pty) Ltd* 2005 (8) BCLR 786 (CC) (2005).

resolve an eviction situation with little court direction and no analysis of the substantive factors that required a delay in the evictions.[36] The Court's cookie-cutter decisions in each case temporarily stopped the eviction, ordered the municipality to submit additional information about its housing capacity and policies and remanded to the High Court for further proceedings following those submissions.[37] Both decisions thus protected the short-term interests of the occupiers first by temporarily preserving their access to housing, and second essentially forcing the municipalities to provide some form of alternative accommodation before evicting them. The analysis in each case, however, was even thinner than *Blue Moonlight*, where the Court at least identified some specific factors to consider under PIE and also explained the bases for rejecting the municipality's policy of excluding evictees from private land from its emergency housing policy.

The Court's sparse analysis of the PIE factors in those cases calls into question the extent of its willingness to develop more substantive principles under the social rights even through incremental, case-by-case, interpretation of legislation like PIE. The details in each case were largely superfluous to the result, and *Golden Thread* even read out PIE's distinction between long- and short-term occupation so that it could consider the lack of alternative accommodation.[38]

Zulu is another, more recent, illustration of the Court's continued reluctance to reach substantive issues where it can provide some procedural relief.[39] The majority cautiously limited its analysis to finding the residents had standing to intervene in the High Court proceeding and refused to address the relatively clear-cut substantive questions of whether PIE and section 26(3) permitted municipalities to rely on a blanket injunction against supposed land invasions by unspecified individuals effectively to evict them and destroy their homes.[40] This temporary measure provided a measure of procedural relief that left open the possibility for more substantive relief, but, as the concurrence noted, it arguably unnecessarily

[36] *Occupiers of Skurweplaas 353 JR v PPC Aggregate Quarries (Pty) Ltd and Others* 2012 (4) BCLR 382 (CC) (2011) ("*PPC Quarries*"), and *Occupiers of Portion R25 of the Farm Mooiplaats 355 JR v Golden Thread Ltd and Others* 2012 (4) BCLR 372 (CC) (2011) ("*Golden Thread*").

[37] *PPC Quarries*, ibid., [16]; *Golden Thread*, ibid., [21].

[38] *Golden Thread*, *supra* note 36, [12–13]. Prevention of Illegal Eviction from and Unlawful Occupation of Land Act 19 of 1998 at 4(6)–(7).

[39] *Zulu and Others v eThekwini Municipality and Others* 2014 (8) BCLR 971 (CC) (2014) ("*Zulu*").

[40] Ibid., [37].

delayed resolution of issues that could have protected a much greater number of people in other pending cases.[41]

Paradoxically that same reluctance to engage in a careful, substantive interpretation of PIE has resulted in the de facto principle that evictions must be delayed where alternative accommodation is unavailable. The Court's consistent refusal to issue an eviction order where a municipality cannot provide temporary accommodation has transformed the management role *Port Elizabeth* described from a case-by-case balancing of competing constitutional rights into a strong principle for enforcing section 26. Equally significant, these cases establish that courts have extensive procedural powers both to join relevant parties and engage in extensive fact-finding regarding government budgets, capacity, and policy-making procedures in eviction cases.

Olivia Road's outline of meaningful engagement and the power it gives courts to interrogate whether and how poor people and their advocates were involved in the policy-development process set the stage for precisely this role. The Court's more extensive use of engagement orders in *Schubart Park, Pheko,* and *Juma Musjid* demonstrate the strength of this authority and also provide important examples of how courts can apply it to affect the underlying policies in a case.[42]

In *Schubart Park* the Court used meaningful engagement to delegate the case-management role to the High Court, but it also defined relatively specific terms of the engagement process, thus exercising some control itself over the process.[43] Both *Pheko* and *Juma Musjid* are unusual examples of the Court itself exercising strong procedural authority by maintaining direct oversight and using engagement to prod the parties to reach a rights-protective resolution.[44] *Juma Musjid* also illustrates the potential flexibility engagement creates for courts to shift management strategies to adapt to changed circumstances. Taken together, these decisions firmly establish meaningful engagement as a tool courts can use to manage individual cases and also hint at the potential for structuring engagement processes in individual cases to effect broader change by addressing the underlying policies.

[41] Ibid., [47–50], [61–62].

[42] *Schubart Park Residents' Association and Others v City of Tshwane Metropolitan Municipality and Another* 2013 (1) BCLR 68 (CC) (2012) ("*Schubart Park*"); *Pheko and Others v Ekurhuleni Metropolitan Municipality* 2012 (4) BCLR 388 (CC) (2011) ("*Pheko*"); *Juma Musjid, supra* note 4.

[43] *Schubart Park,* ibid., [53].

[44] *Juma Musjid, supra* note 42, [2–5], [73–79].

B. Patterns and politics

Though focused internally on the Court's own analysis in the social rights decisions, the limits in the Court's approach the three second-wave patterns identify closely track Theunis Roux's analysis of the external political factors that he argues consistently constrain the Court's decisions.[45] Roux develops a comprehensive account of the Constitutional Court's decisions from 1995 to 2005, when Justice Arthur Chaskalson headed the Court. He argues that the Court in this period both developed a "strong legal-professional reputation" within the domestic and international legal communities and asserted a relatively strong institutional role in South African politics in several cases by applying constitutional principles to uphold challenges to government legislation and policy.[46] Roux argues these achievements are remarkable in light of the ANC's political dominance and the lack of strong popular support for the Court as an institution in this period and thus require some explanation.[47]

In highly simplified terms, Roux attributes the Court's success to a set of adjudicative strategies he argues the Court strategically developed to carefully assess the political consequences of each decisions. These strategies preserved the Court's capacity to issue legally principled decisions in individual cases but avoided establishing strong abstract principles that could put the Court's long-term institutional security at risk. Specifically, Roux argues that the Court calibrated both its substantive interpretations and the standards of review it adopted across a broad range of constitutional issues to minimize the possibility of institutionally damaging confrontations with the ANC in future cases. At the same time, however, the Court consistently found ways to assert a stronger institutional role in individual cases where the "micro-politics" created political alignments that supported such a role.[48] In particular, the Court was able successfully to exploit the ANC's own political and ideological commitment to the social and economic transformation promised by the new constitution by characterizing many of its stronger interventions as implementations of the ANC's own political mandates.[49]

Roux argues that the social rights decisions are a classic example of the Court's strategic approach, and that viewed from a political perspective "the reasonableness review standard emerges as a largely successful strategy [that allowed the Court] to assert an institutionally sustainable role

[45] Roux, *supra* note 6, 15. [46] Ibid. [47] Ibid., 112.
[48] Ibid., 387–88. [49] Ibid., 388.

for itself."[50] Roux says the Court deliberately crafted the context-sensitive reasonableness review as part of a "managerialist strategy" that allowed it to ratchet the level of scrutiny up or down in each case while avoiding strong abstract principles that could invite unsustainable conflict with the state in later cases.[51] The Court's strategy of maintaining flexibility across cases, Roux argues, also explains its rejection of the minimum-core model, which would have required some inflexible, substantive interpretations that could invite future conflict with the ANC.[52] The Court instead embraced the "deferential, rational justification approach" first articulated by Etienne Mureinik for precisely the same reason.[53] Although conceptually Mureinik's approach positioned the Court consistently in a more deferential role, the Court also carefully articulated reasonableness review as a context-sensitive standard that enabled it in decisions like in *TAC*, to exploit favorable political dynamics to more closely scrutinize particular policies and use the social rights to force changes in them.

Roux's analysis focuses on the first-wave decisions, and he only briefly touches on several second-wave cases in his closing chapter. Nonetheless, the general patterns in the second-wave decisions identified here largely fit his account. For example, Roux highlights the Court's use of procedural rights and remedies and avoidance of substantive interpretations as evidence of its strategic concern with preserving flexibility.[54] Thus he argues *Modderklip*'s shift from the right to adequate housing in section 26 to the more procedural right to access courts in section 34 to uphold the SCA's award of constitutional damages was a deliberate adjudicative strategy to avoid balancing the substance of section 26 against the right to property in section 25.[55] Likewise, he argues the Court in *TAC* was much more "ambivalent" than the High Court in its analysis of section 27 and that it "consciously exploited the slippage between the negative and positive dimension of social rights" to avoid clearly establishing a positive obligation on the government even while applying a more searching standard of review.[56] Roux also argues that the flexible remedy in *TAC* shows the Court was "evidently thinking of its longer-term relationship with the ANC and the need, even in this most pressing of cases, to engage the political branches as partners in the constitutional project."[57]

Roux's analysis applies easily to many of the second-wave decisions as well. For example, the Court's reluctance to intervene in high-profile policies intended to provide housing and basic services in *Joe Slovo* and

[50] Ibid., 9. [51] Ibid., Ch. 7, 388. [52] Ibid., 284–92. [53] Ibid., 265, 289–90.
[54] Ibid., 300–301. [55] Ibid., 330–31. [56] Ibid., 300–301. [57] Ibid., 303.

Mazibuko could be explained in Roux's terms as examples of the Court's refusing to uphold challenges to policies that would cause direct and substantial conflict with the ANC. *Joe Slovo* involved a challenge to a prominent pilot project for the ANC's new national housing policy, Breaking New Ground, and so upholding it directly would involve a high-stakes confrontation with the ANC. The Court's backdoor incorporation of meaningful engagement in the remedy, however, permitted it indirectly to enforce the resident's rights and mitigate the effects of the policy.[58]

The prepaid water meter policy in *Mazibuko* was municipal, not national, but it represented a cost-recovery model for basic services that was a central part of the national government's overarching shift toward a more neoliberal set of policies that began with GEAR.[59] Reversing that policy would have indirectly challenged the overall shift to a neoliberal economic approach to basic services and opened the door for social rights to ground challenges to cost-recovery programs across a broad range of services and programs that were part of that shift. In addition, *Mazibuko*'s clear concern with what the Court perceived as an attempt to revive the minimum-core approach also is consistent with Roux's observation that the Court consistently rejects inflexible interpretive frameworks that could establish principles requiring more direct conflict in later cases.[60]

Nokotyana fits Roux's framework for somewhat different reasons. The case did not involve a policy that had strong national political support, but the residents' argument that the Court should expand its interpretation of section 26 to include an obligation to provide essential basic services, including adequate security, would have constrained the Court in precisely the ways Roux argues it consistently avoids. An expansive interpretation of this kind also would have required the Court to apply it both to other essential services and in cases brought by other communities under varying political circumstances that could involve more significant opposition by the ANC.

The Court's focus on procedural rights and remedies even in cases where it upheld social rights challenges likewise fit Roux's analysis. Thus, the Court's recognition of a thinly defined, procedural right to process before municipal services are cut off in *Joseph* could be interpreted as an

[58] *Joe Slovo*, *supra* note 19, Order at [7], [24].

[59] *See* Patrick Bond, "When Commodification Annuls the Human Right to Water," (2006), at www.ohchr.org/Documents/Issues/Water/StudyContributions/Universities/UniversityofKwaZuluNatal.pdf.

[60] *Mazibuko*, *supra* note 13, [50–60].

example of the Court's issuing a principled decision on limited, largely procedural, grounds that deliberately avoided a direct conflict with the government.[61] Although that new right could invite future litigation challenging decisions to cut off basic services in other more politically fraught situations, the right the Court recognized incorporates a context-sensitive balancing test that is focused on the procedure used rather than the state's obligation to provide services. Both aspects provide escape valves for courts in later cases to uphold a municipality's decision to cut off services without formally changing the legal standard.

On first glance the Court's decision in *Abahlali* to overturn portions of provincial legislation seems like an anomalous example where the Court engaged in direct conflict with an ANC-controlled provincial legislature.[62] That decision, however, could be read to reflect the Court's determination that the provincial government's legislation was inconsistent with national ANC policy, evidenced by its clear conflict with PIE. Alternatively, the Court's careful narrowing of the issue to a single section of the legislation that it interpreted to require landowners to seek eviction in all circumstances might be another example of a principled decision carefully limited to the facts of a specific case. By focusing on the procedural defect in the legislation, the Court minimized both the immediate conflict with the provincial government and avoided the risk of that conflict recurring.[63]

Roux's framework also helps explain the prominent features of the eviction-related cases. The Court's consistent refusal to revisit *Grootboom* despite the growing number of eviction decisions, the development of meaningful engagement and related shift toward *Port Elizabeth*'s model of managerial judging through application of statutory balancing tests each are consistent with Roux's argument that the Court consistently seeks to preserve flexibility in its relationship with the ANC. Collectively these features reinforce the Court's deep reluctance to develop substantive principles – even as part of a democratic dialogue – and the corresponding preference for flexible, context-sensitive tools that allow for targeted strong interventions in individual decisions without committing the Court in later cases.

The second-wave decisions thus largely support Roux's analysis, and the patterns identified earlier, although analyzed in terms of the strong separation-of-powers concerns, the Court consistently cites in the social

[61] *Joseph*, *supra* note 3, [34–39]. [62] *Abahlali*, *supra* note 23.
[63] Ibid., [91–98].

rights cases rather than the political environment, are generally consistent with Roux's account. Both analyses argue the Court adjusts its role in relatively consistent ways in response to an identifiable set of constraining factors and that the results in each case can be explained to a large extent as driven by the combination of those factors.

Focusing on the internal patterns in the Court's own analysis and specifically on the social rights decisions, however, provides a finer-grained view of how those constraints interact. The differences that emerge, although relatively minor, suggest some potential refinements to Roux's account. In particular, the second-wave patterns show that the Court sometimes adopts a stronger role and develops procedural requirements that invite rather than minimize potential political conflict in future cases. Specifically, where the Court was able to characterize the issues and shape its interventions in ways that fit a more traditional judicial role by enforcing procedural norms, it has been willing more consistently to confront the government in each case and to establish principles that increase the risk of confrontation in later cases. This has been especially evident in cases where there was evidence the government refused to acknowledge the obligations that social rights impose or actively sought to avoid those obligations.[64]

Significantly, in several of these cases, including most of the eviction decisions, there was not an obvious source of external political support for the Court's confrontation, such as the public opposition to the government's stance on HIV-AIDs that Roux argues created the political room that permitted the Court to adopt a stronger role in *TAC*.[65] Nor was there apparent support from within the ANC itself, another political factor Roux argues the Court exploits as an alternative source for its stronger interventions.[66] Despite this, the de facto strong-form rule the Court has consistently applied in its eviction decisions has carved out a role for courts that clearly increases the risk of conflict with the government in the future. The Court's decisions open the door to litigation in every eviction situation because the residents can first argue that there was insufficient engagement and second that the municipal government is required to provide alternative accommodation before a court can order their eviction under PIE. The consistently strong role the Court has adopted

[64] Katherine Young similarly argues that the Court consistently adopts a stronger adjudicative role in response to evidence that the political process has ignored the social rights. Young, *supra* note 10, 177.

[65] Roux, *supra* note 6, 296–99.

[66] Ibid., 390.

in these decisions and the sheer volume of claims that they have invited, however, suggest that, in the eviction decisions at least, the Court was willing to invite future political conflict.

A similar pattern emerges in decisions where the Court created new categories of claims or even entirely new rights. Like the de facto principle in the eviction decisions, these new rights have the effect of expanding judicial authority in situations that are likely to recur and so increase the risk of future political conflict, but they also limit the scope of that authority to enforcing procedural rights and remedies. The meaningful engagement requirement in *Olivia Road*, especially the authority for courts to independently evaluate whether there was adequate consultation, is one example. *Joseph*'s independent right to receive municipal services and *Maphango*'s expansive interpretation of the Rental Housing Act are two others. In each of these cases, the Court deployed the procedural creativity described earlier in ways that not only strengthened its role in those individual cases but also established new judicial powers or expanded existing ones. The common thread running through these decisions is the confidence the Court displays when operating within a substantively limited role to enforce the social rights in more authoritative ways.

In several other respects, however, Roux's political analysis helps explain the results in these cases and reinforces the limited circumstances under which the Court is willing to exercise this stronger role. First, the Court has carefully structured these new powers in ways that preserve the flexibility Roux identifies as the touchstone of its approach.[67] The Court consistently avoids acknowledging that it has adopted a relatively strong principle that evictions cannot proceed absent alternative accommodation, and it creates the appearance of flexibility by instead attributing the result in each case to the specific facts of each case.

This is clearest in the Court's reliance on PIE's context-specific balancing test, which allows it to distinguish each case on its individual facts and ratchet back its role where necessary. The stronger authority *Maphango* established relied on the Rental Housing Act's similarly flexible test. And in *Joseph*, where the Court limited the scope of this new right to trigger only the application of PAJA, it even read out PAJA's more onerous and inflexible procedural requirements.

Second, the stronger procedural authority the Court adopted in these decisions often explicitly draws on the ANC's own commitment to the Constitution's transformational project. The Court's strong preference

[67] Ibid., 290–92.

for constitution-enforcing legislation like PIE over direct constitutional interpretation is evidence of that connection in two respects. Enforcing the terms of legislation allows the Court not only to minimize the democratic-legitimacy concern but also to characterize itself as enforcing the ANC's own political priorities. In addition, because the eviction decisions apply PIE primarily to municipalities, the Court has been able to depict itself as acting to enforce the ANC's legislative mandates against local governments that have failed to comply with them.

These examples, thus, do not show that the Court has an open playing field or that it acts without any regard for the political consequences of a decision where it can avoid or minimize the justiciability concerns. They merely illustrate that the interaction between the internal constraints these patterns point to and the external political concerns Roux identifies is more complex than either set of variables alone can capture. That complexity creates somewhat more flexibility than Roux's account suggests within individual cases. It also highlights that the Court is less consistently strategic across cases than Roux's analysis depicts. Instead the range of relatively stronger and weaker approaches seems to emerge more from the Court's intuitive reaction the specific mix of internal and external factors in each case rather than an overarching strategy.

C. Revisiting the "curious divergence"

This section revisits the two sides of the debate over the first-wave cases and reassesses that debate in light of the patterns in the second-wave cases. These patterns confirm the critics' predictions that the Court would avoid developing the substantive content of the social rights. Indeed, the Court has avoided even the more limited substantive role offered by the weak-form model of judicial–political dialogue that several commentators argued the Court's early decisions, especially *Grootboom*, seemed designed to initiate. Conversely, however, the Court's stronger procedural interventions show that it is not committed to the consistently deferential role implied by the administrative-law model.

Although analyses of the Court's second-wave decisions generally agree that the Court has failed to develop a clear substantive account of the social rights, several prominent commentators point to the more authoritative aspects of the second-wave decisions to argue the Court could develop a more substantive role with only relatively modest changes to its existing approach. The stronger roles described previously draw on several of these arguments, in particular the context-specific approach Sandra

Liebenberg has developed.[68] My analysis of the second-wave cases, however, is more cautious regarding the likelihood that the Court will adopt a more consistently substantive adjudicative approach. *Blue Moonlight* provides the best example of the Court engaging in a stronger interpretive role, but even that role was fairly limited and depended heavily on legislative interpretation of statutes like PIE. More importantly, as the *Blue Moonlight* companion cases illustrate, the Court has been very inconsistent in engaging even in this more limited interpretive role.

Equally important, arguments in favor of a stronger substantive role generally fail to recognize the confidence and creativity the Court displays when it relies on procedural rights and remedies. As a result, they do not fully explore the potential for the Court to more effectively enforce the social rights even without developing a more substantive jurisprudence. The stronger roles this chapter identifies and the next two chapters develop focus on the potential procedural techniques created for the Court to more effectively enforce the social rights.

1. *Administrative-law review*

As Chapter 4 noted, one prominent analogy most famously drawn by Cass Sunstein's analysis of *Grootboom* is that the Court's social rights decisions adopt an "administrative-law" approach to the social rights.[69] This label captures the same idea as weak-form review that the Court deliberately leaves room for broad legislative and executive discretion, but it implies a more consistent level of deference and stricter emphasis on procedural regularity. The Court's approach in the second-wave cases, in particular its emphasis on procedural rights and remedies and their relationship to democratic accountability, reinforces the perception that it has moved even further toward a purely administrative-law approach.[70] Although apt in many respects, the administrative-law analogy does not completely capture the full range of interventions – even the purely procedural

[68] Liebenberg, *supra* note 5.

[69] Cass Sunstein, *Designing Democracy: What Constitutions Do* (2001), 234. *See, also*, Dennis M. Davis, "Socio-economic Rights: Has the Promise of Eradicating the Divide between First and Second Generation Rights Been Fulfilled?," in Tom Ginsburg and Rosalind Dixon (eds.), *Comparative Constitutional Law* (2011) 522 (characterizing *Grootboom* as representing "an administrative law model"); Marius Pieterse, "Procedural Relief, Constitutional Citizenship and Socio-Economic Rights as Legitimate Expectations," 28 *S. Afr. J. Hum. Rts.* 359, 360 (2012) (noting that commentators on the first-wave decisions "mostly agreed that the reasonableness approach seemed to be rooted in administrative law").

[70] *See* Pieterse, ibid., 362–63; Wilson and Dugard, *supra* note 8, 222.

interventions – the Court's existing decisions encompass.[71] More importantly, the label implies a consistently deferential role that is inconsistent with the strong procedural authority the Court has applied in several of the second-wave decisions.

The second-wave cases more closely track an administrative-law approach because they more consistently focus on procedure rather than substance. Furthermore, *Mazibuko*'s description of the Court's secondary role plainly reflects many aspects of an administrative-law model. Even within the second-wave cases, however, the level of deference implied by the administrative-law label fails to capture the stronger authority the Court exercised in the eviction cases to protect poor people's interests against the state and private property owners. It also ignores the authority that meaningful engagement gives courts to scrutinize, manage, and reconfigure policy-development processes to ensure adequate participation by poor people and their representatives. The incremental substantive development illustrated by *Blue Moonlight* and possible under the eviction model likewise involves something more than the purely procedural review under administrative law.

More significantly, in cases where the Court enforced procedural standards or imposed procedural remedies it did not apply the same deferential standard that it purports to apply when evaluating the state's substantive choices and that the administrative-law model implies. Instead, in the case of evictions, the Court has enforced a limited but substantively strong rule that effectively requires provision of alternative accommodation regardless of the reasons a municipality has for failing to provide it. At the same time, it has established broad authority to reconfigure individual cases and to require the government to provide extensive information regarding its policies and budgets to support its positions. Finally, the Court's close scrutiny of recent "backdoor" eviction attempts by municipalities applied very little deference to those arguments.

The Court's description of meaningful engagement in *Olivia Road* likewise gives no indication that courts should defer to the government's decisions regarding whether and how to ensure people whose rights are affected by new policies can meaningfully participate in the decision-making process. Even *Mazibuko* suggests that deference is

[71] Pieterse argues that the second-wave decisions implicitly deploy "the *logic* and *method* of the doctrine of legitimate expectations" rooted in administrative law. Pieterse, *supra* note 69, 368. He, however, distinguishes the "'constitutional' conception that seemingly underlies the socio-economic rights decisions" as both substantively and methodologically richer than the administrative-law doctrine. Ibid., 369.

required only where the Court assesses the substance of challenged policies and legislation, and that the Court has a stronger role to play both in evaluating whether the state's decision-making process was sufficiently participatory and for imposing remedies to ensure adequate participation. Moreover, the Court has repeatedly insisted that it has the power to independently assess whether the engagement process was sufficient and to reject even substantively adequate policies where the process was flawed.

2. *Weak-form review*

The Court's enforcement approach often has been described as a version of weak-form or dialogic review. The weak-form model allows courts to adopt both stronger substantive interpretations and to impose stronger remedies than a pure administrative-law model and so better accounts for the range of interventions represented by both the first- and second-wave decisions. It also implies, however, a relatively consistent substantive role for courts that creates a judicial-political constitutional dialogue over the content of rights provisions.[72]

Descriptions of the Court adopting a weak-form approach emerged primarily in response to *Grootboom*, although *TAC* also is cited as containing significant weak-form elements.[73] The declaration in *Grootboom* clearly invited – and prompted – precisely the kind of legislative response filling in the difficult details of a constitutionally compliant policy that weak-form review contemplates.[74] *TAC* issued a much stronger remedy than *Grootboom* but incorporated some modest weak-form elements by giving the government discretion to change its policy without returning to the Court. The Court's analysis was deliberately narrow and did not establish any broad principles under section 27. The Court's refusal to retain jurisdiction further weakened the remedies in each case.[75]

[72] Mark Tushnet, "The Rise of Weak-Form Review," in Tom Ginsburg and Rosalind Dixon (eds.), *Comparative Constitutional Law* (2011) 326 (explaining "the idea of judicial-legislative dialogue" under weak-form review).

[73] *See* Landau, *supra* note 2, 196. *See, generally*, Malcolm Langford and Steve Kahanovitz, "Just Tick the Boxes? Judicial Enforcement in South Africa," Think Piece/Emerging Paper, 2 (2010) (noting that "most of the focus has been on two early landmark decisions" *Grootboom* and *TAC*), at www.escr-net.org/sites/default/files/Langford_and_Kahanovitz_-_South_Africa_0.pdf.

[74] Langford, *supra* note 22, (describing and analyzing these legislative and policy responses).

[75] *TAC, supra* note 14; *see* William Forbath, "Cultural Transformation, Deep Institutional Reform, and ESR Practice: South Africa's Treatment Action Campaign," in Lucie E. White and Jeremy Perelman (eds.), *Stones of Hope: How African Activists Reclaim Human Rights to*

The second-wave cases generally and the recent eviction-related cases in particular, however, have received much less attention in the comparative constitutional law literature on the Court's social rights decisions and discussions of weak-form review. Several of the second-wave cases – and the shift toward enforcing procedural rights generally – incorporate a combination of relatively weaker rights and remedies that leave room for legislative or executive discretion and sometimes even invite legislative or executive responses. The Court's description of its secondary role and emphasis on social rights as tools for policing democratic accountability in *Mazibuko* reinforce the connection to weak-form review. Like weak-form review, that description recognized the need for courts to respect democratic decision-making authority even in constitutional matters and the creative role the legislature and executive could play in interpreting the Constitution. Other aspects of the second-wave decisions, including the Court's frequent acknowledgment of the authority of constitution-enforcing legislation, further reinforce that connection.

Despite these similarities, however, the Court's consistent avoidance of substantive principles generally and deliberate shift to procedural options in cases that presented opportunities to consider legislative and policy responses to *Grootboom* suggest that it's not interested in establishing a sustained dialogue with the political branches over the substance of the social rights. The extended description of its secondary enforcement role in *Mazibuko* and recharacterization of social rights as democracy-promoting devices rather than substantive entitlements, although consistent with weak-form review's concern with democratizing judicial review, arguably goes much further and appears to shift interpretive authority definitively in favor of democratic control.

The eviction-related decisions are inconsistent with weak-form review for the opposite reason. Although they illustrate most clearly the Court's unwillingness to engage in a substantive dialogue, the procedural authority the Court has exercised in them adopts a limited strong-form role in two respects. First, these decisions have transformed *Grootboom*'s abstract principle that the state is required to have policies that address emergency housing needs into a strong right enforced through a strong but temporary remedy that prevents eviction where the state is unable to provide alternative accommodation. Second, they strengthened the Court's managerial authority in a range of ways, most significantly by recognizing the

Challenge Global Poverty (2011) 49 (describing *TAC* as establishing a "more polity-based, less juristocratic or court-centered" approach).

power to join state entities and require them to provide information on social-welfare policies and the capacity to deliver specific services.

The expansive managerial authority these decisions established could provide the basis for judicial interventions that indirectly influence substantive policies and develop positive claims for increased services. The patterns in the second wave suggest, however, that this is unlikely to involve an explicit dialogue between a court and the government. Instead that potential comes from the authority that courts now have to temporarily stop an eviction and to structure and manage a negotiation that could result in broader policy changes. The power to join all relevant government entities to a case and order them to provide relevant information about their policies, budgets, and the procedures they used to develop them further expands that authority.

The net result is a judicial approach that shares the flexibility of weak-form review because courts exercising this authority do not apply a constitutional standard to definitively reject a particular policy and instead apply pressure on the government to change the policy in light of its own evaluation of what the social rights require. It also gives parties challenging the policy leverage to propose their own changes. Rather than beginning an iterative judicial–political dialogue over what the social rights mean in the context of a particular dispute or series of disputes, however, the court's role is limited to enforcing the strong but limited right to temporary accommodation and only indirectly prompting and possibly managing a resolution that reaches these broader issues.

3. *A stronger interpretive role*

The other side of the "curious divergence" over the first-wave decisions is a set of critiques centered on the lack of conceptual content in the Court's interpretive approach. The critique has persisted – and in several respects deepened – in response to the second-wave decisions, in particular *Mazibuko*.[76] Whereas the first-wave critiques frequently called for the Court to adopt something like the minimum-core approach, however, prescriptions from more recent commentary have developed alternative suggestions that work to some extent within the Court's existing approach.

Sandra Liebenberg has been at the forefront of developing these more nuanced suggestions for expanding the Court's existing social rights jurisprudence to incorporate a stronger interpretive role that could begin

[76] *See* Pieterse, *supra* note 69, 362; Wilson and Dugard, *supra* note 1.

to develop the content of the social rights. Liebenberg argues that courts in every social rights case should independently develop "the content and values" not only of the social rights themselves but also their connection to other rights, especially the founding rights to equality and human dignity as well as the right to life the Court frequently cites.[77] She also identifies a range of remedial approaches that courts could use to give social rights more substantive effect without completely preempting the legislature's and executive's roles.[78]

Rather than critiquing the Court's increasingly strong commitment to using social rights as tools to promote democratic accountability, Liebenberg argues it could modify reasonableness review to incorporate an incremental substantive development of the social rights that takes advantage of the kinds of the participatory democratic devices the Court has relied on and still respects the leadership of the political branches in identifying their content.[79]

The interpretive framework Liebenberg describes mirrors in several respects the incremental, context-specific interpretative role that *Port Elizabeth* featured. Liebenberg emphasizes that substantive interpretations tied closely to the specific facts of a case allow the Court to develop a stronger interpretive role while still respecting the coordinate authority of the democratic branches. Such context-bound interpretations both leave room for the Court to recalibrate its interpretation to respond to concerns raised by the legislature or executive in a later case and also for the political branches to affirmatively respond by expanding or modifying the interpretation through legislation and policy.[80]

In her discussion of remedies, Liebenberg argues that the Court's consistent concern with enhancing participatory democracy could be adapted in a different way to incorporate a more substantive approach. Drawing from democratic experimentalism, Liebenberg argues an experimentalist court could use structural interdicts as a tool to "catalyse a structured process of dialogic engagement between the parties and other stakeholders on the precise standards and [remedies]" required in a particular case.[81] This kind of participatory process would allow a court to avoid

[77] Liebenberg, *supra* note 5, 224. [78] Ibid., Ch. 8.

[79] Ibid., at 173–74 (arguing reasonableness review "provides the courts with a flexible and context-sensitive basis for evaluating socioeconomic rights claims" that "allows government the space to design and formulate appropriate policies" to fulfill them).

[80] Ibid., 179–80 (calling for a more substantive approach to interpretation that still leaves the content of the social rights "contingent and incomplete, allowing space for the evolution of new meanings" in response to changed circumstances).

[81] Ibid., 436.

directly identifying the policy changes that flow from even an incremental, context-specific interpretation of the rights at issue.[82] Liebenberg, however, calls for courts to exercise much greater control in this process and thus hews much more closely to the public-law examples Sabel and Simon use to illustrate the experimentalist model.[83] She also cautions that more flexible remedies like meaningful engagement must be tied to some "substantive evaluation of the rights at stake" to avoid the risk that vulnerable litigants will "negotiate away their constitutional rights."[84]

Liebenberg thus describes a set of changes that respect the Court's concern with maintaining a large measure of democratic control over the social rights but that also establish a stronger interpretive framework that could, over time, develop the substance of the social rights. The balance Liebenberg strikes, however, calls for fairly substantial changes to the Court's existing approach. In particular, Liebenberg strongly argues that the Court must abandon its decision to read the substance of the major social rights together with the resources and progressive-realization qualifications in them.[85] The Court's failure to make a sharp analytical distinction between the content of the right and these limitations, she asserts, "detracts significantly" from the Court's capacity to instigate and engage in more democratic substantive development of the social rights.[86] The Court has left the social rights in a "normative vacuum" that not only diminishes its own interpretive role but also inhibits the political branches from independently developing a substantive account of the social rights.[87]

Wilson and Dugard – who first identified this set of cases as representing a distinctive "second-wave" in the Court's approach to the social rights – draw on Liebenberg's arguments to identify a related set of changes that they argue largely accept the broad parameters of the Court's existing interpretive approach but modify it in a more substantive direction.[88] In contrast to Liebenberg, they take direct aim at the Court's preoccupation with democratic legitimacy and its corresponding reliance on procedural rights and remedies. They first argue the Court should abandon the view most completely articulated in *Mazibuko* that social rights are primarily aimed at establishing a deeply participatory form of democracy, and second, the Court must develop "an account of the particular interests

[82] Ibid., 434–38.

[83] Ibid., 435–38 (citing Charles F. Sabel and William H. Simon, "Destabilization Rights: How Public Law Litigation Succeeds," 117 *Harv. L. Rev.* 1016 (2004).

[84] Liebenberg, *supra* note 5, 421–24. [85] Ibid., 175–77. [86] Ibid., 176.

[87] Ibid. [88] Wilson and Dugard, *supra* note 8.

socio-economic rights exist to protect and promote."[89] Like Liebenberg, however, they argue the Court could maintain a context-specific approach by starting with the actual circumstances faced by individual claimants in each case and "assign[ing] meaning to the socio-economic rights" in light of those circumstances.[90]

Wilson and Dugard argue that the Court's limited substantive role flows from its unduly constrained understanding of its own institutional limits and the separation-of-powers problems social rights raise. They point out that the Court has acted far less constrained by those same concerns in other cases and different contexts. Using *Mazibuko*, *Joe Slovo*, and *Nokotyana* as examples, they argue the Court easily could have modified its approach in each case to develop a more substantive account of the rights at issue without excessively intruding on legislative or executive prerogatives or addressing issues outside the normal bounds of judicial competence.

In *Mazibuko*, they argue the residents developed a clear, largely uncontested, factual record that the new water policy did not provide sufficient free water to meet the individual residents' needs.[91] If the Court had started its interpretation of section 27 with that simple, uncontested fact, it could not have avoided finding that the policy created a prima facie violation of the right to sufficient water – under any quantification of "sufficient." Finding that the uncontested water shortages the residents faced established a clear violation of section 27 would not have ended the analysis. The state could still justify its policy by relying on the progressive-realization and resources-limitation provisions in section 27(2). Following Liebenberg, they argue that analytical distinction would have appropriately distinguished between the substance of the right and the merits of the state's reasons for failing to provide sufficient water to the residents.[92] This simple change would create analytical clarity over the related but distinct questions of how much water individual claimants require to sustain themselves, the City's capacity to meet those specific needs while administering a comprehensive water program, and the geographic priorities the City had set. Equally important, it would appropriately place a specific burden on the City itself to raise and justify those arguments.

By taking a programmatic approach the Court instead started with the overall policy and asked only if it violated the right to water on an aggregate level. This abstract approach paradoxically allowed the Court

[89] Ibid., 230. [90] Ibid., 239. [91] Ibid., 232–33. [92] Ibid., 235.

to cite the uncontested insufficiency of the amount of water provided to the Phiri residents as a reason the policy did not violate section 27. Taking the relatively larger Phiri residents' households into account, the Court found, would inappropriately skew the analysis of section 27 and "disproportionately benefit stands with fewer residents."[93] More broadly, ordering the City to provide more water to these residents could potentially divert resources away from the City's capacity to provide even this limited amount of free water to informal settlements many of which the Court noted lacked even the insufficient level of service they were provided.[94]

The Court's analysis thus simply ignored the interests of the residents, and consequently the Court was unable "to hold the City to any meaningful standard of reasonableness."[95] By defining the City's obligations under section 27 at such a generalized level – rather than considering those competing obligations under a resources analysis tied to the circumstances of the individual plaintiffs – the Court effectively accepted the City's concerns as valid and justified without any scrutiny. This significantly limited the scope of section 27. It also prevented the Court from assessing whether the priorities the City has set are consistent with section 27 and to what extent its resources claims are supported by the facts.[96]

Dugard and Wilson show that the Court adopted this same generalized analysis in both *Joe Slovo* and *Nokotyana*. Like *Mazibuko*, the analytical structure in each case ignored the individual effects of the challenged policy.[97] They conclude that "the Court has deprived itself of the conceptual tools necessary to forge a sufficiently rich account of the interests protected by socio-economic rights" and that "it is neither appropriate nor coherent . . . to leave a substantive account of socio-economic rights to supposedly 'democratic' processes beyond the Court's purview."[98]

The patterns in the second-wave cases reflect the substantive limits Wilson and Dugard identify and critique. The Court's own stronger interventions in the later first-wave cases demonstrate those limits are not required by either the structure of the social rights themselves or the separation-of-powers principles in the Constitution. Those same cases also support their argument that the Court has taken a much less constrained approach to separation-of-powers concerns when enforcing

93 *Mazibuko*, *supra* note 13, [88] (quoted in Wilson and Dugard, *supra* note 8, 234).
94 Wilson and Dugard, *supra* note 8, 234–35. 95 Ibid., 236.
96 Ibid., 235–36. 97 Ibid., 236–39. 98 Ibid., 239.

social rights as well as other rights. Indeed, in the first-wave cases the Court frequently emphasized that the overarching goal of transformation requires a flexible approach to separation of powers. *TAC* explained that the Court's "duty" is to decide whether a particular policy "has given effect to [the state's] constitutional obligations" and if doing so "constitutes an intrusion into the domain of the executive, that is an intrusion mandated by the Constitution itself."[99]

As the preceding discussion highlighted, that theme drops out in the second-wave cases replaced by a narrow focus on assessing the process used to reach a challenged policy rather than its substantive effects – a focus justified by the need to avoid intruding into the constitutional domains of the executive and legislature. The Court's shift in emphasis to social rights' role as democratic accountability mechanisms and its related emphasis on the relationship between social rights and the overarching democratic values in section 1 of the Constitution, rather than their relationship to the substantive rights to human dignity and equality, reinforces this narrow focus. These patterns and Wilson and Dugard's own analysis, however, suggest the Court is unlikely to adopt the clear analytical separation that they advocate.

The stronger procedural dimensions of the second-wave cases could nonetheless incorporate, at least to some extent, an analysis of the kind of interests Wilson and Dugard identify. The Court's interventions in the eviction model are one illustration of this stronger substantive potential. Those decisions typically start at the opposite extreme from the generalized approach Wilson and Dugard critique because the Court, under PIE, focuses specifically on the effects of the eviction in each case and only secondarily considers the underlying policies and justifications for the eviction. By focusing on PIE's multifactor balancing test and the need to minimize the unconstitutional effects of each eviction on the individuals involved, the Court in these cases has been able to protect poor people and enforce section 26 without abandoning its current interpretive framework or clearly developing even a set of statutory standards under PIE.

In some cases, like *Port Elizabeth* and *Blue Moonlight*, the Court has engaged in analyses that look something like what Liebenberg and Wilson, and Dugard advocate. Those decisions arguably have identified some important principles that could apply in other cases. The most significant

[99] *TAC, supra* note 14, [99].

of these more substantive principles, however, is the de facto principle that any eviction that risks homelessness is a violation of section 26 enforced through PIE. By consistently refusing to allow an eviction where the state cannot provide alternative accommodation, the Court has directly – if only temporarily and incompletely – enforced *Grootboom*'s basic principle on an individual basis, while still minimizing the institutional-competence and separation-of-powers concerns in the ways Liebenberg describes. By simply stopping an eviction until alternative accommodation is available, the Court stays out of the institutionally straining business of scrutinizing the adequacy of the underlying policies and avoids directly second-guessing the government's priorities.

But those benefits also incur the same costs as the generalized model Wilson and Dugard critique. Both approaches lack any nuanced, contextual analysis of whether and how individual needs in each case implicate the social rights. The only factor that seems to matter is whether alternative accommodation is available, thus eliminating the need to evaluate the content of section 26. Because the default in the eviction model is rights-protective, whereas the default in the generalized approach is deferential to government, that lack of context works in favor of poor people and creates stronger authority for courts. Nonetheless the lack of individualized analysis in both approaches severely limits the potential for further substantive development of section 26, even in a context-specific way. The eviction model starts and stops with *Grootboom* enforcing it in a closed substantive loop.

The eviction cases point to two complementary routes out of this closed loop. The first, most direct, route is for the Court – and lower courts – to identify specific substantive principles in the context of each case either as independent constitutional principles or through constitutionally attentive interpretation of legislation. *Port Elizabeth* is the model for using PIE to identify constitutional principles, and *Blue Moonlight* applied that same approach. *Maphango*'s creative expansion of the Rental Housing Act follows a similar pattern, but there the Court failed to develop the more substantive aspects of the Act. In *Zulu* Justice Van der Westhuizen called for something similar by directly addressing the constitutionality of the arguments surrounding municipal anti-land invasion units, but the majority remanded the case to avoid doing that more substantive engagement with the issues.

As Liebenberg points out, this case-specific, incremental interpretive approach offers the potential for greater substantive development while still preserving substantial flexibility for the Court in later cases and for the political branches to respond.[100] *Port Elizabeth* similarly illustrates that the Court further democratizes its modestly substantive interventions by grounding the principles it identifies in constitution-enforcing legislation rather than directly on social rights. Chapter 8 argues that courts in individual eviction cases could adapt Liebenberg's prescription and more consistently engage in the kind of comparative factual analysis under PIE that would incrementally expand section 26 in that context.

The second, indirect, route is for the Court to take a more active managerial role over the underlying policies in eviction cases. The procedural authority to join responsible government entities to scrutinize budget and policy-development processes, and to structure discussions among the parties gives courts considerable indirect influence over those policies. The *Blue Moonlight* companion cases set up this possibility and the Court's stronger management in *Pheko* and *Juma Musjid* clearly allows for this role.

Neither approach goes as far as either Liebenberg or Wilson and Dugard advocate in terms of formally restructuring the Court's analysis to clearly separate the substance of the social rights. But both approaches could incorporate greater attention to the needs of individual claimants and also give courts greater authority to scrutinize the government's programmatic justifications in light of those needs. The next two chapters develop these possibilities. The eviction model in Chapter 8 describes the incremental substantive effects that case-specific interventions can have and also how those same interventions can extend to systemic policy issues. Chapter 9's description of democratic engagement argues that it can provide a basis for even more direct interventions at an institutional level and has significant potential to make even a proceduralized enforcement approach effective.

D. Experimentalist and catalytic courts

Before proceeding to develop the two routes just identified – an incrementally substantive role under the eviction model and stronger procedural authority using meaningful engagement – I want to turn to two other adjudicative models that more accurately capture the stronger authority

[100] Liebenberg, *supra* note 5, 174.

the Court has developed in the second-wave cases.[101] The brief discussion here first helps to clarify the distinct features of that stronger authority and also lays the groundwork for the more detailed discussion of how the Court could expand that authority in the next two chapters.

1. Democratic experimentalism

The strong procedural authority the Court has developed and its emphasis on using social rights to create a direct form of participatory democracy shares strong affinities with the experimentalist model of public-law litigation described by Charles Sabel, William Simon, and others.[102] Chapter 1 discussed democratic experimentalism as a variant of weak-form review that relies on broadly participatory processes to design and implement measures for fulfilling constitutional rights. Unlike weak-form review more generally, experimentalist review is not concerned primarily with democratizing the substantive development of constitutional norms through judicial–political dialogue. Instead it focuses specifically on the role courts can play in instigating and managing processes in which parties, the state, and other stakeholders themselves develop flexible substantive standards and experimental remedies that fulfill public-law requirements.

Sabel and Simon argue that an experimentalist court's "principal contribution is to indicate publicly that the status quo is illegitimate and cannot continue."[103] This "very general intervention" then destabilizes entrenched public institutions and opens them up to reform proposals generated through participatory processes rather than judicially directed solutions.[104] The roles that the Court has developed in the second-wave cases seemed designed to have a similarly indirect destabilizing effect. The broad procedural powers the Court has developed allow it to intervene in social rights cases in ways that prevent the state (or private parties) from taking action that might violate the social rights. But by avoiding direct constitutional interpretation and limiting even its statutory analysis

[101] The richer "constitutional conception" of the doctrine of legitimate expectation that Pieterse develops comes the closest among existing accounts of the second-wave decisions to the procedurally grounded approaches the next two chapters develop. Pieterse, *supra* note 69.

[102] E.g., Charles F. Sabel and William H. Simon, "Destabilization Rights: How Public Law Litigation Succeeds," 117 *Harv. L. Rev.* 1016 (2004).

[103] Ibid., 1056. [104] Ibid.

to context-specific factors, the Court leaves open both the content of the rights at issue and even the remedial measures necessary to fulfill them.

The meaningful engagement requirement is the paradigmatic example of this combination. Michael Dorf and Charles Sabel describe experimentalist judging in terms that closely track the requirement: "experimentalist courts ask whether the parties whose actions are challenged have satisfied their obligations to grant those rights of participation revealed to be more effective by comparison to rolling best practices elsewhere."[105] In *Olivia Road* the Court specifically recognized that engagement establishes the power for courts to review not only the substance of challenged policies but also whether they were developed with sufficient community participation.[106] *Joe Slovo* failed to enforce that requirement directly but the Court's detailed engagement order applied it to give the residents leverage over the relocation process.[107]

The Court's managerial role in the eviction cases reflects a similar experimentalist structure. By temporarily stopping an eviction, the Court destabilizes the situation and creates uncertainty over the state or private party's authority to evict. Where the Court goes further and orders an existing, or involuntarily joined, state party to provide information regarding its housing policies and resources, it expands that uncertainty to those underlying policies. The net effect disrupts the existing power relationship, in which the state or private landowner has nearly complete control subject only to the threat of physical resistance, by creating some leverage for the residents to negotiate. The flexibility of the meaningful engagement requirement allows courts to calibrate that leverage in the ways Chapter 9 describes by structuring the engagement and setting substantive parameters for it.

Experimentalism's emphasis on democratizing bureaucratic structures and administrative procedures by giving citizens and other stakeholders a legally recognized role in developing solutions to reform public institutions also echoes the Constitutional Court's own shift to identifying social rights as tools for democratic accountability in the second wave. Rather than enforcing the social rights by defining them to establish substantive legislative or policy goals, the Court has reinterpreted its role as ensuring that the procedures used by the state to develop policies to fulfill the

[105] Michael C. Dorf and Charles M. Sabel, "A Constitution of Democratic Experimentalism," 98 *Col. L. Rev.* 267, 403 (1998).

[106] *Olivia Road*, *supra* note 18.

[107] *Joe Slovo*, *supra* note 19, [7].

social rights include direct participation by the people and communities affected by those policies.

The Court's consistent failure to develop the content of the social rights even at a very general level, however, distinguishes it from Sabel and Simon's model of experimentalist judging because the Court does not predicate its experimentalist interventions on the violation of any substantive constitutional norm.[108] Sabel and Simon emphasize that the experimentalist, participatory components come in at the remedial stage. Those experimentalist remedies "are induced and fueled by the intense destabilization that results" from the court's finding of a substantive legal violation and "it seems unlikely" the parties could define the remedies themselves without the court's initial strong intervention.[109] The examples of public-law litigation that Sabel and Simon cite all follow this structure in which courts predicated experimentalist remedial processes on a strong, if abstract, determination that there was a constitutional violation. Courts in those cases also assumed a relatively high level of procedural control over the remedial process through strong remedies like structural injunctions.[110]

The Constitutional Court consistently avoids the kind of strong-rights declarations that these examples feature, and the Court has never issued a structural injunction in a social rights case despite recognizing its power to do so. Indeed, the Court has only selectively exercised even more modest forms of procedural control. *Joe Slovo* and the *Pheko* enforcement orders arguably establish the high-water mark in this respect. The Court's refusal in *Blue Moonlight II* to supervise implementation of that decision shows that it may be reluctant regularly to assert that same supervisory authority.[111]

The Court's reliance on a thinly substantive interpretive role overlaps to some extent with what Jeff King calls the "incrementalist" model.[112] Incrementalist courts avoid broad-based comprehensive decisions in social

[108] Sabel and Simon, *supra* note 102, 1056 (an experimentalist judge "having found a violation of some broad norm . . . imposes the single remedy the liability phase has shown to be appropriate: institutional destabilization").

[109] Ibid.

[110] Ibid. They examine public-law litigation in several contexts, including schools, prisons, mental-health facilities, and public housing and conclude that remedial practice in all of these areas has moved "away from command-and-control towards experimental methods." Ibid., 1052.

[111] *Occupiers of Saratoga Avenue v City of Johannesburg Metropolitan Municipality and Another* 2012 (9) BCLR 951 (CC) (2012) ("*Blue Moonlight II*").

[112] Jeff King, *Judging Social Rights* (2012).

rights cases and instead either issue particularized decisions that directly affect a narrow group or to preserve flexibility in cases that affect broad policies or large groups.[113]

King identifies incrementalism as a close cousin of experimentalist review in that both emphasize a pragmatic judicial approach that relies on nonjudicial actors for developing both constitutional norms and specific remedies. But he argues that experimentalism overemphasizes the judicial leadership role in developing and managing consultation processes. For this reason, King says experimentalist review ignores possibilities for greater inter-institutional collaboration. He also faults experimentalism's exclusive reliance on participation over substantive interpretation by courts and questions the legitimacy of courts dictating the amount and kinds of process required in particular bureaucratic contexts.[114]

King is correct that the cases Sabel and Simon cite as examples of experimentalist review frequently involved strong remedies like structural injunctions. Experimentalist judging does not necessarily require that level of control, however. Indeed, the distinctive characteristic of the experimentalist model is the shift it makes *away* from a court-centered command-and-control model toward one that relies principally on nonjudicial actors to identify solutions. The experimental nature of the model comes from the fact that "experimentalist remedies contemplate a permanent process of ramifying, participatory self-revision" by those outside actors rather than "a one-time readjustment to fixed criteria" by a judge.[115] It thus promises both to alleviate the significant demands that institutional-reform litigation places on judicial competence and capacity and to increase the democratic legitimacy of judicial interventions – precisely the issues that drive the Court's shift to proceduralization in the second-wave cases.

The more expansive application of meaningful engagement that Chapter 9 describes shares significant features with experimentalist review and that chapter further explores the lessons the Court could draw from the experimentalist literature. In keeping with the internal constraints evident in the second-wave cases, however, that expanded account of engagement emphasizes indirect judicial interventions that extend the rights of social rights activists, local communities, and social movements to participate in the policy-development process on an ongoing basis outside of courts and specific litigation. This less direct judicial role shares some characteristics with King's incrementalist model, in particular King's

[113] Ibid. [114] Ibid., 308–10. [115] Sabel and Simon, *supra* note 102, 1020.

strong emphasis on political development of social rights content. On the whole, however, the stronger authority the Court has developed in the second-wave decisions more closely resemble experimentalism. The Court in theses decisions has engaged in relatively close scrutiny of the specific processes government entities have used to develop policies and has also ordered relatively stronger remedies requiring changes to those processes.

King's critique of the engagement order in *Joe Slovo* helps illustrate this difference. King specifically criticizes the detailed engagement order in *Joe Slovo* as an example of an unsustainable and overly intrusive procedural intervention. He argues that the general engagement order in *Olivia Road* worked well and was justifiable in light of the situation in that case, but the oversight and detailed order in *Joe Slovo* were both illegitimate and counterproductive. King concludes that engagement is most appropriate when de-coupled from supervision and enforced indirectly through damages. Even there, he argues engagement is best reserved as a remedy of last resort because it requires extensive judicial control over political processes and limits the flexibility of the political branches to respond.[116]

Chapter 5's analysis of *Joe Slovo* shows that, far from undermining the remedy, the stronger oversight role the Court played was critical to getting the City to seriously consider the residents' concerns over relocation. As just noted, the Court's detailed order arguably destabilized the power relationship between the residents and the state in precisely the ways Sabel and Simon describe.

The second-wave patterns and the Court's refusal in *Blue Moonlight II* to provide that same oversight show that the Court will not frequently use engagement itself in this way. But *Joe Slovo* plainly stands as precedent for lower courts to do so. The success of democratic engagement depends on the possibility that, where government entities fail to provide meaningful access, courts will intervene to create that access. Those interventions could be indirect as King advocates – indeed lower courts already have started to use their contempt powers in social rights cases in a similar fashion.[117] But, as the City of Johannesburg's failure to implement *Blue Moonlight* shows, it will sometimes, especially in the short term,

[116] King, *supra* note 112, 274–76.

[117] *See Mchunu and Others v Executive Mayor, eThekwini and Others* 2013 (1) SA 555 (KZD), *discussed in* Socio-Economic Rights Institute, "Evictions and Accommodation in South Africa: An Analysis of the Jurisprudence and Implications for Local Government," (2013), 43, at www.seri-sa.org/images/Evictions_Jurisprudence_Nov13.pdf.

to overcome entrenched cultural and political opposition, require more direct control. Because that control is focused on enforcing procedural rights rather than imposing substantive requirements, however, it is still consistent with the second-wave cases and the role *Mazibuko* described. Chapter 9 elaborates this expanded, policy-making version of engagement and the lessons it can draw from the literature on experimentalist review.

2. *Catalytic courts*

Katherine Young has developed a typology of judicial review based on the Court's social rights decisions, including several of the second-wave cases that build on the concept of weak-form review to describe a more diverse range of court interventions that involve interactions with nonjudicial actors, including the political branches.[118] Young's typology is useful in conceptualizing the role the Court has developed in the second-wave cases and distinguishing it from weak-form review.

Like weak-form review more generally, Young plots the different roles a court can adopt along a spectrum from weak to strong but includes the interactions they create with nonjudicial actors, including social movements and civil society as well as those between a court and the political branches.[119] Young argues that the Constitutional Court's social rights decisions reveal a deliberate strategy that guides its choice of relatively stronger and weaker interventions that she calls "catalytic."[120] Young defines a catalytic court as "one that sees itself in productive interaction with other political and legal actors."[121] Catalytic courts resolve cases in context-sensitive ways that shift standards of review and deploy diverse remedies to enforce constitutional rights by stimulating other institutions and actors independently and interaction with each other to act in rights-protective ways.

In Young's account the varying levels of scrutiny and remedial devices the Constitutional Court has employed in the social rights cases reflect a catalytic approach driven by the Court's desire to prompt the social and economic transformation the Constitution promises and its recognition that transformation requires the active participation and commitment of all three branches to the new constitution and bill of rights.[122] This means that the Court calibrates its interventions in response to how well and to what degree the government and other political actors are

[118] Young, *supra* note 10, Ch. 5. [119] Ibid.,136–39. [120] Ibid., Ch. 6.
[121] Ibid., 172. [122] Ibid., Ch. 6.

situated to fulfill the social rights. In some cases, like *Khosa* and *TAC*, this required stronger interventions.[123] In others, including *Grootboom* and *Soobramoney*, that meant relatively deferential approaches.[124] Young argues that the Court's shifting standard of review and diverse remedies reflect the Court's assessment of how best to catalyze transformation in each situation and its recognition that transformation often requires the cooperation of the legislature and executive.[125]

Young argues that the diversity of the Court's interventions demonstrates that it does not limit itself to a deferential form of review when faced with social rights claims.[126] Instead, the common element that explains the Court's selection of a relatively stronger or weaker form of review in social rights decisions is the state's own stance toward its obligations under the right in question.[127] Where the state was deliberately obstructive, as in *TAC*, the Court was more likely to adopt a more stringent standard of review and/or issue a more direct remedy. Mere inattention, like the state's failure to recognize its obligations to address emergency needs in *Grootboom*, allowed for a weaker approach that created room for political response after the Court highlighted the state's failure to recognize a particular obligation. Conversely, policies that appear motivated by the political or social status of the parties and thus implicate other rights – the situation the Court addressed in *Khosa* – moved the Court back toward a stronger role. For Young, even *Soobramoney* was an example of a catalytic approach because the Court calibrated its role in response to the evidence that the government had crafted a policy in response to legitimate budget and capacity concerns that justified judicial deference to the state's allocation decisions.[128]

The three patterns in the second-wave cases overlap to a large extent with Young's description. First, both accounts recognize that the Court's interventions in social rights cases have not been uniformly weak. Instead the Court has operated along a spectrum that ranges from highly deferential to relatively demanding scrutiny of the government's justifications for challenged programs and decisions.

Both accounts argue that we can identify a relatively consistent set of factors that influence where the Court positions itself along this spectrum in each case. The classic justiciability concerns with respecting and maximizing the role of democratic processes in fulfilling social rights and maintaining an appropriately limited institutional role when the Court

[123] Ibid., 162–66. [124] Ibid., 143–47. [125] Ibid., 166, 174–77.
[126] Ibid., 175. [127] Ibid., 175–177, 188–91. [128] Ibid.

perceives a case to raise complex technical and policy issues tend to push the Court toward the deferential end. However, where the Court either perceives those concerns as weaker (or finds ways to shape the case to minimize them) it is more willing to closely scrutinize government decisions and issue remedies that require direct and indirect changes to challenged policies. Evidence of state failure to consider the social rights also appears to push the Court toward the stronger end of the spectrum.

The patterns identified here, however, suggest that the Court's interventions, even when it operates at the stronger end of the spectrum, have increasingly focused on the procedural tools the Court has developed in these cases and that the Court strongly prefers to enforce existing legislation or policy as the substantive basis for those interventions rather than the social rights themselves. The Court in these decisions has largely abandoned the more direct engagement with the social rights that first-wave cases like *Khosa* and *Jaftha* featured, even where there is strong evidence of deliberate avoidance of the social rights obligations by the state and even where there are overlapping claims under other rights.[129] The patterns in the second-wave cases instead show that the Court has found ways to use the set of procedural tools it has developed to strengthen its interventions while actively limiting the substantive effects of even those stronger interventions.

Blue Moonlight and its two companion cases are the clearest examples of the Court shifting to a stronger interventionist stance by using a set of largely procedural tools. In each decision the Court described at some length and with obvious impatience the municipal failures to responsibly address their constitutional obligations.[130] The Court's willingness to stop the evictions in each case with no meaningful consideration of the different facts arguably resulted in part from the Court's impatience with those failures. The Court's conclusion in *Blue Moonlight* that the City of Johannesburg's interpretive error made its resources arguments legally irrelevant also could be explained in part by its obvious impatience with the City's argument that it lacked any legal obligation to provide housing for people evicted from private land.[131]

[129] *Khosa and Others v Minister of Social Development and Others, Mahlaule and Another v Minister of Social Development* 2004 (6) BCLR 569 (CC) (2004) ("*Khosa*"); *Jaftha v Schoeman and Others, Van Rooyen v Stoltz and Others* 2005 (1) BCLR 78 (CC) (2004) ("*Jaftha*").

[130] *See Blue Moonlight, supra* note 33.

[131] The Court found that the City's budget "was the product of its incorrect understanding of Chapter 12 [of the Housing Act]" and therefore it was "not strictly necessary to consider the attack" on the SCA's holding that the City had sufficient resources. Ibid., [69].

The later eviction cases and *Juma Musjid* each involved similar situations in which a municipality either refused to recognize its obligations or employed creative methods and arguments to avoid them.[132] These cases also show that the Court uses stronger interventions more frequently to actively check policies or decisions likely to result in deprivation of goods or services guaranteed by the social rights and seems willing to permit greater incursions on competing private rights to avoid such deprivations.

The Court did not significantly develop the content of section 26(1) in any of these cases. Instead, it enforced existing – or developed new – procedural rights and remedies. Even the de facto strong right to emergency housing before eviction that the Court has consistently applied reflects these same limitations. First, the Court has consistently refused to acknowledge the principle by formally applying a multifactor balancing test, usually PIE. Second, the Court applies the principle primarily to assert some procedural control to prompt the parties to develop a rights-protective solution. The Court in these cases temporarily stopped an eviction and either left any resulting policy change up to the parties to negotiate or, less frequently as in *Pheko* and *Juma Musjid*, ordered direct relief but tied it to the specific facts of the case. The *Zulu* majority's decision to address only the procedural question of standing and to avoid the substantive rights of the residents as Van der Westhuizen argued is consistent with this same pattern. Likewise, *Maphango*'s creative revival of the Rental Housing Act's procedure to temporarily stop a private landlord's attempted eviction allowed it to avoid both directly interpreting section 26 or developing the common law of contract in light of the right to adequate housing.

The second-wave decisions also demonstrate that the Court is reluctant to use even these stronger procedural tools when faced with social rights claims in situations it perceives as raising particularly strong separation-of-powers and democratic-legitimacy concerns. There was strong evidence the state deliberately ignored its constitutional obligations in several of the second-wave cases where the Court not only avoided a substantive role but also reverted to deference. For example, in *Mazibuko* the High Court found that the City had deliberately deceived the residents regarding the prepaid meter policy, and yet the Constitutional Court still refused to uphold even the more limited procedural challenges the residents raised.[133] Likewise in *Joe Slovo* several judges highlighted

[132] *See* discussion in Ch. 6.

[133] *Mazibuko and Others v City of Johannesburg and Others* [2008] 4 All SA 471 (W) (2008) [106–12].

evidence of significant administrative and bureaucratic failures in implementing the housing project and communicating with the residents, and in *Nokotyana* both the municipality and the provincial government had essentially ignored the residents' situation and even failed to timely decide the upgrade application.[134]

These examples reinforce the conclusion that the Court views social rights differently than other rights and shapes its role accordingly. This does not mean the Court always applies a deferential mode of review, but it does mean that the Court consistently and increasingly has been reluctant to adopt clear substantive principles or to assess the adequacy of specific policies or programs. Indeed, the patterns in the second-wave cases show that the Court actively shapes the issues it addresses in social rights cases and the role it plays to avoid dealing directly with the substance of the social rights precisely because doing so frees it to intervene in the stronger ways Young describes.

These patterns thus put a slightly different light on Young's analysis that the Court strategically calibrates the strength of its interventions in response to government intransigence and inattention to the social rights. Those failures represent the kind of breakdown in democratic accountability the Court has said the social rights are primarily intended to police. But the Court's role is still primarily to restore that accountability by forcing the government to pay attention to the people whose interests it overlooked or deliberately ignored, not to identify the substantive changes the social rights require.

The combination of this concern with addressing political failures to take the social rights seriously and the substantive limits in the Courts approach helps explain the mixed results in several of the decisions just discussed. For example, in *Joe Slovo* and *Nokotyana* the Court balanced its refusal to uphold the substantive claims by the residents with at least modest forms of procedural relief that were tailored to remedy the blatant administrative failures in each case. *Joe Slovo*'s managerial engagement order both mitigated the effect of the Court's decision to permit the eviction to move forward despite the government's documented unwillingness or inability to effectively consult with the residents and also ensured effective consultation in the relocation process. *Nokotyana*'s order failed to redress the past failures of the municipality and provincial government to seriously address the residents' concerns but imposed a specific

[134] *See* Wilson and Dugard, *supra* note 8, 231–39 (highlighting the evidence of government recalcitrance in all three of these cases).

deadline that was intended to force a decision the Court plainly expected would address at least some of those concerns.

E. Conclusion

This chapter has shown that the Court's role in the second-wave cases does not fit neatly within either side of the divide that developed in reaction to the first wave. On one hand, the patterns in these decisions show that the Court remains committed to the formal analytical structure and context-specific approach to reasonableness review that were the focus of the first-wave critics. They also show that the Court has deepened its reliance on procedural rights and remedies and redefined its enforcement role as primarily to ensure the democratic accountability of the processes the state uses to develop policies to fulfill the social rights. These features have received the most attention in analyses of the second-wave cases and those analyses have, with good reason, focused on the various ways that they further diminish the Court's interpretive role.

At the same time, however, this emphasis on the Court's continued failure to develop a more substantive account of the social rights masks the stronger procedural authority the Court has developed and, equally important, the confidence with which it consistently exerts that authority. These patterns are evident in the remarkable string of pro-poor decisions where the Court has enforced the social rights to challenge government policies and decisions without clearly elaborating their substantive content. In doing so, the Court has managed to avoid adopting the strongly deferential role that many argued would inevitably follow from its failure to identify concrete substantive principles.

The following two chapters build on these more authoritative patterns. They describe in greater detail two complementary approaches the Constitutional Court and lower courts could employ to exert even stronger authority to enforce social rights while still largely working within the constraints the Court has identified.

PART III

Procedure's potential

8

The eviction model

Chapter 5 analyzed the string of eviction-related decisions beginning in 2011 in which the Court relied on constitution-enforcing legislation – most often Prevention of Illegal Eviction from and Unlawful Occupation of Land Act (PIE) – to avoid or delay a potential eviction and also developed a range of procedural powers courts can employ to manage evictions. These decisions are consistent with the other second-wave cases because they all feature substantively limited analyses and an emphasis on procedural rights and remedies. At the same time, however, the Court also exhibited an increasing confidence when working within the confines of this approach by consistently intervening to stop evictions that could result in homelessness and by expanding its power to manage eviction processes to protect the interests of poor people.

This chapter first summarizes the two basic components of the enforcement approach these cases represent – shorthanded as the "eviction model": (1) enforcing *Grootboom* through PIE (or other legislation) by temporarily enjoining eviction until alternative accommodation is available (or at least to permit further negotiations over alternative accommodation) and (2) expanding the procedural powers of courts in eviction cases to obtain information about housing planning and resources and manage the cases in rights-protective ways that ensure access to temporary accommodation and could lead to broader policy change.[1]

[1] The "eviction model" label is appropriate for two reasons. First, the Court developed this model and has applied it most consistently in eviction and eviction-related decisions. Although this chapter argues that this model is adaptable to enforce other social rights, in particular in the context of service-delivery cutoffs, evictions raise distinct practical, jurisprudential, and historical issues that may pose challenges for doing so. Second, the term "eviction" helpfully captures the limitations of the model, especially its procedural focus. This chapter argues that the model could be refined and expanded to address those limitations but also recognizes that the model's limits may create a cul de sac where courts apply the authority it creates fairly narrowly.

Both components reflect *Port Elizabeth*'s style of managerial judging rather than the abstract, programmatic approach of *Grootboom*.[2] The first transforms *Grootboom*'s weak, programmatic declaration into an individually enforceable principle that section 26(3) rights at least temporarily trump section 25 property rights where the state is unable to provide temporary accommodation to potential evictees.[3] The second uses legislation like PIE as the basis for a set of robust, but largely procedural, protections that give courts broad powers to manage evictions in individual cases.[4]

The Court's demonstrated willingness to stop evictions until temporary accommodation is available is the core of this model. By enforcing this limited but strong right through a temporary injunction, courts directly enforce section 26(3) and indirectly protect the occupiers' section 26(2) rights to continued occupation until an alternative is available. Amplified by the range of procedural powers these cases also established, this aspect of the eviction model gives courts considerable power to protect poor people's interests without developing broad constitutional principles or scrutinizing government policies and so stays within the general limits of the second-wave cases.

Malcolm Langford describes the substantive move that turned *Grootboom* into a limited but strong individual right as a kind of "jujitsu."[5] In these cases the Court addresses negative infringements of section 26(3) in ways that implicitly establish positive entitlements under section 26(2), including both the right to temporary accommodation and, in some instances, permanent housing.[6] By purporting to enforce only

[2] *Port Elizabeth Municipality v Various Occupiers* 2004 (12) BCLR 1268 (CC) (2004) ("*Port Elizabeth*"); *Government of the Republic of South Africa and Others v Grootboom and Others* 2000 (11) BCLR 1169 (2000) ("*Grootboom*").

[3] Stuart Wilson, "Breaking the Tie: Evictions, Homelessness and the New Normality," 126 *S. Afr. L. J.* 270, 278–79 (2009).

[4] Steve Kahanovitz was among the first to identify the significant procedural protections the Court's application of PIE in *Port Elizabeth* created. *See* Steve Kahanovitz, "An Urban Slice of PIE: The Prevention of Illegal Eviction from and Unlawful Occupation of Land Act in South Africa," case study prepared for the *Global Report on Human Settlements* (2007). Sandra Liebenberg has analyzed these protections extensively as part of a "new paradigm" for evictions law that could form the basis for a more substantive section 26 jurisprudence. *See* Sandra Liebenberg, *Socio-Economic Rights: Adjudication under a Transformative Constitution*, Ch. 27 (2010).

[5] Malcolm Langford, "Housing Rights Litigation", in Langford *et al.* (eds.), *Socio-Economic Rights in South Africa: Symbols or Substance?* (2013), 207.

[6] S. Afr. Const. 1996 § 26(3). This provision states, "No one may be evicted from their home, or have their home demolished, without an order of a court made after considering all the relevant circumstances. No legislation may permit arbitrary evictions." Ibid. The

the negative aspect of section 26(3), however, the Court does not explicitly articulate these positive-rights implications and so avoids the strong justiciability concerns it consistently sought to avoid in the second-wave cases.

The enhanced procedural powers these cases establish strengthen the indirect positive-rights effects of enforcing section 26(3) by allowing a court to scrutinize the underlying policies at issue. The Court already has used these powers to sketch out an important set of principles governing both the eviction process itself and the state's obligations to budget and plan for evictions. Thus far these principles are still largely procedural in the sense that they do not require specific services or expenditures. Instead they enhance the state's obligation to justify its policies and create indirect leverage for forcing change in those policies. Lower courts could expand these principles through careful attention to PIE's factors and their constitutional basis in section 26.

Even greater substantive potential, however, lies in combining the strengthened procedural requirements these cases established with carefully structured meaningful engagement orders to directly address the broader housing-policy questions that the Court consistently has refused to revisit following *Grootboom*. The implicit expectation where a court intervenes to stop an eviction is that the municipality will change its policies and reallocate its resources to provide temporary accommodation so that the eviction can proceed. As *Pheko* illustrates, a structured engagement process could make that expectation explicit and also give occupiers, private landowners, and civil society groups a voice in deciding what changes are necessary to satisfy PIE and balance competing rights under sections 25 and 26.[7] The Court's use of engagement to give the parents greater input into alternative school placements and transportation options in *Juma Musjid* provides another illustration of the potential substantive effects engagement orders can generate.[8]

Court and commentators refer to this as a "negative" right or obligation because it protects against deprivation of existing access to housing by prohibiting arbitrary evictions and conditioning all others on a court order. E.g., *Grootboom, supra* note 2, [34] (recognizing "a negative obligation placed upon the state [by section 26] and all other entities and persons to desist from preventing or impairing the right of access to adequate housing" and explaining that "negative right is further spelt out in subsection (3) which prohibits arbitrary evictions").

[7] *Pheko and Others v Ekurhuleni Metropolitan Municipality* 2012 (4) BCLR 388 (CC) (2011) ("*Pheko*"). *See* discussion in Ch. 6.

[8] *Governing Body of the Juma Musjid Primary School & Others v Essay N.O. and Others* 2011 (8) BCLR 761 (CC) (2011) ("*Juma Musjid*"). *See* discussion in Ch. 6.

Structured engagement orders like these also could go further by requiring the parties to negotiate over aspects of a municipality's overall housing-policy and budgeting processes. *Blue Moonlight*'s analysis of the City of Johannesburg's policy-planning and budgeting processes established that courts can inquire into these broader issues when asked to issue an eviction order.[9] Initiating an engagement process that considers those broader systemic issues rather than only the measures necessary to resolve a particular case would build on *Blue Moonlight* and give communities and their representatives an even greater role in changing policies that affect their interests. The more structured use of engagement in cases like *Schubart Park* and especially *Juma Musjid* provide the starting points for expanding engagement in these ways.[10]

After describing these two aspects of the eviction model, this chapter identifies possibilities for adapting the model to enforce other social rights. *Grootboom* is now widely recognized as an unusual example of the Court establishing a broadly applicable substantive principle.[11] Moreover, eviction cases may be particularly suitable for this kind of limited strong-form role. Nonetheless, the eviction model is consistent with the broader patterns in the second-wave cases Chapter 7 identified, and it could be the basis for the Court to take a stronger role in other contexts while still working within those overall constraints. The free-standing right to receive municipal services *Joseph* recognized provides one obvious doctrinal basis for extending this role.[12] The Court's education-rights cases also provide evidence of the Court adopting a stronger procedurally focused role to enforce other social rights.

Finally, I consider some possible limits to this model, in particular the concern that the Court may be unwilling to continue to exercise even the incremental substantive authority the eviction model establishes. The Court's failure to carefully apply PIE in constitutionally attentive ways in *Blue Moonlight*'s companion cases, as well as its refusal to exercise

[9] *City of Johannesburg Metropolitan Municipality v Blue Moonlight Properties 39 (Pty) Ltd and Another* 2012 (2) BCLR 150 (CC) (2011) ("*Blue Moonlight*").

[10] *Schubart Park Residents' Association and Others v City of Tshwane Metropolitan Municipality and Another* 2013 (1) BCLR 68 (CC) (2012) ("*Schubart Park*"); *Juma Musjid*, *supra* note 8.

[11] *See* Stuart Wilson and Jackie Dugard, "Taking Poverty Seriously: The South African Constitutional Court and Socio-Economic Rights," in Sandra Liebenberg and Geo Quinot (eds.), *Law and Poverty: Perspectives from South Africa and Beyond* (2012) 222, 225–26.

[12] *Joseph and Others v City of Johannesburg and Others* 2010 (3) BCLR 212 (CC) (2009) ("*Joseph*").

jurisdiction to enforce its order in *Blue Moonlight II*, provide some support for this concern.[13] The practical problems litigants have faced enforcing several of these decisions also highlight the limits of direct court intervention. Finally, the internal debate in *Zulu* illustrates how the third-generation eviction cases will test these limits in the future.[14] This discussion sets up the argument in the next chapter that deploying meaningful engagement to address underlying institutional and policy issues could begin to address these limitations.

A. *Grootboom*'s transformation

Writing in 2009 after *Olivia Road* and *Joe Slovo* were decided, Stuart Wilson described what he called the "new normality" of property rights in South Africa.[15] The traditional common law conception was replaced with a deep-seated constitutional conflict between the right to private property in section 25 and the prohibition against arbitrary eviction in section 26(3). Those seemingly irreconcilable rights were fighting a "war of attrition" in the new constitutional order.[16] Section 26(3) began to gain the advantage in this war with *Grootboom*'s seemingly modest principle that the state address emergency housing needs and *Port Elizabeth*'s transformation of that principle into a tool for wide-ranging enforcement of PIE. These two decisions laid the groundwork for a new substantive understanding of the relative rights of property owners and poor occupants of their land as well as a set of robust procedural powers to enforce those rights.[17]

Grootboom's reputation as a paradigmatic example of weak-form review rests on the Court's combination of that highly abstract interpretation of section 26(2) paired with a limited declaration that gave the political branches the power to determine how to satisfy the broad requirement that policies address emergency housing needs and how to

[13] The companion cases are *Occupiers of Skurweplaas 353 JR v PPC Aggregate Quarries (Pty) Ltd and Others* 2012 (4) BCLR 382 (CC) (2011) ("*PPC Quarries*"), and *Occupiers of Portion R25 of the Farm Mooiplaats 355 JR v Golden Thread Ltd and Others*, 2012 (4) BCLR 372 (CC) (2011) ("*Golden Thread*"). *Occupiers of Saratoga Avenue v City of Johannesburg Metropolitan Municipality and Another* 2012 (9) BCLR 951 (CC) (2012) ("*Blue Moonlight II*").

[14] *Zulu and Others v eThekwini Municipality and Others* 2014 (8) BCLR 971 (CC) (2014) ("*Zulu*"). *See* discussion in Ch. 6.

[15] Wilson, *supra* note 3. [16] Ibid., 270–71.

[17] Ibid., 273. Liebenberg identifies this same shift. *See* Liebenberg, *supra* note 4, Ch. 27.

balance those needs against section 25. This combination democratized enforcement of section 26 because it only minimally constrained the state's discretion to determine how to balance property rights and section 26(3) in the new constitutional order.[18] At the same time, however, the Court's order looked like an invitation to begin a much greater substantive – but importantly still democratic – elaboration of section 26 over the long term through an ongoing dialogue with the legislature and executive. Numerous analyses of *Grootboom* have identified it as the start of a democratic dialogue and even called it a canonical example of weak-form review.[19]

Despite the growing number of eviction cases that the Court has decided in the second wave, the kind of substantively rich, iterative conversation that weak-form review promises over what *Grootboom*'s principle entails and whether particular policies or legislation comply with it or other aspects of section 26 has almost completely failed to materialize. Instead the Constitutional Court has demonstrated a marked reluctance to revisit *Grootboom* or to interpret the housing legislation and policies that have emerged in response to that decision to further elaborate a set of constitutional principles. As Chapters 5 and 6 described, the Court was faced with several opportunities to consider whether and how new housing legislation or policies promulgated in response to *Grootboom* complied with its broad requirements and section 26 more generally. In each case, the Court resorted to developing new or enforcing existing procedural rights or remedies that failed to materially advance a substantive conversation over the meaning of section 26.[20]

In each of these later eviction cases, however, the Court has relied on *Grootboom*'s core principle that the state is obligated to address emergency housing needs in tandem with PIE to enforce section 26 directly by

[18] Mark Tushnet, *Weak Courts, Strong Rights: Judicial Review and Social Welfare Rights in Comparative Constitutional Law* (2008) 240–44; Rosalind Dixon, "Creating Dialogue about Socio-economic Rights: Strong-Form versus Weak-Form Judicial Review Revisited," 5 *Int'l J. Const. L.* 391 (2007).

[19] E.g., Dixon, ibid.; Tushnet, ibid.; Cesar Rodriguez-Garavito, "Beyond the Courtroom: The Impact of Judicial Activism on Socioeconomic Rights in Latin America," 89 *Tex. L. Rev.* 1669, 1688 (2009) (citing *Grootboom* as a decision that has inspired a "growing literature" calling for "democratic deliberation" and "dialogic activism"); Heinz Klug, "*Grootboom* at Home and Abroad: Adventures in the Construction of a Global Constitutional Canon" (2012), at http://digitalcommons.law.umaryland.edu/schmooze_papers/150/; David Landau, "*Grootboom* the One-Case (or Country?) Canon on Social Rights" (2012), at http://digitalcommons.law.umaryland.edu/schmooze_papers/142/.

[20] *See* discussion in Ch. 5 and 6.

temporarily stopping evictions until the government provides alternative accommodation. Instead of applying some combination of weak rights and remedies, these cases enforce a strong right to alternative accommodation in all (or almost all) cases with strong but temporary injunctive relief.

These decisions also established a range of procedural powers courts can exercise in eviction cases that build on the meaningful engagement requirement in *Olivia Road*.[21] These include the power to join other government entities and relevant parties and to require government officials to report not only their efforts to provide accommodation in a specific case but also their general planning and budgeting processes.

This combination of the authority to stop an eviction and to require detailed information regarding housing-policy and budgeting processes creates a procedurally focused version of strong-form review. These cases combine the strong substantive principle that evictions trigger a nearly unqualified obligation to provide alternative accommodation with the strongest remedy – an injunction temporarily stopping the eviction until alternative accommodation is available.[22]

The principle is substantively strong and individually enforceable but severely limited in scope. It strengthens *Grootboom* by transforming it from a general obligation to develop new policies into a specific requirement to provide services directly in the form of temporary accommodation to people facing eviction.[23] But it does not further elaborate what section 26 requires. Rather than continuing a democratic dialogue between the court and the government over the meaning of section 26, this principle effectively cuts off consideration of whether and how section 26 should be interpreted on the specific facts in each case, including the state's efforts to develop constitutionally compliant policies. In other words, rather than weak-form dialogue, *Grootboom*'s clearest legacy is a model that applies a tightly circumscribed version of strong-form review to enforce a set of procedural norms.

Port Elizabeth laid the groundwork for this transformation of *Grootboom*'s weak remedy into a strong, individually enforceable right. *Port Elizabeth* first shifted from section 26 to PIE as the principal mechanism

[21] *Occupiers of 51 Olivia Road, Berea Township and 197 Main Street Johannesburg v City of Johannesburg and Others* 2008 (5) BCLR 475 (CC) (2008) ("*Olivia Road*").

[22] In cases like *Pheko*, where the eviction occurred and return is temporarily impossible, the Court has deployed the same procedural authority to ensure the state provides an adequate alternative. *Pheko, supra* note 7.

[23] *See* Wilson, *supra* note 3, 275–76.

for addressing housing-rights claims in eviction cases.[24] This created a democratic basis for the stronger interventions that followed and minimized the separation-of-powers concerns that the Court identified in *Grootboom*. Second, although the Court in *Port Elizabeth* analyzed at some length the "constitutional matrix" of PIE, it focused on the flexibility of PIE's multifactor test and the need for creative judicial management to reach humane solutions rather than on establishing constitutional or even statutory principles.[25]

Notably the more definitive constitutional principles that *Port Elizabeth* established in the constitutional discussion are primarily examples of this flexibility. The Court found that section 26(3) is not self-enforcing and permits evictions even where homelessness will result, and that in combination, sections 25 and 26 strike a careful balance requiring fact-specific resolution on a case-by-case basis.[26] The Court included substantial qualifiers throughout the judgment that hint at more concrete limits. Most significantly, it cautioned that a court should be "reluctant to grant an eviction against relatively settled occupiers unless it is satisfied that a reasonable alternative is available" even if only interim accommodation.[27] But the overall approach is designed to leave options open in each case.

The Court also emphasized that judges are required to go behind claims of general statistical progress and consider the actual circumstances of people challenging their eviction. Here, however, the emphasis was not on establishing a broad-based section 26 principle for challenging government policy but instead on "reasonable application of judicial and administrative statecraft" to avoid human distress.[28] The power to protect individuals facing eviction permits a court to intervene even in a case challenging clearly constitutional policy that houses the maximum number of people in the most efficient way but nonetheless permits short-term homelessness. That intervention, however, is limited to managing the details and timing of the actual eviction to protect the human dignity of the people involved. It does not include ordering changes to the policy.[29]

[24] *Port Elizabeth, supra* note 2. *See* discussion in Ch. 6.

[25] *Port Elizabeth, supra* note 2, [14].

[26] Ibid., [20–23]. [27] Ibid., [28]. [28] Ibid., [29].

[29] Ibid. Justice Sachs says that the existence of a policy designed to house the maximum amount of people in the most efficient way would "go a long way towards establishing a context that would ensure that a proposed eviction would be just and equitable. It falls short, however, *from being determinative of whether and under what conditions an actual eviction order should be made in a particular case.*" Ibid. (emphasis added).

The stronger authority the Court asserted in *Port Elizabeth* thus didn't primarily involve constitutional interpretation but instead rested on this creative and flexible judicial role that is keenly sensitive to the situation of real people facing homelessness and that actively works to mitigate that situation in individual cases. Justice Sachs described powerful tools judges can use in this role, including the possibility of blocking the government from evicting a person and ordering the government to devise a humane solution. Moreover, this shift to addressing the specific situations of individuals facing homelessness transformed *Grootboom*'s exclusively programmatic right into a limited individually enforceable one.

That same emphasis on individual situations, however, also avoids easily identifiable constitutional principles that apply in future cases. *Grootboom*'s focus on overall policies essentially ignored the specific circumstances of the plaintiffs in the case but set a significant precedent that has shaped legislation, policy, and a substantial jurisprudence around evictions.[30] *Port Elizabeth* sets up an approach designed to do the opposite. Rather than identify concrete constitutional or statutory requirements, judges balance a set of "interactive, complementary and mutually reinforcing" rights through "a close analysis of the actual specifics of each case."[31]

B. The eviction model

The eviction model closely tracks the judicial role *Port Elizabeth* prescribes. The model incorporates two complementary roles that give courts considerable authority to enforce section 26: (1) the power to intervene directly through a combination of *Grootboom* and PIE (and sometimes other statutes) to temporarily stop evictions based on the strong principle that evictions are never permissible unless alternative accommodation is available; and (2) procedural tools to manage the dispute closely, including by ordering meaningful engagement, joining relevant government entities (and others), and requiring those entities to submit information about policy-planning and budgeting processes related to housing.

The first role turns *Port Elizabeth*'s suggestion that courts should be reluctant to order evictions where no alternative accommodation is

[30] Liebenberg points out that this programmatic focus was enabled by the settlement that the parties reached addressing their specific situation. Liebenberg, *supra* note 4.
[31] *Port Elizabeth, supra* note 2, [35].

available into a strong principle that occupiers' section 26(3) rights temporarily trump property owners' section 25 rights in all such cases. The second expands the managerial role *Port Elizabeth* recognized by creating explicit procedural powers that allow courts to more effectively resolve eviction challenges in rights-protective ways.

Both roles establish concrete obligations on the state that are connected to section 26 and so involve some indirect substantive elaboration of the right to housing. But the substantive principles the Court has developed operate primarily to strengthen its procedural authority under the eviction model. This is first because they do not depend on – and indeed risk actively constraining – any further elaboration of either PIE or section 26. The principle that PIE never permits eviction without temporary accommodation allows a court to stop an eviction without analyzing PIE's factors or saying anything about section 26. A court also can join other parties, order parties to submit information, and structure and manage an engagement process without further elaboration of either the statute or the constitution.

The combination gives courts substantial powers to manage eviction processes in ways that could prompt state parties to change policies and reallocate resources to make accommodation available in the short term. But by focusing on the eviction process itself rather than on the policies that either prompted the eviction or resulted in the state's failure to provide housing, the model largely abandons the potential for broader dialogue over the relationship between section 26 and housing policy that *Grootboom* initiated. Instead the Court limits its role largely either to preventing negative infringements that disrupt existing access to housing, or more often, to ensuring that the state provides alternative accommodation and otherwise executes an eviction in a more humane, dignity-protective way.

1. *Incremental substantive development*

Port Elizabeth's description of a keenly sensitive court willing to step in to protect individual dignity in every eviction case enforces section 26 without entangling courts in the much messier task of assessing the constitutional adequacy of housing legislation and policy. Asserting the power to deny an eviction – and especially to deny it even where there's no apparent constitutional defect in the overall legislation or policy – carves out a significant form of judicial power. By intervening directly in individual eviction situations, courts can protect individuals and enforce section 26(3) without questioning the underlying legislative or executive policies.

Evictions lend themselves particularly well to the exercise of this kind of case-specific procedural authority. Even where temporary accommodation is available, an eviction means displacing a person and disrupting their life in dignity-compromising ways. Merely by delaying the eviction process, a court addresses the most urgent aspects of the constitutional claims evictions raise. By making the delay temporary, however, a court can avoid analyzing both the reasons for the decision to evict as well as the policies behind that decision. This authority to grant significant, immediate relief while placing only limited and temporary constraints on executive and legislative discretion, thus turns the deference to legislative and executive substantive decisions required by *Mazibuko* into a tool for strong enforcement of the procedural authority it recognized.[32]

This combination of stronger procedural authority that avoids the justiciability concerns fits the patterns Chapter 6 identified and explains the Court's shift from *Grootboom*'s more substantive analysis to *Port Elizabeth*'s hands-on, procedural approach. Those same patterns suggest that the Court is unlikely to build explicitly on *Grootboom* to engage even in a weak-form substantive dialogue over section 26. Nonetheless, the eviction model offers at least modest potential for greater substantive development of section 26 while still operating within the limited interpretive role Chapter 7 identified. *Port Elizabeth* and *Blue Moonlight* are the best examples of the Court moving in this direction. In both decisions the Court relied primarily on legislation to identify a set of principles that enforce constitutional norms. Using legislation provided democratic cover and also created flexibility for legislative response. Moreover, the primary legislative vehicle in both decisions was PIE's multifactor balancing test, which, as Chapter 6 explained, allows the Court itself to tailor the application of those principles in each case.

Although *Port Elizabeth*'s constitutional analysis largely reinforced the flexible management role Justice Sachs described, the Court's explicit identification of the constitutional issues at stake and also its integration of constitutional and statutory analysis in the interpretation of PIE provide a model that could, over time, incrementally develop more substantive constitutional principles in eviction cases. *Blue Moonlight*'s constitutionally attentive analysis of the statutes and policies at issue in that

[32] *Mazibuko and Others v City of Johannesburg and Others* 2010 (3) BCLR 239 (CC) (2009) [72–73].

case applied *Port Elizabeth* to reinforce several important principles that were implicit in earlier cases and also to extend them in modest but significant ways, in particular by explicitly recognizing that municipalities have independent planning and budgeting obligations under the Housing Act.[33] Both cases – and this general approach – reflect a more modest version of the flexible, context-specific elaboration Liebenberg argues could develop out of the Court's existing jurisprudence.[34]

Blue Moonlight's companion cases, *PPC Quarries* and *Golden Thread*, provided opportunities to continue this more substantive mode of analysis in the way Liebenberg advocates.[35] The Court could have engaged in an extensive analysis of the factual differences among these cases and identified how those differences changed the PIE analysis in light of section 26's overarching principles.

Both decisions clearly reinforce two of the central constitutional principles *Blue Moonlight* established: (1) municipalities have an obligation to provide and fund emergency housing even for people rendered homeless from privately instituted evictions, and (2) PIE may constitutionally limit private landowner's section 25 rights to evict even unlawful occupiers where those occupiers may be rendered homeless. But there was no meaningful comparative analysis of the cases and even individually very little discussion of the specific facts.

If we put all three decisions together and compare their facts, it is possible to identify some implicit extensions of *Blue Moonlight*. When it comes to municipal obligations, *Blue Moonlight* stops with the principle that a city's complete failure to consider homelessness from private evictions during its planning process renders the resulting policy unconstitutional.[36] In combination, *PPC Quarries* and *Golden Thread* lay the groundwork for arguing that municipalities are obligated not just to consider these situations in their budget and planning processes but actually to provide alternative accommodation through their own resources in some situations possibly irrespective of whether the planning processes were themselves constitutional.[37]

Furthermore, the simple fact that the Court temporarily stopped the eviction in each case should mean that under each particular factual configuration PIE's factors dictate striking the balance between section 26(3) and section 25 in favor of the occupiers. Courts applying PIE in

[33] *See* discussion in Ch. 6. [34] Liebenberg, *supra* note 4, 179–80.
[35] *PPC Quarries, supra* note 13; *Golden Thread, supra* note 13.
[36] *Blue Moonlight, supra* note 9, [95]. [37] *See* discussion in Ch. 6.

future cases under similar facts could build on these cases to develop a set of principles for more precisely striking that balance by identifying which facts matter in the outcome and why.

The Court's failure to closely analyze the PIE factors in *PPC Quarries* and *Golden Thread*, however, missed the opportunity to explicitly engage in this more substantive analysis. The Court provided no direct comparison of the cases and very limited discussion of which facts were significant under PIE's factors. In this respect the decisions are consistent with the Court's general reluctance to engage with the substance of the social rights in the second-wave cases and underscore the risk that the eviction model could fail to develop in a more substantive direction.

The accretion of fact-specific principles into a set of harder constitutional standards that work within PIE's framework depends on careful and specific attention to not only the constitutional dimensions but also the statutory factors themselves. The Court's analyses lack that interpretive precision and depth. In *PPC Quarries* – where the Court's direct order could have provided the most authoritative guidance – the Court tells us only that the combination of a property owner with no short-term plans for using the land and the absence of evidence the City would fail to provide alternative accommodation reasonably quickly mattered in the PIE analysis.[38] The summary treatment of even those factors and the failure to specifically analyze other, seemingly significant but countervailing factors, such as the existing interdict and the relatively short time frame of the occupation, provide very little guidance as to how to balance those same factors under different circumstances. The lack of any comparative analysis across the three cases further limits the guidance they provide for future cases.

Golden Thread is somewhat better on this score. The Court's detailed recounting of the facts the High Court considered (with occasional commentary) gives some indirect hints that these facts were legitimate considerations, and Justice Yacoob's conclusion that the landowner's lack of short-term plans to use the land should have significance in the PIE analysis reinforces the significance of this fact.[39] But the opinion explicitly refused to engage with the High Court's PIE analysis. Sweeping aside

[38] *PPC Quarries*, *supra* note 13, [10–12].

[39] *Golden Thread*, *supra* note 13, [8] (the High Court "remarked, correctly in my view, that it was unfortunate" the occupiers "had not said anything about the conditions that existed whence they came."; ibid., [18]("It is of some significance in this context that Golden Thread has not put the land to any use, nor is there any evidence that it intends to subject the land to use in the foreseeable future").

the applicants' "various interesting submissions and criticis[ms]" of the judgment, Justice Yacoob limited the issues he would address to the High Court's failure to order "the City to provide particulars of the applicant's housing situation and whether the City could provide emergency housing" and whether mediation was appropriate.[40] The Court's order was then limited to requiring the City to provide this information.[41] Nothing in the judgment suggests the High Court should reweigh PIE's substantive factors or how it should do so. The only real question left for the High Court on remand is whether to order the City to provide alternative accommodation in light of the information the City must now provide. This seems to assure the occupiers will obtain temporary accommodation, but it provides neither a model for careful exposition of PIE nor a sense for how to weigh the same facts in another case.

This lack of specific analysis strengthens the principle that courts should never order an eviction without alternative accommodation by essentially treating PIE's other factors as irrelevant. The Court's functional elimination of PIE's distinction between long- and short-term occupation in *Golden Thread* reinforces the impression that PIE's provisions do not qualify the state's obligation to provide accommodation in every eviction case. The applicants in *PPC Quarries* and *Golden Thread* argued for the Court to adopt exactly that principle, and the results in each case are consistent with it.[42] But the Court specifically refused to take up that argument in *Golden Thread* and tied the holding in *PPC Quarries* specifically to "the circumstances of this case" without saying much about which circumstances mattered or why.[43]

For courts trying to take seriously the mandate to apply PIE's test on the facts of each case, the dearth of specifically identified reasons for why the City incurred the obligation to provide accommodation provides little additional guidance.[44] It also suggests that these results may be better viewed as instances of ad hoc court management to bring some measure of dignity and humanity into messy situations attributable as much to

[40] Ibid., [12–13]. [41] Ibid., [21].

[42] *Golden Thread, supra* note 13, Applicants' Heads of Argument at [72]; *PPC Quarries, supra* note 13, Applicant's Heads of Argument at [88].

[43] *PPC Quarries, supra* note 13, [13].

[44] Compare the Supreme Court of Appeal's more careful treatment of these factors in the Supreme Court of Appeal (SCA) judgment in *City of Johannesburg v Changing Tides 74 (Pty) Ltd and Others* 2012 (11) BCLR 1206 (SCA) (2012). *See* Shanelle van der Berg, "Meaningful Engagement: Proceduralising Socio-economic Rights Further or Infusing Administrative Law with Substance?" 29 *S. Afr. J. Hum. Rts.* 376 (2013).

informal factors such as the City's extreme and persistent recalcitrance and the parties' concessions. In either case, the failure to develop a careful analysis missed the potential for establishing an interpretive approach that could begin to develop an incremental substantive jurisprudence based on *Blue Moonlight*.

These decisions thus mirror *Maphango* more than *Blue Moonlight* itself in the sense that all three decisions deliberately avoid substantive analyses that could create broadly applicable principles.[45] A similar reluctance to engage head-on with the substantive implications of the eviction model is evident in the majority opinion in *Zulu*. As Justice Van der Westhuizen's concurrence pointed out, there seemed little reason for the majority to limit its holding to permitting the occupiers to intervene and refuse to address the constitutionality of the interim order itself.[46] The majority in both *Maphango* and *Zulu* clearly wanted to reach only the issues directly necessary to leave open the possibility for the claimants to secure some relief and to avoid resolving the cases in ways that would limit its options in future cases.

Even where courts do nothing more than continue to stop evictions until temporary accommodation is available and manage the cases in rights-protective ways, that creates a significant tool for enforcing both 26(3) directly and 26(2) indirectly by implicitly recognizing the new normality Wilson described in 2009. But as Wilson also recognized, simply permitting illegal occupiers to remain on existing land until a municipality can find temporary accommodation is not a sustainable solution in the long term.[47]

On one hand, the situations that lead to these standoffs typically involve poor people living in desperate conditions for whom the state has failed to provide even basic shelter.[48] Equally problematic, the increasing number of court decisions applying this model to prevent evictions has not prompted systematic reform even within relatively well-resourced municipalities like the City of Johannesburg.[49]

45 *Maphango and Others v Aengus Lifestyle Properties (Pty) Ltd* (CC) 2012 (5) BCLR 449 (CC) (2012) ("*Maphango*"). *See* discussion in Ch. 6.

46 *Zulu*, *supra* note 14, [50].

47 Wilson, *supra* note 3, 282.

48 Ibid.

49 As discussed later, the South Gauteng High Court took the City to task for its repeated failures to fulfill its obligations following *Blue Moonlight*. *See Hlophe v City of Johannesburg*, [2013] ZAGPJHC 98 (May 3, 2013) [5] ("*Hlophe*") ("The City has had potential indication of its general responsibilities for a period of some 38 months and final indication of its specific responsibilities for a period of some 16 months").

If municipalities continue to be unable to provide even temporary accommodation for extended periods of time, private landlords in cases like *Blue Moonlight* are likely to return to court to seek to proceed with the evictions, raising the more difficult questions that the Court has so far managed to avoid.[50] Combining structured meaningful engagement orders with the broader procedural powers these cases recognized could begin to address these broader issues.

2. *Procedural authority and engagement*

The enhanced procedural powers the Court recognized in these cases and the meaningful engagement requirement the Court established in *Olivia Road* considerably strengthen a court's role beyond the basic power to stop an eviction until the state provides alternative accommodation. On a procedural level these tools expand the scope of the issues a court can seek to manage when resolving a particular case. Adding state parties and ordering them to submit detailed policy and budget information are significant tools in their own right.

As Wilson notes, simply joining municipalities to an eviction from private land proceeding turns a formerly purely private action into a public law matter that implicates the constitutional protections of section 26.[51] It also configures the case so that the court can take into account the state's constitutional obligations when deciding how best to balance the occupiers' rights against the private owner's. Incorporating the authority to order the state to provide information about its policies and resources gives the court even more options and requires municipalities to justify claims that they lack the resources to provide housing in a particular case. Combining those powers with a structured engagement order could extend judicial power beyond an individual case and into those larger policy questions.

By ordering parties to address the underlying policy issues rather than simply come to an agreement on alternative accommodation in a single case, a court also can use these powerful procedural tools to develop some substantive protections.[52] In the first instance a set of procedural

[50] *See* Langford, *supra* note 5, 218 n. 62.

[51] Wilson, *supra* note 3, 284–85. *See also* Gustav Muller and Sandra Liebenberg, "Developing the Law of Joinder in the Context of Evictions of People from Their Homes," 29 *S. Afr. J. Hum. Rts.* 554 (2013).

[52] Shanelle van der Berg argues in a similar vein that courts could use the meaningful engagement requirement's connection to administrative law to develop a more substantive

norms could flesh out both the process for negotiating alternative accommodation and the baseline requirements for such accommodation. The occupiers in *Blue Moonlight* attempted to use *Joe Slovo*'s detailed engagement order in precisely this way arguing it established a set of minimum requirements for emergency accommodation following an eviction.[53] A consistent focus on the underlying policy and budgeting process in individual engagements could turn eviction litigation into a forum for negotiating housing policy more generally and thus for enforcing section 26 outside of PIE. Rather than simply negotiating the details of the accommodation provided in an individual case, the parties, supported by civil society groups joined to the negotiation, could also address longer-term municipal plans and budgets.

These powers focus on the negotiation process itself and so put an even greater emphasis on procedural control over substantive interpretation of constitutional and statutory principles. This creates the risk that courts will continue to avoid directly elaborating constitutional or statutory norms in favor of managing individual cases. The meaningful engagement requirement formalized and expanded the managerial role *Port Elizabeth* established, but it also expressly disconnected that role from substantive interpretation of either PIE or section 26. Like PIE, engagement gives courts a tool to manage the effects of social-welfare policies in individual cases. Unlike PIE, however, which creates the case-specific opportunities to interpret the statutory factors just described, engagement focuses solely on the process the state used to develop a challenged policy. For this reason engagement in many respects represents the culmination of the shift toward proceduralization that characterizes the second-wave.

The procedural authority to join state parties and order state entities to report on the resources available for housing as well as their policy-planning and budget process shares this same procedural focus. This authority expands judicial power to scrutinize government decision-making processes without identifying statutory or constitutional requirements related to the substantive entitlements themselves.

As the eviction cases going back to *Olivia Road* illustrate, however, exercising these procedural powers can have significant substantive effects.[54]

set of principles. Van der Berg, *supra* note 44. The more substantive effects I identify here, however, do not depend on the Court engaging in the more explicit normative analysis van der Berg advocates.

53 *Blue Moonlight II*, *supra* note 13.

54 Marius Pieterse observes that substantive fulfillment of a right is often a side effect of the Court's procedural remedies and cites *Joe Slovo* as an example. "Procedural Relief,

Moreover, as earlier chapters discussed, where the Court is able to focus on procedure it has demonstrated increased confidence in its capacity to adopt a stronger role precisely because it can minimize the justiciability concerns and operate within the constraints *Mazibuko* articulated. This comes at some risk that the Court will give undue deference to the substantive decisions at issue and unduly limit the scope of its authority – a risk that *Mazibuko* illustrates. But the eviction model has the potential both to limit the risk of deference and to create opportunities for courts to take a more substantive role when exercising these procedural powers.

To begin with, simply by stopping an eviction until a municipality provides temporary accommodation and joining the municipality to the case sets up a situation that requires some substantive change to existing housing policy. In *Olivia Road*, the City ultimately agreed to provide a broad range of services despite initially taking the position that it could provide none.[55]

The Court's determination in *Blue Moonlight* that a private landowner's right to evict temporarily could be trumped by the section 26(3) rights of illegal occupiers to allow a municipality to find temporary accommodation is premised on only a temporary delay in eviction. This assumes that the municipality will change its policy or reallocate resources to provide temporary accommodation in a relatively short period of time. All three of the *Blue Moonlight* cases incorporate this same assumption that the municipalities in each case will reconsider their claims that no resources are available to house the people threatened with eviction and find some solution that provides housing at least in the short term.

Adding the procedural power to require a municipality to survey the needs of the people facing eviction and to provide information regarding its existing housing plans and the resources available to house those people enhances the potential for this exercise of procedural control to prompt substantive change in several ways. First, merely requiring a municipality to formally report on its policy and budgeting processes incentivizes close scrutiny of those processes to ensure they comply with the obligations section 26, the Housing Act and PIE impose. Second, courts can use that

Constitutional Citizenship and Socio-Economic Rights as Legitimate Expectations," 28 *S. Afr. J. Hum. Rts* 359, 371 (2012) (citing *Residents of Joe Slovo Community, Western Cape v Thubelisha Homes and Others* 2009 (9) BCLR 847 (CC) (2009)).

55 *See* Stuart Wilson, "Planning for Inclusion in South Africa: The State's Duty to Prevent Homelessness and the Potential of 'Meaningful Engagement,'" 22 *Urban For.* 265 (2011) (describing the settlement negotiations in detail).

information themselves to identify specific solutions to a particular case and also to give the occupiers and their representatives the power to argue for an alternative.

More broadly, courts can use that information to move beyond the particular facts of a case and identify systemic failures to comply with constitutional or statutory obligations that might have resulted in the unavailability of housing. *Blue Moonlight*'s analysis of the Housing Act and rejection of the City's resource arguments because its budgeting process failed to recognize the obligation to plan for the needs of people evicted from private property establishes the power for courts to interrogate and order changes to the underlying substantive policies in eviction cases.

Lower-court decisions, in particular by the SCA, have already started to develop this procedural authority in creative and potentially effective ways.[56] In *Changing Tides*, the SCA held that in eviction cases under PIE local authorities are required to do more than "file with the court a general report detailing its current housing policy" and that the report must instead "must deal directly with the facts of the specific case," including informing the court "what steps the local authority proposes to put in place to address and alleviate such homelessness by way of the provision of alternative land or emergency accommodation."[57] The SCA then ordered the City of Johannesburg to file a detailed report, including the steps it took to engage with a group of residents and their representatives before seeking to evict them.[58]

Changing Tides illustrates how courts could use this new procedural power to require municipalities to provide specific information and also how they can use that information to make engagement more effective in individual disputes by reducing the information asymmetry between residents and the government. Muller and Liebenberg argue that the same decisions the SCA cited go even further and establish that municipalities are obligated to provide the kind of broader policy and budgeting information that could expand negotiations beyond individual cases.[59] Specifically, courts can order municipalities to provide their housing policies; to identify the housing needs in the area and the government's capacity to address those needs; "[w]hether and to what extent the local

[56] *City of Johannesburg v Changing Tides 74 (Pty) Ltd and Others*, 2012 (11) BCLR 1206 (SCA) (2012).

[57] Ibid., [40]. [58] Ibid., [65].

[59] *See* Muller and Liebenberg, *supra* note 51, 567–68.

authority has sought financial and other assistance" from other levels of government; and the "availability of alternative land or housing for temporary accommodation."[60]

The leverage the eviction model creates to indirectly produce broader policy changes is the same leverage Duncan Kennedy argues antieviction groups could use to capture some of the economic surplus for communities that are being evicted from inner-city land because it is slated for new higher-value development.[61] Kennedy hypothesizes a range of substantive benefits a community – or the government on the community's behalf – could extract from a private developer that reflects part of the increased value. In the eviction model, a court judgment temporarily delaying eviction combined with the expectation the state will provide alternative accommodation creates a similar kind of leverage to bargain for beneficial policy changes.

Meaningful engagement provides a formal basis for exercising these procedural powers that strengthens the control courts can exercise and enhances the potential for substantive policy change. The eviction model begins with a temporary injunction that, as just noted, creates a strong incentive for a municipality to change its policies to provide temporary relief. In private-eviction cases that incentive is strengthened by the landowner's interest in obtaining an eviction order. By ordering engagement among the occupiers, the municipality, and the landowner, and also possibly other government entities and private organizations, a court can maintain a procedural role but still guide the substantive direction of the process.

The engagement order in *Joe Slovo* offers some useful examples of the kind of control a court might exercise over the engagement process to push for this kind of substantive change.[62] The order included an agenda for the engagement that specified seven issues for discussion.[63] Among other things, the parties were required to decide "the exact time, manner and conditions [of relocation]" and "the precise temporary residential accommodation units" for relocation.[64] By identifying specific substantive

[60] Ibid.

[61] Duncan Kennedy, "Comment on Anti-eviction and Development in the Global South," in Lucie E. White and Jeremy Perelman (eds.), *Stones of Hope: How African Activists Reclaim Human Rights to Challenge Global Poverty* (2011) 41.

[62] As Ch. 5 discusses, the Court's failure to exercise this control by requiring further engagement over the relocation decision itself was a missed opportunity to establish even greater procedural authority.

[63] *Joe Slovo*, *supra* note 54, [11–11.7].

[64] Ibid., [11.2–11.3].

issues the engagement has to address, a court first indicates the issues it considers relevant to the constitutional and statutory claims. Doing so at least implicitly interprets those rights in ways that could be applied in other analogous cases.

Second, establishing a specific substantive agenda can shift the balance of power in the negotiations by forcing the municipality to address issues it might have refused to negotiate over and potentially to provide concessions on those or other issues as a result. Analyses of *Joe Slovo* suggest that the City's policy reversal resulted at least in part from the constraints the Court's order placed on both the process for relocating residents and the substantive requirements it imposed on the mix of housing in the final development.[65]

A court also could combine engagement with resolution of specific substantive issues. The engagement would then focus on the remaining issues and establish a framework for implementing the final resolution. The Court's ruling in *Joe Slovo* that 70 percent of the new development would be reserved for displaced residents is an example of this combination.[66] Likewise the two engagement orders in *Juma Musjid* assumed the province was required to provide local placements for the children and were designed to implement that requirement in a way that gave their parents some meaningful input in the decision.[67] The Court's engagement orders in *Pheko* and *Schubart Park* followed the same model. In each case, the engagement was framed by a ruling that the original relocation order could only be temporary and that the government was required either to restore the residents to their homes or provide alternatives as soon as possible.[68]

To make engagement and these procedural tools effective, courts must be willing to closely scrutinize the engagement process for compliance with the principles *Olivia Road* identified. The Court recognized this in *Olivia Road* when it required a record of engagement efforts by municipalities and emphasized that "[t]he absence of any engagement or the

[65] E.g., Pierre de Vos, "Sanity and Humanity Prevails – For Now," *Constitutionally Speaking* (December 8, 2009), at http://constitutionallyspeaking.co.za/sanity-and-humanity-prevails-for-now/comment-page-1; Anashry Pillay and Murray Wesson, "Recession, Recovery and Service Delivery," in Aoife Nolan (ed.), *Economic and Social Rights after the Global Financial Crisis* (2014) 335, 347 ("It is possible to read the *Joe Slovo* decision as a narrative of success for meaningful engagement – after all, the government's ultimate capitulation resulted from further engagement ordered by the Court").

[66] *Joe Slovo, supra* note 54.

[67] *Juma Musjid, supra* note 8.

[68] *Pheko, supra* note 7; *Schubart Park, supra* note 10.

unreasonable response of a municipality in the engagement process would ordinarily be a weighty consideration against the grant of an ejectment order."[69]

Finally, the eviction cases demonstrate that all of these procedural tools are more effective where a court, at least initially, exercises greater control by enjoining the challenged activity and overseeing the engagement process. The Court's willingness to exercise this kind of control in *Joe Slovo* appears to have played a significant role in the City's change in policy. In contrast, the Court's refusal to reassert control in *Blue Moonlight II* made the order much less effective and resulted in protracted enforcement litigation in the High Court.[70] Increasing court control over the process, imposing sanctions for failures to engage, and deploying temporary injunctions during engagement each could enhance the effectiveness of the remedy.

By deploying engagement and these related procedural powers in a more structured and assertive way, courts also could expand the incremental substantive potential of the eviction model in two ways. First, by refining and expanding *Olivia Road*'s criteria, courts can develop procedural requirements that could be used in other cases even absent engagement. As noted, the occupiers in *Blue Moonlight* argued the *Joe Slovo* engagement order established a substantive baseline for negotiations over alternative accommodation.[71] Second, close scrutiny and careful analysis of the agreements reached in successful engagements can begin the same kind of case-specific but flexible elaboration of section 26 that is possible through a more explicit analysis of the PIE factors advocated earlier. This kind of careful analysis is likely to come as part of a formal endorsement of the resulting agreement that could reinforce its connection to section 26 and thus its precedential effect.[72]

Several features of the process the Court described in *Olivia Road* could further enhance the substantive potential of structured engagements. First, the Court's requirement that the state involve civil society

[69] *Olivia Road, supra* note 21, [21].

[70] *Blue Moonlight II, supra* note 13. Stuart Wilson describes the efforts to enforce *Blue Moonlight*'s order in "Curing the Poor: State Housing Policy in Johannesburg after Blue Moonlight," 5 *Const. Ct. Rev.* 279 (2014).

[71] *See* Applicants' Notice of motion in urgent application to Constitutional Court (March 8, 2012) in *Blue Moonlight II*, available at www.seri-sa.org/index.php/litigation-9/cases/12-litigation/cases/36-blue-moonlight-properties-39-pty-ltd-v-occupiers-of-saratoga-avenue-and-another. *See, generally*, Michael Clark, "Evictions and Alternative Accommodation in South Africa: An Analysis of the Jurisprudence and Implications for Local Government" Socio-Economic Rights Institute of South Africa (2013) 32–34.

[72] I am grateful to Sandra Liebenberg for this point.

organizations in the engagement process brings broader perspectives into it. Civil society organizations active on housing issues will understand how the results of these individual negotiations may affect the broader policy landscape. Thus these groups can negotiate for policy changes that extend beyond the individuals involved in the specific engagement. At the same time, they can help alleviate the disparity in bargaining capacity between the municipality and vulnerable populations. The active and sustained role that the growing number of social rights advocacy organizations have played in eviction and service-delivery cases illustrates the importance of systematically including civil society organizations in the engagement process.[73]

For civil society organizations to effectively and legitimately fulfill this role will require close and careful coordination with local communities and social movements to ensure civil society organizations genuinely facilitate direct access to government rather than merely representing their views. Steven Friedman and Eusebius McKaiser have noted that the systematic exclusion of the majority of citizens from civil society organizations under apartheid has resulted in relatively shallow connections between most civil society organizations and the majority of poor South Africans.[74] Although acknowledging that groups active on poverty issues have engaged in much greater grassroots organizing and also that several social movements based in poor communities like Abahlali baseMjondolo have emerged and started to serve the same function, they argue civil society needs to continue to expand its grassroots constituency to provide an effective voice for local communities.[75]

The public-reporting requirement reinforced by the progressive-realization requirement in section 26(2) could allow individual engagements to establish broad norms through a similarly incremental process as careful interpretation of PIE's factors. Progressive realization requires, at a minimum, that the state cannot decrease the level of benefit provided without substantial reason.[76] The public-reporting requirement requires municipalities to document their engagement efforts and also the result of

[73] I develop this point further in Ch. 10.

[74] Steven Friedman and Eusebius McKaiser, "Civil Society and the Post-Polokwane South African State: Assessing Civil Society's Prospects of Improved Policy Engagement," 18–122 (2009), at http://za.boell.org/2009/11/10/civil-society-and-post-polokwane-south-african-state-assessing-civil-societys-prospects.

[75] Ibid.,17–19, 40–41.

[76] *See Grootboom*, *supra* note 2, [45]. The Court adopted the interpretation of "progressive realisation" put forth in paragraph 9 of the general comment to Article 2.1 of the International Covenant on Economic, Social and Cultural Rights: "'Moreover, any deliberately retrogressive measures . . . would require the most careful consideration and would need

any engagement. Citizens in a subsequent dispute will have access to that result and can argue that it establishes a minimum level of benefit from which any municipality cannot depart without substantial justification.

The reasonableness and resources limitations in section 26 give the government flexibility to argue either that a different level of benefit or modified program is more appropriate to address the particular circumstances in that dispute, but it must support those claims in the engagement process. During engagement, residents and civil society groups will have the opportunity to argue for alternatives not considered by the government that may adequately address the basis for that modified program or diminished benefit.

The detailed information that courts can now order could enable this process. As Muller and Liebenberg argue, requiring municipalities to disclose all relevant information regarding not only their existing policies but also other potential resources creates significant leverage for residents to identify alternative solutions.[77] Those arguments and alternatives could be the basis for implicit development of the obligations section 26 creates in other cases.

The Court's interpretive framework linking the substantive right in sections 26(1) and 27(1) to the internal limitations clause when interpreting them largely has been criticized as diminishing its force.[78] But through engagement, the progressive-realization qualifier has the potential to act as a tool for courts to enforce the standards developed through negotiations among the state, affected citizens, and civil society groups rather than mandated by courts. By managing a process through which these other actors engage with the state to develop substantive requirements that fulfill section 26, courts can operate within the confines of the role *Mazibuko* described while still effectively enforcing section 26 directly and over time develop a set of generalizable principles.

to be fully justified by reference to the totality of the rights provided for in the Covenant and in the context of the full use of the maximum available resources.'" Ibid.

[77] Muller and Liebenberg, *supra* note 51, 568 ("An individualized report of this nature would also contribute to a substantive interpretation" of section 26). Liebenberg and Muller argue that this information could be the basis for a judicial interpretation, while I am arguing it could serve the same function for party-developed solutions that could be used to frame arguments in later cases with similar facts.

[78] *See*, e.g., Liebenberg, *supra* note 4, 180 ("In the absence of a principled attempt to develop the content of [sections 26 and 27] in the first sub-section, the criteria of reasonableness review amount to little more than a list of 'good governance' standards for the State as opposed to fundamental human rights analysis").

For this structured approach to engagement to work effectively requires not only a process for documenting the individual engagements, which the Court recognized, but also a publicly accessible repository of those reports. This will give municipalities the longitudinal information they will require to make engagement more than a merely ad hoc process. More importantly, access to the results of engagements is necessary for individual engagements to serve as potential precedents for future engagements and also to allow for public assessment of the results.

Civil society can play a key role here as well. Groups that are consistently involved in engagements can both be a repository for successful engagements and advocate for rules and procedures to provide broader public access. Those same groups can, in turn, use those records as the basis for negotiations in subsequent engagements.

Finally courts could incorporate a more substantive analysis of the constitutional and statutory grounds for approving individual engagements in the same way *Port Elizabeth* and *Blue Moonlight* incorporated substantive statutory and constitutional analyses when applying PIE. *Olivia Road* specifically recognized the need for courts to carefully review the substantive results of each engagement process, noting that "[i]t will not always be appropriate for a court to approve all agreements entered into consequent upon engagement."[79] If courts explicitly identify the statutory and constitutional norms at stake and how a particular settlement satisfies those norms they can elaborate and refine them across cases. Doing so will complement and expand the close analysis of PIE's factors in the initial decision to issue a temporary injunction and order engagement.[80]

Over time, then, engagement can establish a generalizable, but still flexible, set of both process norms and substantive requirements for section 26 that can be applied and modified in later cases. The public-reporting requirement would permit broad access to these norms. The involvement of civil society could help ensure that the government does not depart from these norms in later cases and that modifications are justified by the particular circumstances in each case. The continuing obligation to engage in social rights cases creates an incentive for the government to incorporate these norms into policy development more generally and also to consult with civil society groups and communities when developing those policies.

[79] *Olivia Road*, *supra* note 21, [30].

[80] The detailed information courts can require also helps inform these kind of case-specific interpretations filtered through PIE.

There is, of course, always the possibility that state entities will decide to engage in bad faith. This could happen in one of several ways. First a municipality could simply refuse to engage. Second, it could go through the motions of engagement without offering any serious concessions and without seriously justifying that refusal beyond simply saying it lacks the resources. A more subtle alternative is if the city goes through the motions of engagement using facially reasonable excuses for refusing to provide additional benefits, such as increased demands from other sectors or legitimate differences in the situations between one set of residents and another that are in fact pretexts.

Those cases will likely end up in court, and the question will be how a court should deal with this kind of recalcitrance once identified. In the first two scenarios – outright refusal or obvious bad faith – it makes sense for the court, at least initially, to order further engagement with additional court control. The court also could exercise the authority *Olivia Road* recognized to reject a challenged policy not on substance but on the procedural ground that the public authorities failed to adequately engage in the policy-development process. The public-reporting requirement will give the court the benefit of a record from which it can assess the process itself and order the parties to return to the bargaining table with specific modifications. These could include a broad range of things, including appointing one of the Chapter 9 institutions with specific expertise to act as a mediator or, less dramatically, ordering more inclusive consultations with groups that were either excluded or not sufficiently included.

The option to modify the specific process also gives the court an opportunity, without directly interpreting section 26, to signal the parties in general terms through informal discussions or formal statements on the record what it thinks section 26 might require in a particular situation and in light of previous engagements. This technique draws on engagement's relationship to alternative dispute-resolution techniques and gives courts the kind of informal power to guide the parties to a constitutionally compliant substantive outcome without definitively resolving a particular issue.

Both *Olivia Road* and *Joe Slovo* provide modest evidence that this kind of repeated engagement under specific court pressure could work, even where a municipality initially ignores its obligations. In *Olivia Road* the very specific pressure the Court exerted forced the City to engage more seriously. In a left-handed compliment, the Court deliberately "commended [the City] for the fact that its position became more humane as the case proceeded through the different courts, and for its ultimate reasonable response to the engagement order."[81] Later in the judgment, the Court itself highlighted the fact that direct court pressure to engage and report back was "the deciding factor" that moved the City to make concessions.[82] But the Court went on to emphasize its preference that "engagement take place before litigation commences unless it is not possible to do so because of urgency or some other compelling reason."[83] In *Joe Slovo* the City reversed its decision to relocate the residents and agreed to upgrade the existing site in large part due to the challenges it faced in complying with both the substantive requirements the Court imposed and the task of engaging individually with each resident.[84]

Juma Musjid and the enforcement proceedings in *Pheko* offer further examples where the Court exercised more structured control to push for rights-protective outcomes but also highlight the problems sustained government resistance can create. The sequenced engagement orders in *Juma Musjid* allowed the Court to move in a different direction once it was apparent the parties could not agree on continuing the lease.[85] As discussed in what follows, in *Pheko* the Court has backed up its softer initial engagement order with more specific substantive orders and also ordered specific municipal officers to participate in the stalled process.[86]

The final outcomes in these cases are still unknown and raise the question of what happens in cases where the process breaks down completely, or the municipality persists in refusing to offer a reasonable program. As an initial matter, the Court has structured the engagement process to try and avoid this result. In particular, the possibility for more direct court control over a renewed engagement process just described will at least ensure that complete breakdown is possible only if the municipality takes an extremely hard line over time. In extreme cases courts can threaten contempt proceedings. Several lower courts have taken this route to force municipalities to take their obligations seriously.[87]

Nonetheless, when faced with repeated refusals to engage seriously (or simply a good-faith impasse) a court will have to assert more extensive control over the process. The key characteristics of engagement – its extended nature, the public-reporting requirement, and the political control it creates – leaves the court in a much better position to assume that role for several reasons.

[81] *Olivia Road, supra* note 21, [28]. [82] Ibid., [30]. [83] Ibid.
[84] *See* citations in note 65. [85] *Juma Musjid, supra* note 8. *See* discussion in Ch. 6.
[86] *Pheko, supra* note 7. [87] *See* Clark, *supra* note 71, 41.

First, the court now has a substantial record before it of proposals and counterproposals, including detailed justifications by the municipality. This enhances the informational base to assess the competing claims and thereby reduces the institutional-competence concerns.[88] In addition, once this process has developed over time, the court will also have the benefit of records of other engagements and can consider the similarities and differences of this particular situation.

Second, in state-initiated engagements, the city will have decided in advance to engage with this particular set of residents. Presumably this choice will have taken into account the larger context of the city's other responsibilities and priorities, and therefore ordering expenditures will not be as potentially disruptive as it would if the case were brought directly by residents. In other words, the political control engagement creates should give the court more flexibility to order some substantive benefit where warranted because it was a political decision to target these groups. For the same reason, any court-ordered relief to a specific set of residents will avoid the queue-jumping problem that the Court has been concerned with and used as a reason to avoid ordering individual relief in other cases.[89] In this way, engagement enhances the power to individually enforce section 26 in ways that extend beyond a simple temporary injunction.

The success of engagement as a procedural mechanism for developing broader substantive norms depends on courts applying it more often and more consistently over time and across different cases. It also requires a more structured and deliberate development of the procedures for engagement. A critical mass of successful engagements is required to begin the incremental substantive development that moves beyond individual case resolution. Developing that critical mass depends to a large degree on courts establishing structured mechanisms for engagement by government, civil society groups, and citizens.

88 *Olivia Road*, *supra* note 21, [30] (noting that engagement ordinarily should take place well before litigation commences).

89 *See Grootboom*, *supra* note 2, [92] ("This judgment must not be understood as approving any practice of land invasion for the purpose of coercing a state structure into providing housing on a preferential basis to those who participate in any exercise of this kind. Land invasion is inimical to the systematic provision of adequate housing on a planned basis"); *Modderfontein Squatters, Greater Benoni City Council v Modderklip Boerdery (Pty) Ltd* (2004) (6) SA 40 (SCA) (2004) [23] (discussing the "queue-jumping" problem identified in *Grootboom*).

C. Extending the eviction model

The eviction decisions are the best examples of the more authoritative role the Court has appeared willing to adopt in the second-wave cases when enforcing procedural rights and remedies. In the eviction model that authority is tied directly to the substantive principle that *Grootboom* first recognized and also to the procedural configuration of eviction cases, which allow for temporary but strong judicial interventions without extensive substantive elaboration of section 26 or PIE.

These aspects explain in large part why eviction cases have occupied a significant portion of the Court's social rights docket in the second wave. The jujitsu that turned *Grootboom*'s principle into an individually enforceable right to resist an eviction invites legal action in every eviction case. By issuing a temporary injunction to delay an eviction, courts can intervene to protect occupiers' rights without directly second-guessing or even closely scrutinizing executive or legislative actions.

Nonetheless, it's possible to adapt this formula and extend that more authoritative role to enforce the negative dimensions of other social rights in ways that have positive effects. *Joseph*'s recognition of a general right to service delivery provides the obvious starting point for applying this model to other basic-services cases. *Juma Musjid* reinforces *Joseph* first because the Court recognized the state's obligation to identify specific policies and measures for providing alternative access to services guaranteed under the social rights, and second because it applied a series of meaningful engagement orders to directly manage the case to reach a resolution that ensured continued access.

Juma Musjid also is one of several recent education-related cases where the Court has employed a largely procedural framework similar to the eviction model.[90] Litigation enforcing various aspects of the right to education in section 29 has grown tremendously since 2008, all but ensuring that more of these decisions will reach the Court.[91] These decisions illustrate another area where courts easily could adapt the eviction model.

[90] *MEC for Education in Gauteng Province and Other v Governing Body of Rivonia Primary School and Others* 2013 (12) BCLR 1365 (CC) (2013); *Head of Department, Department of Education, Free State Province v Welkom High School and Another* 2013 (9) BCLR 989 (CC) (2013).

[91] *See* Yana van Leeve, "Mobilising the Right to a Basic Education in South Africa: What Has the Law Achieved So Far?" (unpublished draft 2014), available at www.nylslawreview.com/wp-content/uploads/sites/16/2014/11/van-Leeve1.pdf.

1. Joseph *and basic-service disconnections*

Joseph established a free-standing, but largely procedural, right to "receive basic municipal services" and relied on that general right to hold that tenants facing potential disconnection of electricity services are entitled to some version of the notice and hearing protections provided by PAJA.[92] The Court grounded its holding in the "'special cluster of relationships' that exist between a municipality and its citizens" and the "constitutional commitment to a responsive and public administration."[93]

Joseph recognized that this relationship requires "the government to act in a manner that is responsive, respectful and fair when fulfilling its constitutional and statutory obligations."[94] Notably, the Court connected this relationship to "participatory democracy," emphasizing that "procedural fairness" in local government is "crucial therefore not only for the protection of citizens rights but also to facilitate trust in the public administration and in our participatory democracy."[95]

The strong presumption against deprivation of existing access to essential services the Court recognized in both *Jaftha* and *TAC* reinforces *Joseph*'s principle and establishes a basis for courts to scrutinize the underlying policies and budgets connected to individual service disconnections.[96] The Court in *Joseph* deliberately sidestepped the tenants' argument that disconnections of essential services violate the negative dimension of the right to housing *Jaftha* articulated by framing the "real issue" as "whether the broader constitutional relationship" between public service providers and local communities triggers application of PAJA's procedural protections.[97] Nonetheless, subsequent cases relying on that relationship and the broad right to receive essential services could bring *Jaftha* and *TAC* back into play by raising that presumption in a PAJA process objecting to a disconnection. Individuals facing service termination should be able to argue not only that the disconnection was the result of procedural unfairness in their specific case – as *Joseph* recognized – but also that the underlying policies and/or the implementation process generally fails to meet statutory or constitutional requirements.

[92] *Joseph, supra* note 12. [93] Ibid., [24], [44] (*quoting Joe Slovo, supra* note 54, [45]).

[94] Ibid., [46]. [95] Ibid.

[96] *Jaftha v Schoeman and Others, Van Rooyen v Stoltz and Others* 2005 (1) BCLR 78 (CC) (2004) ("*Jaftha*"); *Minister of Health and Others v Treatment Action Campaign and Others (No 2)* 2002 (10) BCLR 1033 (2002) [38] ("*TAC*").

[97] *Joseph, supra* note 12, [32–33].

The procedural powers the Court has developed in the eviction context likewise easily could apply in other service-disconnection or limitation cases to expand the range of options for a court. To begin with, *Joseph* itself provides for a minimum fourteen-day notice of service termination and the right to make representations objecting to the termination. This creates a more limited version of the temporary injunction that is critical in eviction cases. More broadly, where a municipality proceeds with termination without giving notice and waiting at least fourteen days, that should itself be grounds for a temporary injunction by a court.

In situations where a municipality complies with the notice and fourteen-day delay, *Joseph* recognized that the level of procedure required will vary in each case.[98] This provides a formal legal analogue to PIE's multifactor test and opens the door to bring court challenges arguing that the process was inadequate in each case. In addition to arguing that the pretermination procedure was inadequate, these cases could also argue that the underlying policies and processes failed to meet the broad requirements *Joseph* itself articulated for government action and also failed to raise other substantive and procedural defects.

Courts in either kind of case could order the government temporarily to restore service and issue engagement orders that are designed to resolve both the immediate dispute over the legality of the termination and to examine the underlying policy challenges. As in the eviction cases, courts also could join necessary state parties and require them to provide reports on the policy and budgeting processes necessary to address these underlying questions.

Applying *Joseph* to extend procedural protections across a range of service-disconnection cases fits within the second-wave patterns Chapter 7 identified because it gives courts a procedural analogue to the "dignified framework" the Court has more extensively developed in the eviction cases. Moreover, as the Court itself emphasized in *Joseph*, this framework also draws on the Court's parallel willingness to adopt a stronger role where it enforces democratic accountability through participatory democracy.

Focusing on the strong connection between participatory democracy and the framework *Joseph* establishes for challenging service disconnections more broadly helps resolve the apparent inconsistency between

[98] Ibid., [56–63].

Joseph and both *Mazibuko* and *Nokotyana*.[99] The next chapter argues that this inconsistency is attributable in large part to the political dynamics that Roux identifies and acknowledges that those dynamics in combination with the second-wave patterns suggest that there are limits to how far the eviction model could be expanded. The following comparison shows, however, that the relatively modest extension of the eviction model in other service-disconnection cases just outlined fits within those limits because it allows the Court to operate in a largely procedural mode and to enforce democratic rather than concrete substantive norms.

2. Mazibuko *and legitimate expectations*

Marius Pieterse argues that the second-wave decisions generally, including the basic-services cases, show that the Court has adopted an interpretive and remedial model that implicitly relies on something very close to the administrative-law doctrine of legitimate expectations.[100] As Pieterse summarizes the doctrine, where circumstances demonstrate that a person legitimately expects an administrative process to result in a particular outcome or decision, that expectation requires, at a minimum, a hearing before the administrative process produces a result thwarting it.[101] The doctrine clearly requires some heightened form of procedural protections where a legitimate expectation exists, but commentators and some courts also have extended it to include a more substantive dimension in the form of a presumption in favor of upholding the expectation "unless a compelling public interest dictates the contrary."[102]

Pieterse argues that "the *logic* and *method*" of second-wave decisions reflect a substantively and methodologically richer version of legitimate expectations.[103] The Court's "constitutional conception" is substantively richer because "it appears to be rooted in a particular conception of constitutional citizenship" tied to participatory democracy. The Court's method is richer because in several cases, including *Joseph* and *Joe Slovo*, it corresponds to the more substantive version that includes a presumption

[99] *See*, Pieterse, *supra* note 54, 368–69; Geo Quinot, "Substantive Reasoning in Administrative-Law Adjudication," 3 *Const. Ct. Rev.* 111, 113 (2010) (arguing *Joseph* and *Mazibuko* "represent contrasting approaches to legal reasoning in administrative law"); David Bilchitz, "Citizenship and Community: Exploring the Right to Receive Basic Municipal Services in Joseph," 3 *Const. Ct. Rev.* 45, 71 (2010) ("It is hard to explain why the [*Nokotyana*] Court avoids considering the right to receive basic services it had articulated only a month before").

[100] Pieterse, *supra* note 54, 368.

[101] Ibid., 364.

[102] Ibid., 364–65.

[103] Ibid., 368–69.

in favor of fulfilling legitimate expectations.[104] Pieterse argues that this richer conception underlies the stronger procedural authority this chapter has tied to the eviction model and meaningful engagement and also the indirect substantive benefits that have resulted from the Court's procedural interventions in several cases.[105]

Although acknowledging these benefits, Pieterse also critiques the Court's apparent reliance on the doctrine as limited by a narrow "concept of neo-liberal citizenship based on the existence of a commercial relationship" between citizens and the government.[106] Legitimate expectations to receive basic services from the government arise under this formulation "only in instances where 'customers' have, in fact, duly paid for them."[107]

Pieterse contrasts this neoliberal view of citizenship with the community-based, relational conception of the government-citizen relationship that David Bilchitz identifies as an alternative conception the Court identified in *Joseph*.[108] That conception elevates the relationship beyond a purely commercial one in which citizens are merely consumers of state-services and the right to receive services is specifically conditioned in the duty to pay for those services. Instead, the relationship is grounded in the founding value of *Ubuntu* and implicates a broad range of reciprocal duties and obligations.[109]

Pieterse acknowledges that the Court in *Joseph* and other cases has articulated both conceptions of citizenship but argues that only the neoliberal conception can explain the apparent anomalies between *Joseph* and the other two basic-services decisions. In *Joseph*, the tenant "customers" had paid for electricity, and the disconnection without notice unfairly burdened them with the consequences of the landlord's default. In *Mazibuko*, by contrast, the Phiri residents, whom the Court also referred to as "customers," could restore service themselves simply by paying for it, so there was no negative infringement.[110] Likewise, in *Nokotyana* the Court implicitly found that the residents had no legitimate expectation to improved lighting or sanitation, but the municipality's own decision to apply for upgraded status required a timely decision on that application by the provincial government.[111]

As Pieterse notes, *Mazibuko* used this neoliberal language, calling the Phiri residents "customers," throughout the opinion and specifically to

[104] Ibid., 369. [105] Ibid., 370–71. [106] Ibid., 375. [107] Ibid.
[108] Ibid. (citing David Bilchitz, *supra* note 99, 63–67).
[109] Bilchitz, *supra* note 99, 56–58.
[110] Pieterse, *supra* note 54, 376 (citing *Mazibuko*, *supra* note 32, [121–24]).
[111] Ibid., 369.

reject their procedural arguments, including that the prepaid meter policy violated either PAJA generally or the more specific procedural requirements the WSA requires for "limitation or discontinuation" of water services.[112] As Chapter 5 explained, the Court adopted an extremely narrow interpretation of both statutes to reject even the residents' procedural arguments.[113]

Pieterse attributes *Mazibuko*'s failure to consider seriously these procedural arguments to the narrow neoliberal conception of citizenship and the corresponding limit it imposes on legitimate expectations in the social rights context.[114] That same combination suggests that the preceding argument for expanding *Joseph*'s framework to other service-disconnection cases may depend on whether the people facing disconnection can establish that they are "paying customers" in the way Pieterse describes.

The eviction model qualifies that conclusion to some extent, however, because the Court in most of those cases was willing to intervene to protect *illegal* occupiers – people with no legitimate expectations under a neoliberal conception of citizenship. Indeed, in *Blue Moonlight* it turned the legitimate expectations doctrine on its head by recognizing that the interests of illegal occupiers temporarily trump private ownership rights in some circumstances. The eviction cases thus present a very different anomaly that requires some explanation.

This chapter has argued that the explanation lies to a large extent in the continued influence of the justiciability concerns and the Court's perception of their strength in each case. *Mazibuko* involved a large-scale program the government argued was designed to fulfill the social rights. Giving the residents even a procedural victory in *Mazibuko* would have required the Court to disrupt that policy in ways that directly implicated the democratic and institutional policy concerns.

By contrast, the Court in *Joseph* dealt with a single disconnection of service. Even in that limited scenario, however, the Court still refused to address the tenants' argument for expanding the scope of section 26(3) and instead recognized the largely procedural right to receive municipal services. This interpretive move mirrors those the Court made in *Olivia Road* and *Maphango* because in all three cases the Court invented or considerably expanded an existing right to bring into play a procedure

[112] *Mazibuko, supra* note 32, [115] (quoting section 4(3) of the Water Services Act (WSA)), [123], [131] (addressing PAJA).

[113] *See* discussion in Ch. 5. *See, generally,* Quinot, *supra* note 99, 124–36 (critiquing *Mazibuko*'s analysis).

[114] Pieterse, *supra* note 54, 376–78.

that has the potential to protect poor people but doesn't provide immediate substantive relief. In *Joseph*, finding a negative infringement of section 26(3) would have come much closer to expanding services by directly requiring reconnection, whereas the right to municipal services simply gives the tenants the opportunity to initiate a process for seeking reconnection. Applying PAJA's protections was one step removed from the 26(3) argument because it mandated only additional process (and notably a diminished process at that). It thus represented a purely procedural route.

The eviction model reflects that same procedural paradigm that keeps courts out of direct substantive decisions. The relatively strong intervention of a temporary injunction in many cases is necessary to enable that additional process. In the basic-services context that is likely to involve temporary reconnection. But reconnection in under those circumstances still fits within the procedural paradigm because it involves only temporary restoration of services contingent on the outcome of that process. The court is thus not responsible for the ultimate decision whether to extend services only for the incidental temporary restoration required for the government to obtain the information necessary to make that decision itself.

D. Limits of the eviction model

The eviction model illustrates the Court's greater willingness to enforce procedural rights and remedies and also how that procedural focus could have both incremental substantive effects and provide a basis for addressing systemic policy and budgeting issues that go beyond individual cases. The Court's decisions establish these more substantive and stronger procedural opportunities, and the general patterns in the second wave suggest the Court could be willing to take them up in later cases. Nonetheless, these same cases also contain some worrying signs that the eviction model might result in only a truncated version of that stronger role.

1. *Substantive limits*

The appeal of the eviction model from the perspective of the procedural approach of the second-wave cases is that it gives courts the power to enforce section 26 indirectly without further elaborating *Grootboom*'s basic principle and without directly reversing legislative or executive judgments or policies. A court simply delays the eviction temporarily and then structures a process intended to resolve the situation and possibly to effect broader changes but without dictating that resolution or ordering those changes. But exercising the procedural authority to delay evictions without at least articulating the case-specific factors that require a delay in each case masks the real role that the court plays and stymies the potential for that role to incorporate even modest substantive constitutional development.[115]

Justice Yacoob's opinions in the two companion cases to *Blue Moonlight* illustrate this problem. The cases expand the circumstances where courts can delay evictions without elaborating either the constitutional or statutory bases for that expansion. Both cases purport to apply *Blue Moonlight*'s principle that PIE's multifactor test can sometimes justify a court limiting private property rights by temporarily delaying an eviction. But *Blue Moonlight* only started the process of analyzing those factors, and rather than elaborating that analysis further, these two cases largely ignore PIE. The result is a de facto general rule – or at least a soft presumption – that courts will not order evictions from private land – regardless of the circumstances and with no reference to the PIE factors – until the municipality can provide alternative accommodation.

This strong, but temporary, right works within the Court's existing reluctance to develop expansive substantive interpretations in social rights cases. The Court maintains a seemingly context-limited approach that operates within the separation-of-powers and institutional-competence boundaries it has set for itself but nonetheless begins to develop a strongly pro-poor jurisprudence that extends across cases. But this unacknowledged and unanalyzed strong-form approach is problematic because it obscures the basis for the pro-poor results. This simultaneously strengthens judicial authority in the ways described earlier while severely limiting the scope of that authority.

On one hand the Court's approach eliminates the democratic benefits of a judicial-legislative partnership by effectively displacing PIE with a de facto rule that fails to even acknowledge, much less attempt to balance, the constitutional issues at play. More significantly, a rule like this misses the opportunity for the Court to build on the active interpretive role it adopted in *Blue Moonlight* and that could form the basis of a genuinely substantive approach to enforcing section 26 and other social rights. By always stopping an eviction regardless of the factual circumstances, the Court is able to assert procedural control without analyzing the particular facts, how they interact with PIE's criteria or what section 26 requires. Although this creates an important tool for protecting poor people from evictions, it provides no foothold either as a matter of judicial process

[115] *See* Liebenberg, *supra* note 4, 180; Pieterse, *supra* note 54, 371.

or constitutional substance for extending those protections beyond the eviction context because it's not grounded in any broader set of principles.

The second-wave eviction cases clearly have pushed eviction law in pro-poor directions and established important new tools for advocates representing potential evictees. In this respect, there is no question the Court has started to develop a meaningful enforcement role within the limitations of the second-wave patterns. But if the Court continues to deploy that role primarily in eviction cases and even in those cases to focus on individual eviction situations over the substantive policies causing evictions, it risks running into a dead end that easily could lead to the deference its critics predict.

Engaging more consistently and deliberately in the incremental substantive development this chapter described offers a partial solution to this problem, but one that the Court seems reluctant to take up. A broader and more promising route is for the Court to take a more active and structured role in establishing procedural rights and mechanisms that create leverage for communities and social rights advocates themselves to address the underlying policies at play in these cases. The next chapter addresses that possibility and argues that an expanded version of meaningful engagement can provide the doctrinal basis and practical framework for that role. Before turning to that possibility, however, it is important to acknowledge the challenges that have emerged in enforcing even the substantively limited interventions under the eviction model.

2. *Procedural limits*

The protracted enforcement battles that have ensued in the wake of both *Blue Moonlight* and *Pheko* provide a set of instructive examples for examining the limits of the procedural side of the eviction model but also the potential for more structured deployment of meaningful engagement to at least partially address those limits. The problems with enforcement in both cases illustrate the deep-seated institutional and cultural hurdles courts face getting municipal governments to comply with their social rights obligations. Addressing those systemic issues calls for more creative application of the extensive procedural powers the eviction cases have established. The Court in *Pheko* started down that road and was at least able to continue pressing the Ekhureleni Municipality for compliance by pairing engagement with a sequence of specific orders.[116] The Court's

[116] *Pheko, supra* note 7.

refusal to order engagement in *Blue Moonlight* arguably magnified the problems the High Court has been forced to address.[117] Despite this, the High Court recently has started to exercise the stronger managerial control available under the eviction model and gone even further than the Constitutional Court by identifying the underlying systemic issues that the City of Johannesburg has displayed dating back to *Olivia Road.*[118]

The Court's role in enforcing *Pheko* presents a stark contrast to *Blue Moonlight* and shows the need for further explicit development of the procedural side of the eviction model. Like *Blue Moonlight*, the occupiers in *Pheko* encountered significant problems enforcing the order, but the Court intervened several times itself by issuing new orders to push the process forward. The case remains pending before the Court, and so the final outcome is uncertain, but the stronger role the Court played seems likely to force an outcome that provides relief to the residents.

Over several years following the Court's original order, the Ekhureleni municipality repeatedly failed to provide alternative land and the parties returned to the Court several times for follow-up orders. In its most recent order on August 28, 2014, the Court found the municipality in breach of its constitutional obligations, ordered it to show cause why the Mayor and City Manager should not be joined in the case, and required it to identify any other officials responsible for complying with the orders to provide housing in the case. It also required the City to file yet another report by late November 2014 detailing steps it had taken to comply with the earlier orders, including purchasing and developing land to provide permanent housing to the residents.[119]

The stronger managerial role the Court developed in this enforcement sequence tracks the active role the High Court eventually developed on its own in *Blue Moonlight.* Both cases illustrate the potential for courts to use this management role to provide concrete relief in specific cases and advance the positive aspect of section 26 and other rights in eviction cases. But they also demonstrate the significant challenges courts face where the state resists compliance. The next chapter takes up both aspects and argues that extending meaningful engagement to reach the underlying institutional issues behind that resistance could help resolve it and maximize the substantive effects of this managerial role.

[117] *Blue Moonlight II*, *supra* note 13. For a detailed description of the enforcement battles, *see* Jackie Dugard, "Beyond Blue Moonlight: The Implications of Judicial Avoidance in Relation to the Provision of Alternative Housing," 5 *Const. Ct. Rev.* 265 (2014).

[118] *See Hlophe*, *supra* note 49.

[119] August 28, 2014, Order, at www.seri-sa.org/images/280814_Pheko_Order.pdf.

In a follow-up proceeding to *Blue Moonlight*, the Court rejected the opportunity to use meaningful engagement in ways that might have prevented serious problems with implementation that later developed.[120] With the deadline for relocation fast approaching and no real communication from the City, the occupiers filed an urgent application with the Court requesting that it enforce or modify its original order.[121] Among other things, the modifications they sought included a delay in the eviction date and a ruling that the original order required the City to meaningfully engage the occupiers over the details of the relocation.[122]

The Court rejected the application on formal procedural grounds, characterizing it as "the usual 'set aside and replace' kind of order made in an appeal" that "effectively became an order of the High Court."[123] It also distinguished the order in *Joe Slovo* where it had retained jurisdiction and issued detailed engagement requirements as an unusual example "that made clear the Court itself chose to regulate and oversee their execution."[124] Finally it declined to consider whether orders like this one that condition eviction on the provision of temporary accommodation implicitly require meaningful engagement over the specific conditions of that accommodation as the *Joe Slovo* order required.[125]

The Court's refusal to follow *Joe Slovo*'s example and exercise some control over the enforcement process in *Blue Moonlight* resulted in considerable problems implementing the judgment. In June 2012 the occupiers secured a High Court order requiring the City of Johannesburg to provide accommodation before they were evicted. The City failed to provide accommodation by the deadline and instead filed a report with the court stating it lacked the resources to satisfy the order.[126] The occupiers then brought a new action to enforce the accommodation order. The High Court confirmed the original order and once again required the City to report back by March 20, 2013, providing details on the accommodation it would provide. In this second report, the city stated it was still unable to provide accommodation and requested an indefinite delay.[127]

Following this second report the High Court "invit[ed]" the Executive Mayor, City Manager, and Director of Housing to attend a hearing to address concerns about the city's reports. Among other things the court was concerned that the city waited eight months after the original High Court order to even begin identifying accommodation; its reports for the

[120] *Blue Moonlight II*, *supra* note 13. [121] Ibid., [1].
[122] Ibid., [5–6]. [123] Ibid., [8]. [124] Ibid., [12].
[125] Ibid., [16–18]. [126] *Hlophe*, *supra* note 49, [1–8].
[127] Ibid., [1–20] (describing the procedural history).

court were prepared by lawyers rather than officials with substantive expertise in "planning, budgetary, town planning, urban development and housing"; and the reports focused on excuses rather than finding a substantive solution.[128]

The court concluded that the reports "indicate an attitude on the part of the city which is only very reluctantly (if at all) compliant with the directions of the Constitutional Court."[129] Rather than giving the City yet another opportunity to find accommodation in this case, the court instead ordered the city to answer detailed questions about its overall emergency housing program and policies, including identifying the "structure or structures [that] implement the housing arrangements required to be implemented in the Blue Moonlight case, with reference to the personnel involved, skills available, liaison undertaken, time availed from other duties, management, and direction of implementation."[130] It also insisted the City could not simply identify alternative accommodation "and then state it is unnecessary to answer" these programmatic questions.[131]

In other words, the High Court embraced the broader procedural powers the Constitutional Court established in its eviction cases to order the City to identify its overall *capacity* and describe its general planning process for meeting the ongoing obligations *Blue Moonlight* imposed. In doing so, the court recognized that the City's failure here was merely a symptom of this broader lack of capacity and refusal to take seriously its obligation to plan and budget in ways that sought to develop that capacity. As the judge explained it, her pointed questions were "premised upon a view that management towards an outcome must be planned, focused and directed toward that outcome" and sought "to address the many difficulties and problems upon which the City relies to explain its failure to take any concrete steps over the past eleven months towards compliance with the court order."[132]

The judge's detailed questions and focus on the City's general capacity to fulfill the obligations created by *Blue Moonlight* is an example of the procedurally active role the eviction model establishes and illustrates the model's potential to extend beyond individual disputes. The judge's insistence that the city answer questions about its overall structures, personnel, and planning for housing delivery reflects a concern with moving beyond individual disputes to get at the root causes behind them. The eviction model is based on the basic premise that municipalities have an

[128] Ibid., [21]. [129] Ibid., [22].
[130] Ibid., Order [34]. [131] Ibid., [32]. [132] Ibid., [33].

obligation to independently consider and develop the capacity for implementing their obligations under section 26. These decisions also recognize that the state is required to incorporate attention to its constitutional responsibilities into its planning and budgeting processes.

E. Conclusion

The eviction model illustrates the rich potential for even a highly proceduralized approach to allow courts first to prevent deprivations of existing access to resources protected by each of the social rights and also to exercise managerial control to begin to address broader policy and budgeting issues. Finally, legislative balancing tests like PIE offer some modest potential for courts incrementally to develop a more substantive set of principles without implicating strong separation-of-powers concerns.

The Court's consistent refusal to permit eviction where alternative accommodation is unavailable and authoritative approach in these decisions creates significant leverage for poor communities and social rights advocates to expand the procedural side of the model. The tools the Court has recognized – including mandatory joinder of government entities and the power to require detailed policy and budgeting information – have set the stage for using individual cases as platforms to press for not only individual resolutions but also for a voice in those broader processes. Meaningful engagement provides a useful framework for that expansion while permitting courts to maintain a largely procedural role.

The Court's shift back toward deference in cases like *Mazibuko* and failure to fully develop this potential itself in cases like *Joe Slovo* where it had the opportunity to do so illustrate that the internal limitations and political environment will continue to shape and limit the Court's role and that case selection could play an important role in developing and cementing this broader approach. The Court's own limits highlight the fact that litigation is limited in its capacity to activate the full potential of the social rights, especially the need for policies that are not only tied to emergency situations like evictions and service cutoffs. The well-documented resistance by even well-resourced municipalities to accept the obligations the Court has imposed in these cases reinforce the limits of litigation and point to the need for leverage that produces more consistent, long-term pressure for reform. The next chapter explores the possibility for meaningful engagement to provide a vehicle for that kind of pressure.

9

Democratic engagement

The previous chapter examined the eviction model and the authority it creates for courts to enforce the social rights within the procedurally focused role *Mazibuko* described and the overall limits of the second-wave decisions. The heart of the model is a flexible approach that uses a set of procedural techniques for managing individual cases to reach rights-protective outcomes. Although it is primarily procedural in nature, that managerial role has the potential to develop modest substantive principles incrementally through legislation like PIE and the Housing Act. The eviction model also creates opportunities for courts to extend that authority to influence broader policy and budgeting processes indirectly. By routinely joining state parties and requiring them to provide information regarding the underlying policies at issue, courts put those policies in play in individual cases.

This broader role could allow courts to use individual cases as platforms to more systematically address broader policies and initiate systemic changes in ways that more effectively enforce social rights. To fully exploit this potential, however, requires first that courts more explicitly recognize this authority and second, that they begin to use it to create routine access for poor communities and social rights activists to policy and budgeting processes. Expanding meaningful engagement – in particular the political opportunities it creates for poor communities and their advocates to influence policy making – offers a related, largely procedural route for the Court to more directly address underlying policies while still operating within the substantive constraints that are characteristic of *Mazibuko* and the other the second-wave cases.

The Court has articulated a strongly participatory conception of democracy and exercised the authority to enforce substantial participation rights in a series of cases dealing with legislative obligations to engage with the public.[1] *Mazibuko* relied on that same participatory conception

[1] *See Doctors for Life International v Speaker of the National Assembly and Others* 2006 (12) BCLR 1399 (CC) (2006) ("*Doctors for Life*"); *Matatiele Municipality and Others v President*

of democracy and identified the social rights as tools for enforcing it.[2] Connecting the second-wave cases to the Court's jurisprudence on participatory democracy expands the doctrinal basis for using meaningful engagement as a tool to create access to state planning and policy processes while maintaining a largely procedural approach.

Drawing this connection capitalizes on *Mazibuko*'s framework in which judicial authority to enforce the social rights is strongest where courts scrutinize the democratic accountability of the state's process for developing a challenged policy and weakest where they assess the substance of the policy itself. This connection further takes advantage of the Court's apparent willingness in both lines of cases to scrutinize political decisions on procedural grounds and to issue relatively stronger remedies to address procedural flaws. It thus transforms *Mazibuko*'s emphasis on social rights as mechanisms for democratic accountability into a hook for an enhanced judicial role that operates within the overall patterns and constraints of the second-wave decisions.

South African legislation and policy recognize the same participatory conception of democracy that the Court has identified in these decisions. Several statutes policies specifically require municipalities to develop and implement mechanisms for citizen participation in all aspects of policy and planning.[3] These statutes and policies provide a thick formal legal framework and a legislative mandate for the Court to extend meaningful engagement into policy making at the local level. This thick framework

of the Republic of South Africa and Others 2007 (1) BCLR 47 (CC) (2006) ("*Matatiele*"). As discussed later, the Court has retreated from this conception in two other democratic-rights cases, *Merafong Demarcation Forum and Others v President of the Republic of South Africa and Others* 2008 (10) BCLR 968 (CC) (2008) ("*Merafong*") and *Poverty Alleviation Network and Others v President of the Republic of South Africa* 2010 6 BCLR 520 (2010) (CC) ("*Poverty Alleviation Network*"). In several more recent decisions the Court has shifted back toward a stronger conception of democracy and a more authoritative role enforcing democratic accountability. *See* Theunis Roux, "The South African Constitutional Court's Democratic Rights Jurisprudence: A Response to Samuel Issacharoff," 5 *Const. Ct. Rev.* 33 (2014).

2 *Mazibuko and Others v City of Johannesburg and Others* 2010 BCLR 239 (CC) (2009).

3 *See* Jaap De Visser, *Developmental Local Government: A Case Study of South Africa* (2005), 99–111; Christopher Mbazira, "Service Delivery Protests, Struggle for Rights and the Failure of Local Democracy in South Africa and Uganda: Parallels and Divergences," 29 *S. Afr. J. Hum. Rts* 251 (2013); Laurence Piper and Lubna Nadvi, "Popular Mobilization, Party Dominance and Participatory Governance in South Africa," in Laura Thompson and Chris Tapscott (eds.), *Citizenship and Social Movements: Perspectives from the Global South* (2010) 217.

creates the same kind of democratic cover that the Court has relied on in the second-wave cases to adopt a more authoritative role.

The national government increasingly has identified participatory governance mechanisms as a key part of the solution to the widely recognized problems that have hampered local governments in delivering basic services and as a response to the related dramatic rise in service-delivery protests dating back to 2004.[4] In practice, however, the extensive participation rights in legislation and policy largely have failed to generate significant community participation in local government.[5] Moreover, the ANC and national politics play a large role in both creating and perpetuating the political-patronage, corruption, and mismanagement problems at the local level.[6] There is a direct relationship between these governance failures – including the lack of meaningful community participation – and the failure of local governments to fulfill their obligations under the social rights.[7]

The connection between service-delivery failures and the lack of meaningful and effective community participation is consistent with the literature on "participatory governance" that argues bureaucratic failures often result from democratic deficits and prescribes expanding participation in state decision-making as a tool to deepen democracy, improve state performance, and increase social justice.[8] Participatory governance is closely connected to the related concepts of democratic experimentalism and

[4] *See* B. Leon and J. Timm, "Strengthening Citizen-Government Partnerships for Monitoring Frontline Service Delivery in South Africa," Citizen-Based Monitoring Paper to SAMEA Conference (2013); National Planning Commission, *National Development Plan 2030: Our Future – Make It Work* (2012) (NDP).

[5] Andrew Siddle and Thomas A. Koelble, *The Failure of Decentralisation in South African Local Government: Complexity and Unanticipated Consequences* (2012), Ch. 9; Mirjam van Donk, "Tackling the 'Governance Deficit' to Reinvigorate Participatory Local Governance," in Good Governance Learning Network, *Putting Participation at the Heart of Development//Putting Development at the Heart of Participation: A Civil Society Perspective on Local Governance in South Africa* (2012) 14; Jackie Dugard, "Urban Basic Services: Rights, Reality and Resistance," in Malcolm Langford *et al.* (eds.), *Socio-Economic Rights in South Africa: Symbols or Substance?* (2014), 275.

[6] *See* Siddle and Koelble, *supra* note 5, 118, 199–200; Piper and Nadvi, *supra* note 3, 234; Patrick Heller, "Democracy, Participatory Politics and Development: Some Comparative Lessons from Brazil, India and South Africa," 44 *Polity* 643 (2012).

[7] Mbazira, *supra* note 3, 252.

[8] *See, generally*, Michael Goodhart (ed.), "Democratic Imperatives: Innovations in Rights, Participation and Economic Citizenship: Report of the Task Force on Democracy, Economic Security and Social Justice in a Volatile World," American Political Science Association Task Force on Democracy, Economic Security and Social Justice in a Volatile World Final Report (2012), 47–50; Heller, *supra* note 6; Archon Fung and Erik Olin Wright, "Deepening

experimentalist governance discussed in earlier chapters.[9] Participatory governance and experimentalist governance theorize that broadly participatory structures not only deepen democracy but also improve state policy-making processes and outcomes by making them more transparent, accountable, and accessible.[10]

The emphasis on institutional reform in these literatures in turn overlaps with what Charles Epp calls the "legalized-accountability model."[11] In Epp's account, formal legal rights in the USA and the United Kingdom became genuinely effective when they were implemented through reform of bureaucracies and administrative processes to make them more accountable to legal norms.[12] Like both participatory governance and experimentalism, legalized accountability identifies a set of common principles for reforming institutional structures and practices.[13] Legalized accountability is focused specifically on making institutions responsive to legal norms, whereas experimentalism and participatory governance identify reforms that make those institutions more responsive, accessible, and effective.[14]

Taken together these theoretical frameworks support the argument that expanding the Court's procedural enforcement approach to instigate institutional reforms aimed at giving poor communities and social rights advocates greater access to policy and budgeting processes could

Democracy: Innovations in Empowered Participatory Governance," 29 *Pol. & Soc'y* 5 (2001).

9 E.g., Charles F. Sabel and Jonathan Zeitlin (eds.), *Experimentalist Governance in the European Union* (2010); Grainne de Burca and Joanne Scott (eds.), *Law and New Governance in the EU and the US* (2006).

10 Participatory governance and experimentalist governance arguably are distinguishable in their relative emphases on different kinds of participation. Participatory governance focuses specifically on opening up elite processes to regular citizens, especially politically marginalized individuals, while experimentalist governance does not distinguish between participation by elites and non-elites. *See* Goodhart, *supra* note 8, 47–50; Charles F. Sabel and Jonathan Zeitlin, "Experimentalist Governance," in David Levi-Faur (ed.), *The Oxford Handbook of Governance* (2012) 169; Grainne de Burca, "New Governance and Experimentalism: An Introduction," 2 *Wis. L. Rev.* 227 (2010). For a critical perspective on the potential for experimentalist approaches to address poverty, *see* David A. Super, "Laboratories of Destitution: Democratic Experimentalism and the Failure of Antipoverty Law," 157 *U. Pa. L. Rev.* 541 (2008).

11 Charles R. Epp, *Making Rights Real: Activists, Bureaucrats and the Creation of the Legalistic State* (2010).

12 Ibid. 13 Ibid.

14 E.g., Fung and Wright, *supra* note 8, 18–24; Charles F. Sabel and William H. Simon, "Destabilization Rights: How Public Law Litigation Succeeds," 117 *Harv. L. Rev.* 1016 (2004).

effectively enforce social rights even in the absence of a more substantive jurisprudence. These same literatures also provide empirically grounded models the Court could draw on when ordering and managing participatory mechanisms to make them more effective.

This chapter first briefly analyzes the democratic-rights decisions in which the Court articulated a strong participatory conception of democracy and connects them to *Mazibuko*'s description of social rights as tools for ensuring democratic accountability. The participatory version of democracy the Court identified in these decisions provides a related doctrinal basis for closely scrutinizing the procedures government uses to develop challenged policies and for requiring greater participation by communities and civil society in those processes.

I then survey the existing statutes and policies that require extensive community participation in local government. These recognize the same thicker, participatory understanding of democracy the Court has identified and establish legislative and policy mechanisms for community participation. This thick legal framework reinforces the democratic legitimacy of the Court's ordering increased access and closely scrutinizing the procedures used to develop social policies.

Turning to meaningful engagement, this chapter identifies the central features of the Court's still limited engagement jurisprudence, which provides a framework for judicial interventions that give poor communities and social rights activists a greater systematic role in local government decision-making and planning. After explaining how the Court's own decisions provide a basis for intervening to make institutional processes more responsive to communities, I connect this expanded version of engagement – called "democratic engagement" – to experimentalism, participatory governance, and the legalized-accountability model. All three theories provide support for the argument that under the right conditions judicial enforcement of constitutional rights may be more effective where courts establish processes in which nonjudicial actors work directly with the state to develop proposals for reforming state institutions rather than intervening directly either to impose specific requirements or identify specific reforms.

Experimentalist review posits that a participatory remedial process like engagement allows official proposals to be tested "against the backdrop of much richer information about the range of arguably feasible choices."[15] Participatory governance applies that insight specifically to

[15] Charles F. Sabel and Jonathan Zeitlin, "Learning from Difference: The New Architecture of Experimentalist Governance in the European Union," 14 *Eur. L. J.* 271, 277 (2008).

poor and marginalized communities and suggests that expanding and systematizing community participation by those communities could "better align expenditures with democratic preferences, increase participation and accountability and decrease leakage, and make patterns of allocation more distributive."[16]

The connections between the Court's meaningful engagement doctrine and these theoretical frameworks suggests that judicial implementation of democratic engagement could instigate institutional reforms at the local government level that address both the bureaucratic failures and lack of effective community engagement that hamper fulfillment of the social rights. Engagement provides a constitutional basis for social rights advocates, community groups, and other organizations to press for systematic access to policy and budgeting processes. In the context of litigation, engagement could create the access necessary to identify systemic problems and propose reforms to make government programs more responsive to the needs of poor communities. Democratic engagement's requirement that the state institutionalize that access and its connection to both the participatory democracy cases and participation legislation opens the door for reform proposals that regularize long-term participation by local communities and civil society.

The chapter closes with a cautionary note. It returns to the Court's democratic-rights decisions to consider two related objections to the argument that the Court is more likely to develop the meaningful engagement requirement in the ways just described because it enforces rather than preempts this participatory vision of democracy through a largely procedural framework. First, in two other democratic-rights decisions the Court reverted to a thinner, representative conception of democracy and adopted a deferential approach.[17]

Second, despite the Court's explicit embrace of the rhetoric of participatory democracy in its social rights decisions, in several instances it failed to take up procedural arguments that could have implemented that vision. The most glaring example of this failure is *Mazibuko*, where the Court adopted a deferential approach to the several procedural arguments advanced in that case.[18] *Joe Slovo* similarly rejected the argument that the government failed to adequately engage with the residents

[16] Goodhart, *supra* note 8, 50.

[17] *Merafong* and *Poverty Alleviation Network*, *supra* note 1.

[18] *See* Geo Quinot, "Substantive Reasoning in Administrative-Law Adjudication," 3 *Const. Ct. Rev.* 111, 124 (2010); Danie Brand, "Judicial Deference and Democracy in Socio-Economic Rights Cases," in Sandra Liebenberg and Geo Quinot (eds.), *Law and Poverty: Perspectives from South Africa and Beyond* (2012), 172, 177.

despite the many problems several opinions identified with the engagement process.[19] The deference the Court afforded not only the substantive policies but also the flawed procedures in each case mirrors the deferential role it adopted in the representative democracy decisions.

These examples illustrate that the Court is still constrained by the external political environment even when it enforces procedural rights and remedies that otherwise fit within the patterns of the second-wave and enforce democratic accountability. Those constraints fit the broader patterns Chapter 7 identified and Theunis Roux's political analysis.[20] Both *Mazibuko* and *Joe Slovo* involved challenges to large programs designed, at least formally, to fulfill the social rights. This suggests that the Court may adopt this stronger role primarily in small-stakes cases with lower political salience. It also suggests the external political environment plays an important role in the scope and range of interventions the Court will make. In this respect, the increasing political pressure the ANC faces from the widespread failure of local governments to effectively deliver basic services could create an opening for the Court more consistently to adopt this stronger role in individual cases challenging municipal failures.[21]

A. Social rights and participatory democracy

In *Mazibuko* the Court identified social rights as tools for enforcing a strongly participatory vision of democracy. Reasonableness challenges under the social rights require the state to explain not only the substance of its decisions but also to "provide the information it has considered and the process it has followed to determine" that policy. Courts are empowered to scrutinize the adequacy of government decision-making processes closely and to "enable citizens to hold government accountable not only through the ballot box but also, in a different way, through litigation."[22] In this view, the primary purpose of social rights litigation is to develop "a form of participative democracy that holds government

[19] *Residents of Joe Slovo Community, Western Cape v Thubelisha Homes and Others* 2009 (9) BCLR 847 (CC) (2009) ("*Joe Slovo*").

[20] Theunis Roux, *The Politics of Principle: The First South African Constitutional Court, 1995–2005* (2013).

[21] *See* Roux, *Politics*, ibid., 392–97; Peter Alexander, "Rebellion of the Poor: South Africa's Service Delivery Protests – A Preliminary Analysis," 37 *Rev. Afr. Pol. Econ.* 25, 37–38 (2010); Mbzira, *supra* note 3, 267–69.

[22] Mazibuko, *supra* note 2, [71].

accountable and requires it to account between elections over specific aspects of government policy."[23]

Criticism of *Mazibuko* has focused on this explicit transformation of social rights from substantive entitlements into more specific mechanisms for enforcing the Constitution's overarching commitment to democracy.[24] As Wilson and Dugard put it, *Mazibuko*'s emphasis on democratic accountability makes social rights litigation "less a process through which claimants enforce entitlements than a particularly elaborate (and expensive) form of participation in policy making."[25]

This critique accurately describes *Mazibuko*'s substantively thin interpretive framework, but it ignores the potential for *Mazibuko*'s embrace of a deeply participatory understanding of democracy to ground a stronger enforcement role that could create leverage for more substantive outcomes. The Court has relied on this same participatory conception of democracy more explicitly to justify close scrutiny of citizen participation in legislative processes – especially participation by citizens who risk marginalization in the electoral process – and to order expanded participation rights. Examining these decisions reinforces the conclusion that the Court may be more willing to adopt a stronger role to enforce democratic norms and to issue stronger remedies to require participation procedures.

1. The participatory democracy decisions

Henk Botha has observed that the Court's jurisprudence on democracy "wavers uneasily between two rival conceptions of democracy and its relationship to the poor."[26] The first is deeply participatory. It "posits a dialogue between the people and their representatives and requires the state to take positive steps to secure conditions under which citizens can exercise rights of democratic participation."[27] The second is formalist and election-centric. Democracy is equated with ensuring procedurally

[23] Ibid., [160].

[24] E.g., Brand, *supra* note 18, 177–79, 182–83; Stuart Wilson and Jackie Dugard, "Constitutional Jurisprudence: The First and Second Waves," in Malcolm Langford *et al.* (eds.), *Socio-Economic Rights in South Africa: Symbols or Substance?* (2013) 54–58.

[25] Wilson and Dugard, ibid., 57 (citing *Mazibuko, supra* note 2, [159–69]).

[26] Henk Botha, "Representing the Poor: Law, Poverty and Democracy," in Sandra Liebenberg and Geo Quinot (eds.), *Law and Poverty: Perspectives from South Africa and Beyond* (2012) 79, 97.

[27] Ibid., 80.

fair and regular elections, and there is little role for people to ensure accountability between elections where the political branches act within the scope of their powers.[28]

The scope of judicial authority differs significantly under each conception of democracy. The participatory model "assumes an active role for the courts in policing legislative and bureaucratic decisions to ensure that they emanate from inclusive participatory processes and do not impinge on basic norms of democratic accountability and responsiveness."[29] The representative model calls for judicial deference to the political process except in cases of clear constitutional violations that undermine the election process itself.[30]

Reading *Mazibuko* as connected to the participatory democracy cases reinforces the possibility that where the Court enforces the social rights to police democratic accountability it may apply a stronger standard of review and exercise stronger remedial control. Although this role would not directly address the substance of particular policies and legislation, it calls for close scrutiny of the underlying processes in which they were developed and allows courts to require extensive participation in those processes. Meaningful engagement provides an obvious, if at present underdeveloped, doctrinal framework for applying this more assertive review standard and for defining the participation rights of poor communities and their representatives in policies designed to fulfill the social rights.

Connecting *Mazibuko*'s characterization of social rights as democratic-accountability mechanisms to the stronger participatory democracy cases first provides a separate doctrinal foundation both for the expanded procedural rights in the eviction model and for using meaningful engagement as a framework for enforcing participatory democracy – what this chapter calls "democratic engagement." Grounding both of these stronger roles in the squarely political right to democratic participation minimizes the justiciability concerns that have limited the Court's interventions in both the first- and second-wave cases. It also allows the Court to characterize interventions in the policy-making functions of the political branches as measures that will deepen and improve democracy rather than as necessary compromises of democratic principle.

The Court's more stringent standard of review and the strong remedies it deployed in the participatory democracy cases reflect the similarly assertive roles it adopted in the second-wave cases where it enforced procedural rights or issued procedural remedies. Viewing both the

[28] Ibid. [29] Ibid. [30] Ibid.

eviction model and an extension of engagement directly into policy making as part of these overlapping patterns reinforces the argument that the Court should be willing to develop engagement in the ways this chapter describes.

The following sections briefly summarize two early democratic-rights decisions where the Court articulated this strongly participatory conception of democracy and the more recent *Glenister* decision where the Court identified democracy with transparent, accountable, and responsive state institutions.[31] It then connects those cases to meaningful engagement and the second-wave cases' redefinition of social rights as mechanisms for democratic accountability to argue they establish overlapping doctrinal bases for democratic engagement.

a. Doctors for Life, Matatiele, and Participatory Democracy

Doctors for Life involved a complaint by the NGO Doctors for Life International, a pro-life group of medical professionals, against the National Council of Provinces (NCOP) for failure to hold public hearings during the passage of several health-policy bills.[32] NCOP is the upper house of the South African Parliament that consists of delegations from each of South Africa's nine provinces.[33] Section 72(1)(a) of the Constitution requires NCOP to "facilitate public involvement in [its] legislative and other processes . . . and [those] of its committees."[34] Doctors for Life based its challenge on that provision and related language in section 118(1)(a).[35]

Justice Sandile Ngcobo wrote the majority opinion that invalidated two of the challenged bills because NCOP failed completely to conduct public hearings despite substantial public interest in the legislation.[36] Both Justice Ngcobo's opinion and a concurrence by Justice Sachs featured extensive discussion of what the Court termed "participatory democracy in our constitutional order."[37]

[31] *Doctors for Life, supra* note 1; *Matatiele, supra* note 1; *Glenister v President of the Republic of South Africa and Others* 2011 (7) BCLR 651 (CC) (2011); *Justice Alliance of South Africa v President of the Republic of South Africa & Others* 2011 (10) BCLR 1017 (CC) (2011) ("*Glenister*").

[32] *Doctors for Life, supra* note 1, [2].

[33] *See* S. Afr. Const. 1996 §§60–72.

[34] S. Afr. Const. 1996 §172(a)(1).

[35] *Doctors for Life, supra* note 1, [4].

[36] Ibid., [211–14].

[37] *Doctors for Life International v Speaker of the National Assembly and Others* CCT 12/05 Media Summary. The Court highlighted this aspect of the judgment in a separate paragraph within the media summary of the case: "In the course of his judgment Ngcobo J dealt extensively with the importance of participatory democracy in our constitutional

In a rhetorical move reminiscent of Sachs's discussion of eviction practices in *Port Elizabeth*, Ngcobo connected the right to political participation to the apartheid struggle and the constitutional founding.[38] In a section titled "The nature of our constitutional democracy," Ngcobo cited the constitutional preamble's "[c]ommitment to principles of accountability, responsiveness and openness" and emphasized that "one of the basic objectives of our constitutional enterprise is the establishment of a democratic and open government in which the people shall participate to some degree in the law making process."[39] He concluded that "the participation by the public [in the legislative process] provides vitality to the functioning of representative democracy."[40] Public participation in lawmaking "promotes a spirit of democratic and pluralistic accommodation calculated to produce laws that are likely to be effective in practice. It strengthens the legitimacy of legislation in the eyes of the people." Finally, Ngcobo noted that participation "is of special importance to those who are relatively disempowered in a country like ours where great disparities of wealth and influence exist."[41]

Ncgobo held in light of this analysis that meaningful and effective public participation in the legislative process is required under the Constitution. The Court's role when faced with a claim that participation was inadequate is to inquire whether the opportunities for and degree of public involvement were sufficient in each case. The government is responsible first for providing "meaningful opportunities for public participation in the law-making process" and second "to take measures to ensure that people have the ability to take advantage of the opportunities provided."[42] The context of each case will dictate the precise level of participation required and can range from "providing information and building awareness to partnering in decision-making."[43] Ncgobo found that the provincial legislatures' failure to hold public hearings was unreasonable under this test and the legislation void as a result.[44]

Justice Sachs concurred separately specifically to draw attention to "the special meaning that participatory democracy has come to assume in South Africa."[45] Like Ngcobo, Sachs connected public participation to foundational constitutional values, including dignity, equality, and tolerance. Sachs went further than Ngcobo, asserting that the people

order and the nature of the constitutional obligation imposed on the legislature to facilitate public involvement." Ibid., [3].

[38] *Doctors for Life, supra* note 1, [108–9]. [39] Ibid., [111].

[40] Ibid., [115]. [41] Ibid. [42] Ibid., [129]. [43] Ibid.

[44] Ibid., [192]. [45] Ibid., [226] (Sachs, J. concurring).

"are accorded the right on an ongoing basis and in a very direct manner to be (and feel themselves to be) involved in the actual process of law-making."[46] Sachs went on to specifically emphasize that active and ongoing public involvement in the government is "not just a matter of legislative etiquette or good governmental manners" it is "a requirement of constitutional government in a legal sense."[47]

The question of the extent to which parliamentary processes implicate a right to public participation was also central in *Matatiele*, a decision handed down just one day after *Doctors for Life*.[48] In *Matatiele*, the Court invalidated a constitutional amendment that redrew a provincial boundary because the amendment process failed to incorporate sufficient public participation as required under section 118.[49] The lead judgment by Justice Ngcobo relied heavily on the *Doctors for Life* decision and featured the same emphasis on the democratic process values as that case.

Ngcobo opened the discussion of public participation with a thirty-line quote from *Doctors for Life* describing the centrality of "the principle of participation and public consultation" in South Africa's new constitutional democracy.[50] After surveying the range of constitutional provisions devoted to the principle of participatory democracy, Ngcobo concluded that South African democracy is founded on both representative and participatory elements that "reflect the basic and fundamental objective of our constitutional democracy."[51] These principles combine to require a "law-making process that will then produce a dialogue between the elected representatives of the people and the people themselves."[52]

b. Democracy and accountability in Glenister

A series of more recent democratic-rights decisions have identified a direct link between constitutional democracy and state institutions that are transparent, accountable, and responsive to citizens.[53] Although these decisions do not directly rely on the same deeply participatory vision

[46] Ibid., [230]. [47] Ibid., [231].

[48] *See Matatiele Municipality and Others v President of the Republic of South Africa and Others*, CCT 73/05 Media Summary, www.constitutionalcourt.gov.za.

[49] *Matatiele, supra* note 1. [50] Ibid., [50]. [51] Ibid., [57]. [52] Ibid., [58].

[53] *See Glenister, supra* note 31; *Democratic Alliance v President of the Republic of South Africa & Others* 2012 (12) BCLR 1297 (CC) (2012) ("*Democratic Alliance*"); *Oriani-Ambrosini, MP v Sisulu, MP Speaker of the National Assembly* 2013 (1) BCLR 14 (CC) (2012); *Ramakatsa and Others v Magashule and Others* 2013 (20 BCLR 202 (CC) (2012). Each of these decisions illustrates this more authoritative role. I focus on *Glenister* because it is directly connected to the social rights.

of democracy, they identify and apply a similarly authoritative judicial role in enforcing democratic values. Notably, they do so in the context of exercises of executive power that threatened those values either by flouting democratic procedures or undermining independent institutions or processes tasked with policing democratic accountability. These cases thus reinforce and extend the stronger judicial role the Court established in *Doctors for Life* and *Matatiele* when it enforces the democratic principles in the Constitution.[54] In *Glenister*, the Court grounded its authority in part on the social rights, thus connecting *Mazibuko*'s vision of social rights as tools for enforcing democratic accountability to this stronger role.[55]

In *Glenister* a majority of the Court upheld a challenge to national legislation that disbanded a specialized independent anticorruption police unit and replaced it with a new arguably less independent unit. A narrow majority found that the Constitution requires an independent mechanism to combat corruption because corruption affects the heart of South Africa's new constitutional democracy by undermining the Constitution's "democratic ethos, the institutions of democracy, the rule of law and the foundational values of our nascent constitutional project."[56]

Both the majority and the dissent rejected challenges based on *Doctors for Life* and *Matatiele* that Parliament failed to provide adequate public participation in the legislative process. Writing for the dissent, Justice Ngcobo quoted both decisions at length and reaffirmed that the participation the constitution requires "does not simply entail holding hearings. It must provide the opportunity to influence the decision of the lawmaker."[57] Noting not only that there were multiple public hearings in this process but also that Parliament substantially rewrote it following those hearings, however, Ngcobo found the legislation reflected a sufficient and meaningful participation process.[58]

The majority agreed on this point but overturned the legislation because its effect undermined an institution set up to provide a different form of democratic accountability by policing corruption in public

[54] E.g., Theunis Roux, *supra* note 1, 33, 62–63; Samuel Issacharoff, "The Democratic Risk to Democratic Constitutions," 5 *Const. Ct. Rev.* 1 (2013).

[55] *Glenister, supra* note 31, [198]. In a 2012 address, Deputy Chief Justice Dikgang Moseneke included *Glenister* in a list of social rights decisions where the Court adopted a "pro-poor stance." Dikgang Moseneke, "A Journey from the Heart of Apartheid Darkness Towards a Just Society: Salient Features of the Budding Constitutionalism and Jurisprudence of South Africa," (2012).

[56] *Glenister, supra* note 31, [166]. [57] Ibid., [32]. [58] Ibid., [34–38].

institutions. The majority emphasized that corruption "fuels maladministration and public fraudulence and imperils the capacity of the state to fulfil its obligations to respect, protect, promote and fulfil all the rights enshrined in the Bill of Rights."[59] Specifically corruption "corrodes the rights to equality, human dignity, freedom, security of the person and various socio-economic rights."[60] The majority acknowledged that the state is free "to choose how best to combat corruption," but emphasized its "choice must withstand constitutional scrutiny."[61] In an extensive analysis that accorded no real deference to Parliament, the majority then easily concluded that the reconfigured anticorruption unit was insufficiently independent.[62] The Court declared the legislation unconstitutional but suspended its order for eighteen months to give Parliament the opportunity to pass new legislation that complied with the features the majority identified.[63]

2. *Meaningful engagement and participatory democracy*

Both *Doctors for Life* and *Matatiele* articulate a conception of democracy that requires extensive participation in legislative and policy-making processes and featured a relatively strong judicial role in enforcing those participation requirements. *Glenister* adds a specific emphasis on the connection between democracy and accountability mechanisms designed to ensure state institutions are transparent and accountable and a similarly authoritative role for courts in policing those requirements. *Mazibuko* relies on that same broad vision of robust, accountable, and responsive democracy and identifies social rights as mechanisms for ensuring that social-welfare policies are developed in transparent, accountable, and participatory ways that respond directly to citizen concerns. The judicial role is similar across each of these decisions, and they collectively assert that courts have the power to closely scrutinize claims that raise democratic objections and to reject policies and institutional structures that are inconsistent with that vision.

This focus on public participation and accountability in turn connects to the procedural innovations the Court developed in the second-wave cases, especially the meaningful engagement requirement. *Schubart Park* recognized engagement's connection to the "[m]any provisions in the Constitution [that] require the substantive involvement and engagement

59 Ibid., [166]. 60 Ibid., [200]. 61 Ibid.
62 Ibid., [208–50]. 63 Ibid., [251].

of people in decisions that may affect their lives" and cited *Doctors for Life.*[64] Extending engagement beyond litigation and turning it into a vehicle for enforcing the strongly participatory version of democracy the Court has recognized in its participatory democracy decisions could expand the stronger role the Court has developed under the eviction model to exert more direct – but still largely procedural – control over social-welfare and related policies.

Olivia Road identified the broad outlines of engagement – and emphasized that the requirement is principally addressed to policy making rather than litigation, but it did not detail what democratic engagement should look like.[65] *Joe Slovo* confirmed *Olivia Road*'s requirement that the state is required to build engagement into the policy-development process.[66] Justice Sachs's concurrence, in particular, fleshed out in modest ways both the contours of democratic engagement and the expansive judicial authority to ensure the state meaningfully engages early in the policy-making process.

First, Sachs criticized "the frequent employment of a top-down approach" by state officials intended merely to report decisions taken rather than "involve residents as partners in the decision-making itself."[67] In a related footnote Sachs cautioned that the emphasis on "mobilizing" communities in the national housing policy "risks treating the communities as recipients of state largesse" rather than "as active partners engaged with the authorities in developing programmes and finding solutions to the problems that emerge."[68] This clearly requires the more substantial level of participation along the continuum the Court identified in *Doctors for Life.* It also highlights the independent dignity-enhancing value of giving poor people a formal role in developing policies that affect them.

Sachs went on to identify several specific problems with the City's limited engagements with the Joe Slovo residents. First, he noted the lack of a clear chain of command among the different governmental entities involved: "there were simply too many rather than too few protagonists on the side of the authorities. At different stages, the occupants had to engage with national and then provincial and finally with local entities."[69]

[64] *Schubart Park Residents' Association and Others v City of Tshwane Metropolitan Municipality and Another* 2013 (1) BCLR 68 (CC) (2012) [43] ("*Schubart Park*").

[65] *Occupiers of 51 Olivia Road, Berea Township and 197 Main Street Johannesburg v City of Johannesburg and Others* 2008 (5) BCLR 475 (CC) (2008) ("*Olivia Road*").

[66] *Joe Slovo, supra* note 19. [67] Ibid., [378]. [68] Ibid., note 49. [69] Ibid., [379].

Second, he cited the shifting and, at times competing policy objectives of the different players that confused the residents and led to their sense that the government had broken its promises about the availability of low-cost housing.[70] This reinforces *Olivia Road*'s requirement that the state develop the administrative capacity to systematically engage and a process for engagement training. It also highlights the need to incorporate poor communities early in the process.

Finally, Sachs emphasized the close scrutiny courts should employ when examining whether the state meaningfully engaged with residents. A court's role in reviewing the engagement process extends beyond traditional administrative-law review. When asked to issue an eviction order a court "would be hearing the matter *de novo* (from scratch), and making up its own mind whether the justice and equity requirements of PIE had been met."[71] This requires "consider [ing] all relevant circumstances and giv[ing] a full hearing to the occupiers."[72]

Together these cases establish the basis for expanding meaningful engagement into a tool for developing the deeply participatory version of democracy the Court has identified in the context of enforcing the social rights. Communities should be treated as partners, not aid recipients. Government departments responsible for engagement are required to develop policies and procedures to provide meaningful consultation on a consistent basis at each step of planning and policy. As the Court noted in *Olivia Road*, meaningful engagement requires a set of formal policies for establishing public participation and state officials trained in engaging with the public. Where multiple governmental entities are involved, they must coordinate with each other in the engagement. Finally, authorities must establish a system for creating and preserving a record of each engagement.

Courts themselves must develop procedures for evaluating the engagement process for compliance with these requirements. And, when an engagement fails and the parties resort to litigation, courts must be prepared to enforce the engagement requirements through sanctions.

Although not expressly connected to engagement, the other procedural innovations the Court developed in the eviction cases create complementary tools for extending engagement to policy making. The basic power to join state parties to social rights litigation provides a necessary predicate for giving courts access to information about policy-making processes. Adding the power to directly order reports about both past processes and

[70] Ibid. [71] Ibid., [393]. [72] Ibid.

future planning then sets the stage for courts to inquire directly about the nature of those processes and, in particular, the extent of meaningful engagement.

Blue Moonlight established that a municipality's outright failure to consider its section 26 obligations is a sufficient basis for rejecting both the resulting policy and any related resources arguments. This places a substantial burden on the state to demonstrate that not only its policy making but also any related budgeting process included consideration of the social rights. It's only a very small step to connect that obligation to the requirement that those processes also include adequate public participation as *Olivia Road* and the participatory democracy cases require.

The Court's criteria for engagement, including detailed reporting on engagement efforts, the need for formal training in engagement, and especially its insistence that engagement should begin early in any large-scale policy development give courts the power to scrutinize the way municipalities develop policies that implicate the social rights. By requiring engagement well before litigation, *Olivia Road* implicitly recognized that courts can and should use the process to address systemic issues, not just to resolve individual cases.

None of the later engagement cases, however, have developed the full potential of this stronger procedural role directly to order expanded access to policy processes. Instead engagement has developed almost exclusively as part of litigation, primarily in the eviction context. The eviction model illustrates that exercising this form of procedural control has real potential to protect the rights of poor people. But limiting the judicial role to resolving individual eviction disputes or even expanding the control to other social rights cases severely limits the power of the social rights to effect long-term change.

The High Court order in *Hlophe* that Chapter 8 analyzed provides some important innovations that set up the expanded procedural role just outlined.[73] The High Court implicitly drew on the expanded procedural authority the eviction cases established and further recognized that municipal planning must include a range of technical expertise relevant to housing delivery. It also recognized the implicit message of *Olivia Road* that individual cases are merely symptoms of the systemic problems within municipalities and that addressing those systemic issues requires

[73] *Hlophe and Others v City of Johannesburg Metropolitan Municipality and Others* [2013] ZAGPJHC 98 (May 3, 2013) ("*Hlophe*").

delving into the policy-making process directly rather than simply resolving individual cases.[74]

The order in *Hlophe* and the court's insistence on obtaining detailed general information even if the City finally complied with the housing order shifts the focus of individual social rights cases significantly closer to that goal. Rather than asking only why the City failed these plaintiffs, the order notes the clear link between this failure and others and the futility of repeatedly ordering the City to deliver a service it failed to adequately plan and budget to deliver.

Throughout the judgment, the court repeated the need for the City to address "planning, budgetary, town planning, urban development and housing" issues.[75] It also highlighted the City's extensive foot-dragging in the face of *Blue Moonlight*'s clear holding that it is required to plan and budget for these situations.[76] The point of demanding information about the City's technical capacity and planning process was to "propel the City into (if not a whirl) at least a flow of directed and focused action" to deal comprehensively with the problem of emergency housing.[77]

But the court stopped short of actually intervening in these larger issues. In other parts of the judgment the court took a constrained view of the scope of its authority as largely limited to resolving this case. Most telling in this respect, the judge insisted that the only purpose of her questions was the "provision of temporary accommodation *for these* applicants sooner rather than later."[78] This echoed her scathing critique of the city's presentation of its general efforts to house evictees as irrelevant to the original order that required only details of the "solution achieved" to the applicants' own pending homelessness.[79] By limiting engagement to a set of case-specific issues and only asking *questions* about the City's overall capacity, the court was left merely hoping to "propel" the City itself to solve these structural problems.

Connecting *Hlophe*'s use of an individual eviction case to interrogate and address systemic housing policy and budget issues to meaningful engagement moves past the mistaken perception that judicial authority is or should be limited to resolving case-specific issues in social rights cases. Rather than stopping with what was, in effect, an attempt to

[74] *See* discussion in Ch. 9. [75] *Hlophe, supra* note 73, [21.a].

[76] Ibid., [5] ("The City has had potential indication of its general responsibilities for a period of some 38 months and final indication of its specific responsibilities for a period of some 16 months").

[77] Ibid., [27]. [78] Ibid., [33] (emphasis added). [79] Ibid., [21.c].

embarrass the City by exposing its failure to take the necessary steps to satisfy *Blue Moonlight*, a court could use the procedural power these cases and engagement establish to initiate and manage a process designed to force the City to make those same changes directly. This wouldn't require, as the *Hlophe* court worried, judges themselves to take on the significant technical issues involved. Instead, the engagement order could structure a multiparty process that allowed the parties and their representatives to investigate these underlying policies and bring in the kind of outside expertise the court identified.

The Constitutional Court has taken only limited advantage of the capacity for engagement requirement to extend to systemic issues. In *Schubart Park* Justice Froneman recognized that engagement can extend to more structural concerns but nonetheless limited the engagement order largely to case-specific issues.[80] In an unreported order in another case the Court ordered outside organizations to participate in and facilitate an engagement process.[81] Both *Pheko* and the successive engagement orders in *Juma Musjid* illustrate further refinements including pairing engagement with substantive resolution of particular issues and managing the engagement process toward a new resolution as the process developed.[82]

Like *Hlophe*, however, the engagement orders in these cases ultimately focused on resolving case-specific issues or implementing case-specific orders. They did not directly address the systemic problems at play, and the outside parties the Court included had some stake in the outcome. As described, the Court's broad description of meaningful engagement and the array of procedural powers it has established through the eviction decisions create the authority to go much further than these examples. The next section connects this more robust version of meaningful engagement with the extensive participation requirements in local government legislation and policy. These legislative and policy mandates provide a thick legal framework for courts to develop meaningful engagement as a platform to require effective community participation in social-welfare planning and budgeting processes at the local government level.

80 *Schubart Park, supra* note 64, [42].

81 *Mamba and Others v Minister of Social Development and Others* 78 CCT65/08, Court Order dated August 21, 2008.

82 *Pheko and Others v Ekurhuleni Metropolitan Municipality* 2012 (4) BCLR 388 (CC) (2011) ("*Pheko*"); *Governing Body of the Juma Musjid Primary School & Others v Essay N.O. and Others* 2011 (8) BCLR 761 (CC) (2011) ("*Juma Musjid*").

B. Social rights, participation legislation, and democratic engagement

The appeal of relying on an expanded model of meaningful engagement to enforce social rights over developing a more substantive interpretive framework role is two fold. First, it responds to the justiciability concerns at the heart of the theoretical debate over social rights by democratizing judicial enforcement and focusing on procedural issues over the institutional-competence straining questions that substantive enforcement is likely to raise. Second, it fits within the confines of the substantively limited role the Court consistently adopted in the second-wave cases and explicitly articulated in *Mazibuko.* It thus takes advantage of the increased confidence that the Court demonstrated when it operated in a largely procedural mode in those cases.

Drawing the close connection between *Mazibuko* and the participatory democracy cases underscores both of those benefits because it highlights the democratic nature of judicial enforcement of participation requirements and also the stronger role the Court adopted when doing so. Both the procedural nature of engagement and its connection to participatory democracy are strong evidence the Court may be willing to extend engagement into policy-making processes and to maintain a more assertive role in both identifying and enforcing expanded participation rights. *Glenister* adds further support for a stronger judicial role to enforce institutional structures that ensure accountable, transparent and responsive government. The strong commitment to participatory democracy in local government legislation and policy provides a specific legislative mandate for using meaningful engagement to broaden community participation in local government. That legislation and more recent policies also provide a thick set of formal legal mechanisms for using democratic engagement to reform existing participation mechanisms or establish new ones. Finally, focusing on local failures to implement national legislative mandates could create greater political space for courts to develop this more intrusive authority.

1. *Community-participation legislation and policy*

According to a recent study "South Africa arguably has one of the most progressive policies on participatory governance in the world."[83] From the

[83] Van Donk, *supra* note 5, 13.

start of the democratic transition local government has been restructured to both serve as the "engine of redistribution and development and the main locus of participatory democracy."[84]

The central role of citizen participation was first formally outlined in two early policy "white papers." The 1998 White Paper on Local Government states "municipalities should develop mechanisms to ensure citizen participation in policy initiation and formulation, and the monitoring and evaluation of decision-making and implementation."[85] The 1997 White Paper on Transforming Public Service Delivery (known as the "Batho Pele White Paper") likewise identified publicly responsive bureaucratic structures as key to effective programs.[86]

Two national statutes implement this vision: the Local Government Municipal Structures Act of 1998 and the Local Government Municipal Systems Act of 2000.[87] The Structures Act defines different types of municipalities and requires each municipality to establish an elected council as the central governing structure. Participation is a central feature of municipal councils. One of three municipal objectives in the Act is to "develop mechanisms to consult the community and community organisations in performing its functions and exercising its powers."[88] The executive body of each council is required to report annually "on the involvement of communities and community organisations in the affairs of the municipality" and also "ensure that regard is given to public views and report on the effect of consultation on the decisions of the council."[89]

Part Four of the Structures Act provides for the creation of locally elected ward committees the sole object of which "is to enhance participatory democracy in local government."[90] These committees are chaired by the local ward councilor and have up to ten community members. The committees are intended to provide citizens with a direct conduit

[84] Tshepo Madlingozi, "Post-Apartheid Social Movements and Legal Mobilisation," in Malcolm Langford *et al.* (eds.), *Socio-Economic Rights and South Africa: Symbols or Substance* (2013) 92, 107.

[85] White Paper Political Committee, "The White Paper on Local Government" (March 9, 1998) 17–20.

[86] Department of Public Service and Administration, "*Batho Pele* – 'People First' White Paper on Transforming Public Service Delivery" (September 18, 1997).

[87] Local Government Municipal Structures Act No. 117 of 1998 ("Structures Act"); Local Government Municipal Systems Act No. 32 of 2000 ("Systems Act").

[88] Systems Act, ibid., § 19(3).

[89] Ibid., §§ 44(3)(g)–(h) (executive councils) and §§ 56(3)(g)–(h) (mayors).

[90] Ibid., § 72(3).

to local government by providing information and advice to individual councilors.[91]

Section 16 of the Systems Act requires municipalities to adopt a "culture of municipal governance that complements formal representative government with participatory governance."[92] Municipalities should "encourage and create the conditions for the local community to participate in the affairs of the municipality," including specifically "(i) integrated development planning; (ii) the performance management system; (iii) performance; (iv) the budget; and (v) strategic decisions relating to services."[93]

In 2012, the national government adopted a new high-profile strategy for reducing inequality by 2030 called the National Development Plan (NDP).[94] One of six "interlinked priorities" that the NDP identifies is "[p]romoting active citizenry to strengthen development, democracy and accountability."[95] The NDP draws a direct connection between community participation and effective service delivery. The plan commits to making it "easier for citizens to hold public servants and politicians accountable, particularly for the quality of service delivery," and "mainstream[ing] citizen participation" as key tactics.[96] In the area of housing and "spatial development," the plan calls for supporting "active citizenship" through a range of interventions "including properly funded, citizen-led neighbourhood vision and planning processes and the introduction of social compacts from neighbourhood to city level."[97]

The NDP also acknowledges the link between corruption, accountability, and the rising number of public protests. In a chapter focused on fighting corruption, it states, "Transparency is an important element of public accountability. Dissatisfaction about lack of access to information on service delivery is prominent in public protests."[98]

In its closing chapter, the NDP links the social rights in the Constitution to the development of "responsible and active citizens" who can be "agents of their own development."[99] One section of that chapter devoted to "Active Citizenry and Leadership," reaffirms the 1998 White Paper on Local Government's commitment to participatory governance and acknowledges that many municipalities "still need to make it happen and are encouraged to do so."[100] It also calls for the state to "focus on engaging with people in their own forums rather than expecting citizens to engage with forums created by the state."[101]

[91] Madhinglozi, *supra* note 84, 108. [92] Systems Act, *supra* note 87, §16(1).
[93] Ibid. [94] NDP, *supra* note 4. [95] Ibid., 26. [96] Ibid., 410.
[97] Ibid., 260. [98] Ibid., 452. [99] Ibid., 460. [100] Ibid., 474. [101] Ibid.

2. *Community participation in practice*

South Africa's extensive community-participation structures were motivated by a deep commitment to participatory politics and were part of a political environment and institutional framework that had many of the components required to create meaningful participation in local government.[102] According to Patrick Heller, these participation structures were remarkably similar to structures in Brazil and India. In all three countries, their establishment was driven by a set of political conditions, including left-of-center dominant political parties and a robust set of civil society organizations with strong track records of promoting participation.[103] Among the three, however, South Africa "had a clear and distinct advantage" because it inherited a government structure with the capacity and decentralized structure necessary to make participation work at the local level.[104]

Despite this advantage, South Africa failed to successfully implement genuinely participatory mechanisms. Heller argues this was the result of the ANC's political dominance and specifically the shift in macroeconomic policy to the neoliberal approach represented by the Growth, Employment and Redistribution (GEAR) strategy.[105] Through GEAR and its related policies, "the ANC has managerialized decision-making processes" and "entrenched a bureaucratic and corporatist vision of urban governance."[106] In the process the "local spaces in which citizens can practice democracy and exert some influence over South Africa's very ambitious project of local government transformation . . . have been hollowed out."[107]

A 2013 report by the Good Governance Learning Network (GGLN) – a consortium of civil society organizations working on local governance – describes a deep disconnect between the state's formal commitment to participatory democracy and the lack of capacity, training, and political motivation to meaningfully implement that commitment at the local level.[108] The report makes clear that the problem lies not with a lack

[102] Heller, *supra* note 6, 652–53. [103] Ibid., 652. [104] Ibid., 650.

[105] Ministry of Finance, "Growth, Employment and Redistribution: A Macroeconomic Strategy" (1996).

[106] Heller, *supra* note 6, 655.

[107] Ibid. *See, also*, Piper and Nadvi, *supra* note 3 (describing political dominance of local participation structures). Piper and Nadvi agree that political dominance of local participation structures is a major reason for their ineffectiveness but argue that is a function of poor institutional design, not merely the ANC's dominant position. Ibid., 234.

[108] Good Governance Learning Network, *Active Citizenship Matters: Perspectives from Civil Society on Local Governance in South Africa* (2013).

of formal participation mechanisms. As one paper explains, the "local government system is designed to ensure participatory planning, responsive service delivery, active redistribution and a sensible balance between the short and long term."[109] Moreover, "a layer of civil society organisations (CSOs) – membership based and NGOs – exist to ensure that these legislative and policy imperatives are adhered to."[110] Nonetheless, "it is a public secret that effective citizen engagement and empowerment is the exception to the rule, and that most municipalities fail to facilitate participatory governance adequately."[111]

A recent study of community participation in inner-city housing policy in Johannesburg and Durban drew similar conclusions regarding the effectiveness of formal participation mechanisms in local government. The study found that, despite an extensive set of formal vehicles for public participation, poor residents frequently expressed significant concerns that these formal processes were inadequate, poorly implemented, and even deliberately structured to exclude them.[112]

These failures to implement meaningful community-participation mechanisms are connected to the widespread problems with service delivery in local government. For example, Jackie Dugard argues that "that the multiple, linked failures of local government and governance – some related to economic and some to political constraints – have fatally undermined the promise of national legislation and policy at the local level, resulting in inadequate services."[113] She connects these failures directly to "the malfunctioning of local democratic institutions [that] has rendered local government increasingly unaccountable and unresponsive to the needs of poor residents, displacing dissatisfaction onto the streets and into the courtrooms."[114] Analyses of local participation structures similarly conclude that the increasing number of local protests "reflect the failure of local democracy"[115] and "the incapacity of the new institutions of participatory governance to change this."[116]

109 Edgar Pieterse, "Rethinking the Purpose and Modalities of Community Development in South African Cities," in Good Governance Learning Network, *Active Citizenship Matters: Perspectives from Civil Society on Local Governance in South Africa* (2013) 19, 20.

110 Ibid. 111 Ibid.

112 Community Agency for Social Enquiry, *Enhancing the Voices of the Poor in Urban Housing: Durban and Johannesburg* (2012) 127–30; *see, also*, Lisa Thompson, Ina Conradie, and Pamela Tsolekile, "Citizen Agency in Khayelitsha: Political Participation for Better Access to Resources?," African Centre for Citizenship & Democracy (ACCEDE) Report (2012).

113 Dugard, *supra* note 5, 277. 114 Ibid. 115 Mbazira, *supra* note 3, 253.

116 Piper and Nadvi, *supra* note 3, 233. *See, generally*, Van Donk, *supra* note 5.

A common set of institutional, cultural, and political factors contributes to both the failure of participatory governance and problems with service delivery.[117] Formal participation structures are widely viewed as deeply politicized, generally disconnected from local communities, and largely ineffective because they lack both funding and have limited formal influence in the actual functioning of municipalities.[118]

The surge in what are often described as "service-delivery" protests – local protests, usually in poor communities that began roughly in 2004 and began to escalate in 2009 – illustrate the close connections between government's disengagement and the lack of adequate basic services.[119] A 2012 study of participation mechanisms notes that "[g]overnance failings in the sphere of local government have been put into stark focus through the phenomenon of community protests."[120] The study documents the steep decline in trust in local government from 2004 through 2009 and connects that decline to "the lack of accountability" and "a dearth of meaningful opportunities to engage with municipal representatives and influence local decision-making."[121]

A 2013 report on housing delivery concludes that the problems of widespread corruption and lack of capacity at the local level are exacerbated by the failure of local governments to communicate even basic information about the housing process to poor people: "research shows that these perceptions relate not only to the amount of real corruption that has been exposed over the years, but also to the 'clumsiness, opacity, confusion and capriciousness that exists within the housing programme.'"[122] Although bureaucratic failures and outright corruption "exist and appear to be widespread, it also appears that much of the anger and confusion – which often culminates in protest – arises from a lack of information and explanation of some very technical and banal processes and systems."[123]

Studies of local protests consistently find that they are motivated not only by the lack of essential services but also unresponsive local

[117] Piper and Nadvi, *supra* note 3, 233; Madlingozi, *supra* note 84, 108–9; Mbazira, *supra* note 3, 265–69.

[118] Piper and Nadvi, *supra* note 3; Pieterse, *supra* note 109, 20–21; Van Donk, *supra* note 5, 13–18.

[119] Van Donk, *supra* note 5, 13–14. [120] Ibid., 14. [121] Ibid., 15.

[122] Kate Tissington *et al.*, *'Jumping the Queue,' Waiting Lists and Other Myths: Perceptions and Practice around Housing Demand and Allocation in South Africa* (2013), 8 (quoting Margot Rubin, "Perceived Corruption in the South African Housing Allocation and Delivery Programme," 46 *J. Asian & Afr. Stud.* 479, 488 (2011)).

[123] Ibid.

governments.[124] Dugard notes that the protests typically feature three common factors: (1) high levels of poverty and unemployment; (2) inadequate basic services; and (3) repeated failures by local authorities to respond to community efforts to engage with them."[125]

The government's own 2009 analysis "paints a picture of local government that is unresponsive and unaccountable, fails to involve communities in their own development, and is characterized by poor political governance."[126] The NDP likewise acknowledges direct connection between local protests and local government's lack of responsiveness and accountability to citizens. The plan concludes that "service delivery protests stem from citizens' frustration that the state is not responsive to their grievances."[127] It further observes that "this is unfortunate as citizens are often best placed to advise on the standard of public services in their communities and to suggest possible interventions."[128]

3. *Local protests and invented spaces*

These studies show that there is a direct connection between the lack of meaningful community-participation mechanisms in local government and the widespread problems with basic service delivery and suggest that instigating reforms designed to make local participation structures function effectively also could help improve services.[129] A parallel line of criticism argues, however, that even well-functioning formal participation mechanisms are insufficient to provide a meaningful voice for poor, marginalized communities because they reinforce existing power structures and relationships.[130] These analyses argue that the local protests represent a set of "invented spaces" that allow for genuine dissent from

[124] *See* Dugard, *supra* note 5, 286–94 (summarizing several empirical studies); Alexander, *supra* note 21, 37–38.

[125] Dugard, *supra* note 5, 291–92 (citing Luke Sinwell *et al.*, *Service Delivery Protests: Findings from Quick Response Research on Four 'Hot-Spots' – Piet Retief, Balfour, Thokoza, Diepsloot* (2009)).

[126] Pamela Masiko-Kambala *et al.*, "Advancing 'Networked Spaces': Making a Case for Communities of Practice to Deepen Public Participation," in Good Governance Learning Network, *Putting Participation at the Heart of Development Putting Development at the Heart of Participation: A Civil Society Perspective on Local Governance in South Africa* (2012) 68, 68–69.

[127] NDP, *supra* note 4, 427. [128] Ibid.

[129] *See* Van Donk, *supra* note 5, 18–20; Piper and Nadvi, *supra* note 3, 233; Mbazira, *supra* note 3, 252–53.

[130] Madlingozi, *supra* note 84; Richard Pithouse, "Rethinking Public Participation from Below," 2 *Crit. Dialogue* 1 (2006).

the status quo.[131] Channeling that critical dissent into formal participation structures undermines its effectiveness by acquiescing to official control and risking cooptation.[132]

This concern that state-controlled participation mechanisms operate to exclude views that genuinely challenge the state and thus to maintain the status quo is underscored by well-documented incidents where local governments and/or local ANC structures have targeted social movements representing poor people that have effectively mobilized outside of official processes. The tactics in these instances have ranged from political denunciation of these movements as "counterrevolutionaries," establishment of alternative, politically controlled organizations to co-opt these movements as well as criminalization and the illegal use of force to intimidate them.[133]

Richard Pithouse argues that mainstream characterizations of local protests as primarily about the lack of basic services reduce the problems to a set of technical, bureaucratic issues and miss the deeper political undercurrents and substantial mistrust between formal government structures and poor people's movements that these more violent confrontations represent. He agrees that the protests are intimately connected to the lack of meaningful participation and show "there is a clear demand for popular democracy against both the technocratic authoritarianism (of bureaucracies) and the politics of clientelism and patronage (of parties)."[134] But he argues the existing participation mechanisms operate to reinforce bureaucratic authority rather than to give poor communities a real voice in them.

Even where they work as designed, government-controlled participation mechanisms "most often function as a means of top down social control aiming to subordinate popular politics to the party and, thereby,

[131] Piper and Nadvi, *supra* note 3. They analyze both "invited" and "invented" participation mechanisms and argue both are necessary to create meaningful participation. Ibid., 233–35. *See, also,* Masik-Kambala *et al.*, *supra* note 126, 70–71 (arguing invented and invited spaces should be viewed as a "dialectic" rather than a dichotomy).

[132] Pithouse, *supra* note 130; Sandra Liebenberg and Katherine G. Young, "Adjudicating Social and Economic Rights: Can Democratic Experimentalism Help?," in Helena Alviar García *et al.* (eds.), *Social and Economic Rights in Theory and Practice: Critical Inquiries* (2015), 237, 251–53; Chris Tapscott, "Service Delivery in South Africa – The Limits to Equity and Participation" Paper to the Sixth European Consortium for Political Research General Conference, August 17–25, 2011, Reykjavik, Iceland (2011).

[133] *See* Madlingozi, *supra* note 84, 109–11.

[134] Richard Pithouse, "Voices of Resistance from Occupied London," The University of Abahlali baseMjondolo (2007), at http://abahlali.org/node/2814/.

society to the state."[135] Pithouse argues that, to be meaningful, participation must involve the state negotiating directly with legitimate community organizations to "enable a bottom up politics that can, in slow, grinding battles with occasional flashes, steadily subordinate the local state to society."[136]

In a related critique Steven Friedman notes that formal mechanisms are biased toward organizations and individuals with the resources to gain government attention even without those structures. These mechanisms thus "are intrinsically hostile to the poor, who most need access to government decisions."[137] Improving the performance of those formal mechanisms or creating new state-controlled ones, in his view, won't meaningfully improve poor communities' access to government unless government entities "develop attitudes and institutions accessible to citizen action."[138]

Friedman identifies two overlapping rationales for participation mechanisms: (1) deepening democracy by providing a voice for the broadest range of people in policy and planning processes, and (2) securing cooperation and support from key organized constituencies for the policy by including them in its development.[139] Both the national legislation described previously and the Constitution's democracy provisions emphasize the first rationale, deepening democracy. In practice, however, those mechanisms have operated – when they function at all – instead to secure support from key organized (and well-resourced) constituencies. The result has been the exclusion of poor communities who make up the vast majority of people in South Africa and who were the intended beneficiaries of these mandates.[140]

The solution, Friedman holds, is to create conditions that enable citizens, especially in poor communities, to engage in their own forms of activism and for government to reach out directly to those communities on their own terms. Creating this kind of "participation from below" requires both open-ended opportunities for engagement and also greater dissemination of information about engagement opportunities and the substantive policy options the state is considering.[141]

[135] Ibid. [136] Ibid.

[137] Steven Friedman, "Participatory Governance and Citizen Action in Post-apartheid South Africa," *International Institute for Labour Studies Discussion Paper* DP/164/2006 (2006) 3, at www.ilo.org/wcmsp5/groups/public/–dgreports/–inst/documents/publication/wcms_193613.pdf.

[138] Ibid. [139] Ibid., 4–6. [140] Ibid., 8–14. [141] Ibid., 19–20.

Laurence Piper and Lubna Nadvi make a similar diagnosis of the failure of local participation mechanisms. They agree that participation "is best led by oppositional movements rather than ruling political parties," but also argue that the key to ensuring meaningful participation by local communities is to strengthen those movements.[142] This can happen both by enabling them both to invent their own spaces for engagement with the state and also by creating the resources and leverage for them to effectively exploit existing formal mechanisms. Reforming those mechanisms – for example redesigning ward committees to make them more independent of political parties – is one tool that could expand the power of local movements and civil society organizations.[143]

But they emphasize that institutional changes by themselves are not enough. The critical piece currently missing in South Africa is broad political support for oppositional movements necessary for government to become truly responsive in South Africa. Like Roux, however, they point to encouraging signs that the conditions are ripe in South Africa for increased mobilization and argue specifically that the very "failure of 'participatory governance'" is creating "pressure for change [that] can only grow."[144]

C. Participation, experimentalism, and legalized accountability

The large gap between official community-participation mandates and actual practice at the local level demonstrates that merely creating participation policies and procedures is plainly insufficient to make them effective. Moreover, as the line of criticism represented by Friedman and Pithouse demonstrates, even well-functioning formal mechanisms are likely to be ineffective by themselves for giving poor communities a meaningful voice in government processes. Rather than giving up on democratic participation as a tool for making local government both more responsive and more effective, however, even critics of participation argue the answer lies in developing stronger, more inclusive participation mechanisms and in providing the resources and leverage to make those opportunities meaningful and effective.[145]

[142] Piper and Nadvi, *supra* note 3, 233–35.

[143] Ibid.; *see, generally*, Heller, *supra* note 6, 650 (arguing "promoting participation requires building new kinds of institutions" and "serious attention to institutional design").

[144] Piper and Nadvi, *supra* note 3, 233.

[145] E.g., Siddle and Koelble, in a comprehensive study of the failure of the decentralized local government model in South African, argue for selectively abandoning the model in municipalities that lack the capacity to fulfill their basic functions but also refocusing the

The connection analyses of local government between genuinely participatory mechanisms that are accessible by and responsive to poor communities and the substantive failings of local government in delivering services suggests that *Mazibuko*'s vision of social rights as tools for policing democratic accountability might not be as far off the mark as its critics suggest. Rather than reducing the social rights to pale shadows of preexisting administrative-law requirements, a serious effort to use the social rights as vehicles for creating genuine participation mechanisms could make local decision-making processes more accountable, effective, and responsive to the voices and needs of poor communities.

Enforcing social rights by creating the leverage for establishing genuinely participatory processes that give poor communities and social rights advocates a formal role in developing policies that fulfill them reflects the same, indirect judicial role envisioned by democratic experimentalism. Several others have identified the close connection between the Court's emphasis on participation mechanisms in the second-wave cases and the democratic experimentalist model of judging. These analyses generally recognize – with substantial caveats – that participatory processes could be one important tool for courts to enforce social rights.[146]

Democratic engagement as described earlier develops these arguments by identifying a framework for courts to experiment with a range of participation mechanisms, including establishing ongoing participation processes that, although initiated by court judgments, operate largely independent of judicial oversight. Establishing participatory mechanisms that extend beyond individual cases and create leverage for poor communities and social rights advocates to participate directly in policy-making decisions and processes incorporates aspects of both experimentalism and participatory governance that advocate for deepening democracy through direct citizen participation to promote social justice by making government more accountable to poor communities.[147]

limited capacity of municipalities on increasing public participation. Siddle and Koelble, *supra* note 5, 234–36.

[146] *See* Sandra Liebenberg, "Deepening Democratic Transformation in South Africa through Participatory Constitutional Remedies," *Nat'l J. Const. L.* (forthcoming); Katherine G. Young, *Constituting Economic and Social Rights* (2012); Stuart Woolman, *The Selfless Constitution: Experimentalism and Flourishing as Foundations of South Africa's Basic Law* (2013); Shanelle van der Berg, "Meaningful Engagement: Proceduralising Socio-economic Rights Further or Infusing Administrative Law with Substance?" 29 *S. Afr. J. Hum. Rts.* 376 (2013).

[147] *See* Goodhart, *supra* note 8, 47–50; Kathleen G. Noonan, Charles F. Sabel, and William H. Simon, "Legal Accountability in the Service-Based Welfare State: Lessons from Child Welfare Reform," 34 *Law & Soc. Inq.* 523 (2009).

The focus on institutional structures and reforms shared by experimentalism and participatory governance in turn overlaps with Charles Epp's "legalized-accountability model," in which activists used rights-based approaches and litigation as levers to instigate managerial reforms that translated legal standards into rights-protective institutional and bureaucratic practices.[148] The intersections among legalized accountability, experimentalism, and participatory governance provide a set of theoretical and empirical frameworks for considering how a largely procedural enforcement approach could be more effective in fulfilling the social rights. Together they suggest that courts could play a meaningful role in reforming local government institutions to make them more responsive, accountable, and effective.

As discussed, the basic capacity problems many municipalities face are immediate and significant hurdles to implementing existing programs and to effective use of available resources intended to provide the services mandated by the social rights.[149] Addressing these problems and finding ways to enable local government to perform critical functions is a necessary starting point for any more ambitious enforcement measures to succeed. One of the most comprehensive studies of local governments by Andrew Siddle and Thomas A. Koelble found that "the current system of fiscal redistribution ought to be adequate to address many of the service delivery issues currently plaguing poorer municipalities."[150] They call for a comprehensive reevaluation of the existing local government structure and extensive institutional reforms to enable municipalities to function effectively.[151]

Requiring structured, long-term access by local communities and civil society representatives can help address these immediate issues by creating greater accountability, professionalization, and access to outside expertise. Those same groups could then use the leverage of the engagement process to propose structural reforms to address the widespread capacity and

[148] Epp, *supra* note 12.

[149] Indeed, a persistent problem across many municipalities and also provincial governments is the failure to spend their full budget allocations for existing programs. *See* Lloyd Gedye, "The Money's There – Spend It!," *Mail and Guardian* (February 25, 2011) ("Local government failed to spend 17c of every budgeted rand it was allocated for infrastructure projects in 2009–10"), at http://mg.co.za/article/2011–02–25-the-moneys-there-spend-it.

[150] Siddle and Koelble, *supra* note 5, 10.

[151] Ibid., 228–40. Siddle and Koelble propose a differentiated system that emphasizes centralization of local government functions in municipalities with fewer resources and less capacity. Ibid.

competence problems that local governments face. The precise content of those reforms is left up to the engagement process itself.

There are definite limits to interventions focused on local government – in particular with respect to funding and macroeconomic policy.[152] Local governments operate within a limited scope both in terms of geography and the overall structure of government. This means they are constrained by fiscal and substantive policies set at the provincial and national level and that judicial interventions aimed at individual municipalities will similarly be constrained in terms of their direct effects. Nonetheless in South Africa local government is directly responsible for front-line delivery of services that fulfill the social rights and many municipalities throughout South Africa have suffered from widespread problems performing those functions.[153] The broad-based accountability, transparency, and responsiveness that community-participation mechanisms were intended to create are particularly well suited to address these issues.[154]

Municipalities also generally are more accessible by local communities than provincial or national government. It is thus relatively easier to establish meaningful participation structures at the municipal level and to make those structures accessible to poor and marginalized communities with relatively fewer resources. More broadly experimentalist governance posits that local changes in one area can have effects that "percolate horizontally and even upwards," serving as models and instigators of broader change.[155] Participatory governance studies go further and argue that there is some evidence to support the claim that properly designed and implemented participation structures can "better align expenditures with democratic preferences, increase participation and decrease leakage and make patterns of allocation more redistributive."[156]

Finally, the institutional reforms that democratic engagement generates are not limited to increasing participation in local government. Democratic engagement allows local communities and social rights activists access to policy-making processes to propose their own solutions to the specific problems that face their own local governments. Although the participatory governance literature argues that increased decentralization through direct community involvement in municipal budgeting and

[152] *See* Liebenberg and Young, *supra* note 132, 253–54.
[153] Siddle and Koelble, *supra* note 5.
[154] Van Donk, *supra* note 5, 20–21; Goodhart, *supra* note 8, 39–45.
[155] Sabel and Zeitlin, *supra* note 9, 180.
[156] Goodhart, *supra* note 8, 50.

policy making can improve the accountability and effectiveness of those functions, it also emphasizes that building state capacity is the most critical element and that participation structures have to be tailored to state and community capacities.[157] The central conclusion of Siddle and Koelble's study is that many local governments in South Africa simply lack the capacity to fulfill even very basic functions, including facilitating participation.[158] Democratic engagement has the potential to create the leverage necessary to propose institutional reforms necessary to build that core capacity and the flexibility for those reforms to be tailored to local needs.[159]

1. *Democratic engagement in theory*

Expanding local government capacity requires reforming institutional structures and also changing institutional cultures. The legalized-accountability model, in Epp's account, can and has, under the right conditions, successfully instigated formal policy reform and real cultural change across a diverse range of institutions and in different societies.

Epp describes development of the legalized-accountability model in three areas: police use of force, workplace sexual harassment, and playground safety in the USA and United Kingdom.[160] In each instance, organizational and bureaucratic reforms to protect civil rights developed in response to social-movement group pressure, including legal pressure. Epp concludes that these bureaucratic reforms operationalized rights protections by translating those rights into administrative procedures and using the perceived risk of litigation to change organizational culture.[161]

[157] Ibid., 29, 45.

[158] E.g., Siddle and Koelble propose reforming the deeply decentralized model of local government by adopting a differentiated approach that emphasizes greater centralization of powers for municipalities with fewer resources and less capacity. Siddle and Koelble, *supra* note 5, 228–40. They argue short-term centralization of essential functions in municipalities with fewer resources and severe capacity problems is necessary to enable effective decentralization in the long run. Ibid. Even those municipalities would retain – and indeed strengthen – their role in facilitating public participation. Ibid., 236. Democratic engagement could create leverage for communities and activists to propose many of the reforms Siddle and Koelble identify and the local participation structures could be reformed to develop, implement and monitor those reforms.

[159] The yearly reports on participatory structures in local government by the Good Governance Learning Networks yearly reports illustrate the range and diversity of approaches that could be developed. E.g., Pieterse, *supra* note 109; Masik-Kambala *et al.*, *supra* note 126.

[160] Epp, *supra* note 11, 216.

[161] Ibid., 25.

Legalized accountability is connected to two key developments. First, reformers in several fields sought to translate formal legal principles established in court victories into a set of bureaucratic practices for implementing those principles in the day-to-day, front-line activities of government officials and private actors. Epp identifies a common set of characteristics that developed across these diverse legal and organizational contexts that are the core of the legalized-accountability framework: "*administrative policies* that state an organizational commitment to legal norms," training and communication intended "to change organizational culture in keeping with" those policies, and oversight mechanisms to enforce them.[162]

Second, interactions between activist pressure for new legal rules and conflict within managerial professions over how to respond to the threat of legal liability created the conditions necessary for developing and implementing these legalized administrative reforms. The direct legal pressure from activists pursuing rights-based litigation interacted with a parallel movement by administrators in each area to establish a set of professional norms: "the activists supplied pressure for change in the form of lawsuit-generated publicity; the administrative professionals supplied practical tools – rules, training, and oversight mechanisms – to produce real, lasting change in bureaucratic practice."[163] The relationship between activists and administrators in targeted institutions was mediated and facilitated by the rise of outside experts with deep knowledge of the bureaucratic structures and practices. These outside experts developed specific reform proposals and advocated for them as both necessary to avoid legal liability and also as professional best practices.[164]

Democratic engagement shares legalized accountability's focus on reforming administrative practices and bureaucratic culture to generate rights-protective policies. That focus is particularly relevant to social rights, which fundamentally rely on appropriately conceived, adequately resourced, and well-functioning government policies and programs. Like legalized accountability, engagement views the state's substantive obligation to fulfill the social rights through the framework of the administrative rules and compliance systems necessary to satisfy those obligations. Rather than relying on a substantive "master norm," however, engagement's underlying principle is the procedural right to play a meaningful role in policy development and implementation.[165]

Engagement's focus on giving communities and social rights activists a role in local government policy also mirrors the experimentalist model

[162] Ibid. [163] Ibid., 3. [164] Ibid., 29–30. [165] Ibid., 3.

where courts convene multiple stakeholders and experts in an ongoing process to identify and refine solutions to structural problems in bureaucratic institutions.[166] At its most abstract, experimentalism is a remedy for requiring and structuring participation by nonjudicial actors to identify and implement these solutions.[167]

Experimentalism in turn shares the legalized-accountability model's focus on institutional reform. The destabilization rights that experimentalist review creates "are claims to unsettle and open up public institutions that have chronically failed to meet their obligations and that are substantially insulated from the normal processes of political accountability."[168]

Both models also recognize that systemic institutional change depends primarily on nonjudicial actors and political processes that courts can influence only indirectly. The destabilization rights experimentalism recognizes "induce [an] institution to reform itself in a process in which it must respond to previously excluded stakeholders."[169] Experimentalist courts do this by "stigmatiz[ing] the status quo" and opening "the defendant institution up to participation of previously marginalized stakeholders."[170] Notably, like the legalized-accountability model, experimentalist interventions often capitalize on internal dissension within institutions and create leverage for internal reformers to press for change.[171]

The principal difference between these models is that, as originally developed by Charles Sabel, William Simon, and others, experimentalism focused on relatively direct judicial interventions in a single case or series of cases that targeted institutional rules, practices, and culture. Experimentalist review is derived principally from a set of institutional-reform cases in the USA, where courts issued structural injunctions to assert control over public institutions. Experimentalist courts in those cases relied on collaborative, participatory processes to identify solutions to the problems that were the basis for those injunctions and also often extended those processes to allow for ongoing monitoring and revision of those

[166] E.g., Sabel and Simon, *supra* note 14, 1067–73. Sabel and Simon cite examples of experimentalist approaches that developed outside of courts, but their focus is on structural remedies issued by courts. Ibid., 1091 (describing legislative reforms with experimentalist characteristics); Ibid., 1098.

[167] Ibid., 1015 ("the experimentalist tendency treats participation not just as an aspect of the initial remedial formulation, but as a core feature of the remedy itself").

[168] Ibid., 1020. [169] Ibid., 1056. [170] Ibid., 1100–1. [171] Ibid., 1092.

solutions. But these cases started with a fairly direct judicial intervention, typically including structural injunctions.[172]

Legalized accountability both takes a longer view and focuses on processes that, although prompted and shaped by litigation and court interventions, operate primarily outside of direct judicial control. This tracks the broader framework of "experimentalist governance" that focuses on institutional reform processes and participation mechanisms outside of the courts.[173]

The judicial role is further decentered in both the legalized-accountability model and experimentalist governance. As Epp describes it "[j]udicial decisions were important less for what they required in precise legal terms than for which direction they pointed, which coalition they endorsed, and whether they exposed defendant organizations to liability."[174] Courts catalyzed the development of legalized accountability principally by recognizing specific but abstract substantive rights and issuing tort remedies. Reformers then used the threat of future litigation as leverage to push for administrative reforms designed to proactively avoid the risk of court sanctions. It was the reforms themselves – rather than judicial pronouncements – that made rights "real" by articulating detailed policies and procedures.[175]

These individual cases brought public attention to the systemic problems that activists identified and tort remedies helped sustain litigation because successful cases sometimes paid for themselves.[176] In most of Epp's examples courts were not involved directly in identifying and ordering the specific administrative reforms that are the hallmark of legalized accountability. Instead the reform proposals came from the interaction between receptive insiders and external professional organizations that seized on the threat of legal liability to press for changes they were already developing.[177]

Democratic engagement draws from both models. Like experimentalism it describes a collaborative and inclusive judicial role that relies primarily on a set of procedural powers for convening and structuring ongoing participatory processes that rely on parties and other stakeholders to identify solutions to the systemic institutional problems at

172 Ibid., 1067–73.

173 E.g., Charles F. Sabel and William H. Simon, "Minimalism and Experimentalism in the Administrative State," 100 *Geo. L. J.* 53, 55 (2011).

174 Epp, *supra* note 11, 218.

175 Ibid., 227–31.

176 Ibid., 217.

177 Ibid., 216–18.

stake. Ordering democratic engagement is an experimentalist intervention because it "opens up [an] underperforming institution to the influence of and participation by dissatisfied citizens through stakeholder negotiation."[178] Engagement and experimentalism both focus on creating "a form of direct rather than representative democracy" by making formal state institutions more accountable to those with the greatest interest in their operation.[179]

Engagement also starts with an experimentalist intervention where a court orders and manages a collaborative and participatory process. The flexibility of the engagement requirement gives courts the option to take a more direct oversight role to monitor and direct that process in ways that closely track the examples Sabel and Simon describe.[180] The Court's use of engagement to date generally has operated in a more direct fashion, although with relatively light control compared to the examples Sabel and Simon describe.

Democratic engagement moves beyond individual case management and focuses on using experimentalist interventions in individual social rights cases to instigate the largely autonomous reform process the legalized-accountability model describes. In that context parties and outside organizations could use the meaningful engagement process in individual cases as the platform to propose substantive reforms that create independent accountability mechanisms. These could include proposing reforms that reinvigorate or restructure existing formal participation mechanisms drawn from participation legislation and the more recent policy frameworks identified previously. They also could include the innovative, community-based mechanisms that critics of existing participation structures have called for or even the broader structural changes that Siddle and Koelble prescribe.[181]

Epp's work demonstrates that courts can provide the leverage necessary for instigating institutional reforms without articulating with any specificity the requirements for those reforms. Experimentalism argues that participatory, experimental processes are potentially effective mechanisms for identifying and implementing legal norms that are the basis for the institutional reforms Epp describes. Experimentalist review focuses specifically on using participation mechanisms to identify flexible, contingent norms in individual cases. Experimentalist governance extends

[178] Sabel and Simon, *supra* note 14, 1094. [179] Ibid. [180] Ibid., 1067–73.

[181] *See* Pithouse, *supra* note 130; Friedman, *supra* note 137; Van Donk, *supra* note 5; Siddle and Koelble, *supra* note 5.

that insight and identifies "experimentalist regimes" within a diverse set of public institutions that "have developed forms of nonbureaucratic administration that try to combine accountability with local initiative in ways that facilitate learning and individuation."[182]

Participatory governance studies complement and reinforce the experimentalist argument but focus on institutional reforms designed to make local governments more responsive to poor communities and produce more progressive policies.[183] A recent report by the American Political Science Association notes that human rights, including social rights, and participatory governance "are linked through their overlapping concern with social justice."[184] It argues that participation and rights are "two sides of the same coin" and that efforts to secure rights "are most effective when they are not confined to the implementation of pre-defined programs," but instead include participatory mechanisms both for defining the content of the rights and for monitoring implementation.[185]

Heller's comparison of local government participation structures in Brazil, India, and South Africa suggests that South Africa has the institutional structure, state capacity, and civil society and community networks that are prerequisites for meaningful participatory governance at the local government level.[186] Heller argues South Africa's failure to effectively develop this potential despite this more favorable institutional and historical context is largely the result of the ANC's political dominance. Successful implementation of meaningful participation structures in the future depends "on getting the politics right, and specifically having a proper balance between political power and civilsociety."[187]

Other studies of participatory structures in South Africa argue that South Africa has "very specific and identifiable 'invited spaces' that have the potential, in theory, to both engender more constructive and democratic state-society relations and enhance the delivery of social goods."[188] That potential is limited, however, by the domination of formal political parties over local popular mobilization.[189]

The political constraints on effective participation these analyses identify track Roux's analysis of the Court, and I return to these in the following pages. Democratic engagement focuses specifically on the institutional

[182] Sabel and Simon, *supra* note 173, 93.
[183] Goodhart, *supra* note 8, 50; Heller, *supra* note 6.
[184] Goodhart, *supra* note 8, 72. [185] Ibid., 5, 72.
[186] Heller, *supra* note 6, 665. *See, also,* Goodhart, *supra* note 8, 46–47.
[187] Heller, *supra* note 6, 665. [188] Piper and Nadvi, *supra* note 3, 214. [189] Ibid., 1.

policies and procedures that experimentalism and legalized accountability argue could create formal opportunities for restructuring the balance among the state, citizens, and civil society in particular institutional contexts. It creates a specific forum and concrete leverage for activists and local communities to press for procedural reforms by giving them greater access to local decision-making processes. These procedural reforms are not limited simply to restructuring existing participation mechanisms. They can and should encompass the kind of innovative processes and institutions Heller and others have identified as more effective in creating genuine participation and that could help develop local capacity to organize.[190] Alternatively, they could encompass the kind of broad structural reforms Siddle and Koelble argue are necessary for low-capacity municipalities to function effectively.[191]

Democratic engagement reinforced by the stronger judicial role established in the participatory democracy cases could provide a mechanism for developing the conditions Epp identifies as necessary for genuinely rights-protective institutional reform by creating the leverage that to allow civil society and local communities to take advantage of the formal commitment to participatory governance that already exist. Equally important, enforcing democratic engagement in these ways capitalizes on the Court's characterization of social rights enforcement as primarily a political rather than legal enterprise. It gives the Court a primarily procedural role to enforce democratic norms, including the participation values in *Doctors for Life* and *Matatiele* and the strong accountability requirements in *Glenister*. Comparing engagement with the central features of the legalized-accountability and participatory governance models illustrates this potential.

2. *Democratic engagement as legalized accountability*

Democratic engagement tracks the legalized-accountability model in three distinct ways: (1) engagement creates a legal framework for using individual cases to identify systemic, institutional problems and to establish ongoing processes for addressing those issues; (2) the engagement process allows local communities and their advocates to bring in outside experts who could address the technical and capacity-related issues that frequently have led to service-delivery problems in municipalities;

[190] Heller, *supra* note 6. [191] Siddle and Koelble, *supra* note 5.

and (3) engagement is a mechanism for enforcing the strongly participatory version of democracy the Court identified in *Doctors for Life* and *Matatiele*and that the national legislation requires. It thus gives courts a tool for enforcing those requirements by identifying and requiring structured, long-term engagement with local communities that goes beyond the existing formal mechanisms and that could make local governments genuinely responsive to their views and needs.

Engagement creates a form of legal liability that focuses directly on institutional policies and practices. The Court has emphasized that the state is constitutionally required to develop administrative structures for engagement. Civil society organizations could use their constitutionally sanctioned role to advocate not only for specific policy changes that resolve a particular case but also to use individual cases to push for more systemic reforms, including procedural reforms that expand participation.

In Epp's account it was the combination of activist pressure and litigation and the development of practical reform proposals by policy experts with knowledge of the relevant field that succeeded in institutionalizing bureaucratic reforms.[192] Activist organizations started the process by redefining the problem in each area as a systemic one rather than a series of isolated incidents. This elevated the focus to the institutional level and turned individual lawsuits into vehicles for institutional reform.[193]

The Constitutional Court's requirement that municipalities build engagement into planning processes from the start and its related recognition that this requires personnel and training in engagement already brings institutional issues into play. The procedural rights the Court has recognized in the eviction cases to join state entities and require them to provide information on broader planning and budgeting processes expands the range of institutional issues courts can address. Connecting both these requirements and engagement to the participatory democracy decisions and legislative mandates for local government processes to broadly incorporate community participation provides both a political mandate and a more specific legal framework for identifying institutional reforms that give local communities and social rights advocates direct access to those institutional structures.

In addition to redefining the problem as an institutional one, individual cases in Epp's account also reshaped the public debate over issues like police abuse in ways that created public pressure for reform. Media stories began to frame coverage of specific incidents of abuse in terms

[192] Epp, *supra* note 11, 90–91. [193] Ibid., 135–36.

of institutional failures to adopt appropriate policies and practices.[194] In South Africa, media coverage of service-delivery failures by local government already depicts a consistent set of systemic problems including lack of capacity, fraud, and corruption.[195] Media accounts frequently connect these protests to unresponsive local governments.[196]

The Court's evolution to a more assertive role in the eviction model is the starting point for creating a legal framework that could draw on this growing political pressure to require institutional reforms. To begin with, eviction cases provide vehicles for not only addressing specific situations but also for highlighting the systemic nature of the underlying causes and the need for institutional reform. Chapter 8 identified the potential for *Joseph*'s recognition of a free-standing procedural right to receive municipal services to extend the eviction model to other service-delivery contexts. Developing that connection in other cases can provide similar vehicles for identifying systemic issues and advocating for institutional reform in other bureaucratic structures involved in delivering basic services.

The expanded procedural powers the Court has recognized – in particular the ability to order state parties to provide extensive information regarding existing and future policies – already extends judicial control into the policy-making arena. *Blue Moonlight* adds the authority for courts to closely scrutinize policy and budget processes to ensure they did not ignore the obligations the social rights impose. *Juma Musjid* expanded that authority to each of the social rights. Enforcing the engagement requirement simply recognizes that those obligations include systematic participation mechanisms as well as substantive obligations.

The Court's recognition in *Olivia Road* that civil society organizations have a specific role to play in the engagement process opens the door for social rights organizations to partner with professional groups, local communities, and social movements to develop proposals for reforming local government. Activists can use engagement in two related ways to

194 Ibid.

195 E.g., Niki Moore, "North West: Service Delivery? What Service Delivery?," *Daily Maverick*, June 19, 2014, at www.dailymaverick.co.za/article/2014–06–19-north-west-service-delivery-what-service-delivery/#.U6Q6QI1dXWZ; Khulekane Mugubane, "Fears That Service Delivery Protests Are Spreading," *Business Day*, February 20, 2014, at www.bdlive.co.za/national/2014/02/20/fears-that-service-delivery-protests-are-spreading.

196 E.g., Sarah Evans, "Local Government Needs More Residents to Get Involved," *Mail & Guardian*, May 27, 2014, at http://mg.co.za/article/2014–05–27-local-government-needs-more-resident-participation.

propose reforms that address the related problems of bureaucratic failure and the lack of genuine community participation identified previously.

Many municipalities simply lack the capacity effectively to perform basic functions or engage with local communities. Epp's model clearly has the potential to address these issues by creating legal leverage to give outside groups and local communities access to local government processes and to offer reform proposals. In other cases, municipalities have sufficient capacity and resources but refuse to employ them to meet their social rights obligations or to reach out to local communities to include them in meaningful ways.

The protracted enforcement battles that have ensued in several of the second-wave eviction cases illustrate that, even with relatively strong court oversight and a substantively limited order, courts face tremendous practical and institutional hurdles that individual decisions can't overcome. As the High Court in *Hlophe* recognized, the City of Johannesburg – a well-resourced municipality with relatively well-functioning administrative structures – failed to build the necessary capacity to house people facing eviction despite a series of Constitutional Court decisions ordering it to do so.[197] The enforcement battles following *Pheko* illustrate the same problem.[198] Engagement gives activists and community organizations the leverage to open up those failed planning processes not only to redirect existing technical expertise and resources toward fulfilling the social rights but also to begin building the long-term cultural changes Epp identifies as key to meaningful rights enforcement.

Using individual cases as vehicles to require institutional reform through democratic engagement provides a partial answer to the concern that the Court's increasing proceduralization in the social rights cases disincentivizes litigation by the poor because it fails to provide concrete relief. The threat of eviction – or any other deprivation of existing access to essential services – creates a direct incentive to litigate to protect that access. As Chapter 8 described, the Court in eviction cases consistently has provided direct, if temporary relief by temporarily stopping an eviction and requiring additional consultation designed to reach a rights-protective solution that either maintains access or provides an equivalent alternative. If courts more consistently provided similar temporary relief in cases like *Joseph*, involving the cutoff of other basic services, it would create that same incentives. Combining temporary protection against deprivation with a more structured application of the engagement

[197] *Hlophe, supra* note 73, [5]. [198] *Pheko, supra* note 82.

requirement that first identifies the systemic problems at issue and also creates mechanisms for participation earlier in policy-development processes uses those individual incentives to amplify the results of each cases.

3. *Participation's pitfalls*

Legalized accountability focuses specifically on largely technocratic, administrative reforms and the ways such reforms have changed both bureaucratic practices and culture to make them responsive to new legal norms. Epp notes that his model accepts the prevailing view that law rarely diverges significantly from elite interests or power.[199] The reforms he describes, while driven by popular pressure created through activist litigation, were a product of elite, professional organizations that translated (and domesticated) new legal norms into administrative procedures that they could control and implement.[200] This inevitably led to conflict between activists and professionals, but that conflict Epp argues was productive in opening up elite professional bureaucracies to popular demands for reform. The relative penetration of popular demands depended in many cases on court decisions that favored particular viewpoints over others "often decisively shaping subsequent developments."[201]

Many of the problems local governments face are amenable to the elite-controlled, technocratic reforms Epp describes.[202] Engagement's value on this level is giving social rights advocates leverage to partially counter the pathologies of political influence, incompetence, and outright corruption that are widespread in local governments and could modestly improve delivery capacity and the general use of resources. Notably, these are similar to the issues that plagued police forces in the USA, and that Epp argues the legalized-accountability model has – to varying degrees – had some effect in reforming.[203] This also can help develop "the necessary managerial, organizational, and technical capacities to make local government work" that the participatory governance literature recognizes.[204]

[199] Epp, *supra* note 11, 216. [200] Ibid., 216–18. [201] Ibid., 216.

[202] The reforms Siddle and Koelble prescribe generally fit within this category, and the legalized accountability model illustrates how democratic engagement could create leverage in individual cases to begin pressing for the structural reforms they advocate. Siddle and Koelble, *supra* note 5.

[203] Epp, *supra* note 11, Ch. 3.

[204] Patrick Heller, "Moving the State: The Politics of Democratic Decentralization in Kerala, South Africa, and Porto Alegre," 29 *Pol. & Soc'y*. 131, 137 (2001); Goodhart, *supra* note 8.

Professionalization by itself, however, will not make bureaucracies responsive to social rights and poor communities. Indeed, it may lead to greater exclusion of poor communities by further strengthening elite control. Critics of experimentalism and participatory governance argue that participation mechanisms are incapable of addressing the structural inequalities and political marginalization that poor people and communities face.[205] Participation requires resources that poor communities lack, and even where they are able to participate the cooperative emphasis in deliberative forums is designed to maintain rather than challenge existing power relationships. Social rights are intended to redress those inequalities, and so enforcing them through mechanisms that depend on a level playing field makes little sense in theory or practice.

Sandra Liebenberg and Katherine Young have applied a version of these critiques to the South African context and argue that relying on participatory processes to enforce social rights raises three specific concerns that illustrate their limits: (1) they dilute social rights by emphasizing process over substance; (2) they risk reproducing rather than redressing structural inequalities and so disadvantage the people and communities social rights are intended to protect; and (3) the literature on participation focuses on decentralized processes, especially local governments and so unduly restricts the capacity of social rights to effect broader change.[206]

As an initial matter, the analysis of the previous chapters suggests that the Court is unlikely, at least in the near term, to adopt the most commonly identified alternative – strong substantive interpretations enforced through direct orders. One premise of both the eviction model and democratic engagement is that they operate within the constraints of the second-wave cases. The principal benefit of relying on a proceduralized approach like democratic engagement is that the Court generally has been more willing to adopt a stronger role in that context and conversely has been deeply reluctant to develop abstract substantive norms.

This chapter also has argued, however, that the connections between democratic engagement, legalized accountability, experimentalism, and participatory democracy suggest that a proceduralized approach focused on developing meaningful participation mechanisms in local government

[205] E.g., Liebenberg and Young, *supra* note 132; Super, *supra* note 10.

[206] Liebenberg and Young, *supra* note 132. They address experimentalist review specifically, but the concerns they raise apply generally to participatory processes and are well recognized in the participatory governance literature. E.g., Fung and Wright, *supra* note 8.

might turn out to be a more effective tool for enforcing social rights than a stronger interpretive role that focuses on establishing clearly defined principles that courts enforce directly.

The central premise of the affirmative defense of democratic engagement is that effective enforcement of social rights requires state institutions that have the capacity to deliver basic services and are responsive to the voices and needs of poor communities. The legalized-accountability model suggests that law-influenced institutional reform primarily involves the development and application of a set of institutional policies and procedures. The courts, and law generally, play at most an indirect role, primarily by creating leverage for activists and professionals to propose their own reforms and to develop connections with reform-minded individuals within specific institutions.

Experimentalism and participatory governance overlap both with each other and the legalized-accountability model by arguing that participatory processes are functionally well adapted to identify reform proposals for making institutions more responsive and accountable. Participatory governance specifically argues that deepening democracy through participatory mechanisms designed to give poor communities real access to state structures is an effective mechanism for developing more redistributive policies and achieving social justice.[207] Experimentalism suggests that incorporating ongoing participation mechanisms and reflective learning processes can both monitor progress toward particular goals and identify generalizable best practices over time.[208]

Advocates of experimentalism and participatory governance acknowledge that participatory processes are not "cure-all[s] to be applied discriminately" and that the success of participatory processes depends on appropriately structured processes that are attentive to potential inequalities.[209] There is an important distinction between participatory governance, which focuses specifically on the capacity for participation to promote social justice, and experimentalism, which identifies decentralized, participatory processes to address a broader range of institutional failures. Studies of participatory governance recognize that relying on participatory processes to achieve social justice requires some mechanism to address the fundamental inequalities between poor communities and the state but also that absolute equality is not a prerequisite.[210]

[207] Goodhart, *supra* note 8, 47–50. [208] Sabel and Simon, *supra* note 173, 93.
[209] Goodhart, *supra* note 8, 3. [210] Fung and Wright, *supra* note 8, 24.

While acknowledging this risk, the participatory governance literature provides multiple examples that "leave little doubt that even citizens with little more capacity than their own commitment to democratic engagement can effectively participate in local government."[211] Fung and Wright argue, based on five case studies, that there are several mechanisms for creating power balances "sufficient for deliberation."[212] First "self-conscious institutional design efforts" that give citizens real power can redress inequality.[213] They cite local citizen councils with the authority to examine and review budgets as an example of a power-balancing design feature.[214] Second, participation by outside organizations, including "community organizations, labor unions and advocacy groups" can prevent both officials and citizen groups from commandeering deliberative processes.[215]

The American Political Science report recognizes that participatory governance structures have to be adapted to reflect the capacity limits of both local communities and the state itself.[216] The report also cautions that participation structures "must be designed with an inclusive pro-poor bias" to promote social justice.[217] It then identifies five design principles derived from successful participatory governance examples that had identifiable pro-poor effects.[218]

Democratic engagement allows courts to draw from these examples and others to adjust power imbalances both in specific court-ordered engagements as well as in the design of ongoing participation mechanisms. The Court in *Olivia Road* recognized the need for social rights advocates and civil society generally to play a power-balancing role, and engagement is sufficiently flexible for courts to craft orders that bring those organizations into the process.[219]

There are clear limits to the extent to which institutional design can counterbalance the power of the state, but it doesn't necessarily follow that participation structures are any more susceptible to those imbalances than the alternatives. Those imbalances arguably are exacerbated as much or more by the litigation process, and there's little reason to think that courts will consistently resist structural power imbalances better than participation mechanisms. A central tenet of participatory governance is that establishing structured, ongoing mechanisms for citizen participation, under the right political circumstances, can itself change those

211 Heller, *supra* note 6, 662. 212 Fung and Wright, *supra* note 8, 24.
213 Ibid. 214 Ibid., 24. 215 Ibid. 216 Goodhart, *supra* note 8, 44–47.
217 Ibid., 48. 218 Ibid., 49. 219 *Olivia Road, supra* note 65.

power relationships in rights-protective ways. Rather than forcing poor communities to rely on courts and litigation – institutions that are structured to magnify those differences – democratic engagement argues it could be more effective to use the courts tactically to create the leverage to reform state institutions themselves in ways that could create ongoing access and influence.

The thick legislative and policy framework for community participation in local government decision-making is the starting point for creating this access. The Court's participatory democracy decisions establish an explicit constitutional norm requiring meaningful consultation with communities. *Mazibuko* connects that norm directly to social rights, and the engagement cases specifically mandate access by poor communities to policy decisions that affect them. As noted, existing participation mechanisms have largely failed to create meaningful access, especially by poor communities. Heller's work suggests that those failures may be as much political as institutional, and so there may be room for reforming those existing structures to make them work as they were originally intended.[220] Siddle and Koelble also prescribe refocusing municipalities on reforming and strengthening public participation as part of a much broader set of structural reforms that they argue could create the necessary capacity for both good governance and improved service delivery.[221]

Others, including Pithouse and Friedman, however, have argued that the existing participation mechanisms are designed in ways that exclude poor communities and that alternative participation mechanisms are necessary to enable genuine participation.[222] Here the Systems Act's general mandate to incorporate community involvement throughout all aspects of planning and budgeting provides a platform for more creative proposals. The NDP calls for "engaging with people in their own forums rather than expecting citizens to engage with forums created by the state."[223] Courts can take advantage of this explicit recognition in official policy that existing formal mechanisms are insufficient to address the concern that participation will become another tool for co-opting local movements that have developed an independent power base within communities and oppose the ANC.[224]

220 Heller, *supra* note 6. *See, also,* Piper and Nadvi, *supra* note 3.
221 Siddle and Koelble, *supra* note 5.
222 Pithouse, *supra* note 130; Friedman, *supra* note 137.
223 NDP, *supra* note 4, 474.
224 Pithouse, *supra* note 130.

Several community-based organizations and civil society groups in South Africa already have developed the capacity to engage with local government as well as alternative models that have had some modest success in penetrating state policies.[225] In many cases, these forms of engagement are deliberately structured in resistance to the existing formal processes. The lines between formal and informal process is not a sharp one, however. Some of the most successful engagements have developed over time and involved multiple interactions among the state, local communities, and social movements.[226] Engagement's flexibility allows activists to draw on these models to develop reforms that both incorporate greater participation into existing structures and also identify new community-led participation structures.

Using engagement to require structured interactions with local communities on their own ground over policies that affect them responds to the critique that community-participation programs channeled through formal state structures and procedures can exacerbate the exclusion of poor people. As discussed, these "invited spaces" often provide only the pretense of community consultation while consolidating state control by marginalizing alternative, community-invented, and controlled forms of engagement.[227] Enforcing social rights through engagement can democratize local government processes by creating the opportunities for local communities to organize and engage with government on their terms.

Creating new participatory spaces that operate outside of state control and even physically take place within local communities is an important step in making those processes meaningful and one that courts can take relatively easily by ordering and carefully structuring engagement processes. Simply creating these spaces is not enough by itself, however. Studies of successful participatory processes uniformly highlight the need

[225] E.g., Van Donk, *supra* note 5; Neil Overy, "The Social Justice Coalition and Access to Basic Sanitation in Informal Settlements in Cape Town, South Africa," *International Budget Partnership Study No.* 11 (2013); Benjamin Bradlow, "Beyond a Legal Framework for 'Meaningful Engagement' in South Africa," *SDI Bulletin* (March 11, 2010) (arguing "victories in court appear almost pyrrhic when compared to the developmental achievements of an organized community armed with its own information and priorities prepared to engage with the state"), at www.sdinet.org/blog/2010/03/11/sdi-bulletin-beyond-a-legal-fr/.

[226] *See* Benjamin Bradlow, "Quiet Conflict: Social Movements, Institutional Change, and Upgrading Informal Settlements in South Africa," Thesis, Masters in City Planning, Massachusetts Institute of Technology (May 23, 2013) 47.

[227] *See* Pithouse, *supra* note 130; Friedman, *supra* note 137; Tapscott, *supra* note 132.

for information, coordination, and resources to enable local communities – especially poor communities – to take advantage of even the most accessibly structured participation opportunities.[228]

The enhanced procedural powers the Court has established in the eviction cases can help address the most basic of these issues – especially the information asymmetry between the state and local communities. Courts already have used the eviction model to order municipalities and other levels of government to provide specific information in individual cases. Through democratic engagement, courts could establish mechanisms that routinized access to information and also apply existing legislation that already requires such access.[229] The strong civil society network focused on social rights and participatory governance more broadly also can help mitigate some of the power imbalance between local governments and poor communities.

Participatory governance studies argue that careful structuring of the participation mechanisms is another tool courts can use to address this imbalance.[230] The rich literature on participatory governance has identified a core set of institutional characteristics shared by successful examples. Courts can draw on these models as well as the range of existing engagement examples in South Africa to identify structural and institutional features that mitigate the power disparity between the state and poor communities. The experimentalism literature provides a related set of models for institutionalizing structured, ongoing learning mechanisms to develop best practices for structuring democratic engagement over time.[231]

D. Conclusion: the limits of democratic engagement

The premise of this chapter's argument for connecting social rights and meaningful engagement to the Court's participatory democracy decisions is that in both lines of cases the Court has consistently been more willing to adopt a more authoritative approach when enforcing procedural

[228] Goodhart, *supra* note 8, 48; Fung and Wright, *supra* note 8, 33–35.

[229] *See* Kristina Bentley and Richard Calland, "Access to Information and Socio-Economic Rights: A Theory of Change in Practice," in Malcolm Langford *et al.* (eds.), *Socio-Economic Rights in South Africa: Symbols or Substance?* (2013), 341, 348–49.

[230] Heller, *supra* note 6, 649–50; Goodhart, *supra* note 8, 44–47.

[231] E.g., Noonan, Sabel, and Simon, *supra* note 147 (analyzing an experimentalist model of reform of US state child-protective services systems that "has potentially broad application to public law").

norms that it can characterize as promoting democratic values. There are two related problems with drawing support from the participatory democratic-rights cases for a more authoritative procedural enforcement role in the social rights context. First, as Botha observes, the Court in two subsequent democratic-rights cases, *Merafong* and *Poverty Alleviation Network*, retreated to a thinner, representative understanding of democracy and a correspondingly deferential role.[232] Second, the Court failed to take up obvious opportunities to rely on procedural arguments in several social rights cases, including *Mazibuko* and *Joe Slovo*.

Danie Brand argues that *Mazibuko* fits within the formal, representative model of democracy side of the split that Botha identifies and that using social rights to police democratic accountability simply means applying deference across the board to state decisions.[233] Brand cites the Court's statement that legislative and executive leadership in fulfilling the social rights "is desirable as a matter of democratic accountability" because "it is their programs and promises that are subjected to democratic popular choice" as evidence that *Mazibuko* embraced a limited, representative conception of democracy that requires deference to political choices.[234]

Brand's critique misses the distinction *Mazibuko* draws between the judicial role in identifying and scrutinizing the substance of social-welfare policies required to fulfill the social rights and its role in ensuring that the processes used to develop those policies are accountable and democratic. *Mazibuko* plainly implies it is inappropriate for courts to craft substantive policies themselves and that they should deferentially scrutinize those developed by the legislature and executive. When assessing challenges to the procedures used to develop those policies, by contrast, *Mazibuko* identifies a deeper, participatory understanding of democracy that connects directly with the stronger judicial role the Court adopted in *Doctors for Life* and *Matatiele*.[235]

The Court's failure in *Mazibuko* to adopt this stronger role despite clear evidence of significant procedural as well as substantive problems with the prepaid meter program at first glance seems to support Brand's view.[236] As Liebenberg and Young explain, however, the Court clearly articulated a more participatory vision of democracy and celebrated "the ongoing

[232] Botha, *supra* note 26, 86–88. [233] Brand, *supra* note 18, 183.

[234] Ibid. (quoting *Mazibuko, supra* note 2, [61]).

[235] *See* Liebenberg, *supra* note 146, 12–13.

[236] For a through discussion and analysis of the procedural arguments in *Mazibuko, see* Liebenberg and Young, *supra* note 132.

accountability, information disclosure, and responsiveness, produced directly by the litigation."[237] The deferential result, however, they contend was driven by a flawed application of this participatory conception, not a repudiation of it.[238] Rather than recognizing the obvious procedural defects the lower-court decisions had identified and the City's failure to recognize the real hardships residents faced, the Court focused exclusively on the "problem of water scarcity, distribution and expense" in a way that excluded the residents' voices.[239]

What explains the Court's deferential application of participatory democracy in *Mazibuko*? Returning to the second-wave patterns Chapter 7 identified, it arguably relates to two aspects of the case that consistently trigger a more deferential response by the Court. First, the Court adopted an unjustifiably narrow view of the case as requiring it to evaluate and set a clear substantive standard related to the minimum core. Second, the decision involved a large-scale program that the government argued was designed to better fulfill the right to water by creating a more efficient and effective delivery system. Rather than demonstrating the Court is committed to deference in all situations, however, these aspects of the case suggest that even where procedural options are available the Court may be reluctant to take them up in situations like *Mazibuko*, which the Court perceives to raise particularly strong democratic and institutional-competence concerns.

As Chapter 7 argued, the patterns in the second-wave cases mirror the political constraints that Theunis Roux has identified across a range of decisions, including both social rights and democratic-rights cases. In the democratic-rights decisions, Roux identifies the same split as Botha between a deeper participatory vision and a thinner representative model. Like Botha, Roux identifies *Doctors for Life* and *Matatiele* as decisions where the Court "articulate[d] a deep, participatory conception of democracy more in keeping with South Africa's political tradition" and contrasts them with several other decisions where the Court adopted a much thinner conception of democracy.[240]

Roux argues that this split reflects the same set of political constraints that also explain the shifting roles the Court has adopted in the social

[237] Ibid., 245. [238] Ibid. [239] Ibid.

[240] Roux, *supra* note 20, 362–63. Roux focuses his analysis on two other democratic-rights decisions, but cites *Doctors for Life* and *Matatiele* as examples of the Court adopting a more principled approach. *See also*, Theunis Roux, "Principle and Pragmatism on the Constitutional Court of South Africa," 7 *Int'l Const. L. J.* 106, 130 (2009).

rights cases.[241] Roux analyzes these more deferential decisions as examples of the Court's responding to the greater political risks the issues raised by flexibly interpreting its commitment to participatory democracy to avoid damaging confrontation with the ANC.[242] In both cases the arguments were not that the process failed to provide for participation but instead that those processes were effectively shams because the provincial government in each case ignored them.[243] Upholding these challenges would have required the Court to assess the motivations behind specific legislative decisions and determine whether and how they took into account the community's views.[244] By contrast in *Doctors for Life* and *Matatiele* the Court found merely that the provincial government failed to provide any participation opportunity at all.[245]

Roux draws a direct contrast between the Court's more deferential democratic-rights decisions and *Grootboom* and *TAC*, where the Court adopted a stronger standard of review in the face of potential political backlash. He argues that other factors created the necessary political space for the Court to adopt a stronger role in these social rights decisions.[246] In *TAC* the domestic and international criticism of the Mbeki administration's stance on the connection between HIV and AIDs was the key factor. In *Grootboom* the Court's own flexible articulation of reasonableness review and limited remedy, which returned control to the government, created that same space.[247]

Roux has updated and refined his analysis of the Court's democratic-rights cases in a comment on an article by Samuel Issacharoff criticizing the Court's consistent failure to recognize and address the antidemocratic effects of the ANC's consolidation of power in several recent democratic-rights decisions.[248] Issacharoff argues that the Court should develop a more substantive theory of democracy and more directly apply it to the ANC's political dominance across a range of situations.[249]

Roux first points out that in both *Doctors for Life* and *Matatiele* the Court reached results that articulated and enforced a substantive vision of democracy threatened by the ANC's dominance, without making the direct political connection between the specific procedural failures and the ANC's politics that Issacharoff advocates. Roux connects these two decisions with a string of democratic-rights cases beginning in

[241] Roux, *supra* note 20, 362–63; Roux, *supra* note 240, 136–37. [242] Ibid.
[243] *See* Botha, *supra* note 26, 86–88. [244] Ibid. (summarizing the issues).
[245] Ibid. [246] Roux, *supra* note 20, Ch. 7. [247] Ibid.
[248] Roux, *supra* note 54. [249] Issacharoff, *supra* note 54.

2009 – most notably *Glenister* – where the Court expanded that role to overturn individual decisions that threatened independent institutions critical to democratic governance.[250] The Court's stronger role in these cases responded directly to the pathologies Issacharoff cites but without explicitly identifying the ANC's dominance itself as a structural threat to that vision of democracy.[251]

In Roux's view the Court's ability to challenge the ANC's substantive policies in these cases was enabled by the substantively limited reasoning it adopted. The Court limited the institutional threat to itself in part by minimizing its authority through reasoning that relied closely on the constitutional text. The Court "never once suggested that the problems it was asked to address were symptomatic of some more general breakdown in the ANC's capacity to govern associated with its ongoing dominance of South African politics."[252]

Combining Roux's analysis with the internal patterns Chapter 7 identified helps refine the conditions likely to enable enforcement of the extensive participation rights democratic engagement entails. It also underscores the importance of the thick legislative and policy framework for participation rights and the growing formal commitment by the national government to enforcing those rights through institutional changes in local government. On one hand, it suggests that the Court will try to minimize direct political confrontation with the ANC even when enforcing procedural rights. On the other, these shifts illustrate the Court's capacity to expand the scope of its authority to challenge the ANC's policies where there is either strong external opposition to the ANC or internal dissension in the ANC itself that could provide support.

Developing democratic engagement by using the social rights to create political leverage works within the political constraints Roux identifies. Relying on meaningful engagement and the premise that a political process has not provided sufficient opportunities for participation allows the Court to articulate a purely procedural set of constitutional standards that are grounded in democratic norms. The thick set of participation legislation and policies provides additional democratic cover for enforcing strong participation requirements as well as formal legal sources the Court can rely on to minimize its independent role in identifying them.

This is not to say that the Court has free rein when enforcing procedural requirements to promote participation. Even where external political circumstances have changed to allow the Court to adopt a stronger role,

[250] Roux, *supra* note 1. [251] Ibid. [252] Ibid., 71.

it is still constrained in the extent to which it can explicitly articulate a substantive constitutional framework for that role. As noted, the Court in the social rights decisions clearly is reluctant to assert even procedural authority in challenges to large-scale programs that are designed to fulfill (rather than evade) the social rights.

Mazibuko plainly illustrates that there are limits to the Court's willingness even to enforce the kind of procedural rights this chapter advocates – limits that are related to and intersect with the external political conditions Roux identifies. There are two related factors in *Mazibuko* that help explain the Court's failure to closely scrutinize these procedural arguments. First, the Court was clearly preoccupied with the adequacy arguments it perceived the case to raise.[253] In particular, the Court seemed concerned that upholding the residents' claims required it to endorse something like the minimum-core concept that the High Court cited with approval.[254]

Even at the peak of its interventions in the first-wave cases, the Court consistently has shied away from assessing the substantive adequacy of particular programs against an independent standard. *Mazibuko*'s rejection of the High Court's adoption of a minimum-core-like standard is consistent with that same pattern and helps explain its refusal to take up the procedural arguments in any depth.

But the Court's consistent avoidance of adequacy claims does not explain its related failure to find a lack of meaningful engagement in *Joe Slovo*. Several of the judgments expressed deep concern over the state's largely ineffective efforts to engage with the community, and yet all agreed that, in the end, those efforts satisfied the newly announced meaningful engagement requirement.[255] Here it seems that the Court was reluctant to apply its newly established engagement requirement with full force to disrupt a large-scale program that was well advanced and that was specifically designed to fulfill the social rights.[256]

[253] *Mazibuko, supra* note 2, [52–57].

[254] Dugard and Langford argue the Court "(re)characterized" the case as raising positive rights claims and "misunderstood [it] as an attempt by the applicants to re-open the minimum core content" approach. Jackie Dugard and Malcolm Langford, "Art or Science? Synthesizing Lessons from Public Interest Litigation and the Dangers of Legal Determinism," 27 *S. Afr. J. Hum. Rts* 39, 51 (2011).

[255] *See* Sandra Liebenberg, *Socio-Economic Rights: Adjudication under a transformative constitution*, 309; Kirsty McLean, "Meaningful Engagement: One Step Forward or Two Back? Some Thoughts on Joe Slovo," 3 *Const. Ct. Rev.* 223, 237 (2010).

[256] This is consistent with Young's observation that the Court calibrates the force of its interventions to the extent there is evidence the state has deliberately ignored or obviously missed the social-rights obligations. Young, *supra* note 146.

Justice Sachs's reasoning supports this reading. After noting that courts will "not normally intervene to decide how well or badly programs are being managed," he found that the failures to engage in this case "were not so disproportionately out of kilter with the meritorious Project" to make its implementation unreasonable.[257] In other words, the government's good intentions required a substantial margin of discretion with respect to the procedural inadequacies in implementation. Both *Mazibuko* and *Joe Slovo* thus illustrate that the Court is likely to revert to a more deferential posture even with respect to procedural arguments in challenges to the implementation of large-scale programs, especially ones intended to fulfill the social rights obligations.

Putting Roux's analysis that the Court reverted to a thinner conception of democracy in cases that raised direct threats to the ANC's political control together with *Mazibuko* and *Joe Slovo* underscores the connection between the eviction model and the possibilities for developing democratic engagement. The eviction model (and also *Joseph*) show that the Court seems more willing to identify and enforce strong procedural requirements in lower-stakes, smaller-scale cases that involve deliberate deprivation of existing access to services. Drawing from the legalized-accountability model, social rights advocates can reframe these individual cases as examples of institutional problems and use them as platforms to push for more substantial participation rights in those processes without asking courts to intervene directly in those larger processes.

First, the relatively small scale of individual eviction cases provides a vehicle for establishing stronger procedural norms that minimize the direct political costs of compliance. Second, evictions generally target municipal policies and procedures rather than national policies. Indeed, a key feature of the eviction model is enforcement of national legislation, especially PIE but also the Housing Act. Using eviction cases to establish more systematic participation requirements at the local government level therefore allows the Court to characterize stronger interventions to enforce the ANC's own policies.

Finally, focusing on local government failures gives the Court more political room under Roux's analysis. Dugard argues that studies of local protests suggest "a critical disjuncture between national and local politics" in which local communities "view local problems as arising from corrupt councilors who are betraying the ANC."[258] Dugard hypothesizes that this disconnect could serve to continue to insulate the ANC from the potential

[257] *Joe Slovo*, *supra* note 19, [381]. [258] Dugard, *supra* note 5, 292.

political pressure these protests have generated by deflecting it to local political representatives.[259]

That same insulating effect, however, also creates the opportunities to leverage national political pressure for local government reforms. It opens the kind of political space Roux identifies as critical for courts to take a more active role by creating a potential alignment between engagement orders targeting local government failures and the national government's own interests. Following the 2014 national elections, there are signs that the national ANC is beginning to view the persistent failures of municipal governments reflected in the sustained increase in service-delivery protests as a more serious political threat than in the past.[260] The next chapter analyzes these political shifts in more detail and argues they increase the likelihood the Court may continue to exercise its procedural role in even stronger ways that could create the incentives necessary for communities and activists to begin developing meaningful engagement to establish a more sustained role.

[259] Ibid.

[260] The ANC's appointment of the well-respected Pravin Gordhan as head of the Ministry in charge of local government generally is perceived as evidence it perceives these problems as a serious political threat. *See* Shanti Aboobaker, "Gordhan Sent to Clean Up Local Government," IOL Online, May 26, 2014, at www.iol.co.za/news/politics/gordhan-sent-to-clean-up-local-government-1.1693611#.VEfJAildXWY; "Municipal Man: Pravin Gordhan Tackles Transformation's Ultimate Test," *Daily Maverick* (October 22, 2014), at www.dailymaverick.co.za/article/2014–09–04-municipal-man-pravin-gordhan-tackles-transformations-ultimate-test/#.VEfLPildXWY.

10

Conclusion

Real rights

In an expansive critique of the comparative constitutional law field generally, Ran Hirschl cites the social rights literature as a paradigmatic example of a general failure to engage with the "realpolitik" factors that political science and social science research have demonstrated exert much greater influence than formal legal doctrine: "in the world of comparative social rights jurisprudence, there are no macroeconomic doctrines, fiscal realities, political interests, legacies of welfare provision, elections, or patterns of executive-judiciary relations."[1] In a related article focused specifically on social rights, he and Evan Rosevear critique that same narrow, doctrinal emphasis and call for empirical and political analyses of why constitutions incorporate social rights and how courts enforce them in different constitutional systems.[2] Applying such an empirical analysis, they argue, reveals that the entrenchment of social rights in a broad range of constitutional systems has not meaningfully improved overall inequality or instigated greater redistributive policies.[3]

Hirschl undoubtedly is correct that "idealist normative accounts" and "insular case-law" analyses cannot by themselves demonstrate the efficacy of social rights, and that it is necessary to "understand these rights as part of a larger matrix of public-policy, economics and policy."[4] The previous three chapters drew some modest and tentative connections between the close case analyses of the earlier chapters and the sociopolitical issues Hirschl raises. Chapter 7 identified the overlap between the Court's own jurisprudential limits and Theunis Roux's political account of the earlier social rights cases. Chapters 8 and 9 then considered how the

[1] Ran Hirschl, "From Comparative Constitutional Law to Comparative Constitutional Studies," 11 *Int'l J. Const. L J.* 1, 9 (2013).

[2] Ran Hirschl and Evan Rosevear, "Constitutional Law Meets Comparative Politics: Socio-Economic Rights and Political Realities," in Tom Campbell *et al.* (eds.), *The Legal Protection of Human Rights: Skeptical Essays* (2011) 220–21.

[3] Ibid., 220. [4] Ibid., 208.

eviction model and democratic engagement could provide enforcement approaches that worked within those overlapping constraints.

Acknowledging that judicial enforcement of social rights is both shaped and limited by a broad range of social and political factors doesn't necessarily mean that broad macroeconomic measures like patterns of income inequality in the Gini coefficient or aggregate levels of development in the Human Development Index are the correct measures of whether and how such enforcement can or has had any meaningful effect. That argument has strong intuitive appeal. Surely the point of entrenching social rights and giving courts the power to enforce them is to reduce overall inequality or poverty, or at least to generate government policies that are more redistributive. But focusing exclusively or even primarily on macroeconomic measures makes the same error that Hirschl critiques by expecting entrenchment and judicial enforcement on their own to have relatively short-term and identifiable society-wide effects.

The macroeconomic measures Hirschl cites are related to the myth-of-rights or "neorealist" arguments that rights and rights-based strategies are effective only if they result in some empirically measurable material change.[5] Chapter 2 outlined the constructivist response. Reliance on empirical measures like these defines the goals of rights too narrowly. Rights can have both direct and indirect effects on a range of actors and institutions. Those effects may be discernible only over time and are likely to be most apparent at a relatively fine-grained level.[6]

Using these broader measures also reflects the macro-level focus typical of political science studies of law and social change. Administrative-law and sociolegal studies, by contrast, have documented ways that court decisions contributed to micro-level changes in bureaucratic structures and decision-making processes.[7] These are the kinds of diffuse and indirect changes that constructivists argue demonstrate that legal interventions

[5] *See* Malcolm Langford, "Introduction," in Malcolm Langford *et al.* (eds.), *Socio-Economic Rights and South Africa: Symbols or Substance?* (2013) 1, 21–23 (summarizing and critiquing "neorealist" analyses); Malcolm Langford, Jackie Dugard, Tshepo Madlingozi, and Ben Cousins, "Concluding Perspectives," in Malcolm Langford *et al.* (eds.), *Socio-Economic Rights and South Africa: Symbols or Substance?* (2013) 421 *See, generally*, Michael McCann, "Litigation and Legal Mobilization," in Keith Whittington *et al.* (eds.), *Oxford Handbook of Law and Politics* (2010) 522, 532–35.

[6] Langford, "Introduction," *supra* note 5, 21–23.

[7] E.g., Keith Whittington, Richard Kelemen, and Gregory Caldeira, "Introduction," in Keith Whittington, Richard Kelemen, and Gregory Caldeira (eds.), *Oxford Handbook of Law and Politics* (2010) 1; Charles Epp, "Law as an Instrument of Social Reform," in Keith Whittington *et al.* (eds.), *supra* note 5, Ch. 3.

can have real and meaningful effects over time. Those effects, however, are only a component of much larger social and political processes.

Understanding whether and how social rights have had meaningful effects thus calls for a much finer-grained examination of their interaction with particular aspects of these sociopolitical processes. These include not just litigation but also political mobilization, community organization, and bureaucratic reforms. Measuring social rights by whether litigation itself succeeds in reducing inequality or generating policies that, in the aggregate, move in a more redistributive direction simply asks too much. The better question is whether social rights have played some identifiable role in mobilizing legal, political, and community efforts aimed at reaching those goals.[8]

Several recent studies of social rights litigation and mobilization in South Africa conclude that the social rights can and have had discernible pro-poor effects not captured by macroeconomic measures. These studies uniformly acknowledge that social rights are not an unalloyed good, but they identify several rights-based strategies that have contributed to meaningful social change.[9]

The patterns in the second-wave cases reflect a similarly modest evaluation of the role social rights can play in shaping political responses to poverty and inequality. The Court has repeatedly acknowledged the limits of its power and the primacy of political processes in fulfilling the social rights and generating social and political change.

These studies and the Court's own decisions, however, demonstrate that conceding "rights alone certainly do not do the trick" does not mean social rights are pointless.[10] Nor does it inevitably lead to the more damning conclusion that relying on rights-based strategies diverts energy and resources away from more efficacious tactics like political mobilization and social-movement development. It does, however, accept that the effects of social rights will be modest, diffuse, and in most cases, incremental.[11]

[8] Langford, "Introduction," *supra* note 5, 21–23.

[9] Langford *et al.*, *supra* note 5; Daniel M. Brinks and Varun Gauri, "The Law's Majestic Equality? The Distributive Impact of Litigating Social and Economic Rights," World Bank Development Research Group Working Paper 5999 (2012); Varun Gauri and Daniel M. Brinks (eds.), *Courting Social Justice: Judicial Enforcement of Social and Economic Rights in the Developing World* (2010).

[10] Hirschl and Rosevear, *supra* note 2, 223.

[11] Jackie Dugard and Malcolm Langford, "Art or Science? Synthesizing Lessons from Public Interest Litigation and the Dangers of Legal Determinism," 27 *S. Afr. J. Hum. Rts.* 39, 41 (2012); King, *supra* note 7, 63–70.

This chapter connects the eviction model and democratic engagement to these studies of the ways that social rights have contributed to meaningful social change. Although it analyzes these studies to reject the strong version of Hirschl's argument, it does not directly address the questions he asks. Instead, the point of drawing these connections is to consider – in a system like South Africa's that includes an array of justiciable social rights – what judicial roles seem more likely to positively influence the broader processes Hirschl argues are the dominant factors in social change. More specifically, the chapter asks, given the constraints that the Constitutional Court seems to be operating within, do the eviction model and democratic engagement have the potential to influence those processes?

Framing the inquiry in this way accepts the argument that the Court operates under real and considerable constraints when it enforces social rights. Chapter 7's analysis of the internal dynamics of the Court's decisions and their connection to Roux's political analysis identified outlined those constraints. But that same analysis also identified patterns where the Court moved toward a more authoritative role. Chapters 8 and 9 analyzed and developed two enforcement models that build on those more authoritative interventions while still working within the limits of the second-wave cases and Roux's political constraints. This chapter shifts direction to consider whether and how these limited, largely procedural, enforcement approaches could effect the kinds of diffuse and incremental changes these case studies of effective legal mobilization identify.

A. Justiciability and social change

Before turning to these studies, it is useful briefly to revisit the connections between the justiciability concerns and the myth-of-rights debate Chapter 2 discussed. Both the neorealist view that judicial enforcement has no meaningful impact on public policy and the constructivist view that it can have some limited but meaningful effects under the right circumstances provide direct responses to the justiciability concerns. Accepting the shared starting point of both realists and constructivists that courts are constrained by their political environment also means that judicial enforcement of social rights will be relatively democratic. This point may seem obvious, but as Hirschl points out, the normative arguments in the justiciability debate often implicitly assume that democratic-legitimacy and institutional-competence concerns hinge principally, if not exclusively, on formal doctrinal limits and that courts are relatively free to move along a continuum of enforcement approaches.[12]

If, as neorealists argue, political, cultural, and economic factors have much greater influence than entrenched social rights on whether and how redistributive policies develop in particular polities, that also must mean courts aren't preempting large areas of democratic decision-making or regularly entangling themselves in issues far outside their expertise with potentially disastrous practical consequences. Likewise, the conditions the constructivists argue are necessary for court enforcement to make some difference suggest that court interventions largely support rather than preempt democratic politics.[13]

Charles Epp's influential support-structure thesis demonstrates that rights-protective judgments require a substantial network of well-resourced organizations with sufficiently broad political support to influence courts.[14] Epp's related "legalized-accountability" model builds on that thesis and shows that legal rights can instigate bureaucratic and administrative reforms but only where those reforms are pushed by active and well-resourced interest groups.[15] Varun Gauri and Daniel Brinks's analysis of case studies of social rights litigation in several countries, including South Africa, similarly concludes "courts can advance social and economic rights under the right conditions precisely because they are never fully independent of political pressures" and that the relative effectiveness of judicial enforcement is directly related to the level of external political support for the outcome and the capacity of the groups it benefits to mobilize within that political environment.[16]

This research shows that courts tend not only to work within existing political currents but also that courts are aware of and responsive to the resources and capacity limits of the state and the organizations involved in a case. As a result courts tailor their decisions and the scope of their orders to reflect both government capacity to comply and claimants' ability to press for compliance.[17] Although not completely eliminating the

[12] Hirschl, *supra* note 1, 2.

[13] E.g,. Varun Gauri and Daniel M. Brinks, "Introduction," in Gauri and Brinks, *supra* note 9, at 1, 28 (arguing "courts will be more effective when they act well within the political mainstream and with substantial support from other political actors").

[14] Charles R. Epp, *The Rights Revolution: Lawyers, Activists, and Supreme Courts in Comparative Perspective* (1998) ("*Rights Revolution*").

[15] Charles R. Epp, *Making Rights Real: Activists, Bureaucrats, and the Creation of the Legalistic State* (2010) ("*Making Rights Real*").

[16] Gauri and Brinks, "Introduction," *supra* note 13, 6.

[17] Ibid., 14–16.

possibility for courts either to make mistakes regarding technical, scientific, or economic questions or to misjudge the empirical consequences of a decision in a specific case, these self-imposed limits significantly minimize the strain on judicial competence that form the other side of the normative objections to entrenching social rights.

The eviction model and democratic engagement outlined in the previous two chapters recognize and operate within the constraints both the realists and constructivists identify. The internal patterns in the Court's second-wave social rights jurisprudence, especially the Court's concern with preempting democratic authority and its consistent emphasis on legislative leadership in fulfilling the social rights, mirror those same constraints. Close analysis of these internal patterns, however, showed that the Court often adopts a more authoritative role when it works within those constraints.

The connection between *Mazibuko*'s redefinition of social rights as tools for policing democratic accountability and the Court's broader participatory democracy jurisprudence identifies a related doctrinal basis that reinforces this more authoritative role.[18] The deeply participatory understanding of democracy the Court articulated in those decisions amplifies the legitimacy of using social rights to enforce extensive procedural rights and order structured engagement. The network of community-participation legislation and policy Chapter 9 analyzed creates a direct democratic basis for courts to use individual cases as platforms to address the systemic problems that underlie both the lack of meaningful participation in local government and the bureaucratic failures that have undermined effective service delivery. By enforcing these legislative mandates rather than an independent judicial standard, the Court further legitimates its role.

Viewed in isolation that enhanced legitimacy arguably comes at the cost of effective enforcement of social rights. By shifting away from a strong interpretive role that establishes clear principles defining the substance of the social rights in favor of secondary, procedural protections – even extensive procedures like a structured engagement backed up by the threat of strong remedies – courts appear to be giving up a defining aspect of judicial review.[19]

[18] *Mazibuko and Others v City of Johannesburg and Others* 2010 (3) BCLR 239 (CC) (2009).

[19] E.g., David Bilchitz, Socio-economic rights, economic crisis, and legal doctrine, 12 *Int'l Const. L. J.* 710 (2014); Danie Brand, "The Proceduralisation of South African

Experimentalism and participatory governance theories complicate that picture. Both literatures suggest that deepening democracy by increasing participation can make government more responsive to marginalized communities and also produce policies that are more effective.[20] Participatory governance studies suggests that stronger participation by poor communities – under the right circumstances and structured in the right ways – could promote social justice by bringing marginalized groups into decision-making processes that affect them and reorienting policy priorities and budgets.[21]

These arguments put both the procedural enforcement model and the democratic-legitimacy concern to which it responds in a different light. They suggest that a judicial approach focused on participatory processes and grounded in a commitment to deep democracy can be effective in changing state institutions and processes. The legalized-accountability model and experimentalist review specifically identify litigation as a forum for local communities and social rights activists first to identify systemic problems and second to create leverage for bureaucratic and administrative changes that can effectively address those problems.[22] The eviction model has the potential to draw on those insights by reorienting the judicial role toward establishing procedural mechanisms that create a forum and leverage for poor communities to challenge specific policies and decisions. Democratic engagement broadens that framework and suggests courts can and should manage those individual processes to reinvigorate existing participation structures and establish new ones that give communities consistent access to local government policy-making and budgeting processes to make them more transparent, accountable, and responsive.

Socioeconomic Rights Jurisprudence, or 'What Are Socioeconomic Rights For?'" in Henk Botha *et al.* (eds.), *Rights and Democracy in a Transformative Constitution* (2003).

20 Patrick Heller, "Democracy, Participatory Politics and Development: Some Comparative Lessons from Brazil, India and South Africa," 44 *Polity* 643 (2012); Archon Fung and Erik Olin Wright, "Deepening Democracy: Innovations in Empowered Participatory Governance," 29 *Politics & Soc'y* 5 (2001); Charles F. Sabel and Jonathan Zeitlin (eds.), *Experimentalist Governance in the European Union: Towards a New Architecture* (2010); Charles F. Sabel and William H. Simon, "Minimalism and Experimentalism in the Administrative State," 100 *Geo. L. J.* 53 (2011).

21 Michael Goodhart (ed.), "Democratic Imperatives: Innovations in Rights, Participation and Economic Citizenship, Draft Report of the American Political Science Association Task Force on Democracy, Economic Security and Social Justice in a Volatile World (2012) 50; Heller, *supra* note 20, 645–48.

22 Epp, *supra* note 15; Charles F. Sabel and William H. Simon, "Destabilization Rights: How Public Law Litigation Succeeds," 117 *Harv. L. Rev.* 1016 (2004).

This is not to say that procedural rights and remedies are always effective, much less to suggest that they are superior to other judicial approaches in every situation. As Dugard and Langford argue, "litigation is always context-specific and judicial outcome is hard to predict."[23] The claim here is far more modest: the enhanced democratic legitimacy that comes from procedural interventions to enforce participation rights may turn what looks like an unalloyed constraint into a tool for effective enforcement of social rights. The remainder of the chapter explores that claim.

B. Social rights and social change

An important recent compilation of studies of social rights mobilization in South Africa concludes that in many instances social rights-related litigation and mobilization have had a positive impact on poor communities.[24] These case studies document evidence that social rights litigation in South Africa has materially improved living conditions, prevented the loss of existing access to basic services, and changed power relationships between poor people and the state in ways that forced pro-poor policy changes or resulted directly in increased benefits. The studies also provide evidence that in some cases the litigation instigated broader political changes and helped prompt more systematic policy and legal reforms.[25] Consistent with the recognition that litigation is not sufficient by itself to create meaningful change, these studies "chart discernable positive impacts flowing from the use of rights-based tactics and strategies" but "also emphasize the wide variation in outcomes, the limits of rights, and in some cases the existence of negative impacts."[26]

The eviction cases discussed in earlier chapters provide representative examples of litigation that resulted in identifiable material effects. These material effects frequently were indirect resulting from "interim settlement orders, court-sanctioned negotiations, or court-ordered compensation for property owners that created monetary incentives" for municipalities to change policies or reverse specific decisions.[27] In the aggregate, however, the housing and eviction cases show how "small communities with minimal legal support and funding" have achieved not only legal victories but also "have successfully resisted eviction, improved

[23] Dugard and Langford, *supra* note 11, 60.
[24] Langford *et al.*, *supra* note 5, 431; *see, also*, Dugard and Langford, *supra* note 11.
[25] Langford *et al.*, *supra* note 5, 431–40. [26] Ibid., 431. [27] Ibid., 432.

their housing situation (and that of surrounding communities), reformed national policy and legislation and forced local municipalities to develop innovative and potentially replicable housing policies and practices."[28]

Beyond the material effects illustrated by the eviction cases, social rights litigation in several contexts changed power relationships in ways that gave advocacy groups leverage indirectly to influence policy changes. In some cases like *Mazibuko*, these changes occurred as litigation progressed so the state could better position itself during the litigation rather than from a favorable court decision. In others they changed the overall approach the government adopted to a recurring issue.[29] Here again, the housing-rights context provides one of the clearest illustrations. An analysis of section 26–related litigation found that *Grootboom* prompted proactive changes by government officials in the housing-policy development process, with municipalities often "*Grootboom*-proofing" new policies to avoid the possibility of litigation.[30]

The authors of these studies identify several conditions that enabled litigation to have these direct and indirect effects. Notably these conditions largely track the patterns in the second-wave cases that limit the Constitutional Court's approach. In particular, claims to new or significantly expanded entitlements were unlikely to succeed either in litigation or advocacy. Litigation defending existing access and incrementally expanding programs or services had much greater effect. Success also was linked to the ability of groups to organize and mobilize others around rights-based strategies.[31]

A set of cross-cutting factors consistently limited the effects of litigation.[32] First, private power was less susceptible to social rights challenges. Progressive court decisions generally failed to change broad social values, and both courts and the government were reluctant to significantly alter existing economic distributions. Second, initiatives targeted at national policies generally had greater success than those focused locally. This was in large part because there is "greater access to sympathetic and capable bureaucrats and politicians" at the national level.[33] Finally, rights-based strategies were more effective in urban than rural areas.[34]

[28] Dugard and Langford, *supra* note 11, 61. [29] Langford *et al.*, *supra* note 5, 432.

[30] Malcolm Langford, "Housing Rights Litigation," in Malcolm Langford *et al.* (eds.), *Socio-Economic Rights and South Africa: Symbols or Substance* (2013) 187, 203–4 ("Housing Rights").

[31] Langford *et al.*, *supra* note 5, 441. [32] Ibid., 442–47.

[33] Ibid., 445. [34] Ibid., 442–47.

C. The support structure for social rights

These studies demonstrate that more nuanced analyses of social rights can "chart discernable positive impacts flowing from the use of rights-based tactics and strategies" in South Africa.[35] Focused as they are on individual case studies, however, these studies do not depict the full range of organizations and activities that draw on social rights.

South Africa's persistently high levels of poverty and inequality have generated a substantial, sustained, and successful range of advocacy and community mobilization activities that focus directly and indirectly on social rights.[36] The influence of social rights in each case is difficult to identify with any precision.[37] Nonetheless, it's clear that social rights "have provided a rich discursive opportunity" for many of these groups and that the number and diversity of organizations focused specifically on social rights is growing.[38]

Several other rights have been the focus of targeted and highly successful advocacy campaigns in South Africa. Among the most famous of these is the strategic litigation around section 9's prohibition against sexual-orientation discrimination that generated a series of favorable decisions culminating in the Court's ruling that the state was required to recognize same-sex marriage.[39] But that was a carefully constructed, largely elite-driven effort that deliberately avoided extensive grassroots mobilization.[40] Arguably, no other area of constitutional law has produced the same sustained judicial attention or inspired the same breadth and level of social-movement and professional–legal organization as the social rights.[41]

That the emergence of this extensive range of social rights influenced activism itself is strong evidence that including these rights in the 1996 Constitution has contributed to changing the sociopolitical landscape in

[35] Ibid., 431.

[36] E.g., Richard Ballard *et al.*, "Globalisation, Marginalisation, and Contemporary Social Movements in South Africa," 104 *Afr. Affairs* 615, 625 (2005); Steven Budlender, Gilbert Marcus, and Nick Ferreira, "Public Interest Litigation and Social Change in South Africa: Strategies, Tactics and Lessons," *Atlantic Philanthropies Report* (2014) 7–8.

[37] Langford *et al.*, *supra* note 5, 429–31.

[38] Ibid., 429.

[39] *See* Pierre de Vos, "The 'Inevitability' of Same-Sex Marriage in South Africa's Post-Apartheid State," 23 *S. Afr. J. Hum. Rts* 432 (2007).

[40] Ibid.

[41] The Atlantic Philanthropies' survey of public-interest litigation in South Africa selected social-rights-related litigation for six of the seven case studies it analyzed. Budlender *et al.*, *supra* note 36, 26.

South Africa. In the immediate transition period, the well-developed public interest litigation structure that had worked to challenge the apartheid system was in a state of flux.[42] Although the extensive set of rights in the 1996 Constitution provided rich fodder for potential strategic litigation, the new government was controlled by the ANC, the presumptive champion of the values the Constitution enshrined.[43] The ANC itself sought to exert influence over civil society and position it as a partner in implementing political and social transformation.[44] In addition many prominent civil society leaders joined the ANC government, creating direct connections that further blurred the lines between the state and civil society.[45] This created a political environment that emphasized cooperation with the new government to achieve the Constitution's goals rather than challenges to it.[46] The demobilizing effect of the transition to democracy and the ANC's dominant position in the new government was compounded by shifts in donor funding to projects aimed at building the state's own capacity to function effectively and deliver the expanded services promised under the new constitutional order.[47]

This environment started to change around the late 1990s. Civil society organizations increasingly began to work in opposition to state policies, and beginning in 2000 there was a marked increase in public interest litigation – much of it focused on social rights – challenging state policies.[48] Among other factors prompting the resurgence of oppositional civil society was the ANC's move toward a more neoliberal economic policy. This policy change was formally enshrined in the ANC's fiscally conservative

[42] Ibid., 8. [43] Ibid., 7–8; Ballard *et al.*, *supra* note 36, 622–23.

[44] Ballard *et al.*, *supra* note 36, 622–23; Theunis Roux, *The Politics of Principle: The First South African Constitutional Court, 1995–2005* (2013) 180–81.

[45] Budlender *et al.*, *supra* note 36, 8; Richard Ballard, "Social Movements in Post Apartheid South Africa: An Introduction," in Peris Jones and Kristian Stokke (eds.), *Democratising Development: The Politics of Socio-Economic Rights in South Africa* (2005); Laurence Piper and Lubna Nadvi, "Popular Mobilisation, Party Dominance and Participatory Governance in South Africa," in Lisa Thompson and Chris Tapscott (eds.), *Citizenship and Social Movements: Perspectives from the Global South* (2010) 212.

[46] E.g., Richard Pithouse, "A Politics of the Poor: Shack Dwellers' Struggles in Durban," 43 *J. Asian & Afr. Stud.* 63 (2008); Tshepo Madlingozi, "Post-Apartheid Social Movements and the Quest for the Elusive 'New' South Africa," 34 *J. L. & Soc'y* 77, 85 (2007); Mark Heywood, "Civil Society and Uncivil Government: The Treatment Action Campaign (TAC) versus Thabo Mbeki, 1998–2008," in Daryl Glaser (ed.), *Mbeki and After: Reflections on the Legacy of Thabo Mbeki* (2010) 5–7.

[47] Ballard *et al.*, *supra* note 36, provide a nice graphical illustration of this shift at 17. *See, also*, Piper and Nadvi, *supra* note 45, 215.

[48] Budlender *et al.*, *supra* note 36, 8–12; Piper and Nadvi, *supra* note 45, 215–16.

Growth, Employment and Redistribution (GEAR) strategy adopted in 1996.[49] GEAR's fiscal austerity and market-based approach conflicted with the ANC's commitment to redressing the economic legacies of apartheid. It also arguably was inconsistent with the social rights' mandate to ensure adequate access to basic services, setting up a conflict that eventually lead to several social rights cases.[50]

Legacy public interest organizations like the Legal Resources Centre and the University of the Western Cape's Community Law Centre were involved in early cases such as *Grootboom*, but increasingly new organizations specifically focused on the social rights are taking the lead role in litigation.[51] The Treatment Action Campaign's multi-pronged advocacy on HIV-AIDS-related issues that resulted in the successful Constitutional Court litigation in 2002 is the most prominent early example.[52] A growing number of social rights-related organizations have emerged since.

The Court's increasing social rights docket in the second wave reflects the development of this support structure. This structure includes organizations with an explicit litigation focus. Among the most active of these are the Socio-Economic Rights Institute (SERI), founded in 2008 by two researchers formerly with the University of Witwatersrand's Centre for Applied Legal Studies (CALS); Section 27, established in 2010 by a leading member of TAC, and, more recently, Equal Education, a community-based organization that started in Khayelitsha in 2008.[53] These organizations have played prominent roles in most of the second-wave cases and have brought a range of lower-court cases.[54] They also each engage in sophisticated social rights advocacy efforts that combine targeted litigation with community mobilization, political activity, research, and education.

49 "Growth, Employment, and Redistribution: A Macroeconomic Strategy," Department of Finance, Republic of South Africa," at www.treasury.gov.za/publications/other/gear/chapters.pdf.

50 *See* Roux, *supra* note 44, 176–79.

51 *Government of the Republic of South Africa and Others v Grootboom and Others* 2000 (11) BCLR 1169 (CC) [17] ("*Grootboom*").

52 *See* Heywood, *supra* note 46, 21–24 (describing TAC as part of "the advent of new social movements" in the early 2000s).

53 *See* www.seri-sa.org/index.php/2013–03–07–10–16–20/about-seri; section 27, "2012–2013 Review," at http://section 27.org.za/wp-content/uploads/2014/10/S27review2014web.pdf; www.equaleducation.org.za/page/what-is-ee.

54 www.seri-sa.org/index.php/litigation-9/cases; Section 27, *supra* note 53; www.equaleducation.org.za/campaigns/legal.

These litigation and advocacy organizations are connected to a broader network of South African and international organizations that engage in applied research and policy analyses of social rights-related issues. On the academic side, several South African universities have social rights-focused research projects that have actively participated in litigation through background research, filing *amicus curiae* briefs, and directly representing parties through their legal clinics.[55]

Notably there is a strong connection between social rights and issues related to governance and democratic accountability. Several of the advocacy organizations listed earlier incorporate these issues into their work. For example, Section 27 is closely involved in the Budget and Expenditure Monitoring Forum, a consortium of civil society organizations that works "to ensure that the South African budget process is transparent and participatory," including by facilitating "constructive engagement between civil society and government" on social service budgets.[56] One of SERI's three thematic areas is "political space," which focuses on protecting "the political spaces within which communities can peacefully assemble, demonstrate, articulate and campaign for the advancement of their socio-economic rights claims."[57]

Organizations that focus primarily on governance issues also frequently connect those issues either directly or indirectly to social rights. Although these groups are not explicitly focused on litigation (and some not even on rights enforcement per se), their work is connected to and frequently builds directly on the work of the rights-advocacy groups identified previously. Equally important, these groups could provide the support structure necessary to generate the policy and institutional reform proposals that are critical in the legalized-accountability model.

Prominent examples include the Isandla Institute, a public interest think tank founded 1994 that describes itself as a "hothouse" for "policy ideas about the reduction of urban inequality, poverty racism and social exclusion."[58] One of Isandla's signature projects is a set of dialogues on the "right to the city," which protests "the growth of inequality, marginalisation, discrimination and a lack of public participation in

[55] Examples include the University of the Western Cape's CLC, the University of Witwatersrand's CALS, and the University of Stellenbosch Socio-Economic Rights and Administrative Justice Centre.

[56] Section 27, *supra* note 53, 76–79.

[57] www.seri-sa.org/index.php/2013–03–07–10–16–20/political-space.

[58] http://isandla.org.za/publications/.

decision-making" in municipalities.[59] These dialogues bring together representatives of the urban poor, NGOs identified by community-based organizations, and government officials.

Planact, a Gauteng-based community-development group founded in 1985, says its mission is "to support and mobilise community processes that enhance good governance at the local level to improve people's habitable environment in ways that alleviate poverty."[60] It has worked extensively on participatory approaches to housing development and informal-settlement upgrading. One of Planact's four program areas is "participatory governance," which aims "to influence bureaucratic systems through improved participation" in particular at the local government level.[61]

In 2003 several of these organizations formed the Good Governance Learning Network (GGLN), an umbrella organization focused on promoting "participatory, accountable and pro-poor local governance."[62] GGLN produces a yearly report on the state of local governance and "has consistently highlighted the shortcomings in the design, interpretation and implementation of the edifice of participatory local governance."[63] GGLN and its member organizations have closely analyzed local government planning processes and documented the problems that plague existing participation structures. A 2012 report focused on the new NDP analyzes these problems in light of the NDP's renewed emphasis on community participation and offers a range of proposals for creating meaningful participation structures.[64]

The rise of these advocacy and policy organizations coincided with similar growth in social movements and community-based organizations that rely in part on tactical use of social rights to promote their goals.[65] A 2009 analysis of thirty-six social movements in South Africa found that eighteen of the organizations were founded after 2000 and eleven

[59] http://isandla.org.za/publications/134/. [60] www.planact.org.za/.

[61] www.planact.org.za/programme-areas/participatory-governance/.

[62] http://isandla.org.za/projects/good-governance-learning-network/.

[63] Good Governance Learning Network, "Putting Participation at the Heart of Development//Putting Development at the Heart of Participation: A Civil Society Perspective on Local Governance in South Africa" (2012) 5, at www.ggln.org.za/publications/state-of-local-governance-research-project/ggln-state-of-local-governance-publication-2012.pdf.

[64] Good Governance Learning Network, "Community Based Planning in the Context of the National Development Plan Research Paper" (2013).

[65] Heywood, *supra* note 44, 23–24; Ballard *et al.*, *supra* note 36, 628–29.

between 1994 and 2000. The large majority of these organizations focus primarily on issues related to land, housing and basic services.[66] Many of the organizations formed after 1996 identified the government's adoption of the GEAR economic policy as a motivating factor.[67]

The 2009 study found that, although these organizations generally did not associate these issues with a lack of rights per se, many used rights and litigation as a strategy to advance their claims.[68] Several of the organizations identified in that study were involved in the second-wave cases. Most prominent and successful among these is Abahlali baseMjondolo.[69] Abahlali baseMjondolo's victory in the Constitutional Court is only a small part of a much broader mobilization effort that includes regular use of litigation to prevent evictions.[70]

D. The eviction model's impact

A recent study of housing-rights litigation by Malcolm Langford in the collection described earlier demonstrates that judicial enforcement of *Grootboom* and PIE has produced real changes in policies at the national, provincial, and local levels.[71] What the Court has identified as the "dignified framework" it established and Chapter 8 calls the eviction model is a major part of the changes Langford describes. Broad measures of society-wide inequality and even narrower assessments of the redistributive effects of government policies completely miss the important, pro-poor changes the eviction model has created. The legal framework for evictions has changed in significant ways, and municipalities in South Africa now increasingly recognize that they are required to plan and budget for emergency housing for people evicted from both public and private land.

[66] Heywood, *supra* note, 46, 13.

[67] Diana Mitlin and Jan Mogaladi, "Social Movements and Poverty Reduction in South Africa," Working Paper (2009), available at www.sed.manchester.ac.uk/research/socialmovements/publications/reports/; *See, also*, Ballard *et al.*, *supra* note 36, 623–26. These authors emphasize the diversity of social movements that have emerged since 1994 but agree "that the most important factor giving rise to contemporary social movements in South Africa is probably the high and growing level of poverty and inequality" connected to national economic policy. Ibid., 625.

[68] Mitlin and Mogaladi, *supra* note 67, 24–25.

[69] Tshepo Madlingozi, "Post-Apartheid Social Movements and Legal Mobilisation," in Malcolm Langford *et al.* (eds.), *supra* note 5, 92, 114–15.

[70] Ibid., 114–22.

[71] Langford, "Housing Rights," *supra* note 30; *see, also*, Dugard and Langford, *supra* note 11.

1. *Municipal policies*

The evolution in the legal arguments municipalities advance in eviction cases illustrate a shift in the formal legal stance they have adopted regarding their housing obligations. Municipalities, at least formally, now recognize that section 26, PIE and national housing legislation collectively limit their power to evict and also impose an affirmative obligation to plan and budget for housing potential evictees.[72] For example, in 2008 the City of Johannesburg defended its mass-eviction program in *Olivia Road* by arguing that PIE did not apply to evictions from buildings it determined presented health and safety standards, and characterized as "untenable" the idea that occupiers' section 26(3) rights were implicated in that situation.[73] Four years later in *Blue Moonlight* the City relied heavily on the policy it developed in direct response to *Olivia Road* that prioritized emergency housing for people evicted from buildings that posed health and safety risks to defend its failure to budget for emergency accommodation for people evicted from private land.[74] In a complete reversal of its position in *Olivia Road* that its constitutional obligations were limited, the City argued this prioritization was justifiable in light of the extensive obligations PIE, section 26, and housing legislation imposed on municipalities to provide emergency housing and the limited resources available to meet those obligations.[75]

The growing acceptance at the municipal level that the state cannot evict people without providing alternative accommodation and that private evictions also implicate state responsibility to provide emergency housing has had several significant effects. On the most basic level it has severely curtailed blatantly unconstitutional policies like the City of Johannesburg's mass-eviction program successfully challenged in *Olivia Road*.[76] It also has substantially diminished the scale and pace of evictions in urban areas. Langford's study concludes that, although there are no systemic data on forced evictions, "it is relatively clear that the number of large-scale

[72] Langford, "Housing Rights," *supra* note 30, 220; Budlender *et al.*, *supra* note 36, 46–47.

[73] City of Johannesburg Heads of Argument, [26–50] in *Occupiers of 51 Olivia Road, Berea Township and 197 Main Street Johannesburg v City of Johannesburg and Others* 2008 (5) BCLR 475 (CC) (2008) ("*Olivia Road*").

[74] City of Johannesburg Heads of Argument in *City of Johannesburg Metropolitan Municipality v Blue Moonlight Properties 39 (Pty) Ltd and Another* 2012 (2) BCLR 150 (CC) (2011) ("*Blue Moonlight*").

[75] Ibid., [34–36], [39–44]. *See, also,* Stuart Wilson, "Curing the Poor," 5 *Const. Ct. Rev.* 279, 282–83 (2014).

[76] Wilson, *supra* note 75, 282.

government evictions has substantially decreased."[77] His interviews with social movements and housing-rights activists consistently confirmed a substantial decrease in inner-city evictions and demolitions.[78]

The eviction cases also have altered municipal planning for informal settlements. The 2004 Breaking New Ground policy that was at the heart of the *Joe Slovo* case generated an explicit policy focused on upgrading informal settlements rather than removing them.[79] That policy has fallen well short of its ambitious goal to eradicate informal settlements by 2014.[80] Nonetheless the formal shift away from eviction and relocation is notable in itself. Moreover, the strict limits the eviction model has established in several cases prompted municipalities to initiate on-site upgrading in specific areas to create alternative accommodation options.[81]

Finally, the eviction cases have indirectly influenced municipal policies in ways that show some signs of evolution toward the legalized-accountability model. One of the significant indirect effects of *Grootboom* has been what Langford calls the "*Grootboom*-proofing" of social policies.[82] In several 2010 interviews housing officials from Cape Town and Johannesburg cited *Grootboom* and subsequent judgments as "helpfully pushing them to review the adequacy of [housing] policy."[83] An earlier study of public interest litigation similarly found that *Grootboom* has prompted the government to carefully consider the possibility of social rights litigation in budgeting and policy processes and also that the decision has made government "far more responsive to lawyers' letters pointing out program flaws and requesting information."[84]

2. *Middle-class capture and regulatory effects*

In an updated analysis of their original study of social rights litigation in South Africa and several other countries, Daniel Brinks and Varun Gauri "predict, and find, that countries and policy areas characterized by judicial decisions with broader applicability beyond the litigants tend to

[77] Langford, "Housing Rights," *supra* note 30, 204.
[78] Ibid., 220. [79] Ibid., 201–2.
[80] Habitat for Humanity, "The Dynamics of Informal Settlements Upgrading in South Africa," Report (2013) 8.
[81] Langford, "Housing Rights," *supra* note 30, 202; Dugard and Langford, *supra* note 11, 61–62.
[82] Langford, "Housing Rights," *supra* note 30, 203–4. [83] Ibid., 204.
[84] Gilbert Marcus and Steven Budlender, "A Strategic Evaluation of Public Interest Litigation in South Africa," Atlantic Philanthropies Report (2008) 65.

avoid the presumed anti-poor bias of courts, while areas dominated by individual litigation and individualized effects are less likely to have pro-poor outcomes."[85] Individual litigation tends to result in greater "high-end state benefits, rather than low-cost goods" because such litigation will tend to be brought by people with resources who seek relief that benefits them.[86] This problem of "middle-class capture" is well documented in the social rights literature.[87]

Brinks and Gauri argue that an individual case can avoid the problem of middle-class capture and have generalizable effects, but only where it either establishes a broad precedent or where it creates "nonexcludable" public goods. This happens when the remedy changes law or policy or expands a program or service in ways that benefit people outside the litigation rather than providing only individualized relief.[88]

Brinks and Gauri identify three categories of cases. "Provision" cases demand a good or service funded by the state. "Regulation" cases require the state to create a new or modify an existing regulatory regime to recognize the obligations a right imposes. "Obligation" cases modify rights and duties between the party asserting a right and some third-party.[89] They argue that Regulation cases have the greatest progressive potential because those cases create public goods that affect large classes of people. Obligation cases are more likely to benefit people with existing access to a good or service. Provision cases focus on individual benefits but sometimes provide a platform for broader policy change.[90] The South African examples in the study show that a very small number of decisions in each area have had significant pro-poor effects largely because they were Regulation cases that affected broad underlying policies.[91]

On first glance the highly individualized eviction model seems to run directly counter to these findings. Each case relates to a single community usually in the context of an emergency proceeding to prevent imminent eviction. The Court has carefully limited the scope of each decision by tying it to case-specific factors and avoided establishing generalizable principles. Several aspects of the eviction model, however, either are, or could be developed, to fit Brinks and Gauri's model.

[85] Brinks and Gauri, *supra* note 9, 7. [86] Ibid., 8–9.

[87] David Landau, "The Reality of Social Rights Enforcement," 53 *Harv. Int'l L. J.* 189 (2012); Octavio Luiz Motta Ferraz, "Harming the Poor through Social Rights Litigation: Lessons from Brazil," 89 *Tex. L. Rev.* 1643 (2011).

[88] Brinks and Gauri, *supra* note 9, 11–14. [89] Ibid., 9–11.

[90] Ibid., 11–12. [91] Ibid., 23–24.

As an initial matter, evictions almost exclusively affect relatively poor people, eliminating the risk that better-resourced people will seek to enforce the right and capture its benefits. More importantly, the eviction model rests on the de facto broadly applicable principle that no person can be evicted unless alternative accommodation is available. These decisions effectively generalized *Grootboom*'s abstract principle by turning it into a right to demand alternative accommodation in every eviction case. This is the core of the "dignified framework" that the Court recognized now governs evictions.[92] Although the Court has consistently framed its interventions as driven by case-specific concerns and left open the possibility that people could be evicted even where no alternative accommodation is available, it has never ordered an eviction in those circumstances.[93]

Enforcing this principle still requires the resources to litigate, and that clearly has limited the effect of the eviction model in precisely the way Gauri and Brinks predict.[94] The growing number of cases challenging illegal eviction attempts by municipalities, despite the formal establishment of this dignified framework, underscores these limitations. Nonetheless, the growth in cases and the Constitutional Court's consistent refusal to grant an eviction without alternative accommodation demonstrates that the principle is working in consistently pro-poor ways for those with the resources to litigate.[95] Moreover, the fact that municipalities are beginning at least formally to acknowledge that every eviction implicates a duty to both house the evictees and provide related services described earlier demonstrates that this principle is starting to develop into something more like a regulatory change that Brinks and Gauri argue has greater pro-poor potential.[96]

Eviction cases thus are potentially hybrids under their model. All eviction cases fall into the individual Provision category because of the Court's

[92] *Abahlali baseMjondolo Movement SA and Another v Premier of the Province of Kwazulu-Natal and Others* 2010 (2) BCLR 99 (CC) (2009) [122] ("*Abahlali*").

[93] Indeed, the only eviction case lost by residents is *Joe Slovo*, and in that case the state sought to relocate rather than simply evict the residents. *Residents of Joe Slovo Community, Western Cape v Thubelisha Homes and Others* 2009 (9) BCLR 847 (CC) (2009). Moreover, the Court's expansive use of engagement in the order effectively provided the same protections that it has extended to potential evictees in the more recent cases in particular the opportunity to delay the eviction and negotiate over the specifics. Ibid.

[94] Brinks and Gauri, *supra* note 9, 15.

[95] Michael Clark, "Evictions and Alternative Accommodation in South Africa: An Analysis of the Jurisprudence and Implications for Local Government," SERI Report (2013); Dugard and Langford, *supra* note 11, 61–62.

[96] Dugard and Langford, *supra* note 11, 61–62; Langford, *supra* note 30, 220–22.

de facto principle that municipalities are required to provide alternative accommodation. Cases involving evictions from public land also are Regulatory cases because they prevent deprivation of existing access to a public good. In addition, these decisions have triggered broader regulatory effects represented by the changes in eviction policies and the "*Grootboom*-proofing" of housing and other social policies that Langford describes.[97] The potential for each individual case to involve the kind of incremental constitutional and statutory development Chapter 8 describes creates even greater regulatory potential by expanding the precedential effect of each case. Finally, cases involving eviction from private land also are obligation cases because they temporarily limit the rights of private landowners to protect the rights of occupiers.

3. *Backlash*

A core argument of the myth-of-rights critique is that progressive legal decisions frequently undermine the achievement of broader political goals by mobilizing opposing forces in society.[98] South Africa's history and political environment make the kind of broad political countermobilization described by Rosenberg and others unlikely in the case of pro-poor social rights decisions. Indeed, in the 2014 national elections the major political parties competed to position themselves as the true champions of progressive social-welfare policies, including housing.[99] There is general skepticism that those political promises will translate into real policy reform.[100] Nonetheless, the widespread adoption of pro-poor political platforms among the major political parties illustrates that backlash against pro-poor judicial decisions is unlikely to materialize in the near term.

A recent analysis of public interest litigation in South Africa found that a conservative countermobilization against progressive policies has

97 Langford, *supra* note 30, 203–4; Dugard and Langford, *supra* note 11, 61–62.

98 E.g., Gerald N. Rosenberg, *The Hollow Hope: Can Courts Bring About Social Change?* (2nd edn, 2008); Michael Klarman, *From Jim Crow to Civil Rights: The Supreme Court and the Struggle for Racial Equality* (2004). For a thorough discussion and critique of the backlash thesis in the social rights context, *see* King, *supra* note, 7, 67–70.

99 *See*, Stephen Grootes, "ANC's 2014 manifesto: promises, dreams, realities," *Daily Maverick*, March 13, 2014, available at www.dailymaverick.co.za/article/2014–01–11-ancs-2014-manifesto-promises-dreams-realities/#.VQMLurPF-OM.

100 *See* Steven Friedman, "South Africa's Election: Same Result, New Future?" Brookings, *Africa* in focus blog, May 5, 2014, available at www.brookings.edu/blogs/africa-in-focus/posts/2014/05/05-south-africa-election-friedman.

emerged in South Africa and is growing in strength and sophistication.[101] The efforts they cite, however, are not specifically targeted at social-welfare policies. More importantly, the conservative organizations lost each case documented in the study, and there was no evidence that these organizations have gained widespread political traction.[102]

That is not to say the Court is politically secure; only that its social rights decisions are unlikely to provoke the kind of issue-specific backlash described in the US literature. Indeed, Roux's analysis of the Chaskalson court's decisions is based on the political vulnerability the ANC's dominance in South African politics creates for the Court.[103] Dugard argues in a similar vein that the Court's political decisions – in particular decisions addressing claims of corruption in the ANC – not only intensified conflict with the ANC but also have been unpopular with the general public. The result is that "the Constitutional Court is a remote institution that is increasingly sandwiched between growing animosity from the polity over its political judgments on one hand and, on the other hand, disinterest and distrust by the majority poor citizenry."[104] This is compounded by the government's own resistance to successful court judgments and increasingly frequent public statements questioning the legitimacy of the courts.[105]

Chapter 7's analysis of the second-wave cases connected the internal patterns in those cases to these external political realities and argued together they reveal substantial constraints on the Court's capacity to enforce social rights. Both the eviction model and democratic engagement, however, are structured to work within those constraints and yet still could generate Court decisions that have important pro-poor and redistributive effects.

The Court's eviction jurisprudence has prompted several municipalities to develop creative legal arguments that avoid the full implications of the dignified framework it recognized in *Abahlali* and, in particular, the de facto obligation to house every evictee. On one hand, these strategies are further evidence that the eviction model has produced real change. The careful – even if spurious – distinction municipalities now attempt to

[101] Budlender *et al.*, *supra* note 36, 13–21.

[102] Ibid. *See, also,* Langford *et al.*, *supra* note 5, 441, note 9.

[103] Roux, *supra* note 44.

[104] Jackie Dugard, "Courts and Structural Poverty in South Africa: To What Extent Has the Constitutional Court Expanded Access and Remedies to the Poor?" in Daniel Bonilla Maldonado (ed.), *Constitutionalism in the Global South: The Activist Tribunals of India, South Africa, and Colombia* (2013) 293, 297–98.

[105] Ibid., note 15; Budlender *et al.*, *supra* note 36, 21–23.

draw between preventing land invasions and eviction show that municipalities are seeking to work within the legal framework the Court has established and have accepted on a formal level the extensive obligations that eviction entails. In the past, municipalities would simply have evicted these people without attempting to justify the evictions in these terms.

In addition, there is evidence that the scope of the evictions implemented under these new legal justifications are in fact limited to some extent by this framework. This has resulted in follow-up litigation that could further extend the effects of the eviction model. For example, litigation over the constitutionality of the City of Cape Town's anti-land invasion unit has focused on the City's limited view of the definition of "home" under PIE and whether it can delegate to front-line police the authority to determine which dwellings they can destroy without a court order.[106] Notably, the City sought to carefully distinguish between "homes," which it acknowledged PIE and section 26(3) protect and "unoccupied" structures recently erected as part of a "land invasion."[107]

More broadly, the emergence of this kind of internal resistance fits Epp's description of the legalized-accountability model's development in the diverse contexts he analyzes. In each instance, existing institutions initially reacted to litigation challenging their policies and practices with strong resistance.[108] But those cases created platforms for exposing systemic problems within those institutions. Successful court decisions then generated pressure for internal reformers to push for systemic change and provided a legal vehicle for an emerging set of stricter professional standards.[109]

4. *Limitations*

The eviction model has helped secure the right to stay in existing accommodation for people facing eviction who challenge their eviction in court. That in turn has prompted direct and significant changes to municipal eviction policies and also has influenced broader shifts in municipal and national housing policies. These effects are specifically targeted at poor people and are unlikely to generate the kind of direct backlash that

[106] *Fischer and Another v Ramahlele and Others*, 2014 (7) BCLR 838 (WCC) (2014). SERI intervened in the case on behalf of Abahlali baseMjondolo and filed several *amicus curiae* briefs in the original case and on appeal to the SCA. *See* www.seri-sa.org/index.php/19-litigation/case-entries/243-fischer-and-city-of-cape-town-v-ramahlele-and-46-others-fischer.

[107] Ibid., [23–24]. [108] Epp, *supra* note 15. [109] Ibid.

would undermine them in the longer term. The eviction model also has prompted significant resistance by municipalities designed to evade these new obligations, but that resistance is itself evidence of the model's effect.

The success of the eviction model in prompting these shifts shows the limits of relying solely on the macroeconomic factors Hirschl cites to assess the impact of social rights enforcement. This success also provides at least a partial response to the myth-of-rights contention that court-induced changes are a waste of time and resources because the same results could be achieved through political means more directly and with less cost.[110] The specific political cover PIE provided and the ANC's rhetorical support for pro-poor policies were necessary predicates for the Court to develop this model. But the legal interpretations advanced to defend mass evictions in the early eviction decisions, and the sustained resistance by municipalities to implementing the Court's decisions are evidence that it would have been difficult to achieve the same level of protection against evictions through purely political means. The changes in municipal policies that have resulted and the more refined arguments they now are crafting, especially the distinction between "land invasions" and evictions, are additional evidence that the eviction model is producing the kind of regulatory effects Gauri and Brinks argue are most likely to generate progressive change.

As noted, however, the eviction model is still limited even in its ability to protect individuals facing eviction by the need for resources to bring litigation. More importantly, courts applying this model still primarily focus on resolving individual cases rather than addressing systemic problems. This significantly limits the model's capacity to expand the regulatory effects identified earlier beyond preventing eviction and requiring alternative accommodation. The policies the eviction model has directly influenced all focus on the very limited area of temporary, emergency housing. In this respect, although the eviction cases have elaborated *Grootboom*'s basic principle in important ways, they have not moved beyond it.

As Wilson points out, people facing eviction typically live in unsecure, inadequate, and outright dangerous situations that do not come close to satisfying any definition of the "adequate housing" that section 26(2) requires.[111] The emergency accommodation that municipalities typically provide in eviction cases is at best a temporary solution that does not

[110] *See* King, *supra* note 7, 66–68.

[111] Stuart Wilson, "Breaking the Tie: Evictions from Private Land, Homelessness and a New Normality," 126 *S. Afr. L. J.* 270, 282 (2009).

fulfill section 26(2). Chapter 8 identified the potential for eviction cases to incrementally develop general principles that eventually could establish principles that apply to permanent housing. Nonetheless, the Court has deliberately avoided directly confronting questions related to the relative adequacy of existing programs that could clearly ground that development. As a result, the eviction model has had at best very modest and indirect effects in securing expanded access to permanent housing.[112]

The limits of the eviction model reflect the overall patterns in the second-wave cases, especially the Court's strong focus on procedure and general aversion to developing strong substantive principles. Those same patterns suggest that the prospects are limited, at least in the short term, for the Court to adopt a substantially more substantive interpretive paradigm. The studies of the impact of the Court's decisions discussed previously similarly show that the Court, and South African courts generally, have been reluctant to order new entitlements, preferring instead to prevent deprivation of existing access or at most to incrementally expand existing entitlements.[113] They also raise difficult questions whether a social rights enforcement model that operates within the constraints earlier chapters identified has the potential to instigate the broader regulatory changes that Gauri and Brinks argue are most likely to produce meaningful redistribution.

Several studies – in particular Epp's account of the development of the legalized-accountability model and Brinks and Gauri's original analysis – provide blueprints for building on the eviction model to address these limits. The conditions that these studies argue are necessary to generate broader policy changes intersect in significant respects with the key features of democratic engagement. Identifying those intersections illustrates how this expanded version of engagement could establish a judicial enforcement role that not only works within the constraints that appear to limit the Court's social rights jurisprudence but also could lead to meaningful long-term changes in government policies and practices.

E. Engagement's potential

Recognizing that the eviction model, despite its successes, has so far failed to significantly influence long-term housing policy and the limited results of other social rights to establish new services or broadly expand access

112 *See* Langford, *supra* note 30, 201–2.

113 Dugard and Langford, *supra* note 11, 41; Langford *et al.*, *supra* note 5.

to existing services requires at least a partial concession to the myth-of-rights view that the effects of rights-based mobilization strategies are likely to be significantly limited at best. It also supports Hirschl's argument that formal rights themselves are unlikely to meaningfully reduce overall inequality in comparison with political developments.

The constructivist view accepts that rights-based strategies are inherently limited and that courts play at most a partial role in effecting social change. Epp identifies three institutional developments that have influenced the constructivist understanding of how judicial enforcement shapes long-term policy processes. First is the emergence of litigation support structures – organized groups with the resources to mount sustained litigation campaigns and oversee implementation of court orders. The second is the development of administrative professions and related professional networks that have melded legal norms with professionalization standards. Third, courts in the USA in particular have shifted away from injunctive relief and managerial control toward remedies like tort damages and statutory interpretation that create incentives for other actors to develop and implement reforms.[114]

All three of these developments recognize that courts play only a partial – and sometimes minor – role in instigating social change. The first – Epp's well-known support-structure thesis – argues rights-protective judicial decisions generally result only where there are well-organized organizations and networks of activists with resources to bring sustained litigation.[115]

The merger of professional and legal norms in administrative procedures and practices – the legalized-accountability model – is in many respects more significant than the support-structure thesis.[116] Like the support-structure thesis, this model recognizes that judicial decisions are only one component of operationalizing rights protections. Where the support-structure thesis focuses on the critical role social movements and resources play in creating the conditions necessary for courts to recognize rights, the legalized-accountability model identifies the external conditions required to turn those legal rights into state (and private) practices that implement those legal norms. As Epp's title succinctly captures it, if support structures establish rights, legalized accountability makes them "real."[117]

[114] Charles R. Epp, "Law as an Instrument of Social Reform," in Keith Whittington *et al.* (eds.), *Oxford Handbook of Law and Politics* (2010) 595, 600–2 ("Law as an Instrument").
[115] Epp, *supra* note 14. [116] Epp, *supra* note 15. [117] Ibid.

The third development focuses directly on courts but, like the first two, decenters the judicial role by moving away from remedies that require direct judicial control and extended oversight of reforms. Instead courts adopt remedies that give the organizations that form the support structure leverage to press for the institutional changes the legalized accountability describes.

1. *Social rights and policy legalization*

In their original empirical study of judicial enforcement of social rights in several countries, including South Africa, Gauri and Brinks developed a new model drawn from Epp's support-structure thesis to identify the conditions necessary for social rights to affect policy development and implementation. They describe this process as "legalization of policy."[118] Rather than displacing or preempting political processes, they argue, court enforcement of social rights simply adds another relevant actor and set of considerations to those processes.[119] By the same token, courts themselves are influenced by the external political environment and the specific institutional context targeted in a case. The result is that legal enforcement of social rights "is neither an unambiguous pathway to social equity nor an illegitimate betrayal of popular democratic processes and outcomes."[120] Instead, their studies show that courts can effectively influence social and economic policies but only under certain conditions and only to a limited extent.

The model they describe adapts and expands the support-structure thesis to identify four interrelated elements that shape the relative effect of social rights litigation. First, they agree with the basic premise that substantial professional legal assistance is always a prerequisite but argue the precise level of support varies depending on both the nature of the claim and the existing institutional environment.[121] Less expansive claims require correspondingly less external support. Claims that work within existing institutional arrangements rather than requiring completely new or substantially altered ones likewise require relatively thinner support structures. These observations are consistent with the broader constructivist literature, which generally finds that, although reform litigation has occasionally resulted in major judicial rulings, cases ordering incremental change are by far more common.[122]

[118] Gauri and Brinks, "Introduction," *supra* note 13, 4. [119] Ibid., 14–20.
[120] Ibid., 34. [121] Ibid., 16. [122] Ibid., 349–51; Epp, *supra* note 114, 607–10.

Gauri and Brinks also argue that the support-structure thesis ignores the substantial variations in judicial institutions that factor significantly in the extent to which litigation can have an impact. These differences include the formal legal framework, especially the range and structure of formal social rights. The more courts can rely on existing formal doctrines rather than construct new ones, the more likely they are to recognize claims.[123] Courts also are influenced by the external political constraints that political science models of judicial behavior like Roux's analyze. Consistent with Roux, they predict courts generally will avoid issuing rulings or providing remedies that produce damaging conflict with the legislature or executive.[124]

The third element in their model is the institutional environment that a case targets. Courts take into account the capacity and political willingness of bureaucracies to implement their decisions and are more likely to order modest reforms where capacity is low or resistance likely. By the same token, courts should be more willing to order reforms that have some demonstrated internal support within a bureaucracy.[125]

Finally, the model assesses the capacity of litigants to press for implementation of a court order. This implicates the strength of the support structure for rights-based litigation but focuses on the capacity of that structure to both monitor bureaucratic compliance and bring follow-up enforcement litigation.[126]

Applying these elements to democratic engagement both highlights its potential as a vehicle for effective change and also suggests specific ways courts could apply it to improve its effectiveness. First, meaningful engagement – even in the expanded form Chapter 9 described – imposes a relatively modest set of largely procedural requirements. Engagement does not require a specific substantive outcome; it does not immediately redirect resources or set substantive policy priorities; and it works within the existing policy and decision-making structures of government. As both the eviction cases and *Joseph* show, a relatively thin support structure may be sufficient to generate the kind of procedurally focused interventions engagement requires.[127] Extending those interventions into policy-making processes and enforcing the kind of cultural changes within local bureaucratic structures necessary to make paper policies effective certainly will require more substantial external support. But the Court has

[123] Gauri and Brinks, "Introduction," *supra* note 13, 6–20. [124] Ibid., 25–28.
[125] Ibid., 19–20. [126] Ibid. [127] *See*, Dugard and Langford, *supra* note 11.

consistently been willing to intervene more directly to enforce procedural rights and remedies as predicted by this first element.

Second, the formal legal resources courts can draw on to enforce engagement are substantial. The social rights themselves obviously are the starting point. Engagement's connection to participatory democracy adds the range of democratic participation rights in the Constitution. More significantly, meaningful engagement's procedural focus fits squarely within the Court's own precedents and the limitations evident in the second-wave cases.

As Chapter 9 explained, the participation obligations in the Municipal Systems and Structures Acts as well as the general political commitment to participatory governance, illustrated most recently by the NDP provide an even broader and more specific array of legal resources. Although studies of these mechanisms generally concur that they are not functioning well – if at all – in most municipalities, the fact that they exist at least on paper and in some instances at least partially in practice makes them even more susceptible to judicial enforcement in this model. Rather than inventing entirely new structures out of whole cloth or dramatically changing existing structures, courts can enforce democratic engagement by reinterpreting these existing structures and by relying on the legislative mandates to increase participation.

On the supply side, the internal factors that influence the Court and Roux's analysis of the political environment both suggest that the Court is more likely to order procedural reforms than substantive ones. Roux argues that political realignment that breaks up the ANC's dominance is required to open political space for the Court to expand its role enforcing the social rights.[128] But engagement's procedural emphasis plays on the existing tension between the national and local governments. This tension helps explain the remarkable result in *Blue Moonlight* and the other eviction model cases. The Court could use that same political space to enforce the procedural requirements of democratic engagement.

Finally, democratic engagement is consistent with the more recent analysis by Brinks and Gauri of the structural factors that influence the potential for litigation to have greater effect because it expands the regulatory aspect of individual eviction cases.[129] As Chapter 9 argued, meaningful engagement gives courts the doctrinal framework to expand individual eviction cases to first identify and then address underlying structural issues.

[128] Roux, *supra* note 44, 394–98. [129] Brinks and Gauri, *supra* note 9.

The central problem for democratic engagement under this model is the institutional environment. Although courts can take advantage of a rich array of formal legal mechanisms and target their interventions at existing structures or at least existing policies, the well-documented problems that have consistently plagued local government's capacity to both deliver services and implement participation mechanisms will not easily or quickly be solved by courts. Perhaps most challenging in this respect is the problem of endemic corruption and its close connection to the ANC's practice of cadre deployment.[130] Changing these practices is likely to raise strong political resistance because they are tools critical to the ANC's political control at the local level.[131]

2. *Legalized accountability*

The legalized-accountability model focuses specifically on this institutional dimension and identifies the conditions necessary for legal pressure to translate into institutional reform. Chapter 9 analyzed the considerable overlap between democratic engagement and the factors Epp identifies are necessary for legalized accountability to effect meaningful bureaucratic reform.

Legalized accountability provides a framework for working within elite institutions by co-opting and redefining professional norms to incorporate legal rights that are responsive to popular demands. The core insights of legalized accountability are first that court decisions act primarily as catalysts for institutional and cultural reforms that make legal norms real to varying degrees in different contexts. Second, courts do not identify the reforms themselves – not even indirectly through the kind of collaborative court-directed process that experimentalism identifies. Instead, those reforms emerge over time through interactions among outside professional organizations, reform-minded insiders and advocacy groups. The threat of legal liability and the abstract principles established in litigation help drive those reforms, but courts generally do not intervene to structure them directly.[132] Put differently, the legalized-accountability

130 *See* Langford *et al.*, *supra* note 5, 11–12.

131 Ibid. *See, also*, Sujit Choudhry, "'He Had a Mandate': The South African Constitutional Court and the African National Congress in a Dominant Party Democracy," 2 *Const. Ct. Rev.* 1, 13–17 (2009). Richard Pithouse, "The Assassination Scourge on Those Fighting Corruption," *Mail and Guardian* (October 3, 2014), at http://mg.co.za/article/2014-10-03-the-assassination-surge-on-those-fighting-corruption.

132 Epp, *supra* note 15, 214–22.

model describes a generic procedural framework that enables institutions to adopt policies and procedures that incorporate substantive legal norms.

Democratic engagement provides a mechanism that capitalizes on both of these insights and focuses specifically on the procedural framework itself instead of the background substantive norms. Rather than exposing institutions to liability that reformers can use as leverage to propose institutional changes, the right to participate recognizes a direct legal basis for outside organizations to participate directly in proposing and even implementing reforms.

Engagement's flexibility allows courts to play relatively stronger or weaker roles in that process. Courts can move toward a more active role by mandating specific processes or requiring participation by particular groups or classes of people. They also can maintain the direct oversight to review both the process and the results that are typical of an experimentalist court. Conversely, courts can issue fairly general engagement orders and leave it to the parties themselves to press for changes with the threat of follow-up litigation as the lever. Regardless of where courts position themselves on that continuum, the focus is always on the institutional framework rather than the substantive policies.

As an initial matter, the focus on institutional structures shared by legalized accountability and meaningful engagement suggests that targeting procedural reforms rather than adopting a more substantive interpretive role may better address the underlying structural causes of local government failures Chapter 9 discussed. Both roles could create the threat of potential future legal liability that instigates legalized accountability. A more substantive approach would create programmatic standards or targets advocates could use both to press for policy changes and rely on in follow-up litigation where the state fails to meet it. The Court's critics consistently have argued that its contentless, case-specific interpretive approach have left social rights advocates with little leverage to press for policy changes that extend beyond individual cases.[133] Adopting a more substantive interpretive framework either by changing this framework or through the more incremental process described in Chapter 8 could create even stronger leverage that could lead to legalized accountability. The patterns in the second-wave cases suggest, however, the Court is unlikely to change its interpretive approach significantly, at least in the short term.

[133] *See* Marius Pieterse, "Procedural Relief, Constitutional Citizenship and Socio-Economic Rights as Legitimate Expectations," 28 *S. Afr. J. Hum. Rts.* 359, 360 (2012).

Doing so would heighten the justiciability concerns that the Court has consistently sought to avoid.

More importantly, the legalized-accountability model illustrates that court decisions are significant primarily because they create leverage for other organizations to identify and propose institutional reforms designed to meet those standards.[134] Democratic engagement can create the same threat of legal liability as a more substantive approach while still working within the Court's existing limits. Democratic engagement also could increase or at least refine that leverage because it targets the institutional processes that are the specific drivers of rights-protective policies in Epp's model.

In the concluding chapter of his analysis of the Chaskalson Court, Theunis Roux briefly addresses some of the second-wave decisions and speculates that the political context in South Africa may have changed sufficiently to permit the Court to adopt the more substantive role advocated by the Courts critics including Bilchitz and Liebenberg.[135] Roux critiques the deeper proceduralization represented by meaningful engagement and *Mazibuko* as examples of reasonableness review's limits.[136] Roux argues this substantively thin interpretive approach makes it difficult to address institutional issues like government corruption and inefficiency because it requires advocates to litigate each individual instance rather than establishing a broad precedent through a single case.[137] He argues that the increasing internal divisions in the ANC and growing popular discontent with its policies could create the necessary political support for the Court to abandon these procedural interventions in favor of a stronger substantive approach that would establish broad precedents applicable across cases.[138]

Connecting Roux's political analysis to the legalized-accountability model suggests that the Court could make better use of these changed political circumstances by issuing decisions that target government institutions rather than adopting stronger substantive norms. First, as Roux recognizes in a more recent analysis of the Court's democratic-rights decisions, even in this more fractured political climate the Court is still substantially constrained in its capacity to challenge the ANC directly.[139] Roux argues that, although "the ANC has lost much of its moral stature,"

[134] Epp, *supra* note 15, 218–19. [135] Roux, *supra* note 44, 392–98.
[136] Ibid., 395–96. [137] Ibid., 379. [138] Ibid.
[139] Theunis Roux, "The South African Constitutional Court's Democratic Rights Jurisprudence: A Response to Samuel Issacharoff," 5 *Const. Ct. Rev.* 33, 62–63 (2014).

the Court remains doubly constrained by "a relatively formalist legal culture" and the external political environment.[140]

The political factors that constrain the Court dovetail with the legalized-accountability model's recognition that court decisions play an indirect role in generating meaningful rights-protective practices and that their most significant contribution is to provide leverage for institutional reforms. Judicial decisions that identify more specific substantive requirements will not by themselves create the institutional conditions necessary for implementing those requirements. The studies cited here consistently emphasized that securing compliance with even the relatively modest requirements in the Court's decisions remains a significant and recurring problem. The High Court's description in *Hlophe* of the City of Johannesburg's continued resistance to embracing the systematic changes necessary to comply with *Blue Moonlight* illustrates the significant political, institutional, and bureaucratic challenges social rights advocates face in implementing court victories.[141]

The legalized-accountability model is premised on the idea that even the most expansive formal rights become real only to the extent there is an administrative structure available to implement them and a bureaucratic culture committed to doing so. Democratic engagement targets those same institutional issues and, carefully deployed, could help develop the conditions necessary for institutional reform.

This more authoritative but still procedural role engagement creates allows courts to identify and assist the growing range of civil society groups, community-based organizations, and social movements that have emerged in the past decade to press for greater and more structured access to local government planning, budgeting and implementation. These organizations already have developed and deployed sophisticated advocacy strategies that integrate strategic litigation, local mobilization, and political pressure. More recently, many of these groups have started to focus more directly on enforcing the existing participation mandates as well as other administrative reforms as part of this multi-faceted strategy for enforcing social rights.[142]

140 Ibid., 63.

141 *Hlophe and Others v City of Johannesburg Metropolitan Municipality and Others* [2013] ZAGPJHC 98 (May 3, 2013) ("*Hlophe*").

142 One prominent example is the Social Justice Coalition's effort to use social audits to press the City of Cape Town to improve services in Khayelitsha. Social Justice Coalition, "Report of the Khayelitsha 'Mshengu' Toilet Social Audit, April 22–27, 2013," May 10, 2013 Report (2013).

Finally, several community-based organizations and social movements both individually and through national and international networks have developed sophisticated strategies and developed the capacity to engage with the government.[143] Collectively, these groups can develop both the professional norms and outside pressure that are critical in the legalized-accountability model to generate administrative reforms that make rights real.

One element in the legalized-accountability model largely missing in the South African context is a group of interested, motivated government insiders with strong connections to these outside groups. Several of the case studies discussed earlier documented isolated examples of sympathetic government officials who played key roles in making legal pressure effective.[144] Accounts of the Treatment Action Campaign's successful efforts also cite the critical role of bureaucratic insiders aligned with the Campaign.[145] These examples show that it should be possible in other contexts to find or develop the insider base that can provide a link between local governments and these outside organizations.

The growing political attention devoted to service-delivery problems and the consistent connection drawn between those problems and the local government's failure even to communicate with affected communities, much less provide for meaningful consultation, could create momentum and open up political space for reform-minded insiders to emerge.[146] In Epp's account, legal pressure by activists succeeded in large part because they were able to shape public debate over the problems identified in litigation and build widespread public support for institutional reforms. Outside experts with close connections and deep understanding of the bureaucratic structures that were the targets of these criticisms developed specific reform proposals that turned these legal norms into concrete policies and procedures.[147]

The rich legal framework for participatory governance Chapter 9 described shows that a formal commitment to the kind of participation

[143] Ibid. *See, also,* GGLN, *supra* note 64; Benjamin Bradlow, "Beyond a Legal Framework for 'Meaningful Engagement' in South Africa," Shack/Slum Dweller's International, *SDI Bulletin*, March 11, 2010, at www.sdinet.org/blog/2010/03/11/sdi-bulletin-beyond-a-legal-fr/.

[144] Malcolm Langford *et al.* "Concluding Perspectives," *supra* note 5, 437–38.

[145] Peter Houtzager and Lucie E. White, "The Long Arc of Pragmatic ESR Advocacy," in Lucie E. White and Jeremy Perelman (eds.), *Stones of Hope: How African Activists Reclaim Human Rights to Challenge Global Poverty* (2011) 172, 178–79.

[146] *See* Friedman, *supra* note 99.

[147] Epp, *supra* note 15, 20–21 and 217–18.

that engagement requires already exists. Enforcing this framework creates rhetorical support for courts to hold the government accountable to its own policies and therefore to avoid the democratic-legitimacy concerns the Court frequently cites.[148] There are some tentative signs that the national government may be more willing to take these commitments seriously and start to address local governance failures.[149]

Formal policies increasingly highlight the need to implement participatory governance mandates at the local level. The NDP describes the state's commitment to community participation in government as both a legal and professional obligation.[150] Following the 2014 national and provincial elections, the new cabinet approved a "Framework for Strengthening Citizen-Government Partnerships for Monitoring Frontline Service Delivery."[151] The Framework, which was made a key focus area of the national Department of Performance Monitoring and Evaluation, is tied directly to the NDP's commitment to greater participation. The explicit "aim" of the Framework "is to institutionalise citizen-based monitoring in the monitoring and performance management of government to support on-going improvements to what, how, and why services are delivered to our people."[152] It identifies the "overall problem" as the lack of consistent, systematic community participation in service-delivery planning processes in many sectors.[153]

Finally – and perhaps most significantly – there are tentative signs that a genuine political commitment to these reforms is beginning to emerge at the national level in response to the political vulnerability that local government failures have created for the ANC.[154] Chapter 9 noted the disconnect between local and national politics that Dugard argues insulates the national ANC from the political effects of court decisions that expose local government failures. This same disconnect also could open the political space Roux identifies as critical for courts to take a more active role. Court decisions that identify specifically local failures

[148] Gauri and Brinks, *supra* note 9, 28.

[149] Langford *et al.*, "Concluding Perspectives," *supra* note 5, 439–40; Steven Friedman, "No Manna from Heaven, but No Reason to Sneer," *Business Day BDLive* (June 25, 2014), available at www.bdlive.co.za/opinion/columnists/2014/06/25/no-manna-from-heaven-but-no-reason-to-sneer.

[150] National Planning Commission, *National Development Plan 2030: Our Future – Make It Work* (2012).

[151] B. Leon and J. Timm, "Strengthening Citizen-Government Partnerships for Monitoring Frontline Service Delivery in South Africa," Citizen-Based Monitoring Paper to SAMEA Conference (2013).

[152] Ibid. [153] Ibid. [154] *See* Friedman, *supra* note 149.

and orders that target local government policies and processes could align with the national government's interests in several ways. As Chapter 9 described, courts can rely directly on national legislation to require these changes and thus characterize their orders as enforcing national policy. This creates a rhetorical framework courts can rely on to highlight the alignment between the ANC's interests and local government reform.

Experience to date has shown that, rather than providing political support for these interventions, the national government has instead facilitated evasion of meaningful reform.[155] The legislative and policy framework Chapter 9 identified has been ineffective in large part because of the lack of genuine political support from the ANC. This lack of support is connected to the strongly centralized control the ANC exercises over provincial and local governments. In addition to setting policy at the national level, the ANC also essentially controls the provincial candidate lists and controls appointment of provincial premiers. The system of cadre deployment, where the party leadership decides who will fill positions in government and government-controlled entities, extends that control even further by making bureaucracies accountable primarily to the party rather than local constituents.[156] Reforms that decentralize control by creating meaningful community and civil society participation and local accountability mechanisms threaten that dominance.[157]

Recent political developments, however, suggest that the ANC may be beginning to recognize the need to produce real reform at the local level to maintain its political dominance. This could create the political momentum necessary to give courts greater support for ordering reforms and also generate the political will necessary for them to actually work. The political reconfiguration Roux identifies, especially the internal fractures in the ANC and the growing popular disaffection with the ANC's failure to effect broad redistribution and economic change for the vast majority of citizens, may create sufficient pressure to change the status quo.[158] Other recent political developments provide further evidence that these political shifts are continuing to create openings in the ANC's political dominance and that the formal policy changes, like the NDP, that mandate greater accountability and participation, may be responses to those shifts.

Writing before the 2014 national and provincial elections, Dugard identified encouraging signs that the growing social tensions the local protests represent were beginning to develop into broader political coalitions that

[155] Piper and Nadvi, *supra* note 45, 233. [156] Choudhry, *supra* note 131, 16–19.
[157] Ibid., 15–17. [158] Roux, *supra* note 44, 392–96.

recognize the linkages between these local government breakdowns and "structural socio-economic and political problems."[159] These more recent political developments are part of a longer trend in diminishing support for the ANC in both national and local elections. The quality of government service delivery has been a central and growing theme in each of these elections, with both the ANC and the Democratic Alliance seeking to capitalize on the other's alleged failures to provide adequate services.[160]

These political developments are evidence that the reconfiguration Roux posits is required to create openings for the Court to issue decisions that risk conflict with the ANC and challenge its policies is emerging in South Africa.[161] Although it's possible this reconfiguration could ground the stronger substantive approach Roux advocates, it appears to more clearly support interventions specifically focused on local government failures.[162] The growing role that service delivery and other social rights-related issues have started to play and the renewed public commitment to reform they have prompted suggest that there is both widespread popular support for such interventions but also that they could attract support from the national ANC or at least avoid outright opposition.

Viewed through the lens of the legalized-accountability model, these political shifts and the attention to local service-delivery protests that have accompanied them create a situation ripe for judicial interventions aimed at reforming local government structures in the ways Chapter 9 described. Social rights activists can capitalize on the media attention local protests have generated by using individual cases as platforms to highlight the connection between these failures and the lack of systematic processes for meaningful community participation. The changed political environment could give courts more room to consistently issue remedies that require democratic engagement and exercise greater control to bring specific individuals and organizations into those processes. Activists could

[159] Jackie Dugard, "Urban Basic Services," in Langford *et al.* (eds.), *supra* note 5, 285–86.

[160] E.g., Neil Overy, "The Social Justice Coalition and Access to Basic Sanitation in Informal Settlements in Cape Town, South Africa," International Budget Partnership Case Study No. 11, SSRN 2333670, 18–19 (2013); Steven Robins, "Toilets That Became Political Dynamite," *Cape Times* (June 27, 2011), at www.iol.co.za/capetimes/toilets-that-became-political-dynamite-1.1089289#.U9aSE4BdXWp.

[161] Roux, *supra* note 44, 392–96.

[162] For more recent analysis of disaffection with the ANC tied to local government failures, *see* Pithouse, *supra* note 131; Susan Booysen, "Ungovernable Government – AG's Local Story," *The Sunday Independent* (August 10, 2014), at www.iol.co.za/sundayindependent/ungovernable-government-ag-s-local-story-1.1733079#.VCA1sWTt8dI.

then draw on the broad range of organizations that have developed models for engagement and expertise in connecting local government and communities to create connections between local officials and outside groups that could lead to practices and policies that generate real reform.

F. Conclusion

A 2014 article in the *Daily Maverick* – a left-leaning digital newspaper – reported a depressing litany of service-delivery failures across the North West Province, a largely rural province that runs along the Botswana border from Gauteng in the east to the Northern Cape in the west and the Free State in the south.[163] The problems the article documented include a water crisis in one municipality that left residents with no water for four days; a new township constructed entirely without water infrastructure; a low-income housing development with no sewer installations; and a rural farming district that has been without water or sewer services since 2005.[164]

The article attributes these myriad problems to "crumbling infrastructure due to inept financial control, corruption, maladministration and lack of skills." It singles out the ANC's practice of "cadre deployment," in which local government officials are appointed and reassigned based on politics rather than merit, which allows incompetence to flourish and leads to widespread corruption in local government as the root cause behind these governance and capacity problems.[165] The article concludes that the solution is not increased resources but "a fundamental shift in the way the ruling party manages its local governments. It will require skill and performance in employees, not loyalty and patronage."[166]

With only slight changes to the details, this description easily could apply in parts of every province in South Africa. As earlier chapters described, even relatively well-resourced and highly functioning municipalities like Johannesburg and Cape Town suffer from some degree of organizational dysfunction and outright corruption. These political, cultural, and bureaucratic issues are the major stumbling blocks to effective realization of the social rights.

[163] Niki Moore, "North West: Service Delivery? What Service Delivery?," *Daily Maverick* (June 19, 2014), at www.dailymaverick.co.za/article/2014–06–19-north-west-service-delivery-what-service-delivery/#.U6Q6QI1dXWZ.

[164] Ibid. [165] Ibid. [166] Ibid.

No matter how carefully crafted and regardless of the depth of outside support, judicial interventions of any stripe simply cannot by themselves solve the kinds of problems the *Daily Maverick* highlights. One of the central themes this book has developed is that courts generally are fairly limited in their capacity to address these complex problems, and that the Constitutional Court of South Africa consistently has approached the social rights with a close eye toward those limits.

This is not news to anyone even passingly familiar with either the literature on courts and social change or the Constitutional Court's social rights decisions. The close analysis of these decisions this book presents – in particular the patterns in the second-wave cases – provides a finer-grained picture of the way those limits have played out in one particular court. But the conclusion that the Constitutional Court, like all courts, has played a limited role in effecting meaningful social change through social rights breaks no new ground.

That same close analysis, however, contested the view that the Court's increasing proceduralization of the social rights necessarily leads to deference and ineffectiveness. To the contrary, it demonstrates that where the Court is able to avoid the justiciability concerns and operate in a largely procedural mode, it frequently adopts a more authoritative role. These last three chapters have argued that role, under the right circumstances and with sufficient political support, might be more effective than a jurisprudence that develops a stronger set of abstract constitutional principles in addressing problems like corruption, mismanagement, and the lack of political commitment that the *Daily Maverick* article highlights.

Procedural enforcement models like the eviction model and democratic engagement respond to the classic objections in the justiciability debate by establishing a concrete enforcement role for courts that neither preempts democratic politics or forces courts to make complex policy judgments. For these reasons, procedural enforcement shares a strong affinity with weak-form and dialogic forms of review, in particular democratic experimentalism. In contrast to these models, however, the Court's proceduralized approach has strongly avoided any substantive dialogue over the social rights.

This aversion to a strong interpretive role has been at the crux of the debate over the Court's social rights jurisprudence dating back to the well-known first-wave decisions like *Grootboom* and *TAC*. Critiques of the Court's interpretive framework have only deepened in reaction to the second-wave decisions, in particular following *Mazibuko*'s explicit articulation of these limits. Those criticisms are warranted, but their focus on the Court's weak interpretive role misses the surprising results that the more authoritative examples of its procedural approach have achieved.

The point of this concluding chapter has been to argue that those surprising results illustrate first that the procedural models the Court has developed can and have been effective even in the absence of a strong interpretive framework. Second, this chapter has attempted to show that these results are consistent with and support the constructivist view that litigation and other rights-based approaches can play a meaningful role in effecting social and political change.

Finally, this chapter has sought to identify connections between the Court's procedural models and several other studies of the conditions and institutional structures that make it more likely that law and policies will change in pro-poor directions. These connections suggest that procedural models are well suited – perhaps better suited than a stronger interpretive role – to instigate the kind of systemic institutional reforms that could lead to more redistributive and pro-poor social policies.

INDEX

Printed in the United States
By Bookmasters